Virgin Territory

CONTEMPORARY APPROACHES TO FILM AND TELEVISION SERIES

A complete listing of the books in this series can be found online at wsupress.wayne.edu

General Editor
Barry Keith Grant
Brock University

Advisory Editors
Robert J. Burgoyne
Wayne State University

Caren J. Deming
University of Arizona

Patricia B. Erens
School of the Art Institute of Chicago

Peter X. Feng
University of Delaware

Lucy Fischer
University of Pittsburgh

Frances Gateward
Ursinus College

Tom Gunning
University of Chicago

Thomas Leitch
University of Delaware

Anna McCarthy
New York University

Walter Metz
Southern Illinois University

Lisa Parks
University of California–
Santa Barbara

Virgin Territory
Representing Sexual Inexperience in Film

edited by
Tamar Jeffers McDonald

Wayne State University Press
Detroit

© 2010 by Wayne State University Press, Detroit, Michigan 48201. All rights reserved. No part of this book may be reproduced without formal permission.

14 13 12 11 10   5 4 3 2 1

Library of Congress Cataloging-in-Publication Data

Virgin territory : representing sexual inexperience in film / edited by Tamar Jeffers McDonald.
  p. cm — (Contemporary approaches to film and television series)
Includes bibliographical references and index.
ISBN 978-0-8143-3318-1 (pbk. : alk. paper)
1. Virginity in motion pictures. 2. Sex in motion pictures. I. McDonald, Tamar Jeffers.
PN1995.9.V55V47 2010
791.43'6538—dc22
2009037066

Typeset by Maya Rhodes
Composed in Adobe Garamond and Myriad Pro

Contents

Acknowledgments vii

Introduction 1
    TAMAR JEFFERS MCDONALD

Gaylyn Studlar
Velvet's Cherry: Elizabeth Taylor and Virginal English Girlhood 15

Ilana Nash
The Innocent Is a Broad: American Virgins in a Global Context 34

Timothy Shary
Virgin Springs: A Survey of Teen Films' Quest for Sexcess 54

Rebecca Sullivan
Postwar Virginity and the "Marjorie" Phenomenon 68

Alisia G. Chase
One Very Chic Hell: Revisiting the Issue of Virginity in *Bonjour Tristesse* 83

Tamar Jeffers McDonald
Performances of Desire and Inexperience: Doris Day's Fluctuating Filmic Virginity 103

Pete Falconer
Fresh Meat? Dissecting the Horror Movie Virgin 123

Nina Martin
Don't Touch Me: Violating Boundaries in Roman Polanski's *Repulsion* 138

Greg Tuck
Orgasmic (Teenage) Virgins: Masturbation and Virginity in Contemporary American Cinema 157

Lisa M. Dresner
Love's Labor's Lost? Early 1980s Representations of Girls' Sexual Decision Making in *Fast Times at Ridgemont High* and *Little Darlings* 174

Shelley Cobb
Was She or Wasn't She? Virginity and Identity in the Critical Reception of *Elizabeth* (1998) 201

Andrea Sabbadini
The Window and the Door 223

Carol Siegel
Irreconcilable Feminisms and the Construction of a Cultural Memory of Virginity's Loss: *À ma soeur!* and *Thirteen* 238

Celestino Deleyto
The New Road to Sexual Ecstasy: Virginity and Genre in *The 40-Year-Old Virgin* 255

Bibliography 269
Filmography 281
Contributors 287
Index 289

Acknowledgments

This edited collection has had a long gestation and has thus garnered a similarly long list of people to whom I owe a debt of thanks. Richard Dyer encouraged me to investigate all things cine-virginal during the years of my doctoral thesis. Robin Larsen, Alisia Chase, and Peter Thomas helped me work through issues of virginity and anthology organizing during and after a lunch at the Society for Cinema and Media Studies (SCMS) in Atlanta. Barry Keith Grant and the anonymous reviewers at Wayne State University Press provided very helpful feedback. To all these I owe my thanks and appreciation.

Colleagues and students at Birkbeck College, University of London, Warwick University, Buckinghamshire Chilterns University College, Oxford Brookes University, and the University of Kent, as well as at various film studies conferences, helped by hearing my ideas as they developed and bore with me as my fascination for disproving Doris Day's perennial virgin status showed no sign of waning.

I am indebted to the chapter authors for their patience with my edits and their high levels of enthusiasm for the project. Special recognition and gratitude is owed to Annie Martin at Wayne State University Press for her keen interest and support throughout, and to the Press's Maya Rhodes and Carrie Downes Teefey and copyeditor Mary Tederstrom for their inestimable assistance in getting the book to print.

And, of course, it is to my family that I owe greatest thanks: my mother for taping odd films for me late at night; Chloë for helping me check the bibliography; and Chloë, Jessica, and Paul for sitting through innumerable bizarre genre products with me because they had some tenuous relation to virginity (*The Dunwich Horror* again, gang?). My love and thanks to you all.

Tamar Jeffers McDonald

Introduction

Does she or doesn't she? Is she or isn't she? Will she or won't she? Should she or shouldn't she? Should I surrender? Have you been bad? As these lines from books, articles, advertisements, and films from the cusp of the 1950s and 1960s demonstrate, virginity resists scrutiny and provokes interrogation.[1]

Although these queries in the popular media can be dated from the 1953 publication of *Sexual Behavior of the Human Female,* popularly known as the "Kinsey Report," a moment that propelled the figure of the desirable and desirous female virgin into the public eye, it would be wrong to assume that this was the first or only incidence of virginity becoming a hot, and hotly contested, topic in popular culture. As chapters in this book explore, virginity was already an important social trope during the early decades of the twentieth century as well as during the years of the Second World War, and it remains so today, despite superficial assumptions about permissiveness.

Indeed, virginity has had a long and vexed history and has never been a simple matter of an ontological either/or. It most often has a chronological, medical, legal, religious, or moral dimension to its loss; frequently its maintenance is seen as being as problematic as its relinquishment. While virginity may seem an "old-fashioned object," it nevertheless remains one of perpetual currency within popular culture and the various cinemas that serve it.[2]

This collection thus considers examples of virginity as produced and marketed in film in order both to prompt discussion about the topic's wider significance within culture and to consider the specific problems

INTRODUCTION

that an internal quality such as virginity presents when it is rendered in a visual medium. This collection is titled *Virgin Territory* for two reasons: first, because all the chapters within are about virgins and, second, because research into the topic of virginity in films is, remarkably, fairly untrodden ground. While there have been a small number of individual analyses of the subject of virginity in film, either looking at specific stars or offering sexually symbolic readings of film moments, to date there has been no comprehensive treatment of the topic.[3] Thus this collection attempts to supply a lack and make a start at opening a dialogue on an important topic.

Virginity fascinates the writers of these chapters because of its paradoxical nature. At first glance, virginity seems such an obvious concept, so personal, private, and natural that it renders discussion unnecessary. But on closer examination, it becomes apparent that virginity is not personal but social, not private but public, not natural but constructed, and not obvious but invisible—a point that causes no less anxiety in the various contexts within the films that we examine here than it does for film as a medium itself, one predicated on "showing." For this reason, while the essays here may take different time frames, genres, and star personae as their topics, they all center on examining how virginity—a lack of experience, a zero—can be made visible to audiences. Unexpectedly, perhaps, this turns out to be as problematic an aim in modern cinema as it was in earlier times when the Motion Picture Production Code in Hollywood mandated that such matters could not be openly discussed on-screen. The inclination to displace virginity from overt dialogue onto the bodies of the actors or the mise-en-scène, or both, can be seen operating not only in Hollywood films before the abandonment of the code around 1968 but also in modern films and those adhering to alternative cinematic traditions. The aim of this volume, then, is to destabilize assumptions about virginity by questioning how it can be performed, externalized, and rendered not only visible but spectacular, across a range of periods, genres, and performances, and through this destabilization to relate the virginity moments outward from their filmic texts to their wider social meanings.

Popular culture has long assumed an association, reckoned in both verbal and visual terms, of the virgin state with innocence and naturalness. This seems at first uncontroversial: we are all born virgin. Yet when questions are raised about who has and who has not relinquished this status—as has been a popular motif in melodramatic films since the beginnings of cinema—relying on outward signs proves misleading, reinforcing again the central question of this edited collection: How can a state before

INTRODUCTION

experience be rendered in a visual medium? Virginity becomes narratively interesting when its loss is threatened and therefore has been accompanied by prurience throughout cinema history. This collection seeks to explore the contrasts and continuities in film's attempts at representing externally this internal state. Using films from different genres, cinemas, and historical periods, the following chapters study representations of virginity in relation to issues of femininity and masculinity; identity; the body; sexual agency and control; stardom and performance; the individual and society; and hysteria, trauma, and psychosis. All contributions thus investigate the strategies elected by various films to represent the unrepresentable, but beyond this the chapters are largely organized chronologically. It is hoped that readers will find connections and convergences, as well as variations of approach and conclusion, across different chapters. In addition, this volume has employed a conscious policy to permit recurrent mentions of some films, in the spirit of fostering more debate, rather than limiting them and thus perhaps implying that any single or final readings have been reached.

Throughout the chapters—and the films that are examined within them—virginity seems to prompt consideration around several core clusters of ideas: about power, desire, and agency or passivity; about the need for, and simultaneous impossibility of believing in, visible signs for this invisible state; about the symbolic register that virginity can operate within; and about the curious qualities it possesses that allow it both to figure as a metaphor for the coherence of the nation-state and to refer to a literal state of sexual inexperience.

The most commonly occurring clusters of ideas prompted by the figure of the virgin in this collection are those of conflict and context. The virgin appears, in chapter after chapter of this anthology, to mobilize conflicting arguments and points of view and does so in contexts that are always both entirely specific to the time of the particular film and connected to longer traditions of beliefs about purity, innocence, and goodness. The "double standard" and the "technical virgin" may seem to be uniquely 1950s concepts; yet essays here show that both are still pertinent to current films and the societies they reflect and serve. Virginity causes, and is revealed and made visible through, conflict: it appears through paradoxes and sets aspects of film style, such as mise-en-scène and costume, against the dominant narratives. Female virgins have been simultaneously enjoined to be go-getting, can-do national citizens yet remain passive and underachieving as girls; the maintenance of virginity is posited as both right for the girl and wrong for her partner. The liminality of the virgin on and as a threshold underlines her position as a central point in a moment it is impossible to sustain. Yet other films indicate that the true discovery of sexual knowledge is more properly understood as a process than as a state reflecting a stark either/or. Finally, virginity can be understood as a state that seems clear-cut but is actually deeply ambiguous—physically, literally, and symbolically—especially when it is taken as the shorthand indication of moral qualities. It seems, therefore, that, as Kathryn Schwartz notes in her provocative exploration of Elizabeth I, the issues raised by virginity have more resonance than we generally acknowledge: "Perhaps the questions precipitated by the apparently archaic institution of virginity have had a longer and more potent shelf life than we might expect."[4] While today sexual sophistication is assumed uniformly possessed by adults and seemingly ever younger and younger teens, virginity can be posited as an anomaly, pathologized rather than naturalized in any but the very young. It is this rarity value that creates the humor in a film such as *The 40-Year-Old Virgin* and the frisson prompting successive starlets such as Britney Spears, Jessica Simpson, and Katie Holmes to market their uninitiate state as remarkable—for as long as it lasts.

Studying the Virgin

As noted, despite the fact that virginity (especially perhaps female virginity) has been such an important and contested area of cultural thought across many historical periods and national and social contexts, there has not been, to date, much academic consideration of the subject, either within film studies or indeed at all. While there are no direct precedents in film theory for this book, the collection does draw on existing research in various areas, including studies of virginity in literature; star, reception, and genre studies in film theory; sociocultural and cultural histories; and a newly emergent thread of academic interest, girlhood studies.[5] Although this book does not assume that virginity is only connected with the teenage years or indeed with the female, but rather seeks to contest and problematize such assumptions, several of the authors have been inspired by this recent turn in cultural and film studies.

Quite late in the gestation of this project, two book-length treatments of the topic were published almost simultaneously: Hanne Blank's *Virgin: The Untouched History* (2007) and Anke Bernau's *Virgins: A Cultural History* (2007). Blank's book looks in detail at the historical, religious, medical, legal, and social definitions and meanings of virginity, uncovering fascinating facts (such as the precise dating of the discovery of the hymen: 1544) and provocatively arranging juxtapositions of information so that the story of virginity's long history never seems random, despite its variations. Beginning with the difficulty of offering a definitive definition of the word and then proceeding to examine the changes in its meaning and importance from Old Testament days forward, Blank brings her topic up-to-date with brief explorations of film and television presentations of virginity, including asides on *Little Darlings* (1980, discussed in this book by Dresner and by Shary), *The Breakfast Club* (1985), *Beverly Hills, 90210* (1990–2000), and *Buffy the Vampire Slayer* (1997–2003). In contrast, Bernau does not offer such useful links from contemporary popular culture to the historical and religious convictions concerning virginity explored in the book—a curious fact, because she confesses in the introduction that she was drawn to studying virginity by researching the topic in film.[6] Bernau is a medieval historian, and her work seems most comfortable when discussing virginity in that time period.

Both Blank and Bernau recognize the importance of the work of Kathleen Coyne Kelly, another medieval historian, on chastity and purity, and indeed we, the cine-virginologists of this collection, must also acknowledge the great debt we owe her. Kelly's book may be titled *Performing Virginity and Testing Chastity in the Middle Ages*, but it convincingly manages to link ideas, assumptions, and superstitions about the topic within current thought and popular media. Kelly traces in detail these ideas through to their visible conclusions in films from a range of periods, including *A Summer Place* (1959) and *Hair* (1979). She also, uniquely among these historians, considers the habitual association of virginity with certain female film stars; Kelly finds that virginity is assumed to be legible on the body of its possessor within cinema just as it is within the stories of saints and martyrs from the Middle Ages.[7] That assumption, and film's attempt to grapple with it in visual terms, informs the work of this edited collection, as various chapters consider the impact of the legible virgin body on the star personae of several actors, including Doris Day, the subject of my own chapter, whom Kelly specifically references.[8]

Another piece that has been of great interest to scholars in this collection is Kathryn Schwarz's article "The Wrong Question: Thinking through Virginity," in which she examines the myth of virginity surrounding the Virgin Queen, Elizabeth I. While Schwarz takes pains to establish that her article explores virginity specifically in a sixteenth-century context, her discoveries have great resonance with portrayals of virginity on film four centuries later, and not only in those films dealing specifically with Elizabeth (as with the 1998 film discussed in this volume by Cobb). Chiming with Kelly, throughout her argument she relies on the idea that both sexual innocence and sexual experience are written on the body and are legible to others. As Schwarz notes, however, "Bodily certainties are precarious, vulnerable to the disruption of the processes that refer. This is the failing of the test: when the structures of proof become visible, proof itself is in some sense under scrutiny."[9]

Tested virginity does not merely cast doubt on its own means of examination, however. This external proof of an internal state is open not only to scrutiny but also to manipulation. Once there are considered to be external signs indicative of internal states, these signs can be manufactured without the internal referent on which they are supposed to rely. In other words, once virginity can be read, it can be faked. This has great significance for film, especially during those periods when the performance of the actor alone was relied upon to convey the sexual status of the character (as, e.g., in Production Code–era Hollywood when the word *virgin* was taboo).

Schwarz also seems to believe that virginity is significant solely as it pertains to women, calling it "a vehicle for misogyny."[10] In this view she is in agreement with Kelly and Blank; as the latter further formulates it, "Virginity . . . is exclusively heterosexual. . . . [It] is also female."[11] While these assertions are based on how religious, medical, and legal doctrine have conceptualized the term, rather than the authors' own beliefs, they all choose not to pursue the idea of the male virgin; this is understandable in the case of Schwarz, who deals with a specific female monarch, but in the book indexes of Kelly and Blank also there are scant or no references to the concept or possibility of the male sexual innocent. By contrast, this collection has actively tried to contest the assumption that the virgin is inevitably female, as the chapters by Shary, Falconer, Tuck, Sabbadini, and Deleyto illustrate.

Chapters in Brief

Initiating the collection, Gaylyn Studlar offers an in-depth consideration of the legibility of the star body as a site of virginity, using Elizabeth Taylor in her early 1940s roles as her exemplar. Studlar relates the virginal girl persona of the child star Taylor to both immediate wartime contexts and traditions within fine art that reach back to the Victorian period. Both settings play on the girl's Englishness and the associative qualities evoked by that national allegiance at a time when America was especially receptive to the idea of preserving its ally's independence and way of life. Studlar finds that the particular piquant quality Taylor brought to three child roles of 1944 locates itself in the paradoxically womanly beauty of the young girl. Conflicting notions of innocence and eroticism, passivity and agency, pricelessness and marketability, swirl around the figure of the beautiful virgin girl, which Studlar ties to Victorian art conventions, referencing Millais' portrait *Cherry Ripe,* itself a mixture of innocence and awareness of the girl child's allure.

Next, Ilana Nash compares paired films from the 1940s and 1960s, finding that the anxieties created by the national circumstances in which America found itself on both occasions—openly fighting the Second World War and more covertly waging the Cold War—can be mapped onto the figure of the virgin teenage girl, an ambivalent source of both prurient interest and disturbing tensions. Her chronologically paired virgins, Janie and Corliss, Scarlett and Molly, are all treated in some way as emblematic of the nation itself: hence fears of their bodily penetration can be seen as revealing a fundamental uneasiness about America's safety and inviolability. Yet the teen girl is finally shown as the nation's ultimate hope for the future. She can be the ideal citizen, as long as her passions are directed patriotically rather than personally.

Timothy Shary, in turn, provides the collection's first examination of male virginity in his survey chapter, which investigates the cycle or minigenre of the teen "sex quest" film. From the 1920s onward, movies most frequently warned against the dire consequences of indulging teen lusts, but with the arrival of the Canadian film *Porky's* (1982), the trope of sex-crazed boys begging to be *Goin' All the Way* (1982), *Losin' It* (1983), and hoping to find *The Sure Thing* (1985) began to proliferate. Later 1980s films abandoned the teen quest with the coming of the AIDS crisis, dwelling instead, as Shary indicates, on the romantic aspects of teen couplings or on their inevitable consequence, pregnancy. Larry Clark's *kids* (1995) caused a crisis within the teen sex genre, as the film reverted to evoking associations with crime and depravity hinted at by 1950s exploitation shockers, but with documentary-style explicitness in the sex scenes. Although the quest film has subsequently returned, most contemporary films that show teen sex have done so in a downbeat manner; while the 2007 summer smash *Superbad* seemed to reverse this trend, the next popular success about teens, *Juno* (2007), returned the emphasis on teen sex to its predictable filmic conclusion, pregnancy.

In her exploration of a similarly widely popular text from the 1950s, *Marjorie Morningstar* (1958), Rebecca Sullivan maintains the focus on the significance of virginity to the couple, not just the female innocent. Sullivan's chapter reveals that the 1950s, far from being the epitome of safe conformism, was actually a time of sexual challenges and exploration, for women as well as men, which anticipated in many ways the turmoil of the sexual revolution of the 1960s. Sullivan compares the film to its source novel by Herman Wouk, finding that the movie text attempts to alter the moral center of the book through its casting and performance strategies, especially by having the charismatic star Gene Kelly play the male lead, Noel Airman, inevitably elevating him from feckless wastrel to tortured artist. Ultimately, however, the film cannot resist compliance with the traditional double standard, finding the maintenance of Marjorie's virginity as vital for her as it is damaging to Noel.

Alisia G. Chase also analyzes a film in comparison with its source novel, examining *Bonjour Tristesse* (1958) for the ways in which director Otto Preminger exploited the contemporary notoriety of the book, and his juxtaposition of its scandalous young author and ingénue star, in order to secure audience interest in his film. Chase further reveals how Preminger attempted to satisfy both the young women who had bought the infamous novel and their mothers, who would prefer the amoral heroine Cecile to be punished in the film for her sexual precocity, as she is not in the book. Chase's chapter explores Preminger's manipulation of codes around the legibility of the virgin, using mise-en-scène and costume to carry affirmations of sexual sophistication and chicness for the young women to enjoy, as the narrative trajectory seems to plod toward a more punitive resolution for Cecile in order to appease their mothers.

My own chapter attempts to problematize the habitual, unthinking fixing of the label "virgin" to the star persona of Doris Day by pinpointing the moment of the label's attribution. Looking at moments of performance from two films, *Pillow Talk* (1959) and *Lover Come Back* (1961), my analysis seeks to demonstrate that virginity was a status that Day consciously adopted for her character, Carol Templeton, in the latter film, but it was absent from her role as Jan Morrow in the former and had not been a factor in her characters before the 1961 film. By analyzing in detail the vocal and somatic choices made by the actor in two comparable scenes from these

INTRODUCTION

films, in which the central female excitedly anticipates, or tremulously debates, her sexual union with the desired male, my chapter challenges the notion that Day "always plays a virgin" and also inquires both how playing a virgin—outwardly manifesting an internal quality, an invisible lack of knowledge—could be executed and why the assumption of virginity is so often made about the star.

Pete Falconer then switches the focus to the horror film, considering how the figure of the virgin has become so associated with and necessary to the genre that films such as *Scream* (1996) and *Scary Movie* (2000) can parody the usage of the trope. Falconer, with his discussion of the "Final Girl," who is the ultimate prey and the vanquisher of the psycho killer throughout the genre's most iconic films, pushes further the association of the virgin victim with the killer, finding that both present bodies that seem inviolable, closed.[12] His chapter also considers how virginity can be conferred on a subject symbolically even though literally it may be missing: Blade (Wesley Snipes), the reluctant vampire hero in Stephen Norrington's 1998 film, for example, is probably not literally a virgin, but his refusal to indulge his own bloodlusts conveys upon him a kind of purity, as the chapter elucidates.

Continuing the association of virginity with horror, Nina Martin embeds Roman Polanski's *Repulsion* (1965) not only firmly within generic borders but also within the specific context of the "swinging sixties." In doing so, Martin investigates how the post-Pill period fostered different, but no less urgent and intense, problems for women seeking sexual autonomy in the 1960s from those in the previous, apparently more repressive, decade. *Repulsion*'s heroine, Carole, attempts with increasing hysteria to cling to her youthful innocence despite attracting male sexual attention; as she begins to imagine threats of invasion and penetration being mounted against her body, her apartment becomes psychically figured as the contested terrain, to be guarded against male intrusion by any means necessary. The chapter considers how the film manipulates the spaces of the apartment in order to portray the unraveling of Carole's sanity and how editing techniques in particular are employed to enable the viewer to share the protagonist's trauma.

Greg Tuck's chapter problematizes the notion of virginity by coupling it with masturbation as a topic in recent Hollywood films across a range of genres. The chapter considers how masturbation affects the subject's sexual status, finding provocative associations between self-pleasure and innocence, and experience and madness, coalescing around the figure of

INTRODUCTION

the desirous virgin. Looking at a number of contemporary Hollywood films, beginning with *American Pie* (1999), Tuck explores the ontological position of the seemingly paradoxical orgasmic virgin, finding that sexual experience is shown in such films as unfolding along a continuum rather than hinging on one single event. While not compromising virginity, then, masturbation does conflict with maturity: adult masturbators are seen to regress to adolescence (as with Lester Burnham's morning shower indulgences in *American Beauty* [1999]), prompting Tuck to conclude that contemporary cinema deems solo sex only excusable as practice for "the main event," heterosexual procreative intercourse. Paradoxically, according to Tuck, only a masturbating mother (Betty in *Pleasantville* [1998]) can risk self-pleasure without sacrificing her adult status.

While Tuck's examination concludes that masturbation is still seen in too highly pejorative terms to have a wholly positive association with virginity, Lisa M. Dresner investigates a rare moment in recent history when female sexuality was portrayed in a positive light and also as a fitting topic for a film's narrative. Against a familiar background of films detailing boys' quests to end their virginity, also considered by Tuck and by Timothy Shary, Dresner considers the more unusual female quest film via two early 1980s examples, *Little Darlings* (1980) and *Fast Times at Ridgemont High* (1982). The female protagonists setting out to gain sexual experience in these films are shown to be obsessed with sex, turned on by nubile bodies, prepared to plan and scheme to achieve their goals: to be very much, then, like their male equivalents in the boy-focused films. The female-centered narratives, however, also tacitly illustrate that the most enjoyable aspect of the quest comes from the homosocial bonding it necessitates rather than any heterosexual pleasures derived from sex achieved.

Shelley Cobb shifts the focus from America to Great Britain but maintains the perspective on the association of the female virgin's body with the nation-state in a specific time frame, as considered in previous chapters. Cobb explores the contemporary reception of the 1998 film *Elizabeth,* directed by Shekhar Kapur, discussing the significance of the film's portrayal of the queen's relinquishing her sexuality as a political move. Showing the young queen first engaged in an active sexual relationship and then making an overt decision to "become a virgin" were the two most contentious facets of the film, which Cobb relates to late 1990s debates in British society around female agency and desire and which she links to the unlikely figures of Princess Diana, Margaret Thatcher, and the Spice Girls.

In his intervention, Andrea Sabbadini brings to film studies insights

INTRODUCTION

from the perspective of psychoanalysis. Considering two sexually uninitiated characters, one female and one male, from a psychoanalytic viewpoint, Sabbadini examines the employment of Freudian notions about virginity in art cinema, as well as examining the use of virginity as an organizing theme within two European films, *A Short Film about Love* (1988) and *Stealing Beauty* (1996). In this divergence from the tenor of the book's largely American focus, Sabbadini neatly reminds us that virginity has been a vexed topic in societies and periods beyond those of the American 1950s, with which it is so often and oversimply associated.

In addition, the book's final two chapters confirm in different ways the importance of virginity outside of the 1950s: Carol Siegel considers two films from the cusp of the new century, one American and one French, which both deal with very young women's sexual initiation. By contrast, Celestino Deleyto concludes the collection with a chapter that reverses both the gender and age of the main protagonist against societal assumptions.

Carol Siegel devotes her attention to two recent female rites-of-passage movies, *À ma soeur!* (2001) and *Thirteen* (2003). While both deal with the coming-of-age of female protagonists, Siegel finds more radical variation between the texts than just their respective American and French provenances. She considers the films' different approaches to virginity, and to female sexual agency and desire, as emblematic of the types of feminist thinking they display. The two texts thus represent the tensions between American and French feminisms at the turn of the new millennium. In *Thirteen* Siegel finds all the traditional associations of virginity still applied in contemporary cinema to enshrine the female and confer innocence and purity upon her, particularly when this purity is under threat. By contrast, the overt horrors visited on the virgin heroine of *À ma soeur!* are, challengingly, held by the film to be less damaging than growing to adult femininity within traditional patriarchal structures.

Finally, the collection concludes with Celestino Deleyto's reading of *The 40-Year-Old Virgin* (2005), a key text in the latest round of filmic obsession with the subject of first sex and one that raises the usually troubling specter of male virginity as a central topic for comedy.[13] Here Deleyto finds a rare positive instance of the inexperienced man and then proceeds to relate this figure to the romantic comedy genre more widely. Deleyto sees the tonal mixture of the film, merging scatological and explicitly sexual talk and imagery with more common romantic notions, as part of a move seemingly to open the genre more overtly to male audience members. Fur-

11

thermore, he reads this blending as indicative of a flexibility, an ability to incorporate new elements as they become popular, within the romantic comedy genre, which bodes well for its continued viability in the cinematic marketplace. Deleyto's concluding piece indicates that, while the topic of virginity remains a recurrent one in cinema, new approaches toward this perennial favorite are still possible.

It bears repeating that this edited collection is intended to inaugurate exploration of this fascinating topic rather than offering any definitive last words on it. There are many other films, historical periods, national cinemas, and specific stars that could very fruitfully be examined by focusing on what part virginity plays in their meanings. Finally, of course, virginity and the ways in which it is portrayed and envisaged continue to have importance, as sexual initiation remains a recurrent topic of interest and currency in films and wider media culture. For example, in late August 2006, Sky Television launched the show "Virgin Diaries." Accompanied by the tagline "There's a first time for everyone," the program followed various teen virgins as they attempted to gain sexual experience, debating with themselves and each other, on camera, the rights and wrongs of "losing it." Britain's BBC2 dealt with the topic in a comparable talking-heads format in May 2008: "Virgin Memories," though presented from a somewhat more sober perspective, also chose to invite people to speak about their "sexual debut[s]," asserting that "each first time has a different tale to tell."[14] In addition, incidents at the 2008 MTV Video Music Awards show fostered interest in the topic when the evening's compere, British comedian Russell Brand, criticized popular Disney Channel boy band, the Jonas Brothers, for prominently displaying their promise rings, only to be attacked in turn by female teen singer Jordin Sparks ("It's not bad to wear a promise ring, because not everybody—guy or girl—wants to be a slut").[15]

Such evergreen currency of the topic will likely remain, as each individual's relinquishing of virginity is an inevitable rite of passage into adulthood and as successive societies continue to struggle with how the individual's sexual identity, desire, and agency intersects with cultural concerns and decrees. As Kathryn Schwarz notes, the state of sexual innocence retains an ambiguous and paradoxical charge: "[Virginity] is in the past, in the future, in the negative, in the subjunctive, an impossibility, a provocation, a performance, a lie."[16] This collection explores in detail these ambiguities and paradoxes.

INTRODUCTION

Notes

1. "Does she or doesn't she?" Clairol, 1955, advertising slogan for Miss Clairol Hair Color Bath; "Is she or isn't she?" Helen Gurley Brown, *Sex and the Single Girl* (New York: Bernard Geis and Associates, 1962), 64; "Will she or won't she?" Jules Archer, *Playboy,* January 1956, 13; "Should she or shouldn't she?" Nora Johnson, "Sex and the College Girl," *Atlantic Monthly,* November 1959, 60; "Should I surrender?" *Lover Come Back* (dir. Delbert Mann, 1961); "Have you been bad?" *A Summer Place* (dir. Delmer Daves, 1959).

2. Kathryn Schwartz, "The Wrong Question: Thinking through Virginity," *differences: A Journal of Feminist Cultural Studies* 13, no. 2 (2002): 1.

3. For examples of those focused on specific stars, see Georganne Scheiner, "Look at Me, I'm Sandra Dee: Beyond a White Teen Icon," *Frontiers: A Journal of Women Studies* 22, no. 2 (2001): 87–106; and Tamar Jeffers, "Pillow Talk's Repackaging of Doris Day: 'Under all those dirndls . . .,'" in *Fashioning Film Stars: Dress, Culture, Identity,* ed. Rachel Moseley (London: British Film Institute, 2005), 50–61. For an example of a study offering a sexually symbolic reading, see the perceptive chapter by Peter Krämer on the relationship of the heroine's loss of virginity to the sinking of the ship in *Titanic* (dir. James Cameron, 1997) in "Women First: *Titanic,* Action-Adventure Films, and Hollywood's Female Audience," in *Titanic: Anatomy of a Blockbuster,* ed. Kevin Sandler and Gaylyn Studlar (New Brunswick, NJ: Rutgers University Press, 1999), 108–31.

4. Schwartz, "Wrong Question," 5.

5. For studies of virginity in literature, see, for example, Joanne Stroud and Gail Thomas, *Images of the Untouched: Virginity in Psyche, Myth and Community* (Dallas, TX: Dallas Institute for the Humanities and Culture, Spring Publications, 1982); Lloyd Davis, *Virginal Sexuality and Textuality in Victorian Literature* (Albany, NY: SUNY Press, 1993); and Marie H. Loughlin, *Hymeneutics: Interpreting Virginity on the Early Modern Stage* (Lewisburg, PA: Bucknell University Press). For sociocultural and cultural histories, see Elizabeth Abbott, *A History of Celibacy: From Athena to Elizabeth I, Leonardo Da Vinci, Florence Nightingale, Gandhi and Cher* (New York: Scriber, 2000); and John D'Emilio and Estelle B. Freedman, *Intimate Matters: A History of Sexuality in America* (New York: Harper and Row, 1988). For girlhood studies, see, for example, Catherine Driscoll, *Girls: Female Adolescence in Popular Culture and Cultural Theory* (New York: Columbia University Press, 2002); Frances Gateward and Murray Pomerance, eds., *Sugar, Spice and Everything Nice: Cinemas of Girlhood* (Detroit: Wayne State University Press, 2002); Sarah Hengtes, *Pictures of Girlhood: Modern Female Adolescence on Film* (Jefferson, NC: McFarland, 2006); Sherrie A. Inness, *Tough Girls: Women Warriors and Wonder Women in Popular Culture* (Philadelphia: University of Pennsylvania Press, 1998); and Scheiner, "Look at Me."

6. Anke Bernau, *Virgins: A Cultural History* (London: Granta, 2007), xi.

7. Kathleen Coyne Kelly, *Performing Virginity and Testing Chastity in the Middle Ages* (London: Routledge, 2000), 131.

8. Ibid.

9. Schwartz, "Wrong Question," 14.

10. Ibid., 25.

11. Hanne Blank, *Virgin: The Untouched History* (New York: Bloomsbury, 2007), 10. See also Kelly, *Performing Virginity*, 15.

12. Carol Clover, *Men, Women and Chain Saws: Gender in the Modern Horror Film* (London: British Film Institute, 1992).

13. Besides its critical and box office success, Judd Apatow's 2005 film can be seen as notable for initiating a new rash of sex comedies, such as his own *Knocked Up* (2007) and also *Superbad* (dir. Greg Motola, 2007), *Good Luck Chuck* (dir. Mark Helfrich, 2007), and *Forgetting Sarah Marshall* (dir. Nicholas Stoller, 2008).

14. Anonymous program review in *Radio Times*, May 10–16, 2008, 108.

15. See note about purity rings in Siegel, chapter 13 in this volume.

16. Schwartz, "Wrong Question," 2.

Gaylyn Studlar

Velvet's Cherry
Elizabeth Taylor and Virginal English Girlhood

> Isn't it a good job of work—just to be beautiful?
> —Velvet Brown (Elizabeth Taylor) in *National Velvet* (1944)

Introduction

The child actress was a familiar staple of the Hollywood studio system by the 1940s. In the 1930s, Shirley Temple set the gold standard for the appeal of child stars to film audiences, becoming the first child star to be declared the industry's number one box office draw, a position she held for almost half a decade.[1] Naturally, other studios tried to emulate Fox's success with Temple. Judy Garland and Jane Withers were among the child performers who garnered box office attention in the 1930s. However, Temple's popularity with audiences was not replicated on a comparable scale until adolescent coloratura Deanna Durbin made a deep impression in *Three Smart Girls* in 1936, initiating her financial boon to Universal over the next twelve years.

In 1942, attempting to follow up on Durbin's success, Universal offered a six-month contract to nine-year-old Elizabeth Taylor, whose parents had returned to the United States from Britain when World War II started. After appearing in one low-budget film, *There's One Born Every Minute* (1942), she was dropped by Universal. As movie lore has it, the studio executive who let her go justified his decision by suggesting that Taylor did not appear enough like a little girl; he observed that she had the eyes and face of a woman.[2]

After Taylor was let go by Universal, her mother kept "pushing" for her daughter's Hollywood career. Taylor's next big break has been attributed to a chance conversation between her father, art dealer Francis Taylor, and MGM producer Samuel Marx as they served together as wartime air raid wardens.[3] In 1943, MGM offered Taylor a contract and a small supporting role as an aristocratic English child in the film *Lassie Come Home* (1943), starring the world's most famous collie. The film also featured British child actor Roddy McDowall who, echoing the Universal executive, later remarked on his first glimpse of Taylor, "It was like seeing a tiny adult walking up with this exquisite face. She was the most beautiful child I ever saw."[4]

The cultural and sexual implications of female child performers remain largely unexamined in film studies. In this chapter I explore these implications as they accrued around the "beautiful" screen presence of Elizabeth Taylor as a child actress in the 1940s, as well as the relationship of three of Taylor's early screen appearances to their historical antecedents. I examine how both conventional aesthetic codes of visual representation and thematic traditions as evidenced in Victorian genre painting influenced cinema's contradictory and complex representations of girls in general and Taylor in particular. In this respect, I am following Raymond Williams's observation, "In a society as a whole, and in all its particular activities, the cultural tradition can be seen as a continual selection and reselection of ancestors."[5] I will focus my analysis on the actress's uncredited but memorable screen appearances in two 1944 films, *Jane Eyre* and *The White Cliffs of Dover*, and her star-making title role in *National Velvet* from the same year.

Taylor was not a "cute moppet" in the Temple mold but an unusually beautiful little girl with qualities that might lead us to call her a "womanly girl" whose womanliness created for Hollywood both a problem and an opportunity. In this exploration, I seek to answer several convergent questions: How did the mixture of childlike qualities and womanly facial beauty play into the construction of Taylor's successful screen presence and ultimate stardom? What markers of sexual agency or appeal were inscribed in her screen performances in 1944? How, in other words, did these three films regulate the contradictions involved in presenting an eleven-year-old child marked as "virginal" or sexually "taboo" by storylines but whose performance and presentation might suggest the feminine as desirable or desiring? What was the textual impact of the reassertion of nostalgic visual conventions associated with the Victorian era made by these three films?

Elizabeth Taylor's "womanly" beauty.

And, finally, what were the possible sexual anxieties and fascinations that Taylor's early screen presence produced, and for whom?

Appealing Antecedents and Fascinated Fans

From the beginnings of Hollywood's studio system, a plethora of child actors achieved varying levels of recognition in Hollywood. The industry liked to link its child performers, on and off screen, with traditional middle-class values of sentimentality and familial affection. In keeping with these values, women and children were frequently thought to be the primary audience for juvenile performers. Nevertheless, in 1915, Betty Marsh, a four-year-old player for Reliance-Majestic Studios, received a letter from a New York man. In his self-declared "mash note," the "old bachelor" said he "never suspected [a] little girl could be so nice and appealing so I am going to wait until you grow up and then I will lay my heart and my fortune at your feet.... [P]lease, oh please, do not promise to be a sister to me."[6] The letter was reproduced in several newspapers, but no one appears to have used its publication to comment on how the male fan's reaction to Marsh might have suggested some of the more unsettling sexual implications in making a profitable spectacle of children—especially girls.

Perhaps there was no comment because of the overwhelming cultural precedent for the commodification of juvenile females in popular media. The late Victorian "cult of the girl" was a historically specific articulation of dominant social norms attached to childhood, imbuing girlhood, as art historian Leslie Williams suggests, with "complicated symbolic value as a meeting-point for subordinance and control, marketability and pricelessness, eroticism and innocence."[7] Many of the iconic codes, values, and meanings attached to young females during this era continued into the twentieth century, Hollywood films of the 1930s and 1940s relying on established visual strategies for representing girls. The Shirley Temple vehicle *Curly Top* (1935), while set in the present, even includes a scene that directly cites famous child paintings by the Victorian era's most famous visual interpreter of girlhood, John Everett Millais, as well as works by Reynolds, Gainsborough, and others. In fact, almost half of Shirley Temple's films at Fox in the 1930s were set in the Victorian period and exploited costumes and situations that would have been at home in the paintings of Millais. *Curly Top* demonstrates how nineteenth-century representational norms as well as specific high art references could attempt to control the overdetermined erotic meaning of girls in motion pictures. The film concerns a very wealthy and handsome single man, Edward Morgan (John Boles), who becomes the youngest trustee of the Lakeside Orphanage. On a visit, he meets Elizabeth (Shirley Temple), an orphan who charms him with her lighthearted antics. Returning home to his mansion, Edward continues to think of the adorable child and sings a love song he has composed, "It's All So New To Me," looking around his room at portraits of children, which are then each brought to life, their faces changing to Shirley's/Elizabeth's. As the subject of Thomas Gainsborough's *Portrait of Jonathan Buttall* ("*The Blue Boy*"), she smiles and waves her hat. As the curly-headed girl sitting on a church pew in Millais' *Her First Sermon* (1863), she blows Edward a kiss.

The way in which the film cites nostalgic cultural icons suggests that the orphaned girl has the beauty and charm that idealized, high art children of the past possessed. Her appearance as the subjects of these revered paintings confirms that she could be at home in the mansion of a millionaire. Because the idea of an adult male singing a love song to a child might seem sexually grotesque (like the letter to Betty Marsh), the high art reference (even in its crossing of gender boundaries, such as Shirley's appearance as the *Blue Boy*) serves another important function. It suggests that the millionaire's appreciation of the attractive little orphan girl that he will eventually adopt is both emotionally and culturally normal (if not "elevated") rather than pedophilic and perverse. *Curly Top* employs these high art references to guide the audience's interpretation of the sexual connotations attached to beautiful, virginal girlhood by an adult male admirer as benign.

Victorian high art's reliance on little girls had largely lacked controversy; Millais had remarked that appreciation of juvenile female beauty was so universal that "the only head you could paint to be considered beautiful by everybody would be the face of a little girl about eight years old."[8] Thus, rather than being questioned or condemned, many of the artistic images of girls in rural settings or at domestic pastimes were the object of both critical acclaim and wide public admiration. In a reciprocal relationship to complicated cultural dynamics involving gender, power, and sexuality, these imaginings of eroticized but innocent girlhood were shaped by and yet also responsible for shaping public response. This points to the potential of such girlhood imagery, carefully controlled by male aesthetic sensibility, to satisfy multifaceted fantasies, including heteroerotic ones involving adult male viewers. Although women might be fans of these pictures, as Leslie Williams reminds us, "the buyers of art, the market for these images of young girls, were men."[9] Artists like Millais relied upon these buyers' appreciation of images of beautiful young girls to guarantee the marketability of their products, so the question of whether that appreciation rested on a sexual element was repressed. In fact, rather than raise questions about the sexual response of owners/viewers to these images of girls, artistic representations were called on to ameliorate fears about the sexual exploitation of children through their sentimentalization of childhood beauty.

That these paintings were expected to function, however unconsciously, in this contradictory manner is given support by the widespread negative response to Millais' painting *The Woodsman's Daughter* (1851). Based on the Coventry Patmore poem about a poor girl who succumbs to the sexual overtures of a squire's son, bears his child, and then commits infanticide, the painting foreshadows these eventual unchaste consequences in an earlier interaction between the young boy and girl. Millais' painting thus overtly addressed the issue of childhood sexuality. Although representations of girlhood were ubiquitous by this time, and this picture is no less technically masterful than Millais' other efforts, *The Woodsman's Daughter* crossed the boundary between what was acceptable according to unspoken codes of representing girls as beautiful icons of erotic innocence and what was unacceptable, even repugnant, to Victorian society in relation to them.[10]

Patmore himself declared the otherwise "charming picture" based on his poem marred because "the girl looked like a vulgar little slut."[11] As there does not seem to be any suggestiveness in the girl's bodily posture or costuming, we can speculate that this negative response was triggered by something as subtle as the facial expression of the girl. No one wanted to buy *The Woodsman's Daughter* until it was finally purchased by Millais' half-brother, and many years later, even he asked Millais to repaint the girl's face.[12]

The Woodsman's Daughter teaches an important lesson about the subtle ways in which the boundary defining acceptable codes and conventions of representing girlhood innocence could be crossed. As I will argue, almost a century later the career of child actress Elizabeth Taylor would call attention to this boundary, her frequent casting as an English girl during the mid-1940s suggesting the long-lived appeal of and complexities in representing girlhood associated with the English rural past and with eroticized feminine innocence. As with Temple's *Curly Top,* Taylor's 1944 films also attempt to "guide" viewers' responses to interpreting the sexual connotations of the child in a benign manner, with performance, costuming, photography, and shot choice resulting, across three texts, in very different meanings of the virginal girl child's filmic presence.

Who Is Cherry Ripe?

To Hollywood screenwriters, the English became especially appealing role models during the war years. British citizens' courageous response to the Blitz and their fortitude in standing firm as a nation against Nazi aggression appealed to American audiences, who identified with their allies and wished to imagine that they, if called upon, could represent Anglo-American ideals with equal vigor. British characters and subject matter were frequently accompanied in Hollywood films of the 1940s by a narrative return to the past, highlighting the conventional association of the British with quaintness and an aristocratic or refined past. In addition, this "pastness" agreeably suited Hollywood's desire to capitalize on romantic nostalgia as part of its ideological endeavor to remind wartime audiences "why we fight." In this respect, children were an important part of Hollywood's construction of the romantic nostalgia used to support wartime morale.

An English child on-screen during this period created a special constellation of ideological meaningfulness.

Starting with *Lassie Come Home*, Elizabeth Taylor's career as a child actress at MGM was marked by her frequent casting as a pure and innocent English girl. Both *The White Cliffs of Dover*, based on a poem by Alice Duer Miller, and *Jane Eyre*, adapted from the Charlotte Brontë novel, were film melodramas aimed clearly at the U.S. female audiences so important to Hollywood's wartime box office revenue. The former was a maternal melodrama chronicling the joys and sorrows of an American woman (played by Irene Dunne) whose English husband is killed in one war and whose son is struck down in another. *Jane Eyre* was a gothic melodrama delineating the by now familiar story of a governess who falls in love with her aristocratic employer. In spite of their radically different generic origins, these two films, like many other Hollywood products released during World War II, both drew heavily upon cultural ideals of personal courage, familial love, and sacrifice to duty. As women's films, they attached these ideals to adult female characters—and even to little girls. It is no wonder, then, that in all of Taylor's screen appearances of 1944—in *Lassie Come Home, Jane Eyre, The White Cliffs of Dover*, and *National Velvet*—Taylor's young characters conform to sentimental notions of the "quintessential English little girl" of "timeless purity," a description applied by art historian Laurel Bradley to another iconic British figure, *Cherry Ripe*.[13]

This figure is the juvenile female subject of John Everett Millais' *Cherry Ripe* (1879), a painting that became one of the most famous representations of childhood femininity in the late Victorian era: a big-eyed, dark-haired girl in old-fashioned mobcap and countrified dress sits with a bunch of cherries on the bench beside her. The image circulated widely in popular culture through cheaply made reproductions, appearing as the commissioned centerfold of *The Graphic*'s Christmas annual of 1880 and in mezzotint form, selling more than a half-million copies.[14] According to Bradley, "The pretty child in old-fashioned dress is meant to embody the positive attributes of English culture" at a time when Britain's influence was spreading throughout the world through imperialism.[15] This beautiful child appealed to the nostalgia of a preindustrial, Edenic England and was constructed to address "the patriotic and emotional needs" of the cultural moment by aligning girlish purity and innocence with the rural past and with "the timeless world of enduring values."[16] Pamela Reis has argued for the visual encoding of sexual connotations attached to feminine sexual desirability in the construction of the painting's appeal.[17] This "pedophilic appeal," says Reis, is suggested in the artist's subtle display of the child, with her gaze rather boldly directed at the viewer and her hands cupped between her legs, as well as in the title of the painting, drawn from an early seventeenth-century poem by Thomas Campion. Campion's poem, *Cherry-Ripe,* speaks of the sexual maturation of the girl through reference to what became commonplace slang for the hymen:

> There is a garden in her face
> > Where roses and white lilies blow;
> A heavenly paradise is that place,
> > Wherein all pleasant fruits do grow;
> There cherries grow that none may buy,
> > Till Cherry-Ripe themselves do cry.

It is not unreasonable to suggest the ultimate compatibility of these two seemingly different approaches to understanding the broad commercial appeal of Millais' *Cherry Ripe.* Likewise, Taylor's representations of beautiful English girlhood frequently convey a similar conflation of ideological comfort and sexual suggestion; like Millais' painting, Taylor's films of 1944 expose some of the contradictions in Western culture's modern "eruptions" of the veritable worship of beautiful little girls and the particular power that such an eruption can acquire during a time of ideological upheaval.

Just as Millais built upon but also revised earlier visual and literary representations of girlhood, the Hollywood studio system articulated standards of child beauty that incorporated visual and narrative conventions and did not undo but built upon the contradictions embedded in earlier representations. Taylor's early films often partake of that "reassuring aura of childhood, culture, and the English hearth" that Bradley finds in *Cherry Ripe* and that audiences no doubt found particularly reassuring in the context of Anglo-American war efforts. However, the three films that I analyze here were also called upon to negotiate the presence of an extraordinarily beautiful little girl whose attractiveness echoed the overdetermined cultural and sexual complexities of Victorian girl painting in general and *Cherry Ripe* in particular. It might be expected that, following the precedent of Millais' painting, and in light of the precociously mature, womanly beauty attributed to Taylor, these screen representations would also convey a promise of feminine sexual desirability, if not the possibility of feminine sexual desire. However, I argue that not all her films presented her in exactly the same terms and that, indeed, those differences of presentation result in very different erotic affect attached to the beautiful, virginal, female child. Embodied on-screen by Taylor and envisioned by different creative collaborations, her characters consistently drew on qualities of girlhood predating cinematic convention to suggest, in varying degrees, the mysterious sexual power of the virginal young girl combined with "the reassuring aura of childhood, culture, and the English hearth" that had characterized *Cherry Ripe*.[18]

Helen Burns as the "Queer Virgin"

Nina Auerbach has identified the "charismatic union of childhood and death" as a ubiquitous feature in Victorian literature.[19] The classic Victorian fetish object, the child doomed to an early death, is found in many Victorian novels, including *Jane Eyre*. In the 1944 film version of Brontë's novel, Taylor is cast as Helen Burns, who embodies this important Victorian narrative and sexual trope. As Jane Eyre's childhood friend at the Lowood orphanage, Taylor appeared in a handful of early scenes in the film: Jane's first day at the orphanage when she is publicly punished as a liar; a lighthearted scene set outdoors, away from the austere confines of the school; a scene in which the school superintendent, Mr. Brocklehurst (Henry Daniell), cuts off Helen's curls; a nighttime scene in which Jane and Helen, weighed down by heavy irons, are forced to walk in the cold rain; and a scene in which Jane, overhearing the doctor's prognosis that Helen will die, goes to her bedside. There is one more scene in which Helen figures posthumously and importantly in the film as she does not in the novel, one that undoubtedly resonated with wartime audiences made all too familiar with death and grief: Jane is found by the kindly Dr. Rivers (John Sutton) as she lies across Helen's unmarked grave. Distraught, she sobs, "I want to be with Helen." Dr. Rivers tells her not to succumb to despair, encouraging her to devote herself to her education in fulfillment of her duty to God. Sublimation of Jane's great despair over Helen's death becomes the fuel for Jane's self-improvement in her remaining years at Lowood.

The beauty of Elizabeth Taylor in her period costume and curls is reminiscent of the visual perfection of female children depicted by Millais and other sentimental Victorian artists. Brontë's novel, however, was considered, on its publication in 1847, to be far from sentimental, and its Helen Burns differs significantly from the film's. In the original novel Helen Burns is older (fourteen), pious, and not very pretty. She is described by Jane Eyre as having "marked lineaments . . . thin face . . . sunken grey eye."[20] Helen's lack of attention to the school's requirements results in humiliation, having to wear "the untidy badge" or a placard that reads "Slattern."[21] In fact, on her deathbed, her remarks to Jane show how much she has absorbed these damaging reprimands: "By dying young, I shall escape great sufferings. I had not qualities or talents to make my way very well in the world: I should have been continually at fault."[22] Brontë's Helen is physically unremarkable and downtrodden in almost every sense except the spiritual.

By contrast, Helen in the 1944 film is an erotically charged, if virginal, presence. This charge depends not only on Taylor's beauty and its visual presentation but also on a narrative that enhances her emotional importance to and intimacy with the young Jane Eyre. Thus the filmic presence of Helen suggests her status as a "queer virgin," a term discussed by scholars such as Theodora Jankowski in a different context, that of early modernism.[23] Applying "queer virginity" to a child rather than to the category of "adult woman virgin," about whom Jankowski employs the term, allows a discussion of the film's presentation of Helen as an exemplar of the force of erotic innocence that moves beyond the "binary axis of homo versus heterosexuality" and acknowledges that this inchoate sexuality has physical consummation in a sexual act as its goal.[24]

Taylor functions quite strikingly as a sexual object to the film audience and to other film characters, in particular Jane, but also Mr. Brocklehurst. Her performative presence as an erotic object occurs because the film, even more so than the novel, makes the friendship between the girls much more intense through acting; the creation of new, highly emotionally charged scenes; and melodramatic visual and aural treatment. The resulting eroticization of Helen suggests an intriguing resistance to the heterosexual cultural positioning of the beautiful little girl as an object of male (pedophilic) lust.

As in the novel, Jane's unsympathetic aunt, Mrs. Reed, banishes her to harsh Lowood School. Accused by Mr. Brocklehurst of being a liar, Jane is forced to stand on the "pedestal of infamy" in an assembly, with the pupils exhorted by the headmaster to shun this child of the devil. At this moment, Brontë's novel gives itself over to Jane's voice and her very private vision at her first glimpse of Helen, who moves past her, amid all the other students, and smiles: "Just as they all rose, stifling my breath and constricting my throat, a girl came up and passed me: in passing, she lifted her eyes. What a strange light inspired them! What an extraordinary sensation that ray sent through mine! It was as if a martyr, a hero, had passed a slave or victim, and imparted strength in the transit. I mastered the rising hysteria, lifted up my head, and took a firm stand on the stool."25

The film stages Helen's entrance for the vision of the film spectator, not that of Jane. While Brontë's novel emphasizes Helen's impact on Jane as imparting "strength," the intensity and tenor of the passage in the film suggests a sensual impact, largely through the choices in shot selection and the visualization of Helen. All the teachers and the other students file out. A lap dissolve collapses time. Jane is left alone on the stool. A long shot reveals the huge hall, its depth exaggerated through long lines of shadow stretching to the background. Soundtrack music quietly begins. A shot reveals the entrance of a small figure on a staircase in the background, the camera waiting as a girl gracefully walks down the stairs, casting large shadows on the wall. Thus Helen comes from the back of the room in what can only be described as a "star entrance." She walks into the midground and hands Jane a piece of bread: "I brought you this from supper." The very leisurely paced timing and depth of field shooting invite our curiosity and suggest the importance of Helen as a character who deserves the camera's (and the audience's) extended attention. When Helen comes into the midground of the scene, our wait to see her is rewarded when we see her beautiful face, her luxuriant hair, and her restrained but graceful movements. Elizabeth Taylor's Helen is a child, but one with a sexual presence. Full shots, then a medium close-up that includes both girls, accompany Jane's dialogue. She recounts very emotionally and quite pitifully how she came to school wanting "people to love me." Close-ups are exchanged, while in a two-shot, Helen puts her hand over Jane's. "Eat your bread, Jane," she says, with a calmness that counterpoints Jane's hysteria.

In a scene in which dialogue is dominated by talk of love and the desire for acceptance, one child, a self-possessed, strikingly beautiful girl, creates a "sensation" in another little girl who is desperate, disheveled, and plain. The passionate friendship between Jane and Helen beginning in this scene is made melodramatically effective because of a number of factors, not the least important being the convincing acting out of unhappiness displayed by Peggy Ann Garner as Jane, emphasized in several close-ups, and its contrast with the cool passivity of Taylor as Helen. Helen possesses that combination of "perfect beauty and tender expression" that Millais thought so crucial to "producing beauty."26 Unlike Brontë's Helen, Taylor's Helen is grace and physical perfection personified.

In contrast to the novel, Jane and Helen are completely alone in the film's rendering of the scene rather than in the midst of others. There is an intimacy in their solitude, and Jane's disappointment in being taken for a liar and rejected is about relations, about love: "I thought school would be a place where people would love me." The stillness of Helen's presence (vs. Jane's hysteria), the calmness of her reactions to Jane, and the measured tempo of her placing her hand on Jane's all impose the attributes of an unexpected adult maturity and therefore womanliness on her not-woman status. Helen is an emblem of purity, of the female child whose purity is presumed to be spiritual (as innocent) and sexual (but untouched by men). Like a figure in a dream, this beautiful little girl comes out of nowhere to fulfill Jane's desire to have someone to love her.

Helen's erotic presence is readable as precociously mature and asserted through Taylor's performance, through the quality of her voice and in her delivery of her lines, as well as in the contextualization of her performance both visually and aurally. Herrmann's hushed, romantic musical score conveys the tenderness of emotion valorized in this scene and confirms the importance of Helen's kindness to Jane. The music, the selection of shots, and their timing all combine to suggest a romantic sensuality that trumps spirituality and the presumption of children's asexuality. Although created by a largely male contingent of filmmakers, this romanticization of the two girls' intense friendship to resemble something that looks like Hollywood's approach to romantic heterosexuality is made doubly interesting because it occurs in a film constructed to appeal to a largely female audience.

Another incident further reveals the film's evocation of the erotic in the girls' relationship: Mr. Brocklehurst's cutting of Helen's hair, which is "one mass of curls." He asks for the scissors and pushes Helen around so he can start cutting her hair. Helen is quiet and betrays emotion only through her eyes, and only to the film audience, which she faces. Jane begs Mr. Brocklehurst to stop, to cut her hair instead. In her analysis of Victorian aesthetics, Elisabeth G. Gitter has called attention to the importance of female hair as an erotic show or exhibition in Victorian art and its luxuriance as a sign of sexuality.[27] In Victorian society, the erotic charge that women's hair carried meant that only little girls were allowed to wear their hair long and flowing. Under the repressed and repressive Mr. Brocklehurst, the girls of Lowood are forced to wear their hair up, in pigtails, or in other configurations. No wonder Brocklehurst rails against Helen's natural curls as a sign of vanity (and nature) that must be conquered, that is, cut. No wonder too that Jane begs that her own hair be cut rather than the curls of her beautiful little friend. The extreme reactions in this scene to Helen's curls, both in Brocklehurst's demands and Jane's impassioned defense, suggest an erotic charge to Helen and her curls that might subvert the order of things, including the conventional order that demands the repression not only of Mr. Brocklehurst's desire but also of Jane's inchoate love for her friend.

Mr. Brocklehurst reacts to what he calls "this insurrection" by sending both girls into the cold rain to march as punishment. When the doctor returns, he demands they be brought in, but it is too late: Helen is felled by consumption. Jane overhears the doctor's prognosis and goes to Helen, who is as beautiful and calm as ever. "Don't cry, Jane. I don't want you to cry," she softly intones. She tells Jane to warm herself under the bedcovers. Jane crawls into bed with Helen and falls asleep. A close-up of their intertwined hands is accompanied by the offscreen voice of Jane attempting to wake Helen; she squeezes her hand, then screams on realizing her friend has died. This scene of intimacy and death is subject to a curious avoidance in the novel: there Jane is removed, still sleeping, from Helen's bed and only later learns of Helen's death.

The identity and presence of Taylor's body are of the female as a little girl, for her body lacks the physical marks of "true womanhood"—her flat chest and diminutive physique indicate that hers is an unwomanly body—so that her sexual difference is unlike that of a woman viewer as well as that of a male viewer. Yet Helen's certainty of purpose and mature grace, conveyed in Taylor's performance as a pure little Victorian girl, convey something otherworldly, erotically charged, and "not little girl."

Unlike Brontë's Helen, the impression that Taylor leaves is not of intense spirituality but of extreme femininity. Her hair, eyes, and skin, as well as her voice, function as heightened signs of conventional feminine beauty and refinement in contrast to Jane and the other girls. The result is that Helen's/Taylor's sexual difference is inscribed in ways partially associated with womanliness rather than completely with childishness. This preternatural womanliness is especially effective in view of Helen's narrative function as that Victorian fetish, the doomed child. Because of the casting and visual treatment of Taylor, Helen is the child without a future (as a grown woman) who nevertheless conveys the woman she would have become. Thus, when she dies, post-Victorian viewers are encouraged to mourn her disappearance as both pitiable girl child and beautiful not-woman woman. To further support Helen's role in "queering virginity," both the narrative point in the story and the original viewing context for the film emphasize same-sex relations (female to female) rather than heterosexual ones.

Cherry-Ripe *Redux*

In *Jane Eyre,* the sexual implications of Taylor's character's presentation are radical and unexpected and move into dangerous territory where the sexual power as well as beauty of a virginal little girl might be wordlessly asserted. By contrast, in *The White Cliffs of Dover* and *National Velvet,* Elizabeth Taylor's casting as a pure and innocent English girl is subject to very different strategies of visual display and performance that work to discourage the audience's interpretation of her characters as possessing anything more than conventional girlhood innocence. However, as I will show, even these two films suggest the difficulties in presenting beautiful girlhood without also engaging in some of the sexual contradictions and discomfitures that beset iconographic depictions of girlhood.

In *The White Cliffs of Dover,* Taylor plays ten-year-old Betsy Kenney, the daughter of English tenant farmers who live on the estate of Lady Jean Ashwood (Gladys Cooper). Lady Ashwood's widowed daughter-in-law, Lady Susan Ashwood (Irene Dunne), lives in the Ashwood manor house with her young son, John Ashwood II (Roddy McDowall). In one scene, John and a male servant peruse the estate from horseback. They stop at the Kenney farm and are greeted by Betsy. The landscape and situation suggest a pastoral fairy tale, but with echoes of the erotic encounter of children from different classes depicted by Millais' *The Woodsman's Daughter.* Betsy gazes with fascination at "Sir John" and exhibits flirtatious interest in him, holding onto the farm fence, stretching her arms as she bends into and away from the gate, moving her head in a submissively feminine position and giggling.

Betsy's flirtations are gauche and unstudied so that her behavior appears excessively childish. Like *Cherry Ripe* in her mobcap, Betsy, in her gingham bonnet, is part of a pastoral idyllic landscape: a thatched roof watermill is featured in the background. Unlike *Cherry Ripe* or *The Woodsman's Daughter,* Betsy Kenney does not invite interpretation as precociously sexual, even though the scene is obviously meant to suggest her romantic interest in another child. We are invited to consider her giddy, girlish, and silly.

In a later scene, the boy, Sir John, appears once again at the farm to say good-bye. He and his mother are moving to the United States. After conversing with her parents and shaking hands with a subdued Betsy, he walks off but then goes to back to the fence, leans over it, and offers Betsy the ring he has been wearing. Over-the-shoulder, shot-reverse shots emphasize

Betsy's more mature, subdued, and quite sincere reactions to John's attentions. Taylor is given two close-ups in shallow focus that emphasize her facial loveliness. She is bareheaded, dressed in a modest gingham pinafore apron, over a dress with a lace collar. Such materials would have signaled (at least to a female audience) self-respecting, working-class feminine innocence. The sweetness of her verbal responses to John as well as her physical poise suggest something more than was expressed in the earlier scene between them. The exchange of the ring recalls the girl's attempt to make an offering to the boy in *The Woodsman's Daughter,* but here the conventions of representing childhood innocence are upheld rather than questioned. The moment prefigures a romance between them, but a fairy-tale romance in which British class differences melt away under the force of Hollywood fantasy.

John and his mother decide to stay in England, and in the final scene of Taylor's appearance as Betsy, we see her, with John, on a windswept hill, gathering flowers as his mother prepares a picnic lunch. Although Taylor and McDowall appear no older, their stances are more mature. He holds her from behind lightly and points authoritatively into the distance as she smiles and holds a bouquet. A lap dissolve indicating the passage of time holds them in the same position but replaces McDowall and Taylor in close-up with more mature ingénue actors, Peter Lawford and June Lockhart. The latter, while clearly older than Taylor, appears less beautiful and significantly less sensual. At this moment, audiences may realize they have just witnessed how on-screen girlhood, embodied by Elizabeth Taylor, has threatened to "speak" the fragile boundary between adult sexual desire and the virgin child, the taboo object.

"What Does It Feel Like to Be in Love with a Horse?"

As I have argued of *The White Cliffs of Dover,* strategies of presentation and performance might work to discourage the audience's interpretation of Elizabeth Taylor's beautiful characters as possessing anything more than the innocence and purity conventionally associated with little girls. However, as I argued of her appearance in *Jane Eyre,* we may also observe strategies that move the film viewer into more dangerous regions where the sexual power of the virginal little girl might also be asserted, with the sexual implications of her character's presentation becoming more radical and unexpected.

National Velvet negotiates between these two positions in its story of a twelve-year-old girl, Velvet Brown (Taylor), who wins an unwanted horse in a raffle and, disguised as a male jockey, rides him to victory in the Grand National. The film takes the ubiquitous girlhood fantasy in which prepubescent females obsess with all things "horsey" and places it within a pastoral dream version of a coastal English village in the 1920s. In this respect, the film nostalgically contextualizes the girl's fantasy within a prewar world scene of familial and national contentment guaranteeing the "purity" and "innocence" of the fantasy to which this idyllic setting gives birth. It is a dream world for a beautiful childhood dream.

Unlike Alfred Hitchcock's *Marnie* (1962), which takes the "horse equals phallus" element of the girl's horse fantasy to its psychosexual limits, *National Velvet* constructs the girl's love of horses as both a phase ("all things in their time," as her mother says) and the positive psychological impetus for striving for greatness. It is because Velvet wants to show the world that her "Pie" is an extraordinary jumper that she concocts the plan to enter the Grand National and enlists the help of ex-jockey Mi Taylor (Mickey Rooney).

Her older sister Edwina (Angela Lansbury) offers a sexual interpretation of Velvet's interests by asking, "What does it feel like to be in love with a horse?" The film raises the issue to dismiss it by making it the object of comedy: at another point, Mi touches Velvet's forehead to feel for a fever when she talks of horses and gazes in rapture at nothing. Nevertheless, *National Velvet* prompted the reviewer for *Time* magazine to suggest the transparency of the heroine's sexual obsession. He noted of the film, "It is also an interesting psychological study of hysterical obsession, conversion mania, pre-adolescent sexuality."[28] Manny Farber detected a painful realism of the heroine's "childhood fanaticism" and suggested that she made him "wonder uncomfortably what her motives are when she says she wants to be 'the greatest rider in the world.'"[29] The film (like the book) also justifies an excessiveness that could be read as sexual by making Velvet part of a family of obsessive collectors and strivers: her brother collects insects; one sister, canaries; and the other, boyfriends. Her mother, identified as the first woman to swim the English Channel, encourages her entry into the Grand National as a "breathtaking folly" that everyone should have once in her life.

So that Velvet's intense feeling for horses remains a buoyant, uplifting emotion rather than a low sexual one, the film works to de-eroticize Taylor at key moments in the film, including the beginning, when she is introduced in a classroom of girls. Her childishness in this scene and later ones is emphasized both in reiterated business involving her retainer for her bite and in the camera's and costuming's emphases on her childish, flat body. However, later scenes of her riding the Pie in long shot capture something of her rapturous feelings for the horse and eroticize her by making them a powerful spectacle of movement as well as of emotional bonding. Of course, the film cannot suggest that an obsessive female rider actually experiences a sexual charge from the physical act of her "horsemanship," as Farber's review alludes and Hitchcock's film ultimately articulates. Similarly, there is no physical sexual relationship suggested between Velvet and Mi, but the film does suggest an emotional sympathy between them that has romantic potential, and the casting of the diminutive Rooney lends a kind of physical symmetry between the two (they are almost the same height) that adds to the viewer's perception that they are destined to be a couple. Their conversations are often held in private and played against the backdrop of intimate or confined spaces, as when Velvet goes to his sleeping quarters in the bar to attempt to persuade him to stay with them and work for her father, or when the two of them attempt to nurse the Pie back from illness. Farber complained, in fact, that MGM displayed a "lack of daring," because the relationship between the two, "one of the more interesting in current movies, is left untouched."[30] Obviously, Farber may be following the film's visual cues and forgetting the taboo of Taylor's age. Nevertheless, *National Velvet* acknowledges and satisfies the audience's perception of deep feeling between the young girl and the ex-jockey with the final shot of the film, in which Velvet, in extreme long shot on the back of the Pie, is shown stopping in the middle of the road to bid good-bye to Mi, who leaves to make his way in the world. In spite of the lack of conventional heterosexual romance in the film, the film's advertising campaign offered posters with close-up portraits of Taylor and Rooney, leaning into each other, and called the film "M-G-M's Great Technicolor Heart Drama."[31]

Conclusion

In 1944, Elizabeth Taylor's screen presence challenged the desexualized cultural significance of the stereotype of the "pure" child and unhinged its moorings. "Womanly" qualities inscribed by narrative and visual strategies as well as her own nuances of performance and physicality complicated the child actress Taylor's textual status as a pure child, an exemplar of virginity to be read as a conventional sign of little sexual desirability and no sexual power. Especially through her screen appearance in *Jane Eyre*, we can observe how Taylor's beauty, in combination with specific textual strategies, has the potential to unfix her textual status as an "asexual" child. As a consequence, the Elizabeth Taylor on-screen in 1944 occupies a "sexual space" that disturbs established categories of sexuality in gendered as well as generational terms, raising the signifying problem of sexual difference in relation to childhood. Sexual power accrues to her by virtue of her eroticized innocence and the desire of others directed toward her, including the desire of the film viewer. This calls into question the cultural fantasy of being able to separate desire for the pure child (taboo) from that for the impure woman (acceptable). Thus Taylor's erotically charged feminine presence creates a tension between what is said and what is left unsaid, openly conveyed and wordlessly implied about the possibilities of sexual desire at mid-twentieth century in a culture that would admit only to a sympathy for, or "appreciation of," the beauty of little girls and so reverberated still with those disturbances in the sphere of sexuality that the Victorians knew so well.

Notes

1. John Scott, "Juveniles Bidding," *Los Angeles Times,* March 13, 1938, C1; Edwin Schallert, "Jane Withers Picture Given Budget Boost," *Los Angeles Times,* June 3, 1940, 9.

2. Richard Schickel, *The Stars: The Personalities Who Made the Movies* (New York: Bonanza Books, 1962), 280.

3. *National Velvet* pressbook, microfiche, Margaret Herrick Library, Los Angeles; Schickel, *Stars,* 278.

4. Quoted in Larissa Branin, *Liz* (New York: Courage Books, 2000), 23.

5. Raymond Williams, *The Long Revolution* (London: Chatto and Windus, 1961), 53.

6. Letter to Betty Marsh, January 14, 1915, vertical file, folder 32, Margaret Herrick Library, Los Angeles.

7. Leslie Williams, "The Look of Little Girls: John Everett Millais and the Victorian Art Market," in *The Girl's Own: Cultural Histories of the Anglo-American Girl, 1830–1915,* ed. Claudia Nelson and Lynne Vallone (Darby, PA: Diane, 1994), 124.

8. Malcolm Warner, "John Everett Millais's *Autumn Leaves*: 'A Picture Full of Beauty and without Subject,'" in *Pre-Raphaelite Papers,* ed. Leslie Parris (London: Tate Gallery, 1984), 137.

9. Williams, "Look of Little Girls," 149.

10. Ibid., 131.

11. Ibid.

12. Ibid.

13. Laurel Bradley, "From Eden to Empire: John Everett Millais's 'Cherry Ripe,'" *Victorian Studies* 34 (1991): 192.

14. Pamela Tamarkin Reis, "Exchange: Victorian Centerfold; Another Look as Millais's *Cherry Ripe*," *Victorian Studies* 35, no. 2 (1992): 201.

15. Bradley, "From Eden to Empire," 179.

16. Ibid., 182, 190.

17. Reis, "Exchange," 201.

18. Bradley, "From Eden to Empire," 182.

19. Nina Auerbach, *Romantic Imprisonment: Women and Other Glorified Outcasts* (New York: Columbia University Press, 1986), 24.

20. Charlotte Brontë, *Jane Eyre* (New York: Modern Library, 1847), 96.

21. Ibid., 96, 106.

22. Ibid., 117.

23. Theodora A. Jankowski, "Pure Resistance: Queer(y)ing Virginity in William Shakespeare's *Measure for Measure* and Margaret Cavendish's *The Convent of Pleasure*," *Shakespeare Studies* 26 (1998): 218.

24. Ibid., 219.

25. Brontë, *Jane Eyre*, 95–96.

26. Warner, "Millais's Autumn Leaves," 137–38.

27. Elisabeth G. Gitter, "The Power of Women's Hair in the Victorian Imagination," *PMLA* 99, no. 5 (1985): 938.

28. "The New Pictures: *National Velvet*," *Time*, December 25, 1944, 44.

29. Manny Farber, "Crazy over Horses," *Nation*, February 3, 1945, 175.

30. Ibid.

31. *National Velvet* pressbook.

Ilana Nash

The Innocent Is a Broad
American Virgins in a Global Context

During the late 1930s and early 1940s, the figure of the teenage girl first began to appear as a staple in a new subgenre of Hollywood films: domestic comedies with teen protagonists. A social category newly discovered (or more properly, invented) in the twentieth century, "the teenager" grew in public visibility and in filmic representation to become one of the dominant American stock figures of comic narratives by the 1960s. Strong discursive patterns in this subgenre emerged, particularly in the articulations of female adolescence during World War II, and remained fairly consistent into the postwar and Cold War periods of the 1950s and early 1960s. Chief among these patterns is a statement of the girl's position as an abstract ideal representing the superiority of the United States in a period of international conflict, as America sought to define and assert its identity in times of shifting global politics. Both during World War II and during the subsequent Cold War, comic films about teen girls often juxtapose the girl's status as a sexual innocent with her status as a marker for shared American fantasies about national identity.

But while America contended with its foreign enemies, it contended with a domestic "enemy," as well: the teenager herself. Youth scholars Joe Austin and Michael Nevin Willard have noted in American culture "the bifurcated social identity of youth as a vicious, threatening sign of social decay and 'our best hope for the future,'" a paradoxical construction that simultaneously acknowledges the idealism that youth could represent for world-weary adults and the threats to established social order represented by the innovations of youth culture and by the increasing erosions of patriarchal authority during the twentieth century.[1] Thus, in comedic films of the midcentury period, teenage daughters are presented as dual figures: while they symbolize prized American values, they are also shown (at first) to challenge or oppose traditional structures of social order, particularly the father-controlled nuclear family. Teen-girl characters are often constructed in opposition to traditional ideals of "the dutiful daughter" and to culturally dominant lessons about proper adulthood. As a result, teen-centered comedies frequently portray their heroines as lively, good-hearted, and fundamentally innocent, but also as constant sources of aggravation and anxiety to their long-suffering parents.

These girls' aggravation of their parents takes on a larger metaphoric significance when we consider the social context of wartime films, for in U.S. history "the family," as Robert G. Lee reminds us, has been "the primary metaphor of the nation . . . the primary ideological apparatus, the central system of symbols, through which the state contains and manages contradictions in the social structure."[2] Thus the teenager's role in her family has implications for her role as a citizen in a patriarchally organized polity: her disruption of her daddy's peace of mind mirrors the disruption of American social order by teenagers, which was a topic discussed frequently in various media throughout the twentieth century. Common to many of the girl-centered comedic films is a plot that presents the teenage girl as initially an enemy of the father-centered authority in the home; but because these are comedies, not tragedies, order is always restored—the teen girl ultimately becomes the savior of patriarchal nationalism by proving the success of American values and interests in a global context. Central to this transformation is the status of the girl's virginity, and her relationship to her father or father figures in the narrative, whose appalled reactions to their daughters' budding sexuality echoes the American patriarchy's reaction to the burgeoning cultural power and visibility of teenagers. Anxiety over the girl's hymen also becomes an index of Americans' fears of "penetration" on a larger scale: the threats posed by international enemies to the American way of life. When her virginity is successfully protected, or her sexuality contained within patriarchally approved channels, all is well with American interests at home and abroad.

This chapter focuses on four representative films, two from the World War II period and two from the early 1960s, when Cold War consciousness pervaded American popular culture. I explore the contradictory tensions in portrayals of teenage daughters during this twenty-year period, illuminating the double rhetoric applied to the virginal American girl: her status as sex-crazed hellion is firmly established but is ultimately recontained by patriarchy, either through her recuperation as a "daddy's girl" or through her marrying. When her sexuality is thus properly controlled or channeled, she becomes the privileged icon of American values. In *Janie* (1944), *Kiss and Tell* (1945), *One, Two, Three* (1961), and *Take Her, She's Mine* (1963), fathers fret about perceived threats to their daughters' chastity (in the guise of military or international influences), only to have their fears allayed at the film's conclusion by the girl's containment within domestic and patriarchal order. These films implicitly suggest that national identity—the oft-celebrated "American way of life"—might be as fragile as a hymen and must similarly be protected against invasion by foreign bodies.

Art historian Marina Warner notes that, in public art, figures of women have historically represented abstract ideals more often than real historical agents.[3] We can find a somewhat parallel pattern in girl-centered movies, where girls' "crazy" activities are drawn too broadly to resemble any real-life teen. Instead, the heroines function as allegories representing a double abstraction: a beloved ideal and a dreaded threat. This doubling appears strongly in the characters of Janie Conway (*Janie*), Corliss Archer (*Kiss and Tell*), Scarlett Hazeltine (*One, Two, Three*), and Mollie Michaelson (*Take Her, She's Mine*). This may seem an odd claim, as ideals and threats are complete opposites: one is the stuff of ardent dreams, and the other constitutes harrowing nightmares. But, like opposite ends of a seesaw, both rely on the same axis: the state of the girls' virginity.

Janie and *Kiss and Tell*, although nearly forgotten today, were widely visible on the radar screens of American popular culture in the 1940s; each film derived from a successful Broadway play, and in turn, both Broadway plays derived from popular fiction.[4] In the case of Corliss Archer, heroine of *Kiss and Tell*, her popularity extended to other media, as well; the radio series *Meet Corliss Archer* debuted in 1943 and endured for more than a decade.[5] The widespread success of these narratives bespeaks audiences' eagerness to view, and re-view, stories about potentially sexy girls in conflict with their fathers and with proper social order. Both films revolve around a father's fear that his daughter has become sexually active with soldiers. Issues of chastity and nationalism intertwine, for the girls defend their flirtations in the rhetoric of patriotism: after all, they are just trying to build morale for young men who may soon be facing their deaths. Her sexuality becomes the key signifier of the heroine's identity: while purity marks her as the ideal future citizen, promiscuity marks her as the ultimate destroyer of social order. The optimum condition seems to exist in between: the teen girl who is sexualized rather than sexual (i.e., the girl whose sexuality is projected onto her by a voyeuristic gaze but does not emanate from within herself) is the girl whom the culture industries fetishized. Her image, in these two films, suggests how the question of teen-girl sexuality functioned paradoxically and contradictorily as an index of American national ideals.

Janie centers on Janie Conway, the teenage daughter of a newspaper publisher. Although the film is named for her, our first impressions come not through direct sight of her but through the reactions of adult male observers, a tactic that tells us the film's key issue will be the juxtaposition of teen-girl antics with the more "rational" perspective of an adult male. A voice-over first gives us a brief tour of Hortonville, Janie's hometown, pointing out the various locations where her adolescent high jinks have sparked minor upsets. We see, for example, the drugstore "where Janie gets her malts and magazines, and breaks a heart on an average of twice a week," and the beauty salon "where Janie had a perm when she was fourteen, and caused two riots: one at school, and one at home." The action begins as Janie Conway's father returns home after a frustrating business trip to find that various forms of mayhem have encroached upon his peaceful existence: the army has installed a base in Hortonville, and the influx of strapping young soldiers causes congested traffic in the streets as well as loose morals in the town's teenage girls. At least, so Mr. Conway fears; he publishes an influential editorial in his paper to this effect. At home—the sanctuary that should be "his castle"—Mr. Conway finds more disruption awaiting him: the castle has been laid siege by his teenage daughter's loud records and her immoderate use of the telephone, which not only prevents her father from making important business calls but also reveals "the Op Language," a teen innovation that renders plain English incomprehensible to adults. This linguistic mutation allows Janie's peer group to avoid parental detection while planning a sexually illicit "blanket party" (or "blopankopet popartopy") during which they sit on blankets and "smooch" with their dates. Mr. Conway finds that war, combined with his daughter's sexuality and her oppositional cultural practices, throws the natural order of his existence into chaos and threatens to unseat him from the thrones of domestic and social authority to which he feels entitled.

When *Life* magazine shoots photos of the illicit blanket party and publishes a close-up on its cover of Janie getting a kiss from her high school boyfriend, her father worries that his daughter's naughty notoriety will make a poor impression on the authorities "in Washington," where he lobbies for a new printing press (a restricted commodity in wartime). His fears of the military's corruption of girlish innocence seem to come true when

Janie throws a boisterous party for soldiers without her parents' knowledge. When her parents and their friends return from an evening out, they arrive just as the police have broken up the unruly party to find their house in disarray. Mr. Conway is so enraged that he too becomes unruly, and the police threaten to arrest *him*—implying again that Janie's "misbehavior" with boys, even if fundamentally innocent, can have negative repercussions for her father's relationship to institutional authority. But peace returns when Janie tearfully invokes patriotism as the justification for her actions: in opening the Conway house to rambunctious soldiers, she only meant to lift their morale. Chastened and moved by her noble speech, the adults praise her as a modern Joan of Arc, and even her apoplectic father finds his faith in his daughter wholly restored.

In *Kiss and Tell*, the action is similarly catalyzed by an instance of public kissing. Corliss Archer and her best girlfriend have volunteered to sell towels at a Red Cross bazaar with many soldiers in attendance. But the girls soon discover that selling kisses yields more lucrative results, and when Corliss's family thus discovers her at the head of a long line of grinning soldiers, she too deflects their outrage by invoking patriotism; she's not indulging in debauchery, she's earning money for war relief. Later in the story, through a series of farcical misunderstandings, her family believes that Corliss is pregnant, suggesting that her dalliances with soldiers have surpassed merely kissing. Like Janie, Corliss inadvertently causes her father to run afoul of institutional authority: defending his daughter's honor against the charge that she's a fallen woman, Mr. Archer punches a neighbor and becomes embroiled in an expensive lawsuit—a painful irony, as Mr. Archer himself is a lawyer. In both films, girls' sexuality appears as an agent of chaos but is revealed to be the projection of anxious adults; the girls are fundamentally innocent and, in fact, embody the noblest of American values.

During World War II, those values were often figured in public discourse through images of the home and the nuclear family, as microcosms of American democracy. Girls have a particular function in the iconography of the home and the state. Lauren Berlant notes that modern-day political discourse routinely evokes the home and the private sphere as the site of real American identity. Within this construct, the young daughter is "the infantile citizen whose naïve citizenship surfaces constantly as the ideal type of patriotic personhood in America."[6] For Berlant, the infantile citizen is literally a child, a helpless creature. Janie and Corliss are hybrids of children and women; as teenagers with mature bodies, they are already marked by sex. But their ability to embody patriotism depends on their being physically, though not morally, capable of sexual activity. Ironically, as with Berlant's "infantile citizen," these girls are still minors—not yet full citizens. Their innocence and immaturity authorize them to represent the abstract ideals of citizenship better than a legal adult could.

Why not make these girls perfectly "infantile," then? Why not figure them as children rather than teenagers whose *potential* sexuality causes so much mayhem? The answer lies in teens' dual role in American discourse. Adolescence was a topical concern in the 1940s, perceived as both a subject of titillation in popular culture and as a threat to social order. Wartime periodicals featured innumerable articles suggesting that the war's disruption of traditional homelife would lead to an increase in juvenile delinquency, even while they also celebrated teenagers and teen culture (a newly developing and lucrative aspect of the U.S. economy in the early 1940s) as a welcome innovation on the American cultural landscape. Films like *Janie* and *Kiss and Tell* partake in these national debates by portraying their young heroines as "typical" teenagers, caught up in a joyful whirlwind of peer culture and their generation's departures from the traditional mores of the past, even while showing that, deep down, teenagers have their hearts in the right place.

Lary May has noted that World War II dramatic films with overtly military or nationalist themes built "consensus" to foster support for the war effort; they interpellated their viewers into a shared sense of national identity.[7] We can read the teen comedies through a similar lens. By playing on contemporary concerns about the interactions between youth and authority, teen-girl comedies purport to reflect a common national identity—that of the exasperated parent—and in so doing, they work to foster a sort of "consensus" on American domestic life, itself a synecdoche of the national polity. In teen-centered domestic comedies of the 1940s, as in so much public discourse of that era, the traditional family unit is assumed to be the "central" identity that defines all Americans. For example, *The Aldrich Family*, a long-running and highly popular teen radio comedy in the 1940s, was set in a fictional town called "Centerville." Similarly, the voice-over that begins *Janie* emphasizes the story's general applicability to all America by telling us that "Hortonville, where Janie lives [is] an average, homey little town, *like yours or mine*" (emphasis added). Teen texts encourage audiences to see themselves as part of a common collective experience. Surely, these narratives suggest, "we all" know the exasperations of living with a teenager; that shared knowing is part of what unites us as real Americans.

During the 1940s, fears about the changes war would bring to American society drew upon recent events in the private and public spheres to create a popular perception that modern youth had too great a sense of entitlement and self-importance. Historian Robert Griswold has spoken of "the new fatherhood" that developed in the early twentieth century, a redefinition of the patriarch's role in American middle-class families. No longer a rigid authoritarian who laid down the law, a father was now supposed to be a companion to his children, who in turn were to be granted more freedom and respect in the home. The voices of experts in sociology and psychology acquired increasing public authority during and after the 1920s, encouraging parents, for example, to discipline their young by reasoning with them rather than spanking them. This new construction of the companionate family served a patriotic purpose during World War II; its image was used as proof that the American family was progressive and democratic and thus superior to its "authoritarian counterparts in Germany and Japan."[8]

But a paradox dwelled at the heart of this new ideal. The father was still supposed to be the "head of the household," still linked explicitly with social order: a father is to his family as the government is to the nation. Images of the family, with Dad as its governor, circulated in wartime culture to symbolize "what the war was all about."[9] In the Janie and Corliss films, the link between fatherhood and social order is explicit in the fathers' professions: a newspaper publisher and an attorney are both figures of social authority, men who work with the tools of patriarchal Logos—logic, the word, and the law. As such, they have considerable power both to enforce and to influence public policies and community standards. But fathers' traditional and continued role as "head of the household" did not mesh easily with the notion of children as people with "rights," a new concept articulated most explicitly when the *New York Times* published a "Teen-Age Bill of Rights" in 1945, explaining to its adult readers that teens were not to be treated as little children, but rather deserved, for example, "to have rules explained, not imposed."[10]

American fathers sometimes reacted to this relatively new social development with bemusement. During the interwar and postwar periods, it was not uncommon to see magazine articles in which fathers complained, albeit with humor, that their crazy kids were making their lives miserable by dominating the domestic space, forcing parents into less comfortable rooms, spending too much money, and acting loud, critical, and bossy. In 1939, the *American Girl,* official magazine of the Girl Scouts of America, published "The Care and Feeding of Fathers," in which noted author Fairfax Downey lamented the "machinations" of his wife and teenage daughter, which deprived him of the authority his father and grandfather had enjoyed in their homes.[11] In 1943, Lester Markel explained "Why Parents Leave Home" to the readers of *Good Housekeeping* magazine, and an accompanying illustration showed a teenage daughter in a posture of aggressive confidence: her chin is tilted up and her hip slung to one side. In her open palm stand two miniature and meek-looking parents.[12] Clearly, even while the democratic family proved American superiority at the global level, it was not a wholly satisfying development to many real fathers at the local level.

The problem of uppity children surpassed the confines of the home, for the war years saw the first large explosion of teen consciousness in American mass culture. Teen girls, in particular, began commanding more attention than ever before. As consumers in a capitalist society, they were seen to wield an important kind of social "power," which sprang from their increased financial resources in the booming wartime economy. During the war, hundreds of thousands of teenagers left high school to take lucrative war jobs; in one of its bulletins in 1942, the YWCA, active participants in a campaign to keep girls in school, reported a 100 percent increase in the number of work permits granted to minors in thirty states.[13] Girls' increasing financial autonomy occurred at the same moment as fears about their sexuality arose. In the wartime discourse of juvenile delinquency, fears of violence and destruction of property attached more to boys, while the most frequently noted form of misbehavior in girls was simply sex. In 1945, *Newsweek* reported J. Edgar Hoover's statement that the incidence of so-called sex crimes among females under twenty-one had jumped 375 percent since 1939.[14]

Many of these crimes were said to involve sex with servicemen; the press spoke of "victory girls" who felt it their patriotic duty to give sexual favors to boys who might be heading off to their deaths.[15] One article in *Reader's Digest,* emphasizing that such behavior was not only immoral but also dangerous to national security, quotes a "post surgeon at a . . . midwestern air base" who stated that, whereas professional prostitutes had once been the primary source of soldiers' sexual diseases, "Good-time girls of high school age are the army's biggest problem today as a potential source of venereal disease."[16] Even as girls were used as images of idealism and patriotic fervor, they also represented a threat to the war effort. By infecting soldiers with syphilis, teen girls were imagined to wage a sort of "biological warfare" against the United States, an extreme manifestation of the same destruction they threatened to other such institutions as traditional morality and the stability of patriarchal order in the home. Girls' increases in financial autonomy, sexual behavior, and publicly enacted peer culture combined in the popular imagination to create a common perception of teen girls as uncontrollable, demanding people who posed a threat to national patriarchy writ large. The culture industries responded with narratives about their threat to patriarchy writ small: domestic comedies where teens torture their fathers.

The victory-girl panic influenced the publicity of *Janie* and *Kiss and Tell*. Posters advertising *Janie* spelled out the protagonist's name in red, white, and blue, even while the tagline boasted "She's the Gleam in the Eye of Every G.I.," a statement with vaguely prurient undertones. The posters for *Kiss and Tell* repeatedly featured two images: one of Corliss kissing a soldier at the bazaar and the other of her beleaguered father spanking her (not reasoning with her). These entertainments raise the specter of the sexually active girl as a selling point for a family comedy about girls who are both idealistic patriots supportive of national authority and mischievous agents of chaos who assault the local representative of that authority—their dads.

This is the paradox that finds redress at the climax of *Janie*, when she delivers her noble speech to the assemblage of army officials, policemen, and her father and his friends (who have just returned, in full dress, from an American Legion dance). As Janie puts it to the soldiers' commanding officer, "All the USOs in the world can't take care of all the boys in your army"; that is, the United Service Organizations (which provided servicemen with refreshments, music, and female dance partners) were not sufficient in themselves to offer adequate succor to the brave boys of the armed forces. "When a soldier has to live in a tent and take orders for weeks and weeks," Janie sobs, "he ought to have a chance to see what a home looks like. I know just about every [punishment] is going to happen to me, but I don't care. If only when the going gets tough those boys can look back and say 'Gee, that was a swell party we had that night in Hortonville.'" Janie's evocation of "home" underscores the metaphor of the nuclear family as the privileged symbol of democracy: the Conway house is, metaphorically, what our boys are fighting for. Janie's patriotic speech makes her the

American Virgins in a Global Context

Joyce Reynolds as the title character in Michael Curtiz's 1944 film *Janie*.

authorized spokesperson of American values—indeed, the only person in the room to see those values clearly, despite the numerous and variously uniformed men who surround her. Out of the mouths of innocent babes comes the essential "truth" about the sanctity of the American home and family. Perhaps this is why Warner Brothers donated copies of *Janie* to be screened for servicemen overseas, as one of their magazine advertisements proclaimed.

Corliss Archer has no climactic speech in *Kiss and Tell*, but her fundamental innocence (and her virginity) remain consistent throughout the film and are vindicated when her community learns the error of its assumptions about her supposed out-of-wedlock pregnancy. Her noble intentions and her preserved innocence allow those around her to celebrate her and to heal fractures in their suburban community; harmony is restored through virginity. It is Janie's and Corliss's childlike qualities—naïveté and chastity—that authorize them as idealistic patriots. Yet, paradoxically, it is their sexual maturity that makes them topical and intriguing, and both films highlight their heroines' sexuality. Critic James Agee, reviewing *Kiss and*

Tell, complained that the camera "develops an almost pathological interest in the girl's hind quarters" (as does the poster that shows her getting spanked).[17] The concluding scene of *Janie* shows its heroine dejected when the army departs Hortonville but happy again when she sees trainloads of marines arriving. As one advertisement put it, "Janie sets the United States Army on their ears. And as the picture closes, she's about to go to work on the Marines." As with the "gleam" Janie ignites in the eyes of every GI, her "going to work on . . . Marines" is a coy phrasing designed to imply a sexual undertone; the girl's sexuality is raised only so as to be disavowed and contained in the filmic text. This deliberate evocation of a false threat in order to dramatize its containment uses girls' virginity to exorcise fears about teens' impact on national order at a moment when the relationship between patriarchal privilege and filial freedoms was in a state of flux.

By evoking the victory-girl panic while ultimately denying it, *Janie* and *Kiss and Tell* suggest, rather optimistically, that *real* all-American teen girls are always virgins. Only a virgin can evoke the qualities noted by Berlant: the innocent, the blank, the home-contained child who is not yet a citizen, whose state of becoming endows her with the clearer vision her elders lack. At the same time, her potential sexuality invites viewers—like the soldiers in *Janie*—to assess her with a gleam in their eye. The films titillate and reassure at the same time. Thus the very same ad that tells us that Janie is about to "go to work on the Marines" also tells us that the film "is a rousing cheer for the things that make America American . . . and another example of how [Warner Bros.] combine[s] 'good picture-making with good citizenship.'"[18] This double goal is accomplished by fetishizing adolescent female sexuality: when let loose it titillates and terrifies; when contained, it affirms the fundamental stability and superiority of the all-American, father-centered home and nation.

A parallel set of social and cultural circumstances coalesced nearly twenty years later, at the height of America's conflict with the Soviet Union during the Cold War. Ironically, the intervening decade of the 1950s—long considered in the popular imaginary to be the moment when "teenagers" came into their own in American consciousness—was almost devoid of films that fit the subgenre of the girl-centered domestic teen comedy.[19] As national concerns turned away from the global stage and toward the celebration of homeownership, domesticity, and the joys of family living, the rhetoric of what Elaine Tyler May has called the "homeward-bound" priorities of American life all but obliterated the public image of a rowdy, peer-identified teenage subculture for girls.[20] Instead, numerous forms of public discourse (such as films and girls' magazines) focused on the importance of marriage and family and the rituals of dating and romance that would lead girls to this obedient, domestically focused identity. But as the United States' tensions with global Communism grew, the image of the domestically contained teen girl began to be disrupted through stories that increasingly showed this containment as the delayed outcome that follows intense chaos. Once again, early 1960s comedies about teen girls emphasized their roles as father-troubling headaches before redeeming them through signifiers of loyalty to American ideologies.

The causes for the resurgence of this specific image of the "virginal young girl" are similar to those that accompanied this image in the 1940s: both periods saw a relative swell in the size of the high school demographic. Born during the optimistic affluence of the 1920s, the first wave of Americans to be called "teenagers" in the 1930s and early 1940s were larger in number than the generation immediately preceding them and thus prompted a good deal of public notice. But the years of the Great Depression led to later marriages and smaller families; the high school population of the earliest 1950s was somewhat smaller in number. Not until the late 1950s—that is, when the first wave of the famed "baby boomers," born in the mid-1940s, reached puberty—did American society once again take widespread notice of teenagers as social agents.

Their agency was not uniformly praised; while the growth of the teen market increased the fortunes of industries that created teen-targeted products, numerous cultural commentators complained that the resultant boom in teen consciousness in American culture was "taking over" society; in 1963 a book called *Teenage Tyranny* explicitly decried this development, complaining that "American society is growing down rather than growing up."[21] In addition, the still-thriving discourse of juvenile delinquency cooperated to sustain the image of youth as destructive barbarians who threatened the sanctity of peace and order. As usual, where girls were concerned, sex was discussed as the most prominent "delinquent" activity that caused adult concern. While there were no more "victory girls" in the early 1960s, there was a newly developed birth control pill; this, combined with the perceived continuing downward slope of national mores after the war, led to a stream of articles in the press that focused anxiously on the moral decay of teenagers in general, and girls in particular. In just one example, *Look* magazine published an alarming tale about teen sex in 1962 called "My Daughter Is in Trouble."[22] Once again, the tone of these articles implicitly suggested that girls' virginity was a bellwether of the health of

American society. Only as a virgin could a girl symbolize good citizenship and the health of the national "family."

The girl's ability to represent ideals of the American way of life depended not only on her virginity but also on her having the values that were assumed to accompany virginity: an acceptance and celebration of traditional sex roles and the father-centered family unit. As Susan Douglas humorously recalls, schoolgirls of the era were exhorted to earn high grades in order to ensure American dominance on the international stage but were paradoxically discouraged from parlaying their brilliance into self-supporting careers, lest such professionalism forestall their more important roles as wives and mothers:

No one painted seductive pictures of us girls growing up to become engineers. The Russians had lots of women engineers, doctors too, and we all knew what they looked like: Broderick Crawford in drag. It was because [of this] that we knew their society was . . . joyless, regimented, and bankrupt. No one was going to let that happen here. . . . Our girls were going to stay feminine, but they were also going to roll up their sleeves and make America number one again.[23]

In the Cold War versions of the "teen-daughter-drives-father-mad" plot, the daughters—who are slightly older than their 1940s counterparts, in their late teens—exemplify proper femininity by actually getting married after terrifying their fathers and father figures with the prospect of their impending defloration. These films don't attempt to portray the preservation of chastity as uniformly as the 1940s films did; instead they compromise by shooing their just-barely-legal heroines into youthful marriages, preserving the girl's virginity only long enough for her to become a sexy young wife. The girl's containment within the heterosexual domestic unit cooperates with her patriotism and her exemplification of America's ideological and economic ideals.

In the 1961 farce *One, Two, Three,* James Cagney plays C. R. Mac-Namara, a Coca-Cola executive assigned to West Berlin during the city's walled division under Communism. MacNamara's name, by coincidence or design, resembles that of Robert McNamara, the former president of Ford Motors who became the U.S. secretary of defense in 1961. The filmic MacNamara played by Cagney sees his position in Berlin as an opportunity to introduce expansive Western-style capitalism into Communist countries, hoping thereby to win a promotion to head of European operations in London. He negotiates with Russian officials to extend Coca-Cola's market behind the iron curtain. Pointing to his wall map of the region, MacNamara excitedly tells his staff that Russia is "virgin territory—300 million thirsty comrades, panting for the pause that refreshes." In this formulation, U.S. business interests are the conquering male hero, poised to penetrate virginal foreign markets.

Ironically, MacNamara is also charged with protecting a teenage virgin from penetration. MacNamara's boss at Coca-Cola headquarters in Atlanta, Georgia, is the blustery Mr. Hazeltine, who sends his boy-crazed teen daughter, Scarlett (associations with the capricious Scarlett O'Hara are encouraged), to Berlin to be chaperoned by MacNamara and his wife. The need is urgent: Hazeltine must separate his flirtatious Southern belle from the alarming succession of unsuitable suitors she has collected at home. MacNamara's hopes of promotion depend on his protecting the innocence of this seventeen-year-old sexpot. Scarlett Hazeltine is portrayed as a stereotypical American teenager and as such at first threatens to disrupt Coca-Cola's business interests and MacNamara's career plans: when she lands in Berlin, she wears cuff-rolled blue jeans and lotteries herself as a "prize" for the male flight crew of her plane (the winner gets her phone number and the promise of a date). The all-American teenager is constructed as not only a hopeless flirt but an utterly brainless one: she gushingly anticipates the "swinging" nightlife of Berlin because, as she tells the puzzled MacNamaras, she's read headlines calling Berlin "the hottest spot in the world." Again, the teenage girl's status as an innocent manifests partly through her lack of mature wisdom—although Scarlett is more of an airhead than either Janie Conway or Corliss Archer, all three are blissfully unaware of the dynamite they play with, the havoc their antics might cause, and the gravity of adult concerns. In these films, the girl's relative empty-headedness echoes her virginity; neither logic nor penises have violated her pristine boundaries, and her brain and body cooperate as symbols of her childlike innocence. That innocence prevents her from functioning as a "real" person, as the adult characters do, and thus clears the way for her representing an abstraction—an allegory of the power of youthful femininity to destabilize patriarchal order.

The stakes of Scarlett's innocence become clear when she wriggles away from the panicked MacNamaras' care and disappears for several weeks across the border in East Berlin. When she returns, she confirms MacNamara's worst fears by revealing that she's been bedded by a zealous, impoverished young Communist named Otto (played by Horst Buchholz). While the loss of her hymen is soon made "all right" when we learn

Pamela Tiffin and James Cagney in Billy Wilder's *One, Two, Three* (1961).

that Scarlett *married* her fiery activist, that hardly comforts the fuming MacNamara: he knows he will be fired if Mr. Hazeltine learns that Scarlett, his prized young blossom, has been plucked by a political and economic enemy. At first MacNamara attempts to annul the marriage, but when he learns that Scarlett is now pregnant with a "bouncing baby Bolshevik," he changes plans and, through a slapstick series of fast-paced ruses, arranges for Otto to be disguised as a European nobleman. At first outraged, young Otto gradually becomes persuaded to join the other side as the comforts and luxuries of the capitalist life are offered to him. By film's end, Otto has so convincingly played his role as "Count Dorste-Schattenburg," supposed scion of a wealthy noble family, that Mr. Hazeltine gives *him* the job that MacNamara had been vying for. Scarlett may be pregnant, but it's her surrogate father who's been screwed.

The weight of the film rests on the state of Scarlett's virginity; once that boundary has been ruptured through Scarlett's breaching the East-West boundary in Berlin, chaos threatens both the microcosm of American patriarchy (MacNamara's professional position, Hazeltine's paternal wishes) and its macrocosm (capitalism itself, the penetration of foreign markets, and the international reputation of one of America's most robust businesses). Wrong can only be righted by putting Scarlett's loss of innocence to work as an agent of American capitalist values. The ending is, indeed, a happy one: though deprived of his London dreams, MacNamara is consoled by a luxurious vice presidency back home in Atlanta, which will restore harmony to his rocky marriage. And, on the global scale, capitalism has been protected too: not only is Coca-Cola safe, but another commie has been seduced into Western ideology, by means of a teenage girl's sexuality. The father's fears of his daughter's virginity, as in the 1940s movies, show us that a teen girl's sexual status is an icon of national values, and—when properly protected or channeled—a vehicle for celebrating America's superiority over its global rivals.

The 1963 comedy *Take Her, She's Mine* expresses the patriotic xenophobia of America in the Cold War era indirectly rather than directly. Teenager Mollie Michaelson (Sandra Dee), in her first year of college, wins a coveted spot studying art in Paris, and much of the film concerns her father's fear of what will occur to his innocent daughter when she is set loose in the debauched Old World. Although Mollie, like Scarlett, is slightly older than the high school girls of the 1940s movies, she still functions as a "daddy's girl." Her daddy—played by Jimmy Stewart, who lends his trademark "average guy" stability to the role—is drawn very much in the mold of the earlier father characters: he is an attorney who finds his reputation and his position in the community at risk because of his daughter's antics.

After Michaelson succumbs to an elaborate reverie in which his daughter is seduced by the sexuality of Paris (he envisions her doing a sanitized version of a French apache dance, and then as a bottom-wiggling dancer of the cancan), he goes to France to keep an eye on her, only to find himself embroiled in farcical mishaps that are portrayed in the press as acts of debauchery—as when Michaelson attends a Parisian costume ball in a rented outfit that literally falls apart at the seams, leaving him publicly exposed in his underwear. These humiliations and misunderstandings are the film's focus; the events of the story unfold in flashback, framed by scenes in which Michaelson must defend himself against his numerous appearances of impropriety to the local school board, which holds a hearing to determine whether Michaelson should be banished from its ranks. As in *Kiss and Tell* and *Janie*, a father who should, by rights, enjoy a high position of respect in his community finds himself compromised and runs afoul of institutional authority because of his daughter. By the time he has completed his tale of woe, Michaelson has persuaded the school board of his innocence; they all begin recounting their own headaches with teenage children, debating whether boys or girls are worse.

Mr. Michaelson's fears for Mollie's safety are stoked by a letter she sends home in which she frankly laments her continued status as a virgin; unsuspectingly reading the letter aloud to his family, Michaelson trips on the word *virgin* and lapses into the dumbfounded stuttering for which Jimmy Stewart was famous. Indeed, although Sandra Dee's own fame among the younger set was well established in 1961, it is "Daddy" who is the true star of this show; in addition to the locution of the title, which posits the father as the central identity in the film, a repeated gag shows Mr. Michaelson approached by random strangers who note his uncanny resemblance to that American movie actor, what's his name. This self-reflexive treatment of Stewart's persona constantly reminds viewers that, in a story about teenage girls and their daddies, it is Daddy who counts more and with whom the audience is most encouraged to identify. The daughter's (potential) sexuality is presented only in terms of the negative effects it has on her father. The film implicitly portrays this problem as a symbol for the larger problem of girls' sexuality for the societal "father," the patriarchy of American polity.

Mollie herself, however, personifies the type of innocence and clear-headed American values embodied by Janie Conway in 1944. Among her other activities, Mollie joins a sit-in on her college campus to protest the censorship of books. Her father's efforts to extricate her from the sit-in lead to his eventually joining it instead, once he comes to realize that the campus administrators are unfairly censoring literature and disregarding the students' peaceful protest. Initially concerned with removing his daughter from the impropriety of a youth rebellion, Michaelson instead becomes reminded of the noble ideals behind his legal profession, as Mollie's naïveté—a function of her innocence—clears the way for her uncomplicated support of a basic, all-American principle: the protection of free speech. Similarly, her actual behavior in Paris is above reproach, while the screenwriters take pains to portray the French and the English as decadent snobs and idiotic bumblers, respectively. Against this decaying backdrop, Mollie shines like a beacon of wholesomeness. Despite her father's hysteria, she emerges as an icon of youthful American "can-do" optimism, the very spirit embodied and promulgated by President John F. Kennedy, whose speeches to youngsters encouraged their participation in global affairs. *Take Her, She's Mine* literalizes that call by placing its American teen girl in a foreign context in order to suggest anew an idea that had circulated in

American narratives for centuries: that the Old World has base, corrupted values and suffers from stiffness in its thinking, while Americans—especially young Americans—are vital, energetic, and morally sound.[24]

The patriotic, pro-American message depends on the innocence of the young girl who embodies that message, and thus the virginity of teen heroines in mid-twentieth-century entertainment remains their defining feature. If the innocent becomes a "broad," a debased or lowly woman operating in the sexual economy, she threatens Americans' cherished notions of national ideals and national interests; purity allows the girl to symbolize "ideal Americanness" in the economy of patriotic rhetoric during times of international conflict. Thus when the innocent *goes* abroad, joining the discourse of her country's interaction with foreign nations, she can serve as an ambassador or icon of American ideals. Yet in the same period that employed such images of wholesome girls, the growth in teens' cultural visibility as demanding consumers and as rebellious delinquents raised substantial public anxieties. By presenting teen characters who threaten sexual misbehavior, only to be safely recontained eventually, films such as *Janie; Kiss and Tell; One, Two, Three; and Take Her, She's Mine* offer adult cultural observers the best of both worlds: a story that scolds the "craziness" of contemporary teen life while also proffering a teen-girl icon of deeply cherished values. The paradox results from excoriating the realities of teens while moving the teen girl into the unreal (symbolic) discourse of iconography. In this way, filmgoers could simultaneously exorcise their teenage demons and exercise their need for reassurance that the younger generation could preserve traditional values. By remaining innocent and wholly contained within patriarchy, teenage girls could appear as the authorized representatives of the ideologies that supposedly made America uniquely great among the nations of the world.

Notes

1. Joe Austin and Michael Nevin Willard, "Angels of History, Demons of Culture," in *Generations of Youth: Youth Cultures and History in Twentieth-Century America*, ed. Austin and Willard (New York: New York University Press, 1998), 2.

2. Robert G. Lee, *Orientals: Asian American in Popular Culture* (Philadelphia: Temple University Press, 1999), 7.

3. Marina Warner, *Monuments and Maidens: The Allegory of the Female Form* (New York: Atheneum, 1985).

4. "Janie," a short story by Josephine Bentham, initially appeared in *Ladies Home Journal* in 1941. Bentham and Herschel Williams revised the story as a stage play;

produced by Brock Pemberton, *Janie* ran on Broadway from September 1942 to January 1944. The screenplay, however, was cowritten by Charles Hoffman and Agnes Christine Johnston. Johnston was a teen-film veteran, having scripted several of the popular Andy Hardy films for MGM. The first Corliss Archer tales debuted as a series of short stories in *Good Housekeeping* magazine in 1943. Their author, F. Hugh Herbert, dramatized Corliss's adventures in the stage comedy *Kiss and Tell;* produced by George Abbott, the play ran from March 1943 to June 1945, closing just a few months before the film version was released, the screenplay for which was also written by Herbert. For further information, see the Internet Broadway Database (www.ibdb.com) and the Internet Movie Database (www.imdb.com).

5. John Dunning, *On the Air: The Encyclopedia of Old-Time Radio* (New York: Oxford University Press, 1998), 444.

6. Lauren Berlant, *The Queen of America Goes to Washington City: Essays on Sex and Citizenship* (Durham, NC: Duke University Press, 1997), 21.

7. Lary May, "Making the American Consensus: The Narrative of Conversion and Subversion in World War II Films," in *The War in American Culture: Society and Consciousness during World War II,* ed. Lewis A. Erenberg and Susan E. Hirsch (Chicago: University of Chicago Press, 1996), 71–104.

8. Robert Griswold, *Fatherhood in America: A History* (New York: Basic Books, 1993), 163.

9. Ibid., 162.

10. "Teen-Age Bill of Rights," *New York Times Magazine,* January 7, 1945, 16.

11. Fairfax Downey, "The Care and Feeding of Fathers," *American Girl,* January 1940, 18.

12. Lester Markel, "Why Parents Leave Home," *Good Housekeeping,* February 1943, 22.

13. "Child Labor," Public Affairs News Service, *Bulletin* 4 (January 27, 1942): 11.

14. "The Second Jazz Age," *Newsweek,* October 29, 1945, 34.

15. Marilyn E. Hegarty, "Patriot or Prostitute: Sexual Discourses, Print Media, and American Women during World War II," *Journal of Women's History* 29 (Summer 1998): 112–36.

16. Eleanor Lake, "Trouble on the Street Corners," *Reader's Digest,* May 1943, 44.

17. James Agee, review of *Kiss and Tell, Nation,* October 27, 1945, 44.

18. *Janie* magazine advertisement, source unknown, author's private collection.

19. While "bobby-soxer" films had thrived as a popular subgenre of comedy in the 1940s, the romantic or domestic comedies of early to mid 1950s focused far more often on girls past the age of high school, old enough to be married. High-school-aged teens as such did not return to the spotlight until after 1955, the year that saw the release of *Blackboard Jungle* (dir. Richard Brooks, 1955) and *Rebel without a Cause* (dir. Nicholas Ray, 1955). Teen-girl comedies, specifically, were resurrected with *Tammy and the Bachelor* in 1957 (dir. Joseph Pevney). For further discussion of postwar youth-film trends, see Georganne Scheiner, *Signifying Female Adolescence: Film Representations and Fans, 1920–1950* (Westport, CT: Praeger, 2000); Thomas Doherty, *Teenagers and Teenpics: The Juvenilization of American Movies in the 1950s,* 2nd ed., revised and expanded (Philadelphia: Temple University Press, 2002);

Timothy Shary, *Generation Multiplex: The Image of Youth in Contemporary American Cinema* (Austin: University of Texas Press, 2002); Sarah Hengtes, *Pictures of Girlhood: Modern Female Adolescence on Film* (Jefferson, NC: McFarland, 2006); and Ilana Nash, *American Sweethearts: Teenage Girls in Twentieth-Century Popular Culture* (Bloomington: Indiana University Press, 2006).

20. Elaine Tyler May, *Homeward Bound: American Families in the Cold War Era* (New York: Basic Books, 1988).

21. Grace Hechinger and Fred M. Hechinger, *Teenage Tyranny* (New York: William Morrow and Co., 1963), x.

22. Virgil Damon, "My Daughter Is in Trouble," *Look,* August 14, 1962, 26–28ff.

23. Susan J. Douglas, *Where the Girls Are: Growing Up Female with the Mass Media* (New York: Times Books, 1994), 22.

24. One could compare also the sequels to *Gidget* (dir. Paul Wendkos, 1959) where the eponymous surfing teen takes her all-American values to the islands (*Gidget Goes Hawaiian,* dir. Paul Wendkos, 1961) and Europe (*Gidget Goes to Rome,* dir. Paul Wendkos, 1973).

Timothy Shary

Virgin Springs

A Survey of Teen Films' Quest for Sexcess

Even though Hollywood seemed to deny it—and the Production Code strictly limited it in films from 1934 to 1968—adolescents were having sex long before the raunchy teen comedies of the 1980s. Certainly premarital intercourse has been considered taboo throughout much of the history of American culture, and prohibited by various laws and religions, yet that has not prevented many teenagers from experimenting with their sexual interests and acting on their impulses. On-screen, such interests and impulses were largely ignored until the 1980s, or perhaps were subtly sublimated into safer activities such as "putting on a show" or displaced into troubling activities such as delinquency. Then, after the celebration of teen screen sex during the early 1980s, adolescent sexual activity all but vanished in movies in the late 1980s and early 1990s. When youth began having sex again in the later 1990s, films portrayed teens as more sexually informed and more aware of their sensual pleasure, even though the loss of virginity remained a troublesome practice. What has been and continues to be suggested in depictions of teenage sexuality—as I argue here by focusing on teen films since 1980—is that, despite the characters' certain progressing maturity, sex remains problematic for youth, and the loss of virginity continues to be represented as a daunting conquest en route to adulthood.

One way that early Hollywood (before the mid-1930s) avoided confrontations with normal adolescent sexuality was by defining youth as a primarily preteen population. Consider the most popular young actors of the time, who were all younger than ten years old: Jackie Coogan in *The Kid* (1921), Jackie Cooper in *The Champ* (1931), Shirley Temple in *Bright Eyes* (1934), and the tots of *Our Gang* who started their run of many short films in 1922. This promotion of the preadolescent naturally kept all issues of youthful sexual activity off screen.

Another tactic that Hollywood famously used was the opposite extreme: depicting teenagers as lascivious and even dangerous, especially the "loose" girls of the flapper era in the 1920s who supposedly threatened male standards with their more open sexuality. Georganne Scheiner has explored this issue in films such as *The House of Youth* (1924), *Campus Flirt* (1926), and *Our Dancing Daughters* (1928) that "helped to perpetuate the popular image of wild adolescence and youth run amuck."[1] Scheiner remarks that 1920s films about true adolescent youth were quite few (as compared with more common college stories), and Hollywood meanwhile dodged any authentic discussion of teenage sexual development by resorting to products such as "white slavery" films, for example, *The Port of Missing Girls* (1928).

With clean teen actors of the 1930s such as Mickey Rooney and Deanna Durbin leading the way, Hollywood continued to preserve its own virginity in terms of youth sexuality, allowing the only teen taboo on-screen to be delinquency, which was by far the dominant teen theme until the late 1950s. Yet after the tension over teen virginity was arguably being vented into domestic strife in *Rebel without a Cause* (1955), rock music in *Rock around the Clock* (1956), and sci-fi conspiracies in *I Was a Teenage Werewolf* (1957), some films did begin to discreetly explore the topic of teenagers' losing their virginity. In the case of *Tea and Sympathy* (1956), a teenage boy who seems to be potentially homosexual is "saved" by an older woman who seduces him, although the supposed act of sacrifice vilifies her. Later films such as *Blue Denim* (1959) and *Splendor in the Grass* (1961) then posed the controversial suggestion of teens' losing their virginity to each other. Of course, as the Production Code essentially dictated, the results of even veiled teen sex in both cases were disastrous. In the earlier film, a girl is saved from a dangerous illegal abortion by her boyfriend and father, and in the latter the protagonists seem to go insane from actually just *wanting* to lose their virginity.

Sublimation of teenage sexuality generally continued through the early 1960s with the popular beach films of Frankie Avalon and Annette Funicello, beginning with *Beach Party* (1963), wherein the duo and their friends spent much time half-naked but were so busy swimming and surfing that they never got past first base. Nonetheless, some movie girls were at least losing their virginity somehow, because the protagonists of *Eighteen and Anxious* (1957), *Unwed Mother* (1958), *Diary of a High School Bride*

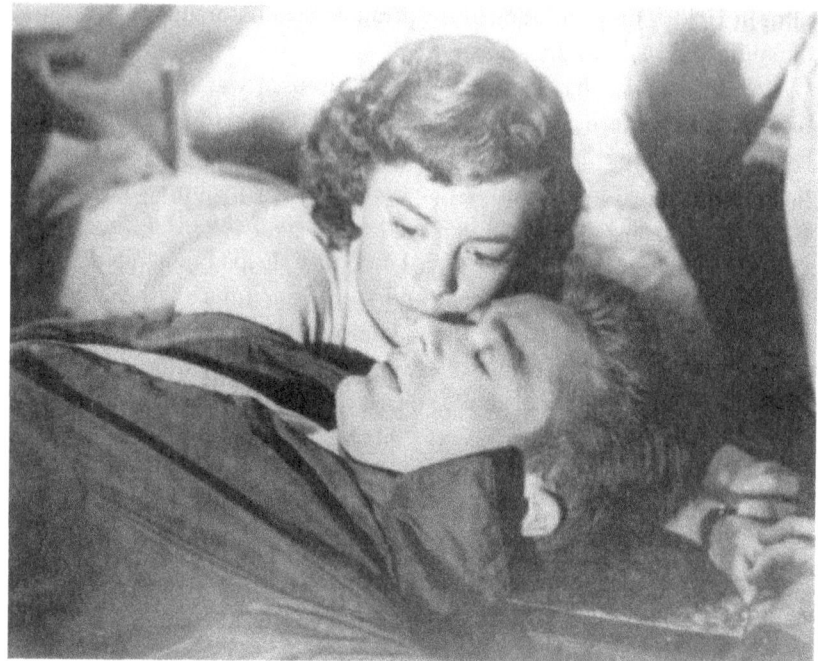

Rebel's 1950s lovers: Natalie Wood and James Dean in *Rebel without a Cause* (Nicholas Ray, 1955).

(1959), and *Married Too Young* (1962) all became cursed with pregnancy. As with *Blue Denim,* the emphasis in these films was on the consequences of having sex before marriage; the prospect of sexual enjoyment or empowerment was still denied to adolescents. One of the few films at this time to even propose that potential was *Lolita* (1962), wherein the teenaged title character fulfills her sexual curiosities—albeit off screen—not only with her stepfather but also with a mysterious middle-aged suitor, leading to the demise of both men and again signaling the dangers of teenage (female) sexual experience.

Most teen movies of the later 1960s did not deliberately ignore adolescent sexuality but rather were consumed by the political energies of the era. One film, however, became a turning point after the strictures of the Production Code had faded: *Last Summer* (1969) was a melodramatic shocker that exemplified the perceived impact of unresolved virginal tensions at that time. In this otherwise sensitive depiction of awkward youth, the idyllic arrangement of two boys and a girl is disrupted when a second girl tries to befriend them, ultimately resulting in the three original friends raping the newcomer. The film explicitly suggests that the swelling sexual pressure among the teens leads to violence and degradation, with no salvation in sight. Such frank depictions—and certainly such excessive reactions—would be rare in youth films until the 1980s, perhaps because teens themselves would likely avoid paying to see such harsh possibilities. The film nonetheless stands at an intersection between the reactionary ethos of previous teen films that addressed adolescent sex and the evolving acceptance of adolescent sex as an inevitably profound experience for most young people.

Teen films of the 1970s dealing with the loss of virginity are thus rather few and inconsequential. When sex did happen for teens in 1970s films, the characters were often assumed to be sexually experienced before the start of the story. *The Last Picture Show* (1971) was different in this regard, as one of the plotlines features a teenage girl pursuing a wealthy boy who does not want her until *after* she loses her virginity. She is then disappointed when her current boyfriend will not have sex with her but nonetheless proclaims her deflowering to her friends as if to finally alleviate the liability of her condition. And the Robby Benson films *Jeremy* (1973) and *Ode to Billy Joe* (1976) are arguably different as well, as he and his girlfriend consummate their virginal relationship in the first film, and he confesses his homosexual affair to another girlfriend in the second film. These films, along with *Summer of '42* (1971)—in which a boy loses his virginity to a grief-stricken young widow—at least indicated that virginity was still an important issue for some adolescents, while most later films of the decade essentially cast that concern aside, as in *The Little Girl Who Lives down the Lane* (1976), *Saturday Night Fever* (1977), *Grease* (1978), *Halloween* (1978), and *The Wanderers* (1979).

Then came the 1980s: as a result of the repressive mentality of the Reagan era and the desperation of Hollywood movie studios, many teen films suddenly featured depictions and discussions of teenage premarital sexual intercourse and on-screen youth going to great lengths to alleviate their carnal longings. This resulted in a conspicuously common plot of youth films throughout the early 1980s: the quest of teens to lose their virginity. Of course, the early 1980s knew little of the AIDS crisis that would erupt by middecade, and as a result, the most serious consequences of teen sexual practice up to that time were pregnancy, emotional distress, and venereal disease (the last of which has been strikingly rare in teen films as compared with real life). After the public learned in the mid-1980s that AIDS could be spread by almost any sexual contact, there was a dramatic decline in the number of youth films featuring the loss of virginity after 1986. (A media-inflamed rise in teen pregnancies, which peaked at 12 percent of American girls in 1990, was also a likely motivator for the movie studios' turning away from depictions of promiscuous teen sex.) In fact, with very few exceptions, the youth sex quest film stopped production altogether from 1986 to the mid-1990s.

While few of the early 1980s tales of losing virginity featured any of the potential medical consequences of sex, many of them did take up emotional issues for their concupiscent characters. To most of the teens in these films, sex was a dark continent to be explored, and most of them faced certain fears and frustrations in that exploration as they tried to find some level of pleasure. Nonetheless, few of these films could be said to have capriciously promoted sex for the population they were directed at, if only because the sex act itself was so rarely portrayed in the positive terms of its anticipation.

The 1980 film *Little Darlings* is a perfect example of a story in which the quest for sex is much more satisfying than its actual attainment, which results in despondency. Here two teenage girls at summer camp compete to see who can lose her virginity first. One girl lies about having sex with an adult counselor while the other is greatly aggrieved when she actually has sex with a teenage boy, and the film, like most others after it, reveals the disappointments of first sex for many teens. Two years later, the more successful Canadian film *Porky's* further capitalized on the group pursuit of first sex from the male perspective, albeit removed to the 1960s. Another 1982 film was *Goin' All the Way*, the title of which suggested the salacious manner in which most of the losing-virginity sagas would operate; the story revolves around a high school senior who can't seem to convince his girlfriend to have sex with him. Like many other youth sex films to follow, *Goin' All the Way* ends with cursory coitus between the protagonists, wherein the loss of virginity and not the sex act provides the ultimate resolution for both teens' tensions, even though the characters remain clearly confused and overwhelmed by sex, a condition that is typical of virtually all these films.

The sex quest film came into its own in American youth cinema of the 1980s with the very successful *Fast Times at Ridgemont High* in 1982. The film takes on high school life in broad terms, and thus sex is merely one aspect of the narrative's matrix, even if the sexual development of Stacy (Jennifer Jason Leigh) is a dominant plotline. First she decides to lose her virginity to a man in his twenties—she tells him she's eighteen when she's really fifteen—and then later has casual ten-second sex with the lubricious Mike (Robert Romanus); in both cases, her enjoyment of the experience is fleeting if even existent. Stacy bears the further brunt of her disappointing sexual initiations when she finds herself pregnant and decides to have an abortion. Sex comes with a definite price for the spacey Stacy, who thinks nothing of birth control, although David Denby accurately notes that while "Stacy and her friends are shucking off their clothes before they've explored friendship or the pleasures of courtship or romance," this theme is "developed satirically, not as a moral judgment."[2] Such satire is also reflected in the loss-of-virginity quest for Mark (Brian Backer), which serves as a foil to Stacy's—it is more arduous and less consequential. Yet Mark is the one character who, by the film's end, does not have sex and seems best off for it: Mike is despised, Stacy is dejected, and her oversexed best friend is ultimately left alone as well. Stacy, having had her fill of troubling sexual experiences, agrees to proceed patiently with dating Mark, portending that this approach will be the best for both of them, and thus Mark's virginal status is rendered more reassuring than frustrating.

The title of *The Last American Virgin* (1982) is both humorous and, within the context of the film's bleak narrative, ominous. Here the protagonist resists his friends' forays into quickly losing their virginity and devotes his heart to a girl whom he helps through an abortion, only to find that she'd rather be with her brutish impregnating boyfriend. Like so many youth films, the division between love and sex is thus enforced—the two rarely occur in the same relationship. *The Last American Virgin* becomes a warning to youth against both the pursuit of sex, which leads to pregnancy and the loss of friends, and the pursuit of love, which is unpredictable and unrewarding.

Risky Business (1983) put a more positive and capitalist spin on the teen sex quest for the Reagan-repressed 1980s. High school senior Joel (Tom Cruise) is left alone at home for a week when his parents go on a trip, and he soon finds himself susceptible to the increasing pressure of his friends, who tease him for his lack of sexual prowess and spontaneity. He thus calls a young prostitute named Lana (Rebecca De Mornay), who promptly fulfills his carnal curiosities. The film thereafter parallels Joel's ambitions to become a successful businessman with his venture into the world of sexuality, as he sets up a one-night brothel with Lana to pay for various damages he incurs during his week of liberation. David Denby observed that when "Joel surmounts his sex and career anxieties by turning himself into a pimp," it is "presented without irony or a hint of criticism, as a triumph of free enterprise."[3] *Risky Business* accommodates its losing virginity agenda within the first third of the story, following Joel through his role as virginity-ender for the young male population around him. Joel's own sexual activity is thus less relevant to the narrative than his selling of sex, and he gains his sense of acceptance and authority accordingly, as when he coolly pitches his service to the diverse range of young men that he meets. That Joel is a salesman of commodified women is obvious, as he claims to be selling "experience" to his eager clients, who see no problem or danger with having sex for money and are happy to lose their virginity with complete strangers and, moreover, with the same complete strangers to whom their friends are also losing their virginity. *Risky Business* thus pitches the morality of young men especially low and makes Joel's chauvinist sex business an acceptable sign of his financial acumen. With such an endorsement being rendered so entertaining by the comic style of the film, Joel's coming-of-age is more a celebration of his daring business education than a questioning of the licentious methods by which it is achieved.

Other sexual adventures abounded in teen films alongside the sleeper success of *Risky Business*, introducing mildly diverse variations. Products such as *Private Lessons* (1981), *Losin' It* (1983), *Class* (1983), and *My Tutor* (1983) offered the services of older women to teenage boys seeking sexual initiation. *Private School* (1983), *Joy of Sex* (1984), and *Paradise Motel* (1985) enlisted larger groups of friends who help each other find sex, which was also the case in *Hot Moves* (1984), a film that provided the now archetypal plot of boys' taking an oath to lose their virginity by a certain deadline. The sex cycle started showing some signs of change by 1985, when the most successful sex quest was *The Sure Thing*, a film about college students who show a certain level of maturity over their predecessors. Further evidence would also come that year with *Once Bitten*, a horror comedy in which a sexually frustrated teen (Jim Carrey in a pre-stardom role) is doubly relieved of his virginity, first metaphorically through the not-quite-sexual blood suckings of a lady vampire, and then literally through his girlfriend, who must finally have sex with him to save him from the virgin-hungry vampiress. The film thus fantastically makes losing virginity a matter of life and death; or on another level, it hints that if teens wait too long to have sex they will be susceptible to monstrous consequences. Yet when the protagonists consummate their relationship in a coffin, the film tacitly hints at the increasingly morbid notions of youth sex that would prevail in the later 1980s and into the 1990s as the threat of AIDS became more prominent and did indeed make sex a matter of life and death.

A low-budget, soft-porn youth film called *The Big Bet* (1986) then became not only one of the most offensive portrayals of teen sexual activity among the many of the 1980s but also effectively its death knell. Yet again a high school student enters into a bet to have sex with a certain girl, and this provides the plot, except that the film indulges in various scenes of the teen protagonist's sexual fantasies about other women. The story suggests that he needs to tame his fantasies and show respect for his potential girlfriend before he will achieve sexual satisfaction, which of course he does, yet this film ends on a note that punctuates teenage sexual practice in movies of the later 1980s, as the characters go on to happily have a child. This bizarre twist may have been an attempt to recuperate a happy ending after the film's otherwise reprehensible imaging of its female lead as a sex toy, yet it also reveals how uncertain filmmakers had become in catering to a teen audience perceived as sexually excitable but supposedly morally vulnerable.

The Big Bet was little seen in theaters and definitely represents the worst of its kind: an unfunny, unfeeling, and ultimately deceptive teen sexploitation movie that further maligned the image of youth. Given that these kinds of products had become so common by the mid-1980s, teenagers simply may have grown insulted at such insensitive stories. However, considering how many the film industry made in the first six years of the 1980s—at least fifteen—the studios' sudden cessation of these films in 1986 remains intriguing. With the more sincere sexual portrayals of teens in John Hughes's films of the mid-1980s becoming more popular, the pornographic quality of a teen-oriented film like *The Big Bet* may have signaled to studios the paucity of options left in portraying teenage sexual discovery in explicit terms.

This is not to say that teenagers did not have sex in films after 1986, but they no longer lost their virginity in the carefree ways of the early 1980s. The few films featuring sexually active teens tended to displace sexual concerns such as by, for example, setting the film in the pre-AIDS past of *Dirty Dancing* (1987) or *Rambling Rose* (1991); by making violence a more dominant plot element than sex, as in *River's Edge* (1987), *Heathers* (1989), and *Boyz N the Hood* (1991); by shifting the focus to romance and away from sex, as in *Say Anything...* (1989) and *The Incredibly True Adventure of Two Girls in Love* (1994); or in the most notable trend of this period, by emphasizing pregnancy as an outcome of sex, as in *For Keeps*

(1988), *Immediate Family* (1989), *Trust* (1990), *Gas, Food, Lodging* (1992), and *Just Another Girl on the I.R.T.* (1993). The one film that did cast humor on the teen sex quest during this time was the straight-to-video oddity *Virgin High* (1990), which still showed sex as immoral and frustrating despite its satirical ambitions.

Then, in 1995, *kids* presented the previously playful loss of virginity as sinister and as reviled as any crime, although like the depictions of much youth criminality, it also retained a cachet of rebellion. The film is a reactionary revision of the teen sex quest story, a faux documentary approach to not only youth sexuality but also general delinquency, drug use, and disease.

The story revolves around two teen boys, Telly (Leo Fitzpatrick) and Casper (Justin Pierce), the first of whom begins the film's day-in-the-life debauchery by deflowering an apparently pubescent girl—Telly prides himself on being a "virgin surgeon" who pursues particularly young girls. Meanwhile, one of his previous conquests, Jennie (Chloë Sevigny), discovers he has infected her with HIV, but she is too late to stop him from having sex with yet another virgin that night, and she's so stoned that she cannot even protest when Casper then rapes her.

The ribald search for hedonistic pleasure that permeates *kids* is based on its distinctly masculinist perspective, or as bell hooks claimed in more assertive terms, "What is being exploited is precisely and solely a spectacle of teenage sexuality that has been shaped and informed by patriarchal attitudes."[4] *kids* does not make sexuality for youth appear effortless; however, the film's one-dimensional perspective—boys are dogs and girls are not much better—denies the psychological intricacy of the issue. The main, if singular, consequence of sex in *kids* is the potential spread of HIV, a serious issue to be sure, but Telly's habitual deflowering practice is left on the moral surface. Within the context of so many vilified images of teen sexuality in the 1990s, the film can appear to be merely marking a moment in the cultural zeitgeist.

Very much like *High School Confidential!* (1958) and other extremely conservative portraits of the "youth threat" in the 1950s, *kids* attempts to inflame the otherwise serious conditions of youth sexual practice by celebrating the unbridled decadence and anomie of ignorant antiheroes like Telly and Casper and in that way is similar to the basest of the teen sex comedies of the early 1980s. As Thomas Doherty has noted, "*kids* can probably be best described as an ethnographic film on urban teen subcul-

The 1990s' version of young lovers: Yakira Peguero and Leo Fitzpatrick in *kids* (Larry Clark, 1995).

ture for an art-house crowd ready to be appalled at what's the matter with kids today."[5]

Teen sex in later 1990s youth films was not nearly as pessimistic or condescending, although it was usually shown to be just as perplexing as it was in the 1980s films, and instances of "first sex" were still portrayed far less often, as teenagers tended to be either virgins for the entire film or sexually experienced before the start of the story. The first case persisted in films such as *Clueless* (1995), *Welcome to the Dollhouse* (1996), *Trojan War* (1997), and *Never Been Kissed* (1999), while the second case was evident in films such as *Hackers* (1995), *Girls Town* (1996), *Wild Things* (1997), *The Opposite of Sex* (1998), and *10 Things I Hate about You* (1999). Even films that did continue to feature deflowering scenes, such as *Fear* (1996),

Titanic (1997), *Can't Hardly Wait* (1998), and *The Rage: Carrie 2* (1999), featured the fated moment as solemn and sincere, quite a remove from the silly and lascivious nature of teen sex scenes in the more immature early 1980s.

Two 1999 films offered bipolar revisions of the teen sex quest film, indicating the fork in the road for teen sexual representation at the turn of the century, the first more aligned with the sinisterism of *kids* and the second an almost nostalgic return to the sex romps of the 1980s. *Cruel Intentions* is a young updating of *Dangerous Liaisons,* in which the wealthy roué Sebastian (Ryan Phillipe) makes a wager with his sexually alluring stepsister Kathryn (Sarah Michelle Gellar) that he will be able to bed proud virgin Annette (Reese Witherspoon). The film plays with ripe sexual tension between the stepsiblings—Kathryn will allow Sebastian to "put it anywhere" he wants if he wins the bet—and the contemptible rich kids are portrayed as unbearably selfish and venal. However, Sebastian finds himself unexpectedly falling in love with the endearing Annette, and even though he does succeed in stealing her prized virginity, he ultimately becomes more concerned with the preservation of their relationship. The resolution of the story then speaks to the moral consequences of the characters' villainous use of sex: Sebastian is killed in a car accident, and Kathryn is exposed in front of her entire school as the vindictive phony that she is. These character assassinations, both literal and symbolic, arise from treating sexual conquest in such a ruthless way.

The sexual conquests of the characters in *American Pie* (1999) are not only more lighthearted but, in many ways, redemptive. Jim (Jason Biggs) emerges as the main character, an inexperienced romantic bumbler who joins his buddies in pledging to lose their virginity before the prom, a mere few weeks away. Given this objective, the story could easily emulate the excessive carnality of the 1980s films it echoes, yet the movie often handles the libidinous boys' travails in an honest, believable fashion, as they realize that their horny desires will take them nowhere. And the girls they pursue want more than to be chased: they want a level of affection and attention not accorded to teen girls in most previous sex comedies, or as Jonathan Foreman makes the distinction, "The girls in *American Pie* are much more than life-support systems for breasts."[6] Thus the boys learn such vital concepts as making foreplay more pleasurable and practicing cunnilingus (as detailed in a secret "sex bible"), thereby introducing the attainment of a girl's orgasm as a plot point in teen cinema, which was also the focus of a less popular but no less intriguing film that year, *Coming Soon*. The hapless Jim, alas, ends up with a nerdy date at the prom and little prospect of losing his virginity, until she shows him the carnal carnivore she really is, resulting in Jim's being used for sex by his date, another twist that is recuperated by his eventual pride in being so used. In fact, as the boys move toward their climactic first times, they each earn a modicum of self-esteem by rising above their initially base impulses and learning to treat the self-assured girls with respect, so that all of their eventual sex scenes are rendered tender and/or humorous. Furthermore, the sex is all ultimately celebratory, a phenomenon that had been minimized in American youth films for over a decade. Perhaps the common acceptance of safe sex (which is clearly practiced in the film) and the refreshing sense of confident *female* sexual pleasure that the film promotes signal further changes in the film industry's attitudes toward teen sex. As Owen Gliberman notes, "It reflects a major shift in contemporary teen culture that the girls in *American Pie* are as hip to sex as the boys."[7]

Yet despite what appeared to be cautious maturation in the sexual initiations of teens in these 1999 films, the majority of youth sex in American cinema remains woefully afflicted well into the twenty-first century. Teenage sex is still confusing and often dangerous for those who do it, leading to death in *The Virgin Suicides* (2000), social mayhem in *Cherry Falls* (2000), drug abuse in *Thirteen* (2003), religious trauma in *Saved!* (2004), and, most consistently, family disintegration in all of these films as well as in *The Door in the Floor* (2004) and *The Ballad of Jack and Rose* (2005). Nonetheless, the film industry clearly maintains its interest in the adolescent deflowering ritual, producing no fewer than a dozen films about teens losing their virginity since 2000, four of which actually had the word *virgin* in their title, including *Virgin* (2003), *As Virgins Fall* (2003), and *Virgin Territory* (2007).

To be sure, the dramatic potential of losing virginity has been mined in films to such an extent that it has become ripe for parody, as evidenced in the excessively tumescent and ejaculatory first time experienced by the young lovers in *Scary Movie* (2000). Yet first sex among youth persists as a primarily serious and very consequential matter. For instance, soon after Lux (Kirsten Dunst) defies her parents and gives herself to her new boyfriend in *Virgin Suicides,* she and her sisters become so distraught at their parents' unbearably repressive response that they all kill themselves. The sex scene itself is of little interest, occurring as it does at night and passing quickly, and Lux offers nary a thought about her pleasure or dread regarding the act, even as she continues to surreptitiously take on other anonymous partners. In fact, as Cynthia Fuchs points out, much of the emotion in the film is conveyed by a group of neighbor boys who long for the girls: Lux's "own feelings remain tantalizingly beyond reach, so that the boys must impute to her a sensitive and self-loathing misery, locked up in her mother's house, sealed away from the corruptions of material desires and consumptions."[8] Indeed, the most significant aspect of her lost virginity is its rupture of parental control and its lethal exposure of her parents' subjugation of their daughters. And the fact that her first sex so deeply affects her entire family in such a tragically unexpected way reveals the stakes involved in our culture's ongoing concern about teenagers'—and especially girls'—loss of sexual innocence.

Other recent films are also revealing of the gender politics that remain inherent to teenage virginity. In *Skipped Parts* (2000), a young teenage boy and girl excitedly take to sexual experimentation out of curiosity, and their first experience of intercourse is appropriately awkward and fascinating for them. However, neither anticipates that she could actually become pregnant as a result, and when she does, the connected families encourage the girl to have the baby—which would have perhaps not been so rare during the story's 1963 setting but seems a suspiciously foreboding decision in the context of teenage life some thirty-seven years later. *A Walk to Remember* (2002) is notable for its heavily veiled handling of its protagonist's virginity, as she is very religious and dying of cancer and yet eventually finds a boyfriend who respects her and marries her at the end of the film. The inevitable consummation of their romance is then completely elided for the sake of preserving a Christian illusion of purity: the couple are not allowed a single minute of on-screen passion after their nuptials, and the girl dies almost immediately thereafter. When a free-spirited girl decides to casually lose her virginity in *The Ballad of Jack and Rose*, her intent is fully realized after she hangs her bloody bed sheets out to dry. Her father erupts in a fit of rage, which works its way inward from his daughter to himself, because his own romantic and sexual hypocrisy is laid bare by his response.

Whether as dramatic turning point, adolescent rite of passage, or political statement, the teenage loss of virginity in American cinema will likely retain its value. Even as social trends in virginity fluctuate and conservative groups continue to promote chastity—as with the popular Silver Ring Thing group—young people will always be eager to explore sexual practice and will always find some level of profound feeling when they do. Films have not been irresponsible in showing young people that sometimes negative consequences arise from the loss of virginity, yet they could be more progressive in suggesting to young people the joys and obligations of sexual experience as well. Thus far, teenage sex in American cinema tends to be either frivolously unenlightened or, more often, torturously somber. Recent films that have even been downright earnest about teens' loss of virginity, such as *All the Real Girls* (2003), *The Sisterhood of the Traveling Pants* (2005), and *Juno* (2007), have had difficulty in representing their characters' ascension to sexual experience in any positively pleasurable or even informative way. If films and media aimed at young people continue to offer them no better alternative to the traditionally serious and silly polarities of teen sex, then we may well wonder if, to paraphrase James Joyce, the virgins will go mad in the end.

Notes

1. Georganne Scheiner, *Signifying Female Adolescence: Film Representations and Fans, 1920–1950* (Westport, CT: Praeger, 2000), 29.

2. David Denby, "Growing Up Absurd," review of *Fast Times at Ridgemont High*, *New York*, September 27, 1982, 50.

3. David Denby, review of *Risky Business*, *New York*, August 22, 1983, 62.

4. bell hooks, "White Light," *Sight and Sound* 6, no. 6 (1996): 10.

5. Thomas Doherty, "Clueless Kids," *Cineaste* 21, no. 4 (1995): 15.

6. Jonathan Foreman, review of *American Pie*, *New York Post*, July 16, 1999, 33.

7. Owen Gliberman, review of *American Pie*, *Entertainment Weekly*, July 16, 1999, 44.

8. Cynthia Fuchs, review of *The Virgin Suicides*, *City Paper* (Philadelphia), May 4, 2000, 17, www.citypaper.net (accessed August 22, 2006).

Rebecca Sullivan

Postwar Virginity and the "Marjorie" Phenomenon

In the decade leading up to the sexual revolution of the 1960s, the subject of virginity, especially as it concerned young single women, became a matter of intense public debate. Tied into larger and competing ideas around American values, women's sexual status was a hotly contested virtue caught between tradition-bound domesticity and new ideals of an autonomous and authentic self. Cinematically, this conflict played itself out most viscerally in the saga of young Marjorie Morningstar, the titular heroine of a best-selling novel that was subsequently turned into a sweeping epic motion picture. The simple plotline of "will she or won't she" may now seem to be a rather flimsy premise on which to base a prestige film, yet it speaks to just how important that question was in the 1950s. The novel by Herman Wouk was released in 1951, and despite its long-winded preachiness (it contains more than five hundred pages), it went on to sell close to five million copies. Warner Brothers optioned the book and in 1958 released the film version starring their brightest young ingénue, Natalie Wood, alongside the considerably older Gene Kelly in a rare dramatic performance. The film was a critical and box office disappointment, earning only six million dollars, compared to the similarly themed *Peyton Place*, which was released four months earlier and earned more than twenty-five million dollars.[1] Nonetheless, it stands as testament to the urgency of the debate on women's virginity and its dramatic shifts as the 1950s wore into the 1960s, the presumed start of the sexual revolution.

The novel emphasized the heroine's Jewish background and the struggle of second-generation immigrants to come to grips with modern American life while still remaining true to their roots. The Marjorie in the novel was a beautiful but spoiled young woman who learned the importance of family, tradition, and old-fashioned womanly virtue just in the nick of time before she almost threw her life away on a misbegotten love affair. By contrast, the film made the religious angle almost disappear and increased the role of Marjorie's object of affection, Noel Airman, as played by Kelly. Clearly identified in the novel as a mediocre and self-absorbed individual who nearly costs Marjorie her chance at happiness, the cinematic Noel is more the victim of Marjorie's virtue than a predator seeking to destroy it. What remains in the film is a deeply ambivalent statement about the value of virginity in an era in which new forms of subjectivity were being established that challenged family-based values such as belonging and togetherness in favor of the individual. Even Wood herself remarked on the film's confused moral message and attitude about its heroine. She complained to the press, "I was in tears during the whole movie. They couldn't decide on a point of view. One day Marjorie was desperately serious about becoming an actress, a few days later it wasn't important to her. So you'd play her one way for several scenes, then they'd change."[2] This confusion over how to play Marjorie speaks to the way traditional and modern sexual mores were defined in significantly dissimilar ways for the different sexes. Thus, in *Marjorie Morningstar*, we can see how virginity was lauded for women but treated as a kind of moral straightjacket that kept men from realizing their true selves.

The story that the film tells is an update of the novel, set in the present day and pared down to focus on the relationship between Marjorie and Noel. The daughter of Jewish immigrants who leave their Bronx community for the upwardly mobile opportunities of Park Avenue, Marjorie Morgenstern is a beautiful, young co-ed at Hunter College, who dreams of a brilliant career as a stage actress. Her would-be lover, Noel Airman, the son of a prominent Jewish judge, has turned his back on his roots in favor of the bohemian lifestyle of a Greenwich Village artist. They meet at a Catskills summer resort catering to well-to-do Jewish families. Noel is the camp's social director, while Marjorie paints scenery and eventually works her way up to performer in Noel's fiesta revue show. On the sidelines is Marjorie's best friend, Marsha (Caroline Jones), a fun-loving and sexually adventurous woman who tries to get Marjorie to give away a few samples herself. She looks up to Marjorie as "God's favorite," having everything she ever wanted: beauty, love, and talent. Marjorie's other unwavering admirer is Wally Wronkin (Marty Milner), the gawky but affable assistant to Noel with theatrical ambitions of his own. Unlike Noel, whom everyone thinks is a genius, Wally is content with commercial success and hopes someday that Marjorie will get over Noel and settle down with him. As these four characters slip in and out of each other's lives, it is the troubled romance between Marjorie and Noel that keeps them all bound to each other. Marsha tries in vain to make everything work between them. She is the one who urges Marjorie to finally give in to Noel's demands and have sex with him or risk losing him forever. And she enlists her wealthy husband to finance Noel's play, perhaps in the hope of a fairy-tale ending for her friend. However, Wally knows better and forces Marjorie to see Noel for what he truly is: a charming failure who can't rise any higher than social director of a borscht belt resort. When Marjorie finally realizes that, she is able to turn her back on Noel and possibly find happiness with his less dashing but more secure former assistant.

This may seem more like the plot of a light romantic comedy than an epic drama. With a running time in excess of two hours, the film charts Marjorie's ultimately doomed struggle to remain chaste until marriage with all the portentousness of a Shakespearean tragedy. However, it is not quite clear what her fatal flaw is: her weakness in the face of Noel's sexual urges or her refusal of them in the first place. Unlike the book, where Marjorie marries a young lawyer who almost leaves her when he learns about how far her affair with Noel really went, there are very few repercussions for her in the film. The novelistic Marjorie "cried a long time, in an excess of the deepest bitterness and shame" over her past.[3] And though her husband forgave her, "She never again saw on his face the pure happiness that had shone there during the drive across the George Washington Bridge in the sunset. He loved her. He took her as she was, with her deformity, despite it. For that was what it amounted to in his eyes and in hers—a deformity: a deformity that could no longer be helped; a permanent crippling, like a crooked arm."[4]

By contrast, the film obliquely suggests that she will find lasting happiness with Wally, who was witness to her entire relationship with Noel and knows exactly what he is getting in Marjorie. There are no tears or shame. If anything, her affair with Noel is presented as a necessary milestone toward the more mature (if less passionate) love that she will now share with his former assistant. Their roller-coaster love affair is buffered by Wally's constant presence, as he tries to both support Noel and steal his girl. It is only once Noel leaves Marjorie for good and slinks back to the South Wind resort that Marjorie finally sees him for who he is. After confidently telling the camp owner that she is now "all grown up," she boards the bus back to the city and sees Wally, sitting a few rows back from her. As the film ends, the camera focuses on Wally's face in the driver's mirror as his expression changes from hopeful anxiety to relief and happiness. It is clear that Marjorie is moving back to sit with him. While the ending may seem ambiguous at first, it is difficult given Wally's role throughout the film to imagine any other possibility than that the two of them will be together. Throughout the film, as Marjorie clings to Noel or what she imagines Noel could be, Wally is there in the background reminding her that Noel is not for the long haul and that he will be there to pick up the pieces once she realizes that for herself. Not even the fact that she and Noel become lovers shakes Wally from his determination to win Marjorie over in the end. In that sense, the film takes a decidedly different direction than the book, treating Marjorie's affair with Noel not as a "deformity" but as an important milestone in her ability to find a mature, lasting love. It thus reflects the beginning of a major change in attitude surrounding women's sexuality that culminated in the sexual revolution of the mid-1960s.

In 1962, Gloria Steinem argued that virginity had ceased to be a major issue for young women. In her classic article "The Moral Disarmament of Betty Co-Ed," she claimed, "*Marjorie Morningstar,* which was taken seriously enough when it appeared to be heatedly denied by many a middle-class Jewish girl ('I'm *not* a Marjorie Morningstar!') is now regarded as a kind of humorless *Much Ado About Nothing* in modern dress."[5] It had been only ten years since the novel was published and five years since the film was released. From this vantage point, the film can be seen as a transitional moment from one short generation to the next. While it can be easier to break cultural moments into decades—the staid and conservative 1950s versus the breakouts in personal, sexual, political, and spiritual freedom of the 1960s—history is rarely so cut-and-dried. The sexual revolution in particular straddles this divide, demonstrating that the moral climate around sexuality changed far more slowly and awkwardly and started much earlier. Certainly, by the late 1950s, co-ed campuses were already experiencing a surge in sexual awareness, an admittance that sex was going on and a certain resignation from administration that they were powerless to stop it. One women's residence at the University of Michigan tried to ban kissing in their common room after complaints that necking sessions were getting out of control. It received major media attention, in particular a photo essay in *Life* magazine that included a staged photo of a couple groping each other on the couch in case the readers didn't quite grasp the situation.[6] Despite such titillation, even the dean of women realized that there was far more at stake than a little hanky-panky. Arguing that sex was merely "the froth on top of the wave of seriousness that grips American students today," she underscored how sex was fast becoming a major factor in larger social and philosophical issues facing young women.[7] As one co-ed writing in *Atlantic Monthly* complained, "Our liberally educated girl is not very likely to be swept away on a tide of passion. With the first feeling of lust, her mind begins working at a furious rate. Should she or shouldn't she? What are the arguments on both sides? Respect or not? Does she really want to enough? And so on, until her would-be lover throws up his hands in despair and curses American womanhood."[8] Films like *Marjorie Morningstar*, therefore, used sex as a device to get to deeper questions about women's social identity in an increasingly modernized and bureaucratized liberal America.

Susan Douglas has identified a spate of sexually charged films that go a long way toward challenging the idea of the 1950s as the chaste decade and the idea that the sexual revolution didn't get under way until at least 1962. She refers to them as "pregnancy melodramas," overwrought tales of good girls who give in to their boyfriends before the wedding night and who defiantly confront social and family disapprobation. Films like *Where the Boys Are* (1960), about a quartet of young women who spend their vacation in Fort Lauderdale looking for love or a near approximation of it, and *Splendor in the Grass* (1961), Natalie Wood's most celebrated role in which she is driven insane by lust, could just as easily have been called "virgin melodramas," as they are more concerned with the consequences of virginity than of pregnancy. In essence, they were confronting more than just disapproving parents. They signaled what Douglas defines as a growing distrust by the postwar generation over "bourgeois hypocrisy about everything from status seeking to sex."[9] Sex, in this popular frame, was a matter of personal decision making that should not be influenced by repressive social mores. Thus it became a public issue because it was at the heart of the individual's relationship to society. Put another way, sex became a major signifier of the rise to dominance of the individual over the family in American postwar ideology.

However, for women, this new emphasis on the individual was not easily accepted. Thus, as many argue, women were essentially caught in a double bind of competing and conflicting value systems. Douglas recalls, "Was I supposed to be an American—individualistic, competitive, aggressive, achievement-oriented, tough, independent? This was the kind of person who would help us triumph over *Sputnik*. Or was I supposed to be a girl—nurturing, self-abnegating, passive, dependent, primarily concerned with the well-being of others, and completely indifferent to personal success?"[10] As she argues, pregnancy melodramas sought to have it both ways, first by offering a critical commentary on smothering American bourgeois values, but then by returning the girl heroine to the suburbs, the bosom of those values, as a kind of reward for having bucked them in the first place.[11] Wini Breines contends that this double bind reflected masculinist anxieties about sexual emancipation—namely, that women wouldn't just be more open and available to men's needs but would also be in direct competition with them because of their increasing education and employment opportunities. In other words, with liberalizing values came the possibility that the division between genders might evaporate.[12] She notes that social commentators across the political spectrum, from Talcott Parsons to Margaret Mead, investigated this conundrum and the restrictions placed on women to preserve a traditional sense of feminine decorum. Mead claimed that, while society seemed to be opening doors for women, it nonetheless construed any attempt to walk through these openings as detrimental to their femininity and therefore their marriageability.[13] Referring to the enormous popularity of the book *Marjorie Morningstar*, Breines highlights changes in popular culture in the 1950s that used sex as a marker not only of social status but also of modern selfhood.[14] Thus women were obliquely encouraged to freely explore their sexuality, with the understanding that an invisible line existed somewhere in their experimentations that, when crossed, turned them from self-reliant individuals, the epitome of the new American, to foolhardy sluts who were responsible for the moral decay of the country.

The film *Marjorie Morningstar* was one of the first of the virgin melodramas, and certainly one of the most explicit. The crisis facing young women in deciding their sexual fates was explored in detail in the opening scene, in which Marjorie is introduced. In a frank conversation with her mother regarding a date with Sandy, the heir to a department store fortune, Marjorie tells her mother that Sandy wanted to make love but that she said no. Nonetheless, she asks plaintively, "What do I do ... about those feelings I get sometimes?" Her mother urges her to "take those feelings and put them in the bank. Save them for the man who'll appreciate them and love you for them after you marry." This straightforward advice in the face of Marjorie's own impulse to refuse Sandy would seem to signal that the film is setting up virginity as a commonsense moral virtue. Yet the camera tells a different story, as it opens on the shot of a scantily clad Marjorie in her boudoir. Her tousled hair, shapely legs, and clingy slip tell the story of an erotically charged young woman yearning to break free, even before she announces to her mother that she is grown up and sophisticated in the ways of love. As they discuss sex, however, Marjorie isn't really talking to her mother but to herself in a mirror and therefore to the women in the audience who identify with her dilemma. However, as she confesses her innermost sexual desires, she puts on a white dress and pearls, the hallmarks of chaste girlhood, in effect covering up her feelings in order to be the good girl her mother wants. The rest of the film, then, seems intent on stripping her back down to her erotic essentials.

As the film progresses, Marjorie is established as a prig in contrast to her fun-loving friend, Marsha. At the summer camp where they work, Marsha is clearly the favorite of the girls while Marjorie is the one who forces them to perform childish skits and sing the goofy camp song on cue. The novel took pains to reveal Marsha as a phony and a user: borrowing money, lying to Marjorie, and sleeping with married men. In the film, Marsha is wild but attractive and fiercely loyal. Yet love seems constantly to elude her no matter how many "samples" she puts out. Eventually she marries for money and security, despite a last-minute panic in which she pours her heart out to her friend:

Why is it I feel that I was destined to never have anything I really wanted? Doesn't seem to me like I've ever wanted much. A friend, a job, a fellow. Oh darling, I'm so alone!" [bursts into tears] Now I'll be alone forever, till the day I

Marjorie in her slip: Natalie Wood and Claire Trevor in *Marjorie Morningstar* (Irving Rapper, 1958).

die. . . . Marjorie, do you have any idea how infuriating it is to me to have you give up on Noel? What is it with you anyway? What do you have in your veins, ammonia? Look, you're madly in love with this man and he loves you like no other girl. Do you know what I'd give up for such a love affair for one hour?

What is interesting about this exchange is that while it sets up Marsha as having lost her chance at happiness by being too free and easy with sex in her youth, it also offers a cautionary tale to Marjorie that she is equally at risk by being too chaste. As Marsha sees it, rebuffing Noel's advances at every turn could destroy their love and drive him away forever. It is a message that resonates for Marjorie, who for the last hour and a half of the film has managed to successfully keep her virginity intact. But the sight of Marsha promising herself in marriage to a man she has just admitted to not really loving pushes Marjorie over the edge. She flees the wedding party and goes to Noel's apartment, where he is lying despondently on the couch. Silently she goes toward him and, in full view of the open bedroom door, draws him down on top of her as the screen fades to black.

The difference between Marsha and Marjorie isn't so much a double standard as a fuzzy distinction between sex as an empty experience of faux sophistication and sex as authentic self-expression. In that sense, then, the double bind to which Douglas and Breines refer was not an unconscious consequence of a transitional morality but a deliberate if subtle form of hegemonic control over women's sexuality in the face of changing national values. Importantly, the apparent liberation of women's sexuality came with a whole new set of convoluted rules that pitted women against themselves and each other, while men were relieved of much of the responsibility for the consequences of sex. "Sex with love" became an acceptable norm on co-ed campuses in the early 1960s; even serial monogamy was possible as long as the girl believed that there was the chance that this partner could be "the one." It made possible women's sexual availability while still remaining true to bourgeois values of heterosexual domesticity. As Steinem notes, the pressure on girls to lose their virginity came more from their peers than from the boys, and women who continued to resist felt the same kind of social disdain that used to be reserved for those who said yes.[15] Furthermore, with this newfound sophistication came additional responsibility, as birth control became the woman's problem. One young teacher told Steinem about her time as a sexually curious co-ed: "In my day, a girl might be having an affair, but it was considered part of chivalry for the young man to look after 'all that.' Now a girl in the same situation thinks it's dumb and even unwomanly to make the man responsible for her not getting pregnant."[16] Thus sex was a way for a young woman to prove her independence and maturity, but at the expense of a responsible commitment on the part of the man. It therefore made her solely accountable for any "mistakes" and to face the consequences if the sex wasn't ultimately backed up by love, usually in the guise of a tidy suburban bungalow.

In her scandalous exposé *Sex and the College Girl* (1964), Gael Greene explained this new morality and noted that the saga of Marjorie Morningstar did more to push women into men's bedrooms than it did to stop the rising tide of permissive sexuality. As one of her interviewees told her, "I suspect Herman Wouk would be somewhat upset if he realized how many nice middle-class Jewish girls lost their virginity because of him. . . . Silly as it sounds, I know for sure at least three girls who gave up the good fight just to prove they weren't Marjories."[17] The dread of ending up in the suburbs with a boring husband for whom they felt no passion was enough to drive women into the bedrooms of Greenwich bohemians like Noel Airman. As one young beat girl asked rhetorically, "What unforeseen catastrophe would send me up the river to decorate a home in Westchester?"[18] This image was the apex of an alienated, disaffected life for women who were afraid to get in touch with their authentic selves. It was even too much for the cinematic Marjorie, as the film diverges dramatically from the book in the end by ignoring the lengthy epilogue in which she is safely ensconced in the suburbs and claims to have little memory of her bohemian past. Instead, by uniting with Wally, Marjorie is shown as a mature woman whose sexual experiences prepared her for the demands of a lifelong commitment, albeit with a much more sedentary and respectable partner. Thus, while freewheeling promiscuity was still frowned upon, sex with love was considered a path to authentic self-hood, even if that love didn't last.[19] In that sense, then, the film seems to challenge the basic premise on which the book was based, turning a rather prurient morality tale on its head and exposing its hypocrisies. However, by changing the character of Noel from an arrogant and untalented seducer to a tortured artist, the film reveals some of its own hypocrisy in its depiction of Marjorie and her desire to stay pure.

Any claims that Noel Airman is little more than a hack are immediately undermined in the film by the casting of Gene Kelly and changing the character from a failed writer to a dancer-choreographer. Widely hailed as one of the greatest of cinematic dancers and choreographers, Kelly's first scene has him going over a routine with his cast at South Wind. It is simply impossible to believe that Airman is untalented when watching Kelly dance. But just in case there are a few doubters in the audience, Wally Wronkin clarifies it by extolling Noel's virtues to Marjorie even as he tries rather clumsily to seduce her. Calling him a genius, a philosopher, and a true artist, Wally validates the adulation that surrounds Noel at South Wind. Later, when Wally agrees to back his former mentor's play, the problem isn't that *Princess Jones* is too mawkish and pretentious (as it is clearly implied in the book) but that it is too good to find a mass audience. Confronted with the realities of commercial theater, Noel breaks down, accusing his backers of being hacks with no integrity. He yells, "Success oozes from all of you. It covers you like a coat of heavy grease. It's disgusting," before collapsing in tears and begging them to support his art, which is "everything I've lived for." By contrast, Wally survives because he is not plagued by such lofty goals, only writing for the audience. He is not an artist, but a businessman.

Presenting Noel as a tortured artist brought low by social convention is an ongoing thread within the film, especially as his relationship with Marjorie is concerned. As they fall in love at the resort, it seems as if Noel is the one resisting the relationship more than Marjorie. He sees her as a trap, as dangerous as the easy money and low-rent fame of South Wind that keeps him from pursuing his artistic dreams. When she first visits his cabin, a nervous little schoolgirl who's afraid to take off her oversized coat, he tosses her out ruthlessly, calling her a "Shirley": "It's a trade name for the respectable middle-class girl who likes to play at being worldly." Even so, he kisses her and they begin a chaste affair as Noel gently nudges her closer to his ideal. Before too long, the good girl in white before the mirror turns into a sultry sex kitten dancing provocatively before her parents and the other guests in a skin-tight black leotard. Ultimately, however, chastity triumphs. After sneering at her mother for wanting him to be in a "gray flannel suit making $20,000 a year," Noel almost induces Marjorie to give in to him, but tragedy stops them in their tracks, quite literally. En route back to his cabin they discover her beloved uncle dead by the fountain. Distraught, Marjorie rebuffs Noel, and he leaves the camp the next morning. When they find each other again, a year after their unconsummated affair at South Wind, Noel has done exactly what Momma Morgenstern wanted him to do: turn his back on the theater and join a Madison Avenue advertising firm. He tells Marjorie with faux jocularity, "Death to the old Noel, that seedy tramp, and long life to the man in the gray flannel suit. . . . Marjorie, you've broken me. I'm saddled, bridled, bitted, and tamed.

Children ride me in Central Park for a dime." This comment on his attire, the gray flannel, is a reference to another canonical novel of the 1950s, *The Man in the Gray Flannel Suit,* Sloan Wilson's story about a returning war vet who cannot face the banality of his life—a home in the suburbs and job in public relations in the city. Wilson's hero is only redeemed when he admits to an affair while stationed in Italy and convinces his wife to help support his love child. Using this parallel, the screenplay thus hints that Marjorie's refusal to have sex with Noel is the root cause for his capitulation to bourgeois conformity. If the film was interested in putting forth a provirgin message, then Noel would be happy in his junior executive position, he and Marjorie would wed, and they'd be rewarded for waiting with a comfortable family life in the suburbs. However, the opposite seems to be true. Deadened by his job and suffering through a chaste relationship, Noel finally collapses into a lost weekend of binge drinking and sex. Marjorie finds him with a sexy young woman, Imogene, but refuses to believe what is right in front of her eyes until he tells her point-blank that it is her fault he has been brought so low. He rebuffs her angrily, "I'm tired of playing the horse to your rider. And believe me Marjorie, whether you know it or not, you've ridden me mercilessly. . . . Don't you understand? I get pleasure right now just touching you. I've been playing the game by your asinine rules, being faithful to you. Do you know what that means to me not to touch you, not to touch another girl? If Imogene hadn't come along and broken the spell . . ." At the realization that Noel has been having an affair, Marjorie flees, but only weeks later she apparently comes to her senses and this time gives in to Noel. No longer tortured by unrequited sexual longing, he is able to rouse himself from his downward spiral, finish his play, and risk his artistic soul on Broadway.

How is it that the film can neatly play Marjorie's virginity as a sign of virtue for her but a source of destruction for Noel? The answer lies in the burst of scientific and social commentaries that sought to undermine traditional morals and values in favor of a newfound sense of authentic individualism, but one that stopped short of affording those values to women in the same measure as men. Foremost among these was the "Kinsey Report," or *Sexual Behavior in the Human Female* (1953), which blew open the sexual double standard and revealed the American woman as a sexual being with needs that were actually being fulfilled either inside or outside the marital bed. Kinsey directly challenged the drive to marriage as the only respectable outlet for women and offered evidence of premarital, lesbian, and elderly sex that defied the conventions tying women's sexual-

Marjorie (Natalie Wood) and a defeated Noel (Gene Kelly).

ity to domestic and reproductive duties alone. However, while voicing his disgust with bourgeois conventions that established restrictive norms for women's sexuality, he capitulated to them by declaring that women's psychosexual makeup was less sophisticated than men's and that their sexual desire was triggered more by material considerations about financial and emotional security than by erotic impulses.[20] This contradictory stance belied his resolute affirmation that science could undo social convention. It also helped establish as scientific fact the belief that men and women were essentially and psychologically different when it came to sex. As is pointed out in *Re-making Love: The Feminization of Sex*, even when the intention was to prove women were fully sexual beings, there was still a sense that "women were asexual, or at least capable of mentally bypassing sex and heading straight from courtship to reveries of Formica counters and cherry wood furniture, from the soda shop to the hardware store."[21] This set the conditions for a clear distinction between the needs and desires of men and those of women that spilled over from scientific treatise to social critique.

Best-selling books such as William Whyte's *Organization Man*, published in 1952, or David Riesman's *The Lonely Crowd*, published one year later, both argued that a numbing sense of alienation was taking over America, striking at the heart of its virility. In Whyte's estimation, the creation of a group mentality characterized by tedious white-collar professions and soulless suburban living was eating away at the national fabric from the inside out. Similarly, Riesman argued that the drive to success in an increasingly bureaucratized, corporate world was changing men from inner-directed—that is, bound by their ego and sense of selfhood—to other-directed, anxious for approval and acceptance by the crowd. In both cases, they blamed the suburbs and the demands of bourgeois domesticity for destroying the American male, yet they did not extend that criticism to women. Whyte acknowledged that women were quickly being left behind while their husbands enjoyed careers and travel but suggested that the suburbs actually helped mitigate their sense of alienation by providing them with a community of similarly repressed and frustrated wives.[22] Riesman went even further and claimed that women's sexual knowledge was creating the conditions for increased sexual competition and putting the other-directed male at risk by turning sex into a mere consumer good.[23] However, as Greene pointed out, it was women's consumer power that gave them autonomy, and so they could use Riesman's philosophy to justify their sexual openness.[24] It was for this reason, perhaps, Riesman argued that women's quest for autonomy only intensified the state of anxiety in which men lived.[25]

It is not that Whyte or Riesman begrudged women their sexual autonomy—far from it. However, they were unable to go so far as to approve of women's using their sexuality as part of their own quest for authenticity and autonomy. Instead, it was something that could be deployed in order to attain certain material comforts such as a home, children, and a savings account. If it was done in such a way that strengthened and supported the man, satisfying his carnal and consumer desires, then that was one thing. But if the woman put her own desires first, then that could result in the emasculation of her partner, especially if sex was only used as a strategy to get the woman that Formica countertop she really lusted after. Thus, while Marjorie thinks she is doing the right thing by prodding Noel to become a Broadway success, they both know that she is really just remolding him into her ideal Organization Man and using sex as both carrot and stick to make him conform to her desires. What is interesting is that while Noel is left in tatters, a failure who retreats to the safety of South Wind where he can pretend greatness, Marjorie is actually rewarded for her part in his destruction with a comfortable middle-class existence as Mrs. Wally Wronkin. After the failure of *Princess Jones*, Noel runs out on Marjorie and flees to Europe. Marjorie duly chases after him, bankrolled by her father, but it seems more out of habit than love. No longer the coltish young girl with theatrical aspirations of her own, Marjorie now dresses like the Park Avenue madam that she always was deep down inside, complete with turban and matching handbag. When Wally meets her at her London hotel to tell her where Noel is, she muses aloud wistfully and somewhat prophetically, "If only it had been you Wally, how simple it would have all been. We're alike, aren't we, so very much alike." Her wavering on the cusp of genuine sexual rebellion and her ultimate refusal of a life on the fringes of respectable society are clearly identified in the film as signs of maturity. However, the sympathetic treatment of the character of Noel makes the ambiguity of the film's ending much more than about whether or not she ends up with Wally. For young women across the country, the idea of a simple life with a simple man must have seemed like giving up. Marjorie's journey into sexual adulthood at the cost of Noel's poetic and passionate soul earned her the disdain of young women everywhere and perhaps even hastened their own acquiescence to the urges of their personal Noel Airmans.

The enormous resonance of *Marjorie Morningstar* for this first generation of sexual would-be revolutionaries speaks volumes about the boundaries of the sexual revolution and how it anticipated its own limitations by never drifting too far from bourgeois conventions. In the end, then, it seems that the message of the film—as it was elsewhere in the culture—was that virginity was a burden not on women but on men, who needed women's full devotion to escape the gaping maw of the deadening suburbs. The mantra of sex with love was a way out of a convoluted social conundrum that still prized the family while extolling the intrinsic worth of the individual. Sex ultimately became the source of salvation for men who had little to look forward to in life other than a cubicle and a commuter train. A wife who combined virtuous chasteness and sophisticated sexual experience would not threaten the other-directed male with her demands for satisfaction. On the contrary, and as Riesman argued, it could be of value to her life partner in staving off "total apathy" without actually contributing to his state of anxiety and alienation by being overly sexually competitive.[26] Thus the journey of Marjorie Morningstar was predestined to end with the likable and eager-to-please Wally Wronkin, no matter how much she imagined herself the erotic muse of a tortured genius like Noel Airman. Even though she loses her virginity, the bohemian life of sexual abandon was more a rite of passage that would ultimately lead her back to the values of home and hearth. Thus the aura of chasteness surrounds her throughout the film, transforming her sexual past from being a threat to her happiness—as it clearly is in the book—into a necessary milestone along the way back to the suburbs. It was a message that many women found hard to take, but ultimately sex with love became the cornerstone of a revolution that was far less about women's sexual autonomy than about a kind of virginal sexual savviness that gave men the best of both worlds.

Notes

1. For box office data, see www.imdb.com and www.the-numbers.com.
2. Gavin Lambert, *Natalie Wood: A Life* (New York: Alfred A. Knopf), 132.
3. Herman Wouk, *Marjorie Morningstar: A Novel* (New York: Doubleday, 1955), 53.
4. Ibid., 553.
5. Gloria Steinem, "The Moral Disarmament of Betty Co-Ed," *Esquire*, September 1962, 97.
6. "Campus Love Left out in Cold," *Life*, March 11, 1957, 49–52.
7. Ibid., 50.
8. Nora Johnson, "Sex and the College Girl," *Atlantic Monthly*, November 1959, 60.
9. Susan J. Douglas, *Where the Girls Are: Growing Up Female with the Mass Media* (New York: Times Books, 1994), 73.
10. Ibid., 25.
11. Ibid., 74.
12. Wini Breines, *Young, White and Miserable: Growing Up Female in the Fifties* (Chicago: University of Chicago Press, 2001), 33.
13. Ibid., 35.
14. Ibid., 86.
15. Steinem, "Moral Disarmament of Betty Co-Ed," 156.
16. Ibid., 153.
17. Gael Greene, *Sex and the College Girl* (New York: Dial Press, 1964), 39.
18. Breines, *Young, White and Miserable*, 137.
19. Greene, *Sex and the College Girl*, 154.
20. Alfred C. Kinsey et al., *Sexual Behavior in the Human Female* (Philadelphia: W. B. Saunders, 1953), 684.
21. Barbara Ehrenreich, Elizabeth Hess, and Gloria Jacobs, *Re-making Love: The Feminization of Sex* (New York: Anchor Press, 1986), 24.
22. William H. Whyte, *The Organization Man: The Book That Defined a Generation* (Philadelphia: University of Pennsylvania Press, 2002), 356.
23. David Riesman, with Nathan Glazer and Reuel Denney, *The Lonely Crowd*, abridged ed. with a 1969 preface (New Haven, CT: Yale University Press, 1980), 146.
24. Greene, *Sex and the College Girl*, 38.
25. Riesman, *Lonely Crowd*, 283.
26. Ibid., 142.

Alisia G. Chase

One Very Chic Hell
Revisiting the Issue of Virginity in *Bonjour Tristesse*

> Hollywood films in those years right after World War II were full of puritan morality. Lovers kissed with their lips closed and were never seen in bed together even if married.
>
> The hypocrisy extended to language, and to the moral code which demanded that anyone who misbehaved in the film had to be punished.
>
> —Otto Preminger, *Preminger*

It could be argued that no Hollywood film director understood better than Otto Preminger the power of language to incite puritanical Americans. Many scholars have even suggested that it was his decision to fight the censors regarding dialogue in *The Moon Is Blue* (1953) by releasing it without their seal of approval, which paved the way for the Motion Picture Production Code's eventual disintegration in the 1960s.[1] According to Preminger, "Looking back, it [was] laughable what all those people found objectionable: the frequent mention of the word 'virgin,' . . . the word 'seduce,' and the word 'pregnant.'"[2] His incredulity is understandable, particularly from our vantage point, when Urban Outfitter T-shirts bear such ironically sanctimonious slogans such as "I'm a Virgin . . . Trust Me." But it is important to remember that the same year that Preminger challenged the Hays Office over word choice, Alfred E. Kinsey published his sociological study *Sexual Behavior in the Human Female,* and his statistical insinuation that more than half of the women in America were not virgins when they married shocked a society that viewed itself as upstanding and virtuous. In Cold War culture, the phrase *unwed young woman* was supposed to be synonymous with the word *virgin*, and anything that suggested otherwise was cause for scandal.

One international scandal in the 1950s that concerned language and the sexual desires of an unwed young woman, and that would later directly involve Preminger, was fraught with far more frisson than Maggie MacNamara's seemingly naïve but clearly calculating "professional virgin" from *The Moon Is Blue*. This was the publication of Françoise Sagan's novel *Bonjour Tristesse*, a shockingly frank story of a young girl's sexual and moral coming of age: quite literally, the loss of her virginity on both fronts. The novel won the *Grand Prix des Critiques* upon its release in France in 1954, broke the country's postwar records for book sales, and incited hysteria among those who believed it signaled the irreparable moral turpitude and emotional lassitude of its postwar youth. Its eighteen-year-old author, whom François Mauriac infamously termed a "charming monster," was suddenly embraced as "an eloquent representative of [the] disaffected generation" referred to as "La Nouvelle Vague," and her image and opinions were soon ubiquitous in the French media.[3]

Bonjour Tristesse fared just as successfully, and no less scandalously, in the United States upon its publication the following year, inflaming worried mothers when it remained at the number one spot for more than thirty-eight weeks and delighting teenage daughters who helped to make it the fourth best-selling novel of 1955. As the *Saturday Review* remarked, the book is "succeeding at once in shocking a lot of old prudes and delighting a lot of young [people]."[4] In another clever turn of phrase, *Time* magazine opined that in Sagan's novel "sin triumphs over everything but syntax."[5] Aside from its seemingly demonic antisentimentality, the novel was considered outrageous precisely because the self-professed existentialist author *de bon famille* did not suggest that a young woman should be ashamed of or punished for her sexual desires, an attitude not surprising given that she was a Parisienne. As Sheila Rowbothom has smartly put it, "Unsuitable sex has a mysterious way of emanating from somewhere else," and for Americans in the 1950s, much unsuitable sex seemed to come straight from France.[6] Simone de Beauvoir's *The Second Sex* (1949), which counseled young women to take their economic and sensual liberty into their own hands; the Broadway and Hollywood adaptations of Colette's *Gigi* (1951 and 1958, respectively), in which courtesans rode through the Bois de Boulogne nodding discretely as their lovers' carriages passed by; and Brigitte Bardot's base physicality in *Et Dieu créa la femme* (1956) were only a few of the many literary and visual images in this period that perpetuated the American cultural mythos that French women were more wanton. *Bonjour Tristesse,* then, was simply further evidence of the sexual immorality of Parisian females. Sagan's idolization by a generation of young American women who found her disillusioned heroine's sentiments illustrative of their own emotional malaise and who were additionally attracted by the author's enviably French sophistication was formidable. By 1958 her book had sold more than 1.6 million copies in the United States.

Given the novel's extreme popularity on both sides of the Atlantic, it is no surprise that Sagan's words and what Molly Haskell has referred to as the author's "well-heeled but barefoot sybarite" of a heroine were eventually brought to the Hollywood screen.[7] As adapted for the movies, *Bonjour Tristesse* bears the traces of the censors' continual influence on punishing "anyone who misbehaved," and specifically, in this case, young women who desired, unapologetically, to lose their virginity. It is my opinion, however, that the film's clearly punitive preponderance on the topic of sexual virginity has been historically overlooked, largely due to the fact that cinema in the successive years quickly moved from "prudery to pornography," and critics frequently underestimate the societal anxiety that surrounded this topic, particularly in a film in which the young woman's loss of moral innocence could easily overshadow the sexual loss.[8] Recently, in an admirable close reading, John Gibbs and Douglas Pye rightly noted that Preminger's adaptation "changes and enriches" Sagan's tale by allowing the spectator access to more than one point of view.[9] However, it is my intention in this chapter to illustrate that Preminger's notable directorial choices, including but not limited to his revision of the relationship between Anne and Cecile; his expressionistic use of both black-and-white and color film stocks; and his pointed choice of mise-en-scène must be considered in the context of American cultural anxiety over Sagan's forthright presentation of a teenage woman's right to guiltless sensual pleasures and loss of virginity upon her own volition. I thus propose that Preminger's choices manifest his attempt to simultaneously satisfy the punitive Production Code and a nation full of apprehensive parents, as well as a young female audience that wished to see the sexually active and, just as important, impenitent heroine of Sagan's text. Mothers were morally assured by the sympathetic portrayal of their generational peer by the elegant Deborah Kerr and by the younger woman's ultimate castigation for her precocious, out-of-wedlock sexual activity. But their daughters saw a chic ex-Iowan, Jean Seberg, wearing the latest in Left Bank style, gambling and making love along the French Riviera, and bebopping at smoky Parisian basement boîtes—all antivirginal mise-en-scènes rife with thrilling implications to young American women in the 1950s and visual consolations that Preminger must have hoped would make up for his morally conventional ending.

To summarize it briefly for the purposes of this chapter, the novel recounts the tale of a spoiled seventeen-year-old French girl, Cecile, who adores her sexually profligate playboy father, Raymond, and their decadent existence, which includes vacations in sun-drenched Saint-Tropez and drunken evenings with flirtatious mistresses. When a highly refined fashion designer (and soon-to-be stepmother) threatens to replace their carefree social life with a regime of dinners at home and afternoons spent studying, Cecile intentionally manipulates her fellow vacationers like a malevolent playwright, and at the denouement of *"ce livre cruel,"* her father's new fiancée drives her convertible off a cliff, a suicide obviously inspired by the malicious drama the young protagonist has wrought. Once Cecile and her father return to Paris, they carry on with their hedonism, self-professedly a little sadder and wiser for the experience. Cecile's sorrow, however, seems wholly self-indulgent, as if the emotion were a fashionable new dress that no one else is wearing. Superficially, it does seem as if the filmic adaptation adheres quite faithfully to the novel: given some of the objections voiced by young female viewers in 1950s periodicals, it would seem logical to deduce that Preminger and screenwriter Arthur Laurents knew that teen movie audiences didn't like some of their "best literature being changed beyond recognition . . . with disturbed sequences and distorted characterizations" and thus adhered as closely as they possibly could to the original narrative.[10] But a more painstaking examination suggests that Preminger's changes shift the narrative focus from Cecile's singular point of view as expressed in the novel to one in which the interplay between the soon-to-be stepmother, Anne, as played by Deborah Kerr, and the soon-to-be stepdaughter, Cecile, as played by Jean Seberg, becomes more pronounced and, at times, outright histrionic. The resultant on-screen relationship can then be read as mirroring that between a concerned parent and a willful daughter on the cusp of sexual adulthood, with each woman increasingly frustrated or infuriated by what she perceives as the other's erroneous definition of moral living. Certainly, in regard to a discussion of cinematic (and other) representations of virginity, the relationship between mother and daughter must also be considered, as in Western culture it was traditionally the mother, or female chaperone, who was deemed responsible for safeguarding a daughter's virtue. Here the mother (figure) is allowed to have her say, insofar as narrative fidelity to a text that spoke for female teens would have permitted.[11]

The period's generational friction in terms of changing attitudes toward virginity and premarital sex were manifest not only in novels and Hollywood films but also in other sociological studies prompted by the landmark "Kinsey Report."[12] In one such study, "Mother and Daughter Attitudes to Premarital Sexual Behavior," Robert R. Bell and Jack V. Buerkle found, not surprisingly, that among college-age and educated women, premarital sexual behavior provides one of the greatest potential areas of mother-daughter conflicts.[13] Their study queried mothers' and daughters' responses to two questions. The first—"How important do you think it is that a girl be a virgin when she marries?"—revealed that, while nearly 90 percent of the mothers thought it "very wrong" not to be married a virgin, only 55 percent of daughters shared their feelings. The second—"Do you think sexual intercourse during engagement is very wrong; generally wrong; or right in many situations?"—revealed that, while nearly 100 percent of the mothers continued to believe that premarital sex was wrong in almost all situations, their daughters were willing to consider it permissible if both love and engagement were part of the conditionals. The authors also revealed that because this was "such an emotionally laden area of human behavior the differences in orientation take on great intensity" and that mothers seemed to become more conservative as they aged, unable to remember their own passions. This is a point Sagan made about *Bonjour Tristesse* when interviewed by *Newsweek* in 1955: "Nobody of my generation finds anything remarkable about my having written the book. It's the older people who forget . . . how they felt at eighteen."[14]

Perhaps Preminger's most explicit revisions to Sagan's text, reflecting these changing mores and subsequent filial tensions, are those scenes in which Anne overtly counsels Cecile on the age-appropriate expression of love and sexuality, and it is not implausible to presume that such moral pronouncements were partially scripted to placate mothers who were anticipating and dreading similar conversations with their own daughters. One such instance occurs when Cecile is expressing to Philippe, her summer boyfriend, how love and the act of lovemaking have visually transformed her father's fiancée. When Cecile tells him, "[Anne seems] as though she has the most wonderful secret in the world. I wish I walked the way she walks now. I wish I had the look she has," it is clear that Cecile believes this enviable aura is due to lovemaking, and her aggressive embrace of

Philippe indicates that she will do what she must in order to appear the same. Preminger skillfully negotiates this moment, as by the time Anne finds the libidinal pair they are half-obscured by the beach umbrella they have knocked over in their lust. When Anne sees their lower extremities prone and pressed against one another, it is made explicit that she imagines more carnal activity than is actually taking place.

A cursory comparison might see this scene in the novel and the film as identical, as in both versions Anne immediately dismisses Philippe and informs Cecile that "such diversions can end up in a hospital," a not so thinly veiled period reference to pregnancy and its inevitably dire consequences. But in the film, the exchange between Anne and Cecile continues at length:

> CECILE: We were only kissing, Anne. That won't end up in any hospital.
>
> ANNE: Please don't see him again, Cecile.
>
> CECILE: What if I say I love him?
>
> ANNE: I don't think you do, darling . . . love doesn't depend on that sort of thing . . . nor is it the only way to express it.
>
> CECILE: But I enjoy Philippe and I want to see him.
>
> ANNE: And I feel a great responsibility towards you now and I cannot allow you to ruin your life.
>
> CECILE: Are you ruining yours?
>
> ANNE: Your father and I are going to be married . . . also I am not seventeen.
>
> CECILE: Seventeen now isn't what it was when you were seventeen. I'm not a child, Anne, and I won't be treated like one.

The dialogue within this sequence very carefully delineates a mother's assessment of the situation: that sex out of wedlock is socially permissible only in certain instances for women of a certain age. The clear insinuation is that a young woman who loses her virginity will ruin her life. But Preminger also permits Cecile to declare what she believes are the sentiments of her generation, as the "Seventeen now isn't what it was when you were seventeen" retort is not found in the novel. Teenage female sexual desire, as the other predominant subtext, is additionally borne out by the fact that Preminger used the most sexually provocative segment of this sequence to promote his film. The trailer begins abruptly, commencing with the moment that Cecile embraces Philippe and kisses him full on the mouth. The only dialogue in this edited version of the aforementioned scene is his confused protest, "I thought you said we weren't supposed to do this anymore," and Cecile's defiant rebuttal, "I don't care." As she embraces his bare chest the music surges dramatically, and their bodies fall to the ground; it is Anne's admonishing cry of "Cecile!" that suddenly jolts the lovers from their bliss. An immediate cut to Cecile's rejoinder about being seventeen years old, and its implication that Anne doesn't understand the difference in mores then and now, function to suggest that the major conflict of the film centers upon generational opinions toward this hot topic.[15]

Another scene in which a mother's moral values conflict with a daughter's desire for sexual liberty, and one that is particularly relevant for the purposes of this collection, occurs immediately after Cecile has lost her virginity. In both the novel and the film, Cecile seeks refuge at Philippe's home after a midday argument with Anne. In narrating her heroine's actual loss of sexual innocence, Sagan's spare prose describes the moment in less than four sentences:

He let go [of] my wrist, but only to take me in his arms and draw me over to the bed. It has to happen sometime, I was thinking in my confusion, it has to happen . . .

For this was the round of love: fear which leads on desire, tenderness and fury, and that brutal anguish which triumphantly follows pleasure. I was lucky enough . . . to discover it all that day.[16]

This moment's cinematic equivalent, while as devoid of actual body parts and specific physical actions as the prose, lacks the poetic insinuations that made the literary version seem so incendiary to moral critics of the period. In the film the scene begins when Anne discovers that Cecile has been playing the Hindu yogi instead of studying for her upcoming philosophy examinations. The older woman upbraids her "daughter" for her dishonesty and, before closing the door, states firmly, "I really don't understand you at all." Cecile remains silent throughout the reprimand, but as soon as the door is shut, she throws her towel across the room and loudly shouts, "And you never will!" She then resolutely changes her clothes and runs to Philippe's house, where they make love for the first time upon his bed. The drama of the event is tritely intimated by the dark bedroom, lack of dialogue, and first ominous, then tentative, and finally crescendoing orchestral score. But the influence of the Production Code and Preminger's attempt to satisfy both mothers and daughters is proved by his major revision to this supposedly monumental occasion in a young woman's life. In the novel, Cecile seems unsure as to why she has gone to Philippe's home and initially panics, hoping to extricate herself before it is too late; ultimately her decision to make love with Philippe seems a weary resignation to the inevitable course of their affair and afternoon kisses. In the director's characterization, however, there is no such hesitation, as Cecile immediately climbs right onto her boyfriend's bed and embraces him with the same desire she exhibited on the beach, as shown in the trailer. It is conceivable to read this as a retaliatory act against the mother figure who repeatedly insists on treating Cecile like a child; she will command her own sexual destiny if she can't control her life.

Preminger and Laurents also revised the conclusion of this critical sequence so that once again, both sides of the generational argument against and for a young women's premarital sexual autonomy were presented, and both audiences were satisfied. In the novel, Cecile's narration suggests that although Anne clearly intuits Cecile's emotional distress and fatigue, she doesn't necessarily attribute it to her newly de-virginized state and allows an affectionate stroke on the cheek to suffice as consolation for whatever ails the young woman. But as might be expected in Production Code–era Hollywood, the equivalent film moment in regard to such a transgression cannot pass without a verbal confrontation and moral rebuke. Instead of the mute but respectful resolution the two women seem to reach in the book, each generational representative declares its understanding of how one should live. Without putting too fine a point on it, it is clear as the scene opens that Cecile's once uninhibited gait has changed; her walk appears stiff and awkward as she nervously approaches the patio where Anne is reading. More telling perhaps, in filling in the elliptical loss of virginity, is that Cecile now attempts to light a cigarette, something she has not done up to this point. Her vain fumbling with the matches, and more blatantly, the fact that she puts the wrong end in her mouth, visually reinforce that Cecile is a neophyte in regard to sophistication, sexual and otherwise, and insinuate that it takes age and experience to elegantly finesse the clichéd postcoital smoke. Anne's words to Cecile, "I sometimes forget that you're still a child," and her slow and deliberate actions as she takes the cigarette out of the young woman's mouth, turns it around, and reinserts it, only serve to underscore who is in power and who truly knows how to behave in the boudoir. Their successive debate on whether one lives for the pleasurable moment (Cecile's opinion) and the eventual loss of respect that such a life brings (Anne's more experienced take) is a veiled warning to young women who give in to their physical desires and would later suffer the consequences of a bad reputation. Here again Cecile is permitted another comeback to a mother's didacticism and answers, "I have another moral, Anne. If you can't accept people as they are, give them up. Don't try to change them. Besides, it's usually too late." With this, she stubs out her cigarette and struts off, mistakenly believing that sexual experience makes her Anne's equal. It is the mother figure on whom the camera lingers, however, and as she rises and looks out onto the sea's horizon, Preminger's camera suggests that it is her point of view that most resonates.

Such circumlocution reveals the difficulty of discussing virginity in an era in which the word alone was thought to indicate degeneracy, but cultural restrictions may have also engendered some of film directors' most creative decisions in representing such a taboo. One innovative directorial choice, I would posit, is also one of the most critically noted elements of Preminger's adaptation—his expressionistic use of both black-and-white and color film stocks, a device that ostensibly demarcates the mood of the two locations in which the film's narrative takes place: Paris after the death of Anne and the French Riviera before it. The film opens in black and white, giving the viewer the melancholy vision of a somber postwar City of Light as if photographed by Henri Cartier-Bresson, then dissolves into the vivid seaside blues of the Mediterranean shore via partial colorization. Nearly all of the film's remaining narrative is in Technicolor, which emphasizes the vitality of the vacationers' idyllic situation and their happiness prior to the tragedy; Preminger reverts back to black and white only intermittently to show Cecile's penitent state of mind as she reflects back upon the summer's events. Superficially, these shifts in stock appear to be visually representative of the vibrancy of life and sobriety of death or, more patently, happiness and sadness, but I believe that they also work to underscore the protagonist's loss of sexual and moral virginity and subtly, perhaps even somewhat insidiously, intimate that a young girl's world is forever colored by her decision to lose her maidenhead. Only in this instance, her world becomes color*less*, a gray and monotonous round of deadened reactions. Certainly this shift in stock can be interpreted as subtly emblematic of Cecile's sexual transformation, as her inability to eternally remain in the sandy and cerulean paradise of the Riviera is metaphoric for Eve's original sin and her banishment from the Garden of Eden. In addition, the rather seedy, smoke curled, black-and-white Paris that Cecile is shown to inhabit from the opening frame is certainly a far cry from the vividly frothy and champagne pink, gay Paris of amorous pleasures that 1950s American audiences were accustomed to seeing on the big screen, and Preminger's gray-toned schema of decadent interiors suggests that the gay, carefree life isn't quite so colorful or appealing once one has lost one's innocence—it's a monochromatic hell.

Cecile's change in outlook as a result not only of Anne's death (the loss of her moral innocence) but also on account of her forthright pursuit of physical pleasures with Philippe (the loss of her sexual innocence) is also supported by a number of other directorial choices concerning the black-and-white sequences. In and of itself, Preminger's decision to add nearly 15 minutes of present-day narrative at the beginning and end of the film, as well as to intersperse three 2- to 4-minute sections throughout the 92-minute picture, suggests that Cecile's anesthetized emotional state is an integral consequence of the summer's affairs that viewers must consider; this is a dramatic revision of Sagan's narrative in which the Paris sequences comprise no more than 4 or so pages of a 128-page novel. The film also insinuates that the change that has occurred is irreversible, as is physical virginity, a clear contrast to the literary work, which suggests that Cecile's life has resumed its normally carefree course with only the most nominal lingering of regret. The mise-en-scène within these additional sequences likewise functions to suggest that the drab and dissolute world in which Cecile now dwells is precisely due to her defilement. One obvious example is the guest performance of the nightclub chanteuse Juliette Gréco, a darling of the existentialist circle who often had songs penned for her by Jean Paul Sartre. Gréco, with her lank black hair and turtleneck, was symbolic of Sagan's disaffected generation and their weary angst. Her cinematic appearance at Maxim's, which was by that point a popular tourist destination meant to evoke the decadence of the Belle Époque, was clearly an attempt to give young female audiences the beret-wearing Left Bank Paris of sensual liberty they desired to see on-screen. Then and now, however, her appearance seems incongruous, and a peculiar directorial choice, for as one 1950s reviewer noted, "[Preminger] inexplicably allow(s) Greco [to sing] the title song and she wasn't supposed to be moral at all."[17] Gréco almost appears conjured up from the point of view of Cecile, whose blank stare as she unresponsively dances with "dear Jacques" is another sign that this is a young woman who "can't feel anything" toward the young men who court her precisely because she has not followed the established order of a chaste

Revisiting the Issue of Virginity in Bonjour Tristesse

courtship and loss of virginity only upon her wedding night. Perhaps the most apparent sign of Preminger's wish to bring a conventional morality to the amoral novel occurs in the middle of the chanteuse's breathy ballad, when the music makes a dramatic pause, and Gréco monotonously intones, "*I've* [long pause] *lost* [another pause] *me*" and then throws up her hands in despair. Her emphasis on this line and the following stanza in which she reveals that after this loss, her "smile is void of laughter [and her] kiss has no caress" reinforces the conservative viewer's understanding that Cecile's present detachment is directly attributable to her loss of virginity.

And yet throughout these sequences, it is possible to argue that despite its monochromatic coloring, this is one very chic hell that Cecile inhabits. When viewed through the lens of a female audience adept at reading the period codes that signified sophistication, Cecile's City of Light existence is le dernier cri.[18] She goes to a crowded art gallery with an impossibly handsome Gallic artist, speeds around the boulevards in her convertible sports car with bejeweled poodle at her side, and wears a sublime Givenchy gown to Maxim's as she kisses and socializes *a la Francaise*. Even if the filmic character completing the activities was shown to be rather immoral, Cecile's on-screen actions and locales were indisputably glamorous to a generation of young women who saw Paris as the world capital of art, amour, and couture. For those American females who were infatuated with the writings of Sagan, de Beauvoir, or Sartre or who had read about their underground nightclubs, the presence of Gréco and the words of her song could likewise be interpreted, not as the moral warnings of a mother fearful for the loss of her daughter's innocence, but as emblematic of their own generation's desire to refute what they considered to be the hypocritical moral code of their parents. Indeed, it is precisely Cecile's blasé petulance that would have been seen as becoming. While the censors might read her throwaway line to a persistent suitor, "You know where I live? In *limbo*," as a deterrent to young women who desired to lead the gay life, most likely it was read by a female viewer—who was also carefully picking up on the visual details, such as the obviously butch-femme lesbian couple bebopping nearby—as the epitome of a sophisticated riposte. The postwar period anxiety over young women's wish to be "sophisticated," however, was evidenced by such warnings as the one in *Seventeen* magazine's article, "Gee, Is She Sophisticated!" in which the author cautioned: "Sophistication has come to mean anything from black lace stockings to the right fork. The dictionary tabs it as phony . . . [but] the visual signs of sophistication to boys translate as 'This is easy!'" Its connection to a girl of questionable sexual mores was further outlined, and its outward signs were seen as something to avoid so that young men wouldn't get the wrong idea.[19]

As Marina Warner has suggested with respect to the medieval period, the virginal body can be inferred via desired qualities or virtues but is also "fashioned, dressed, adorned, and accoutred" in such a way as to be legible to its particular culture.[20] Similarly, 1950s filmmakers often relied on such glamorous loci as that discussed earlier, or more typically clothes and accessories, to outwardly express this truly internal quality and its subsequent loss, a point Jeffers and I have noted elsewhere.[21] Likewise, in *Bonjour Tristesse*, Preminger relies on costume to show the young female protagonist's descent into postvirginal debauchery. In the novel, Anne is a fashion designer, and her refined sense of dress is noted more than once. As translated to the screen, however, it is Cecile's clothing that becomes the integral component that describes her sexual status and transformations, and this is evident from the first scene onward. When the viewer is introduced to Cecile, she is accoutered in what was thought to be the height of French fashion for the period, as immediately it is the miniature French poodle with its rhinestone-encrusted collar that functions as period shorthand for a worldly woman, and later it is her black couture gown by Hubert de Givenchy that suggests this same sort of cosmopolitanism. But when the film shifts back in time, to the idyllic blue sky and water of the Riviera prior to Cecile's sexual coming-of-age, her clothing is far more casual, a beachside wardrobe that largely consists of Capri pants, boat-necked tees, sailor shirts, and short shorts. Most frequently, Cecile is costumed in an ocean blue–hued man's shirt, tied at the waist over her maillot style swimsuit. Her status as a blithe and untroubled tomboy is the most obvious indication of such outfits—all of which permit this still child of nature her freedom of movement—but the last is also unmistakably meant to be a feminine copy of her father's preferred mode of seaside attire, as the shirts that she so casually ties around her waist belong to him, their monogram legible to accentuate this point.[22] Their matching costumes visually indicate that Cecile sees herself as a junior version of the womanizing libertine. In addition, Cecile's androgynously short hair further underscores her visual affinity with men and, by proxy, their social positioning as the more sexually aggressive of the genders. In the filmic moment that Cecile decides to lose her virginity, however, she selects a shirt that reads as a visual harbinger of her eventual prison. In stark contrast to the aquamarines, vivid tangerines, and sunny yellows of her virginal vacation wear, its thick black-and-white stripes function as a symbolic cage, and she visually becomes a body entrapped by her willful transgression.[23]

In the realm of costume, a more self-evident but nevertheless significant indication of Cecile's virginal status is also suggested within the revised sequence of Anne's arrival at the seaside villa. As Kathryn Schwartz has theorized regarding virginity, the body is always "a privileged site of information, evaluating women through the material signs of what they have and have not done."[24] Given the Production Code limitations of what was permissible to be shown on-screen, and the impossibility of representing absence, it is logical to deduce that the dress becomes the visual substitute, the literal material sign, for the virgin or de-virginized body. In the novel, when Anne comes to visit, she brings Cecile a sweater from her latest collection, and the moment warrants one sentence. In the film, however, the haute couture gift is one that implies far more concerning female sexual status and incites far more debate. As she unpacks, Anne gives Cecile a large white box, which contains an organza party dress. The white dress has a voluminous midcalf skirt and tiny sprigs of multicolored flowers embroidered all over it; the color and the minute floral pattern both are traditionally symbolic of maiden innocence in the cinema.[25] In addition, the demure bodice appears to be boned and rather stiff, with wide halter straps that further emphasize its sweet modesty. The verbal exchange between the two women suggests that this gown doesn't fit Cecile's idea of what a woman of her age and supposed worldliness should be wearing, as her spurious exclamation, "The dress is marvelous . . . it's really marvelous, Anne," is immediately recognized by Anne as insincere, and the older woman's counsel functions to remind the younger generation that their ideas of what looks "sophisticated" are misguided. "But you think it's too young for you, hmm?" says Anne. "You're wrong you know—a more sophisticated style would only make you look younger—*more* of a child." Cecile's exclamatory refutation, "I'm not a child!" further elucidates the tensions regarding each woman's misconceptions about one another. Although Cecile does wear the dress to the casino one evening, it is before she loses her virginity; it is the film's sequences in Paris that show her dressed in the black Givenchy that suggest a fashionably insinuated deflowering.

The final element of mise-en-scène that I believe reveals Preminger's desire to suggest more sex than censors would have permitted him to show, and inarguably illustrates his attempt to have his filmic cake and eat it too, is evidenced by his decision to cast Jean Seberg as Cecile.[26] A number of biographers have recorded that he reputedly wanted Audrey Hepburn to play Sagan's heroine but had doubts about the older actress's ability to play a seventeen-year-old. Whatever the real reason, Hepburn would have been seen as far too virtuous to play such a character, as her portrayal that same year in *Love in the Afternoon* (1957) proved that even when playing a French girl, she remained incorruptibly virginal.[27] In addition, one of the more seductive qualities of literature is that the reader can readily put oneself in the place of the protagonist, especially if there aren't too many specific visual descriptives given by the author, and it would have been a particularly easy substitution in the case of *Bonjour Tristesse,* as Sagan reveals virtually nothing about her first-person narrator's physical appearance. In terms of female audiences and filmic identification in 1957, Seberg was still America's "real-life Cinderella," a big-eyed, small-town girl who had won the titular role in *Saint Joan* over eighteen thousand other contestants. *McCall's* described her as having "a round perfect American girl face," and it is conceivable that Preminger knew that stateside viewers who had read the book wanted to believe that it was their own French Riviera vacation they were watching; the choice of an American actress such as Seberg made this type of substitution more plausible.

But more probable than either of these reasons is Preminger's astute recognition that the renowned French author and Iowan ingénue shared more than a few physical similarities. Aside from their mere three-year age difference, they were both petite blondes with short, tousled haircuts and a penchant for the pedal pushers and slouchy poorboy sweaters favored by those Left Bank existentialists, and their undeniable likeness to one another is apparent when one examines a publicity photograph taken while shooting on the Riviera. Side-by-side, the author and actress could be fraternal twins, with Seberg as the beauty and Sagan as the brain.[28] Given the rumor that the literary narrator's liberal attitude toward physical pleasures reflected the real-life author's, hearsay that only served to heighten prurient interest in Sagan, it is difficult not to believe that Preminger desired to bank on the public's fascination with the infamous French teen.[29] David Richards, Seberg's biographer, believed that Preminger understood the power of their resemblance and writes that "before 75 photographers, [Preminger] arranged for Jean to meet Francoise Sagan during the *Saint Joan* premiere at the Paris Opera House in 1957 in order to pump up interest in his adaptation of *Bonjour Tristesse.*"[30] Both Seberg and Sagan were constant features in the popular press, and their visual convergence, as one might call it, probably helped Preminger insinuate that there was more naughti-

Revisiting the Issue of Virginity in Bonjour Tristesse

ness to the on-screen character of Cecile than his moralizing revision let on. For if Seberg was seen as a virginal saint at this point, largely because of her role as Joan of Arc and the attendant press portraying her as a corn-fed innocent, Sagan was viewed as a sinner, not only because of her syntax, but also on account of her professed love for Johnny Walker Black Label and independence.[31] In *Life*'s introductory article, "Precocious Parisienne: She Reaps Rewards of Writing a Best-Seller at 18," the periodical reported that Sagan liked "to drive fast cars, use up the afternoons shooting dice, have drinks on café terraces, and spend whole evenings listening to jazz," desires that seem rather tame now but that in 1955 were indicative of the continental sophistication that equaled loose morality. The accompanying photos of Sagan only magnified her purported decadence and extreme chic: the author is shown on a boat zipping from the isle of Capri, playing

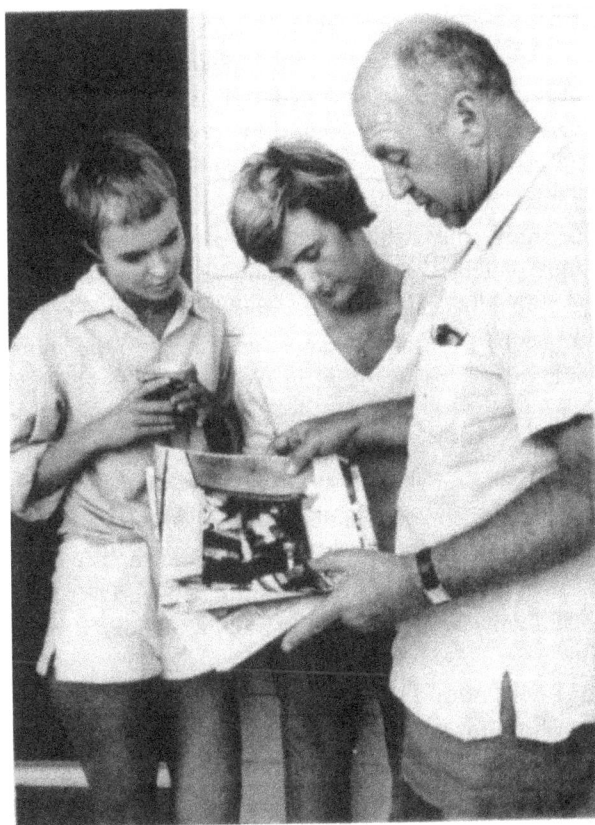

The physical similarities between scandalous author and Preminger's wholesome star played up: Jean Seberg and Françoise Sagan.

shuffleboard for drinks, and wearing a modish leopard-skin coat as she stands by her Jaguar sports car.[32]

In her biography, written nearly thirty years after her novel became a worldwide succès de scandale, Sagan attempted to assess why *Bonjour Tristesse* incited such fury:

> I can only think of two ridiculous reasons for [the uproar]. It was unconceivable that a young girl of seventeen or eighteen should make love, without being in love, with a boy of her own age, and not be punished for it. People couldn't tolerate that idea that girl should not fall madly in love with the boy and not be pregnant by the end of the summer. It was unacceptable too in this way that a young girl should have the right to use her body as she wished, and derive pleasure from it without incurring a penalty, one which had always been thought inevitable.[33]

Her words bear out that it was neither the heroine's naïve plot to rid herself of a stepmother that was the moralists' real concern nor Sagan's whiskey drinking or gambling in Cannes that made her such a cultural icon. Rather, it was that the novel and the author spoke for a generation of women who desired to be sexually liberated—to use their bodies as they wished and to derive pleasure from using those bodies—in a period in which doing so was certain to bring the type of ruin that Preminger's punitive ending illustrates. Immediately following the tragic denouement, in which Anne's once shiny convertible is hauled up from the seaside's rocky depths, Preminger switches back to black-and-white stock and the locale of Paris for the concluding five minutes. After an indifferent, fairly heartless goodnight to Jacques, the now jaded Cecile walks into the home she shares with her father. Her first words as she closes the door, "I never heard from Philippe again. I suppose he finished law school," revise the novel's ending, in which Sagan makes it clear that it is Cecile who no longer desires her summer fling's affections. As she sits at her dressing table, she stares at her reflection: a tortured, relentlessly tear-filled face in which regret is visually palpable. Preminger's insinuation that she is wholly defiled by the summer's monumental events is further confirmed by Cecile's closing voice-over: "So here I am, surrounded by my wall of memory. I try to stop remembering, but I can't. And so often I wonder, when he's alone, is he remembering, too? I hope not." The use of the ambiguous pronoun *he* presumably refers to Raymond, whose philandering was the real reason for Anne's death, and the word *memory* is a reference to the horrid sight of Anne's car being pulled from the bottom of the sea. But to young female viewers constantly reminded of the bad reputation that was presumed to follow one's premarital loss of virginity, the ambiguous *he* could just as easily refer to Philippe and the word *memory* to Cecile's guilty comprehension that she will forever be a girl who gave in to her desires and thus is no longer desirable. Not only has she lost her virginity, but because of her aggressive actions she has also lost her chance to marry a young man who once adored her.

In summary, the director's extensive, and ultimately punitive, revisions to Sagan's best-selling novel sanction the period's cultural anxiety over teenage female sexual desire and illustrate the cinematic need for a mother or mother figure to police those pleasures during that same period. Preminger may get historical credit for defending his use of the word *virgin* in *The Moon Is Blue,* but in retrospect the protest wasn't as radical as it may have seemed then. After all, being a virgin was fine; it was being sexually active that was problematic. The long view regarding teenage female pleasure in *Bonjour Tristesse* is that Preminger was just as conservative as the Production Code. As explicated earlier, Preminger totally expunges the liberal tone of the novel's ending from his film's closure and, in doing so, clearly sides with the moral majority—and the mothers in the audience. And I would argue that it was this decision that finally made the film a failure. To paraphrase Cecile's retort to Anne, seventeen in 1957 certainly wasn't what it was twenty years prior—it was a whole new market, supported by the fact that there was a magazine of that very same name that allowed these young women to voice just how much they disliked their "best literature ... being changed beyond recognition." Given the baby boom generation's escalating power as a paying audience, Preminger should have followed Sagan's lead and done more to satisfy those sexually desirous daughters.

Notes

1. Gerald Mast, *A Short History of the Movies* (New York: Macmillan, 1986), 289; Jeanine Basinger, *American Cinema: One Hundred Years of Filmmaking* (New York: Rizzoli, 1994), 242; Peter Lev, *History of the American Cinema*, vol. 7, *Transforming the Screen, 1950–1959* (New York: Charles Scribner's Sons, 2003).

2. Otto Preminger, *Preminger* (New York: Doubleday and Co., 1977), 108.

3. Susan Weiner, *Enfants Terribles: Youth and Femininity in the Mass Media in France, 1945–1968* (Baltimore: Johns Hopkins University Press, 2001), 82–83.

4. "A Certain Smile," *Saturday Review*, August 13, 1956, 13.

5. Review of *Bonjour Tristesse, Time,* August 20, 1956, 94. This *Time* review also compared Sagan's heroine to the "sophisticated Gallic equivalent of a rock n' roller"

and said that her second novel, *A Certain Smile*, was "a petition in spiritual and emotional bankruptcy." A review in *America: The National Catholic Review* also noted that Sagan was a skilled stylist, but one who lacked moral virtue: "The artistry of the book makes it all the more a matter of regret that the young author chose this subject matter . . . it is a shock that she discusses [it] with such cynical assurance." Harold C. Gardner, review of *Bonjour Tristesse*, *America: The National Catholic Review*, March 12, 1955, 623.

6. Sheila Rowbothom, *A Century of Women: The History of Women in Britain and the United States* (London: Penguin Group, 1997), 303.

7. Molly Haskell, *From Reverence to Rape: The Treatment of Women in the Movies* (Chicago: University of Chicago Press, 1987), 296.

8. Haskell, quoted in Thomas R. Atkins, "Troubled Sexuality in the Popular Hollywood Feature," in *Sexuality in the Movies*, ed. Thomas R. Atkins (Bloomington: Indiana University Press, 1975), 125.

9. John Gibbs and Douglas Pye, "Revisiting Preminger: *Bonjour Tristesse*," in *Style and Meaning: Studies in the Detailed Analysis of Film*, ed. Gibbs and Pye (Manchester: Manchester University Press, 2005), 124.

10. Adrath Perkins, then a freshman at Stanford University, wrote a letter about film censorship and adaptations to *Seventeen* magazine and quoted one of her friends: "We don't like how some of our best literature is changed beyond recognition by adaptation to the screen with disturbed sequences and distorted characterizations. Many of these stories are dear to our heart and it hurts." Perkins, "A Look at New Movies," *Seventeen*, January 1954, 14. Another teenage writer also revealed her frustration with adaptations: "Movies sometime lose that certain feeling the printed page conveys. Often the film writer throws out characters and places and changes the entire plot to suit the movie [producers'] demands." Arnetta Pfiefer, "Movies Make Me Sentimental," *Seventeen*, January 1958, 12.

11. Regarding Sagan's literary treatment of older women, more than one critic saw her as impious, and in a period in which father and mother knew best, it's not surprising that such disrespect was cause for alarm. One 1956 review noted, "In both [of Sagan's] books we have the immoral young girl, her counterpart the amoral older man, and the foil to these two, the older woman who personifies middle-class morality. In both books, the mother figure is done in." Robert Parris, "Grin, Grimmer, Grimace," *New Republic*, August 20, 1956, 19–20.

12. See Dean D. Knudsen and Hallowell Pope, "Premarital Sexual Norms, the Family, and Social Change," *Journal of Marriage and the Family* 27, no. 3 (1965): 316, in which the authors maintain that although "standards intolerant of promiscuous premarital sexual intercourse" still remain, strong affection is becoming a permissible condition for women who wish to justify their actions.

13. Robert R. Bell and Jack V. Buerkle, "Mother and Daughter Attitudes to Premarital Sexual Behavior," *Marriage and Family Living* 23, no. 4 (1961): 390–92.

14. Françoise Sagan, "By a Charming Monster," *Newsweek*, March 7, 1955, 92.

15. It is also notable to consider that in this very short preview the characters of Cecile and Anne are afforded equal screen time, approximately thirty seconds each, as the middle thirty seconds are devoted to Anne and Raymond dancing together

at one of the seaside resorts. Their romance and Anne's charming character were evidently considered as much of an audience draw as the illicit sexuality of the young protagonist.

16. Françoise Sagan, *Bonjour Tristesse* (New York: E. P. Dutton and Co., 1955), 84.

17. "F. De St E.," review of *Bonjour Tristesse, Films in Review* 9, no. 2 (1958): 87–88.

18. Alisia Chase, "'Like Their First Pair of High Heels...': Continental Accessories and Audrey Hepburn's Cinematic Coming of Age," *Abito E Identita: Richerche di Storia Letteraria E Culturale*, ed. C. Giorcelli, Palermo: Ila Palma 5 (Spring 2004): 215–43; and Rachel Moseley, "Dress, Class and Audrey Hepburn: The Significance of the Cinderella Story," in *Fashioning Film Stars: Dress, Culture and Identity*, ed. Rachel Moseley (London: British Film Institute, 109–20.

19. "Gee, Is She Sophisticated!" *Seventeen*, January 1946, 82.

20. Marina Warner, *Monuments and Maidens: The Allegory of the Female Form* (New York: Atheneum, 1985), 250.

21. Chase, "'Like Their First Pair of High Heels'"; and Tamar Jeffers, "Pillow Talk's Repackaging of Doris Day: 'Under all those dirndls...,'" in *Fashioning Film Stars: Dress, Culture, Identity*, ed. Rachel Moseley (London: British Film Institute, 2005), 50–61.

22. More than a few critics have noted that the relationship between Raymond and Cecile (especially as it is illustrated by Preminger) is so complicit in sharing sexual information as to be deemed all but (physically) incestuous. Although the parameters of this chapter don't permit me a more detailed exploration of this topic, it's a point well taken and can be considered another subtext that probably contributed to the reading of the story and subsequent film as immoral.

23. The black-and-white graphics of this teenager's T-shirt as symbolic of her entrapment would be resurrected by Jean-Luc Godard in *A bout de souffle* (1959) when Cecile transmogrifies to a grown but still naïvely malicious woman in a black-and-white striped Christian Dior gown.

24. Kathryn Schwartz, "The Wrong Question: Thinking through Virginity," *differences: A Journal of Feminist Cultural Studies* 13, no. 2 (2002): 13.

25. Maureen Turim, "Designing Women: The Emergence of the Sweetheart Line," reprinted in *Fabrications: Costume and the Female Body*, ed. Jane Gaines and Charlotte Herzog (London: Routledge, 1990), 212–28.

26. I believe it is altogether too facile to take at face value his suggestion that he wanted to give her another chance after critics disparaged her performance in *Saint Joan*.

27. Cameron Crowe, *Conversations with Wilder* (New York: Alfred A. Knopf, 2001), 145–48.

28. I would further note that the documents they are looking at in the picture are upside down, a clear indication that this was a staged photograph to be used for publicity purposes.

29. Lev, *History of the American Cinema*, 7:209.

30. David Richards, *Played Out: The Jean Seberg Story* (New York: Random

House, 1981), 54.

31. Judith Graves Miller, *Francoise Sagan* (New York: Twayne, 1988).

32. In addition to her coverage in *Life*, she was also pictured in *Vogue, Mademoiselle,* and *Harper's Bazaar* throughout 1955–58. Her visage was familiar to young American women not only because of such extensive press but also because some American editions of her novels frequently pictured the author on the cover of the dust jacket.

33. Françoise Sagan, *With Fondest Regards* (New York: E. P. Dutton and Co., 1984), 41.

Tamar Jeffers McDonald

Performances of Desire and Inexperience
Doris Day's Fluctuating Filmic Virginity

> Doris Day's purity is one of the best-known facts about American life. No matter what she does, no matter what anyone tries to do to her, in the mind of the audience, Doris Day will ALWAYS be a virgin!
> —Al Capp, "The Day Dream," *Show*

Introduction

Al Capp, writer of the cartoon strip *Li'l Abner*, here concludes an iconoclastic 1962 article on Day with some humorous hyperbole. The article presents the earliest instance of the assumption of Day's mature virgin persona that I have been able to find in writing, an assumption that has persisted into the present time, nearly forty years after Day made her last film. Capp's observation implied that Day's virginal persona was an accepted fact, but it was actually of relatively recent suggestion at the time of his writing. In this chapter I look at two films, *Pillow Talk* (1959) and its unofficial sequel or remake, *Lover Come Back* (1961), and suggest that the lasting virginal myth attached to Day's star persona actually dates from this latter vehicle, over halfway into her twenty-two-year film career.

While I acknowledge that, as Dyer has noted, the star persona can be made up of extrafilmic events and moments as well as on-screen ones, Day's lasting chaste reputation seems to have very little to draw on from either sphere.[1] Though it is a commonplace that Doris Day "always plays a virgin," neither offscreen facts nor film roles support this reading of the star.[2] Yet it seems incontestable that this is the dominant image of Day:

from the moment that her star persona became fused with the virgin until now, more than thirty years after her screen career finished, Day's association with the maiden has been almost total. A byword for coy, pre-Pill prudery and out-of-touch morality, the star's name is usually invoked to indicate her own films' inane and unrealistic cheeriness ("the noir heroine is no Doris Day") or our (assumed) more sophisticated distance from 1950s morals: "By the time [teenagers] are 13 they already know more about sex than Doris Day had ever figured out."[3]

That this view of the Day persona is postconstructed, however, is indicated by a look at her pre–*Pillow Talk* career. Examining characters from among the twenty-four Day films released prior to this one shows an interesting heterogeneity of sexual status: it cannot be claimed that she earned the virgin tag by endlessly repeating the ingénue role. By 1959's *Pillow Talk* she had played a married woman eight times and a widow three, and she was a mother in five of these eleven films. Thus Day's earlier career noticeably does not contribute to the now-dominant virgin myth. However, her very great popularity as a star indicates that the public were able to find a settled cluster of meanings produced by her image, one that was not affected by the vacillations in her sexual or marital status from film to film.[4] Two specific factors seem to reappear that leant the star persona some coherence: the consistent use of Day's earlier established stardom as a popular singer and a marked quality of independence in the personalities of the women she played. Seventeen of the twenty-four films before *Pillow Talk* are musicals, and two more employ scenes that narrativize Day's singing, including Hitchcock's *The Man Who Knew Too Much* (1956), which foregrounds Day's voice as the ultimate instrument of her kidnapped son's rescue.[5]

Across the wide range of genres she appeared in and her characters' differing personalities and employments, Day continuously projected a quality of independence and self-reliance that provided a coherence to her persona. While other commentators have seen the darker films—*Storm Warning* (1951), *Love Me or Leave Me* (1955), *The Man Who Knew Too Much* (1956), and *Julie* (1956)—as ones anomalous to her career trajectory, exploration of her characters within these films reveals the same core trait of self-determination, just set within more dramatic narratives.[6] Before *Pillow Talk*, then, Day's name on the cinema marquee told the audience that the woman she played would be feisty, hardworking, energetic, independent. These elements were there from her first role as Georgia Garrett in *Romance on the High Seas* (1948) and continued throughout her film roles, whether she was playing a chorus girl, an heiress, or a settled family woman.

Day's persona was more associated with "energy and independence" than with ignorant or innocent sexuality in the years before *Pillow Talk*. Examining this film and its follow-up reveals a new emphasis on her characters' sexuality, an emphasis that has, over time, entirely eclipsed the other factors of her persona. By closely examining these two performances by Day, I intend to rupture assumptions about her perpetual maiden status, such as those raised by Capp in this chapter's opening quotation, by indicating that she does not always play a virgin. In both *Pillow Talk* and *Lover Come Back*, Day tangles with Rock Hudson, negotiating the boundaries of their relationships without ruling out premarital sex but insisting that it must be on her terms. However, only the second film explicitly acknowledges the initiatory nature of the sex she desires. Looking at the two films in chronological order indicates that Day's filmic virginity was fluctuating, first not there, then present: unlike the characters' independence or the probability that Day would sing, it was not an unchanging essential part of either her vehicle's narratives or her own performances. In oscillating, her maidenhood acknowledges its status as achronologically constructed by the studios and media rather than as an inherent part of her screen persona. By contrasting first the two narratives and then two specific scenes, I interrogate how *Pillow Talk* attempted to affirm her character as a maturely sexual woman, while *Lover Come Back* intentionally derives humor from an aged virgin persona.

The Original and Its Problematic Copy

Following close to a decade of box office success in rural-based family films and musical comedies (as well as, less popularly, roles in more dramatic productions), Day's stardom was perceived to be in decline by 1959. Her manager-husband, Marty Melcher, thus cast around for a project that would renew her star potential. He and *Pillow Talk*'s producer, Ross Hunter, both felt that it was time for Day to shift her persona in a different direction; Hunter later told Day's biographer he "felt that it was essential for Doris to change her image if she was going to survive as a top star."[7] Undertaking a role in a risqué sex comedy was new for Day, as was Hunter's insistence that her makeup, hair, and costume should be totally modish and chic. While critics noticed that Day's persona had been subject to a makeover, the star herself was initially unsure if she could convincingly portray someone so different from her usual roles: "[*Pillow Talk* was] very sophisticated, very chic, the leading lady an interior decorator, an 'in' lady very much tuned in to the current New York scene. The plot, for 1959, was quite sexy. I was not sure I was right to depict this rather sexy, beautifully dressed, sophisticated New York career lady."[8] Despite Day's initial misgivings, however, *Pillow Talk* transformed her into an adult, sexually mature star, giving her a career boost that resulted in her being "acclaimed by Theatre Owners of America as the world's number one box office attraction" just before *Lover Come Back* was released.[9] It was perhaps inevitable that due to *Pillow Talk*'s enormous box office success the studio, producers, and writers would be keen to make another film with the same stars and the same salacious plotline in the hopes of repeating its very healthy return on investment outlay.[10] Significantly, however, by early February 1961, when *Lover Come Back* went into production, the idea of the Day figure actively maintaining her virginity had been consciously recruited into the text. In Hudson's biography, *Lover Come Back*'s director, Delbert Mann, later confided that he felt, with this film, "the assault on Doris's fiercely guarded virginity was where the humour came from."[11] Thus *Pillow Talk* established the mature, sexual Doris Day without indicating any sexual inexperience, while *Lover Come Back,* two years later, consciously affixed the old maid label to Day's character.

Exploration of the similarities and differences in the two films' narrative structures serves to underline the contrasting presentations of the central female's sexual desire, agency, and experience. The varying of Day's performance of sexual knowledge stands out especially clearly given that the texts otherwise have so much in common. Because this chapter provides close readings of the two texts, brief synopses are included here as refreshers.

Pillow Talk employs a real late 1950s problem, the lack of available telephone lines, as its motor: without sufficient lines in New York City, complete strangers have to share numbers. Thus interior decorator Jan Morrow (Day) and playboy songwriter Brad Allen (Rock Hudson) become enemies: because of Brad's telephone womanizing, Jan can never make calls. When Brad finally sees—and desires—Jan, he realizes he has no hope of wooing her as himself, so he invents the persona of "Rex Stetson," shy Texan millionaire, and successfully dates her. Brad's best friend, Jonathan (Tony Randall), is one of Jan's clients and wants to marry her; he hires a detective to discover who Jan's new boyfriend is. Finding Brad masquerading as Rex, Jonathan banishes him to his own country cottage, but Brad sneakily manages to take Jan along: the scene is set for a weekend of sexual indulgence. Ensconced in the cottage, Jan is enjoying the mutual seduction when she realizes Rex's true identity; furious, she returns to New York. She refuses to see Brad again; he tries to win her back by having her redecorate his apartment, assuming she will understand that this will be home for both of them. But unaware of his intentions, Jan redecorates it like a brothel. Storming into her apartment, Brad seizes Jan and carries her across town to his place, berating her for turning her future home into a cathouse: Jan understands this proposal and the pair reconcile.

The first few moments of *Pillow Talk* present a *coup de cinéma* in displaying a new Doris: the scene opens, after the credits, on Day smoothing a nude-colored stocking over her thigh. While beautifully (un)dressed in her lavish, chic, urban apartment, her character is also presented via other methods in conveying that she is to be understood as a modern, sophisticated woman-about-town. First there is her name: "Jan Morrow" is obviously a play on the name of the French star, Jeanne Moreau, rendered clipped and brisk in American English but still retaining the European connotations of mature adult sexuality. During *Pillow Talk*'s production, Moreau had appeared in two films released with much media hoopla in the United States: *Ascenseur pour l'échafaud/Frantic* (1957) and *Les Amants/The Lovers* (1958), both texts that associate the French star with adultery and a drive toward her own sexual fulfillment. Because the usual films of the two women were not of similar genres, it seems that the *Pillow Talk* character's name is more a joke specific to the film than to the woman playing her, intended to emphasize that the difference between Day's usual persona and role here is as great as that between the usual Day and the usual Moreau—intended, that is, to signal to the audience that here she is a woman experienced in love.

Further strategies used to underline the new maturity of the Day character are the inclusion in the script of direct references to past relationships and encounters with men and the establishment of a comparison with Brad, the suave seducer. The former proliferate throughout the film: Jan talks to her maid, Alma, about the "very nice men" she goes out with and to "Rex," Brad's alter ego, about other experiences she has had: "I'm sorry, Rex, I should have known you're not like the others." Jan's frequent comments that she can trust Rex are simultaneously comically ironic and indicative of past experiences with men who did not employ such elaborate ruses in order to capture her affections. Jan's apology indicates that other men have tried wolfish behavior on her in the past: significantly, while Jan says nothing to deny that such tactics may have been successful, at least one contemporary reviewer decided to believe this: "A fine healthy young woman, *who has so far fought off the passes of many men,* Doris now begins to be kept awake by the primary urge."[12] Jan's later comment to Rex, "I should be able to trust you by now," should thus surely be read not as her acknowledging her awareness that he will not make a pass at her, but that he will, differing from other men in that he will not run away or end the relationship after she has yielded. This view of the likely outcome of the climactic scene in the Connecticut cabin, had Jan not discovered the masquerade, is borne out by a comment later made by Day herself to Hudson's biographer, Sara Davidson: "I was a businesswoman. I don't think I was a virgin. I went off to the country with him and I probably would have succumbed, except I found out he was a phony and ran away. The audience— *you* thought I was a virgin. *You* thought, oh, she'll think of some way to wiggle out."[13] Further overt comments on her past amatory experiences occur in Jan's sung interior monologue, "Possess Me!" discussed in the following paragraphs, and when she is contemplating manipulating Rex into asking her to go away with him for the weekend:

> JAN: Gosh, I feel guilty! I practically tricked him into taking me along! You know, you've gone out with a lot of men in your time, but this! This is the jackpot.

While the line "gone out with a lot of men" does not necessarily imply that she has had sex with any of them, it does underline the context of Jan's familiarity with male company. Furthermore, by tagging this comment onto the end of her guilty glee about going to Connecticut, it can be seen to imply that she has been in similar intimate situations before.

Jan's comments heard in voice-over, then, serve to reveal to the audience her attraction to and feelings for Rex in both a seemingly authentic and comic manner, the latter especially, given that the viewer knows about the true identity of the man. Jan's happy self-admissions that Rex is handsome, charming, and trustworthy are funny in the context of our awareness that he is really handsome, charming, and *untrustworthy* Brad. But the presentation of the interior commentary does more than provoke laughter at Jan's innocence of the plot and mistaken confidence in Rex: it directly establishes a parallel between the couple, as we are permitted to hear the thoughts of both. Frequently this continues the laughter at Jan's expense, which arises from our possessing greater knowledge than she—as when

Brad/Rex cynically calculates, "I'd say five or six dates ought to do it," while the woman comments internally, "Oh, it's so nice to meet a man you feel you can trust!"—although we are also privy to the thoughts of each when the other is absent.

Allowing both Brad and Jan moments of interiority where the audience can hear their thoughts and desires establishes a parity between the characters that is easily overlooked amid the more overt contrasts the film attempts to build up between them. While external publicity concentrated on opposing the future lovers, the film itself is careful to establish parallels between Jan and Brad to confirm their aptness as partners.[14] For example, both are successful in their careers and derive pleasure from their work: their jobs are more arty than practical, allowing them to be creative, Jan with color, texture, and design and Brad with music and words. Both enjoy life in the metropolis, and both are provided with a character who voices criticism about their single status: friend Jonathan tells Brad, "You oughta quit all this chasing around and get married," while Jan's maid, Alma (Thelma Ritter), voices similar admonishments. It is interesting that while no critic has assumed that Jonathan's homily on marriage to Brad should be meant other than ironically, Alma's parallel remarks about Jan's misguidedness in enjoying her career-woman life—"If there's anything worse than a woman living alone, it's a woman living alone and liking it"—have been taken to be the film itself indicating disapproval of her singleness.[15] It seems to me that, far from setting up Alma as a source of worldly wisdom, the film intends her comments to be read in light of her own context (as a single, lower-class, alcoholic woman of advanced middle age) rather than to reflect on Jan. The film's paralleling of Alma and Jonathan underlines the unlikeness of their status as seers: both unmarried Alma and thrice-divorced Jonathan are meant to act as comic comparison rather than clear-sighted soothsayers.

Two further strategies mark Day's character in *Pillow Talk* as a new, sexually mature persona: the witty use of split screens saucily suggests that the couple are in bed together, or sharing an extra large bath, with the innuendo provided by the split screens serving as the visual accompaniment to the script's suggestive jokes. Finally, there is the little joke about mistaken identity and virginity after Jan has realized Brad's imposture. Driving back to New York with Jonathan, Jan cries all the way, even in a stop at a roadside diner for some coffee. Here they discuss Brad's deception, and Jonathan urges Jan to stop berating herself. Without knowing it, however, the pair are overheard by several burly truckers who read this scene between two friends as one between lovers, taking Jonathan's briskness as a sign of postcoital callousness:

> JAN: I've never done anything like this before.
>
> JONATHAN: All right—there has to be a first time! You don't have to go to pieces over it!
>
> JAN: I'm so ashamed. . . . I thought we were going to get married!
>
> JONATHAN: Forget it!

The film invites us to laugh at the truckers' misplaced response (they nearly break Jonathan's jaw punching him), their presumption of a Victorian melodrama of seduced innocence and sneering villainy. But the scene and the truckers' response are only funny if Jan is *not* a virgin. If she were still a virgin and had nearly been duped by Brad, the truckers' physical punishment of Jonathan might seem transferred from right to wrong man and, while out of proportion, still an apt retribution. The scene can only be funny if the old-fashioned response is being held up as the wrong one, thus indicating again *Pillow Talk*'s commitment to a modern Day playing a woman who is sexually mature and sufficiently postvirginal to be distanced in time from this posited scene of ex-maidenhood.

It seems to me, therefore, that *Pillow Talk* does not posit Jan as a virgin, does not even address the subject of her virginity except, as in the scene mentioned previously, in assuming it to have been yielded in the past. Instead the film seeks to create a postvirginal persona by the several strategies mentioned earlier. In this reading, Jan's wariness of wolves can be seen to exist not because she does not want to yield her virginity but precisely because she has already done so and has been disappointed before. *Pillow Talk* thus presents a new Doris playing a character whose possible trepidation over initiatory sex is no more mentioned than Brad's. In *Lover Come Back*, by contrast, this moment is put center stage in the film's narrative.

Lover Come Back consciously revisits many of its predecessor's plot mechanisms: again Day and Hudson star as successful businesspeople who have not met in person. This time they play rival advertising agents: Carol Templeton devotes creativity and boundless energy to her projects; Jerry Webster uses psychology and sex, invariably winning the contract. Webster creates a campaign for "VIP," a nonexistent product. Carol schemes to win the VIP account and visits the laboratory of the man responsible for inventing it, Dr. Linus Tyler; encountering Webster there, she takes *him*

Doris Day's Fluctuating Filmic Virginity

for the Nobel Prize–winning scientist. Jerry, realizing whom he is duping, permits the mistake and spins out a lengthy performance as the shy chemist. Eventually, one night in her apartment, "Linus" plots to spring the trap, telling Carol he doubts his masculinity. She is set to prove him a real man by sacrificing her virginity, but then his imposture is exposed. Carol avenges herself by telling the Advertising Council that Jerry is promoting a fake product, and a hearing is called, but at the last minute the real Tyler does invent a VIP—an alcohol-saturated mint. Overindulging in these, Carol and Jerry awaken the next morning together in a honeymoon suite. Carol is horrified and has the marriage annulled; but nine months later she consents to remarry Jerry—on the way to a hospital delivery room to have their baby.

This second Day-Hudson pairing can be seen not only to repeat the plot exigencies of the earlier film but also to make them more extreme. Thus, where the original picture presents the necessity for masquerade arising from Brad's need to court Jan in a different persona because she knows and detests his "real" self, in *Lover Come Back*, Jerry takes on the "Linus" persona solely to make a fool of Carol, not in order to win her. While *Lover Come Back* rather transparently repeats many of the points deemed to be successful in the earlier film so as to re-create the box office success of its predecessor (including stars, scenario, split screen, soliloquies, etc.), it alters the character played by Day in two significant, and significantly linked, ways. First it undermines Carol's business skills; then, having eroded any professional acumen she might have, the film also explicitly removes the past personal experiences that Jan acknowledges.

Where Jan was a successful interior decorator, shown to be creative, decisive, good at making contacts, and important to her boss for all these reasons, Carol the advertising executive is mocked by the narrative for her excessive but unfocused zeal, her unwillingness to use sex to sell products, her lack of creative vision. Unlike *Pillow Talk* too, which gave Jan and Brad different careers and allowed each to be a success, *Lover Come Back* makes the two business rivals and shows clearly that Jerry Webster vastly outranks Carol in experience, skill, and importantly, guile.

The greatest difference between Jan and her descendant, Carol, however, is the emphasis placed on the latter's virginity. The later film underlines this by presenting the woman's desire for sex in a sung soliloquy, as did *Pillow Talk*, to which the audience is privileged witness. However, instead of sensuously confirming her desires, as the earlier film does, it indicates her complex array of conflicting emotions. Having manipulated

Carol into installing him in her spare bedroom for the night, Jerry now attempts to goad her into seducing him by baiting the trap with the promise of a lasting commitment:

> "Linus": I'm afraid I could never get married. . . . I'm afraid. Afraid I'll be a failure. . . . Am I the kind of man a woman could love?
>
> Carol: Any woman could love you!
>
> "Linus": If only I could be sure of that.

Torn between fear of her first time and wanting to prove to Linus that he is adequate, sacrificing her maidenhead on the altar of his ego so that he will marry her, Carol's tumultuous feelings find expression in song. The film thus establishes Carol's "crisis of virginity." It is noteworthy, however, that unlike *Pillow Talk*, where the masquerade plot is exploded partly through Jan's own agency and partly through Brad's bad luck, Carol has to be saved from sacrificing her virginity entirely by outside forces. It is an eleventh-hour phone call from her boss, sacking her for entertaining the wrong Linus Tyler at her apartment, which exposes Jerry's true identity. Carol's business and personal ambitions are thus linked again at this moment of joint failure: she loses her job instead of winning a client and keeps her virginity instead of exchanging it for sexual experience.

Again the film copies the original in positing a scenario after the explosion of the masquerade plot where listeners overhear a conversation and draw the wrong, salacious conclusion. In *Lover Come Back*, however, the audience, two cleaning ladies at the honeymoon motel, are not as wrong in their guess as were *Pillow Talk*'s eavesdropping truckers. While they assume that Carol's horror is due to the realities of sex—"It's like olives, dear, it's something you acquire a taste for"—but her actual misery is caused by who her sexual partner has been, the point of each, the assumption and the actuality, is that sex has occurred.

Looking at the outline of the narratives of these two films in chronological order thus demonstrates that, despite their obvious parallels at many levels, the two texts do present female characters of very different experience. Specific examination of Day's performances in the two films' matched presex scenes will work to affirm both the occasional, rather than inevitable, nature of Day's performance of a maiden state and her skill in varying these enactments of desire and (in)experience.

Not "Always Playing a Virgin": Performances of Desire and (In)Experience

In *Pillow Talk,* Jan's moment of internal pondering of the anticipated sexual act comes in a scene of sung soliloquy: in the car with Rex on the way to the weekend alone together, Jan outwardly enjoys the nighttime drive in the convertible. While checking her makeup, and eventually snuggling up to Rex, denote the physical actions she performs, in voice-over she sings a song that the audience is meant to interpret as her internal thoughts. Thus establishing a split between Jan's outward behavior and her inner feelings, the film goes on to elaborate this split by showing the woman's outward actions as seemingly innocent but her inner words, in her performance of the song "Possess Me!" as underlining both her current desires and her past experiences.

Furthermore, throughout the film we have been allowed access to both Jan and Brad's/Rex's internal voices and have usually seen him acting out gallantry while his inner voice demonstrates his cynical awareness of how this impacts Jan. In this scene, however, the similarity rather than difference between the two would-be lovers is stressed, through Jan's passionate thoughts contrasted with her quiet outward demeanor. In this way, both characters are shown as being prepared to use subterfuge to get the desired goal, and for both characters this goal is sex. The scene gives us Jan's outwardly innocent performance—the makeup checking that allows her to snuggle up to the man—while her inner voice thrillingly details what she wants from him:

> Hold me tight
> And kiss me right
> I'm yours tonight
> My darling, possess me.

In this scene Day's performance can be seen enacting Jan's desires, both through her vocal treatment of the song played as a voice-over and through her acting work, thus continuing the film's construction of Jan as a character with past sexual experience. Three separate factors work together to build up this idea of Jan's desire: the song lyrics, Day's vocal treatment of them, and her physical performance; that this last is different from the words sung needs stressing, as there are no direct correspondences on this occasion between the lines delivered and the business Day enacts.

Lover Come Back's similar scene creates much closer ties between lyrics and physical performance, but in *Pillow Talk* the split between internally avowed passion and externally performed innocence is the precise point. The lyrics establish a past history to Jan's sexual desires. For example, her command "Kiss me right" implies that there is a wrong way and that she is experienced enough to know the difference. Further, the line "I'm yours tonight" can be read as implying that the woman is aware of the potentially temporary nature of the relationship: there might not be a tomorrow or a forever, but this is not what she demands. Jan is not only acknowledging here that there may only be tonight but also does not insist on the physical acts being excused by love. While admitting her attraction to the man she addresses, she does not say she loves him or ask him to love her. Both times the word *love* is used, it is made by its position in the lyric to sound like a command to *"make* love."

Day's voice further connotes Jan's status as sexually experienced: her treatment of the lyrics is sensual and caressing. Singing simply, without embellishing or drawing out any particular note, she works her way through each line as though it were a spontaneous outpouring of feeling from Jan. In the middle lines, the tune works itself up to a climax, the notes rising higher and higher, and Day's voice becoming louder and stronger, as if in excited anticipation of the proximity of that which she sings. On "my heart . . . forgets . . . to beat," she holds the top note and the final word, emphasizing the strength of her feelings. For the final lines, shimmering violins underscore the physicality of what she is demanding with pizzicato caresses.

While Jan couches sex in terms of the man's activity, "make love to me," the fact that she is commanding him to do these things undercuts any idea of passivity, as does the fact that while she is singing she is pressing herself close to Rex, enacting with her body language her desire for him. Day's physical business in the scene strengthens the links between Jan and Rex by showing both capable of performance to get what they desire, because, while she is behaving innocently outwardly, her voice-over indicates the depth of her inner passion. Jan is seen looking happily at Rex, checking her makeup, her hair, but this is a performance carried out in order to obfuscate the fact that she is continually moving nearer to him. This *performance* of innocence is foregrounded by the way that the camera records her eyes sliding calculatingly to the left to look at him before she begins her migration. The humor of the scene thereby comes from the

Doris Day's Fluctuating Filmic Virginity

Calculating Jan (Doris Day) in Michael Gordon's *Pillow Talk* (1959).

contrast between Jan's ostensibly demure behavior and the very passionate commands she is singing in her head, revealing her underlying motives.

What the scene does not provide is any hint that Jan doubts what she wants: there is no hesitation on her part, no dramatization of a crisis or loaded choice. I do not think, therefore, that Day is performing virginity here. Even without the ironic contrast between her ostensibly modest behavior and the lyrics that indicate her passionate desires, her actions are still not readable as those of a tremulous virgin, because Jan so clearly has designs on Rex and is getting close to him via the classic "creeping nearer under the pretext of doing something else" maneuver. Jan is thus undoubtedly performing "innocence," but it is an entirely obvious performance supposed to be read by us as the character, and not just the actor, performing.

Day's overt assumption of virginity in *Lover Come Back* is a retrograde one: her persona is not seen evolving naturally, getting bolder and older from film to film, but rather Carol's innocence revokes the experiences to which Jan laid claim. What was conscious sexual desire and the determination to act upon this in the earlier film becomes in the later one an uncertainty, a self-questioning, bound up with questions of morals and a sense of crisis. Ostensibly presented in a similar way, through repeating the device of the sung soliloquy, Carol's acknowledgment of her feelings is presented as a torturous moment of decision rather than a sensual anticipation of known delights. Having been duped by Jerry Webster into believing he is shy scientist "Linus Tyler" and tricked into ensconcing him in her apartment, Carol prepares an intimate dinner for two. Webster then launches his master plan to seduce her: by avowing anguish over his own lack of experience, he hopes to make Carol abandon hers. Thus deciding to "Surrender!" Carol is about to don a lacy negligée and prove to Linus that he is a "real man" when her phone rings and the cruel plot is exposed. The film then spirals off into more comic exigencies as Carol takes her revenge and the two adopt openly antagonistic positions. What the scene has done, however, is demonstrate clearly both that Carol is a virgin and that she no longer wants to be one. In another skilful performance, Day presents bodily and vocal signifiers that make overt both the emotional emergency and the physical arousal her character is experiencing.

Lover Come Back thus revisits *Pillow Talk*'s sung soliloquy with significant modifications. In place of Jan's confident commands to Rex, here we have Carol's tremulous questions to herself, and, where before the man she desired was with her, now he is physically absent, in a different room. This means that, alone in her kitchen, Carol can more openly act out the conflicting emotions besetting her. Unlike the careful array of seemingly innocent actions calculated to bring her closer to Rex that the confident Jan performed, here Carol can be seen trying to dissipate her anxieties through action, hence her constant pacing, wringing of hands, crossing and recrossing of the kitchen space. This location marks another difference with the earlier scene: whereas Jan's avowal of desire had been staged in the

Innocent Carol (Doris Day) in Delbert Mann's *Lover Come Back* (1961).

glamorous, sophisticated, and modern setting of Brad's fast-moving convertible, a sexy space of consumerism and affluence, Carol's occurs in the kitchen of her own apartment, a domestic arena seeming to connote that, however real and sensual her physical promptings may be, she sees them in the context of a settled (married) relationship. However, two factors potentially counteract a reading that posits Carol's desires here as neatly confined within a safe, mundane context, suggesting instead that sexual awakening has taken her into a realm of exciting fantasy, away from the everyday. Fittingly, given the split between vocal avowal of her virginity crisis and physical performance of business meant to dissipate it, these two factors are similarly separated, one being on the soundtrack and the other present in the mise-en-scène.

When Carol emerges from the spare bedroom where she has left Linus, she shuts the door, then leans back on it, her eyes sliding off to the right to where the open-plan kitchen is located. At the same point on the soundtrack a glassy, bell-like note rings out in a rising scale. This signifies the beginning of the sung monologue, but it also introduces a fantasy, an almost fairy-tale-like quality, as Day's voice and the music that plays under it sound very far away. Whereas Jan's soliloquy sounded very much in the here and now, Carol sings quietly, almost as if not to alert Rex to her thoughts, the distant quality of her voice seeming to suggest that she has entered a realm far from her normal, mundane reality. This is further supported by the fantasy aspect of the kitchen space she now enters: it is spotlessly clean and tidy, and implausibly so, given that she has just cooked dinner for two and, as the dialogue makes clear, not yet done the dishes. Not a pan or dish, smear or crumb remains to remind the audience that this is a working kitchen; instead, the literally twinkling clean surfaces and harmonious color scheme suggests that Carol has left the everyday at the door to the spare bedroom and stepped out of time into a symbolic arena in which to debate her options.

As the lyrics of the song overtly and repeatedly pinpoint the stark dichotomized choices Carol feels she has at this moment, to yield now or to end the relationship, her body responds to the words to enact the different options she is listing:

> Shall I resist my heart?
> Shall I deny its splendor?
> Shall I insist we part?
> Should I surrender?

The song's rhyme pattern and repeated should/shall questions at the start of each line binds the whole piece together very tightly and serves to indicate how intensely the dichotomies are warring inside her. Further, while her voice-over sings about the opposing polarities of behavior she could adopt, one accepting sexual contact, one rejecting it, in the second verse (Should I be fire or ice? / Should I be firm or tender?), Day's physical performance conveys these alternate poles through hardening or softening her facial expression. As she poses these questions, Day's voice redoubles this emphasis on the two polarized personae, by hardening and sliding onto the notes for the passionate, sexualized half of the options and by hitting them precisely for the contrasting anxious doubter. Thus Day's physical and voice acting work together to reinforce the existence of the two Carols, each predicated on one of the radically different outcomes of this moment: either giving up her virginity ("Is this the night that love *finally* defeats me?") or parting from the man she loves. Simultaneously, Carol's questioning over which of these roles to adopt conveys that she can choose: the capability of being either fire or ice means that she realizes her potential for both.

While acting out the words of the song, Day also manages to add some stage business to convey still further the dilemma besetting the character: getting a half-bottle of champagne out of the refrigerator, finding two glasses, and shutting the cupboard door all provide occasions for her physically to embody the sense of crisis—through her pacing, clasping and wringing of hands, and, as her voice-over sings the last line of the middle section of the song, turning her head from side to side as she leans against a cupboard door.

At this point acting and mise-en-scène coalesce: the hitherto self-controlled Carol in pearls and yellow dress matches her refrigerator. Her kitchen cupboards illustrate the dichotomy with their bicolored doors, in red/blue, further indicating her polarized desires and the different hot/cold outcomes that Carol anticipates, while the side-to-side motion of her head expresses the extreme moment of her virginity's trial. Facing now one way, now the other, Day's physical enactment shows us a woman caught between desire and fear. As she sings the final line of the section, however, she smiles and seems to gain in confidence. Returning to the central kitchen island, she opens the champagne and pours it out, giving a tiny shake of her head as her voice-over asks its final set of questions: "Should I avoid his touch?" As Day's voice on the soundtrack soars and swoops in the aural climax ("Surrender! Surrender! Surrender!"), her physical acting underlines the idea of a decision taken in favor of agency, as she drinks the champagne decisively, radiating resolution coupled with sensuality.

Here the scene calls for Day to make Carol's virginity visible, which she does through a very economical, nuanced performance, made all the more remarkable because the film, though not the actor, is playing it for laughs. Carol's mature virginity is further affirmed via the business with the champagne bottle: once uncorked, the liquid is not very fizzy, implying that it has been waiting in the fridge for a very long time and thus parallels Carol's virginity, similarly neglected too long, stale and past its "sell-by" date.

This performance conveys the dilemma Carol's virginity is undergoing: alternating in seconds between a hard-eyed raunchy persona and a more tremulous, doubting one in her pantomimic responses to the lyrics' questions, Day's acting underlines that both women—"bad" and "nice"—are possible roles Carol could enact. Her assumption of the sexually assertive persona with Linus would therefore necessitate her performing a role, but no more so than her habitual personification of the self-controlled, wary virgin. Carol is therefore rehearsing the different demeanors to adopt, depending on her choice of sex or separation. Because her performance also conveys the spontaneity of her desires, via alternations of stillness and sudden outbursts of energy, she does not seem calculating in her rehearsal but rather as if discovering her own potential for different behavior as she enacts it.

The scene shows how important the actor's performance can be in determining our understanding of the competing pulls on the character. The actor's body bears the burden of performing the problematic virginity; here, through the rapidity of the alternation between expressive/repressive attitudes to sex, the traditional split between good girl and bad girl is exposed as a false dichotomy, as Day's Carol is so evidently, earnestly both. This acknowledges that clear binaries are rare and that emotions and personae are more ambivalent. Day's performance problematizes not only a distinction between bad and nice but also, by association, other putative polarities such as active/passive, desirous/fearful, and even before/after, as the breathless, excited head rolling of the still-virginal Carol can be seen to evoke and anticipate the motions of sex.

The absence of any similar demonstration during the comparable moment in *Pillow Talk* demonstrates Jan's confidence in her own desires, providing good reason to infer that her character is postvirginal. In *Pillow Talk*, Jan overtly voices her desires but performs a contrived "innocence";

in *Lover Come Back,* both Carol's desire and hesitancy seem spontaneous and are acknowledged by the character to herself: she is not feeling one thing and acting another, but feeling both.

Conclusion

In this pair of comparable moments, then, Day performs the desires of her characters for sexual intimacy, but only in the latter scene, from *Lover Come Back,* is this overtly posited as an initiatory event. *Pillow Talk* consciously attempted to leave behind the old Day persona of the rural girl next door, repackaging the star as a modern urban woman. *Lover Come Back* followed its predecessor in this, as in so many things, but allowed hints of the country girl's unfitness for the metropolis to creep in, in a narrative that showed her inexperience with both business and amatory wolves in the advertising jungle.

The new accent on the glamour and allure of both characters, and the star who played them, was thus played out on a foundation of the earlier connotations; the independence and feistiness, the hardworking determination to get ahead, were now channeled into career progress. The new persona revisited elements of the traditional characterization in order to recruit Day fans' support for this new incarnation. It is thus perhaps understandable that some critics chose to ignore the messages being put out by *Pillow Talk*'s various sexualizing mechanisms and to read Jan's single status as conclusively indicative of maidenhood. This promotes a reading of the film that privileges effects (Jan departs from the weekend cottage without sleeping with Brad) over their causes (Jan has discovered the true identity of "Rex"). Concentrating on Jan's actions rather than her motivations, it becomes possible to view her trying to avoid sex, despite the narrative clearly indicating that her reason for leaving is wounded pride rather than neurotic sex aversion. Such a reading is, for example, advanced by Al Capp, the Doris skeptic who penned this chapter's opening perpetual-virgin hyperbole. He notes earlier in the same article that "in *Pillow Talk* . . . [Day] eagerly accepted Rock Hudson's invitation to visit him alone in his country place at midnight to examine his roofing. When it developed that he wanted to examine her foundations, she flounced out, shocked and indignant."[16]

What I find so ironic in this and other assertions of Day's constant maidenhood is the inflexibility of stance ("Day will ALWAYS be a virgin!"), made evident in the torsion necessary to the narrative to make it fit this précis, in contrast to the fluidity with which Day herself performs the various states of sexual experience and knowledge her characters possess. In the first two films following *Pillow Talk*, Day portrayed a mother of four married to a would-be philanderer (*Please Don't Eat the Daisies*, 1960) and an American heiress recently married to an English businessman, desperate to be granted her "honeymoon" (*Midnight Lace*, 1960). In this latter film it is possible to see Day's character as a mature virgin, but she is definitely an unwilling one. Interestingly diverging from the source play, *Matilda Shouted Fire!* (1961), *Midnight Lace* makes the husband, not the wife, the party who is unwilling to consummate.[17] Although Day's skillful performance of the woman's increasingly urgent demands for sexual relations with her husband is undercut by a standard mystery plot that narrativizes fear of violence rather than desire for sex as the cause of her hysteria, these two very different roles show that Day retained the potential for enacting the maiden after *Pillow Talk*, but it was not inevitable. Appreciating that it is the performances that endow some characters with virginity and others with experience prompts the recognition of tensions within Day's star persona: tracking the fluctuations in sexual status also provokes greater awareness of the actor's skill.

Notes

1. Richard Dyer, *Heavenly Bodies: Film Stars and Society* (Basingstoke: Macmillan Press, 1986), 3.

2. See Al Hotchner and Doris Day, *Doris Day: Her Own Story* (London: W. H. Allen, 1976).

3. James Naremore, *More Than Night: Film Noir and Its Contexts* (Berkeley and Los Angeles: University of California Press, 1998), 20; Joe Joseph, "Sex Aplenty, But Little Sensibility," *Times*, October 21, 1998, 47.

4. She appears in the top box office position in 1952, 1959, 1960, 1962, and 1963, and second in 1951 and 1961. Jeanine Basinger, *A Woman's View: How Hollywood Spoke to Women, 1930–1960* (London: Chatto and Windus, 1994), 509–10.

5. Besides *The Man Who Knew Too Much*, the other film that includes singing is *It Happened to Jane* (dir. Richard Quine, 1959), the Day vehicle before *Pillow Talk* and a box office flop that caused the star and her manager, husband Marty Melcher, to rethink her career path.

6. Jane Clarke and Diana Simmons, *Move over Misconceptions: Doris Day Reappraised* (London: British Film Institute, 1980), 12–14.

7. Hotchner and Day, *Doris Day*, 230.

8. See, e.g., "The New Doris Goes Sexy," *Hollywood Reporter*, September 16, 1959, unpaginated advert after 3. For quote, see Hotchner and Day, *Doris Day*,

222–23.

9. "Star of Star Awards," *Motion Picture Herald,* January 28, 1961, 8.

10. Bruce Babington and Peter Williams Evans, *Affairs to Remember: The Hollywood Comedy of the Sexes* (Manchester: Manchester University Press, 1989), 200.

11. Rock Hudson and Sara Davidson, *Rock Hudson: His Story* (New York: Morrow, 1986), 59.

12. Review of *Pillow Talk, Hollywood Reporter,* August 12, 1959, 3 (my italics).

13. Hudson and Davidson, *Rock Hudson,* 79.

14. One of the publicity lines for the film opposed Day's "careful career girl" with Hudson's "carefree bachelor." See Donald Chang, "Pillow Talk," script and scrapbook accompanying soundtrack of *Pillow Talk,* Bear Family Records, Germany, 1996.

15. Cynthia Fuchs, "Framing and Passing in *Pillow Talk,*" in *The Other Fifties: Interrogating Midcentury American Icons,* ed. Joel Foreman (Urbana: University of Illinois Press, 1997), 238–39.

16. Al Capp, "The Day Dream," *Show,* December 1962, 72.

17. Janet Green, *Matilda Shouted Fire!* (London: Evans Brothers, 1961).

Pete Falconer

Fresh Meat?
Dissecting the Horror Movie Virgin

In *Scream* (1996), an impromptu lecture on slasher movies arises (naturally) out of a discussion of Jamie Lee Curtis's breasts. Video store worker and horror film aficionado Randy (Jamie Kennedy) is incensed at his friends' ignorance of generic conventions. "You don't know the rules?" he yells incredulously. According to Randy, "Only virgins can outsmart the killer in the big chase scene at the end." From his summary, we can extrapolate the following points. First, virginity is of sufficient importance in horror films to be referred to intertextually. Second, it is easy to make glib generalizations about the treatment of virginity in the genre and pass them off as credible. Finally, however, Randy's guide to surviving a murderous cinematic rampage reveals that things are rarely so simple. Making "the rules" so explicit as to be almost a joke simultaneously disavows and reaffirms them. This kind of contradiction is central to the horror genre, in both film and literature, and across a number of national cinemas (although my focus is on Hollywood). Virginity in horror movies resists being treated schematically. Instead, it is one of the elusive and ambiguous themes that characterize the genre.

Horror narratives establish binaries and juxtapositions, exploiting the tensions between them. In horror, we are often shown an alternative side to apparently normal existence, whether it is the "dark side" of human nature, the "other side" of life beyond death, or one of many other variants. In its sustained deployment of polar opposites, the genre is strongly mythic. Carol Clover observes that the plot of many slasher films (in its closing stages, at least) "is a standard one of tale and epic."[1] Like other overtly mythic genres, the horror film is highly codified. These codes, however, change and shift with time, reflecting different, often contradictory cultural impulses and trends. Thus *Psycho* becomes *Halloween* becomes *Scream*. Within these shifts, it is unsurprising to find that virginity recurs as a central theme and that it is often treated with a profound ambivalence. The aim of this analysis is to discuss and evaluate some of the ways in which virginity functions in horror movies, in order to illuminate why it has endured as an important and complex element within the genre.

> Casey Becker (Drew Barrymore): What do you want?
> Unidentified sinister telephone caller: To see what your insides look like.
> —*Scream*

A major structuring opposition of the horror film is that of the physical versus the intangible (or metaphysical). The concept of "horror" itself is rooted in this relationship—the reaction the word describes combines the amorphous uncertainty of fear with a more visceral reaction in which "threat is compounded with revulsion, nausea and disgust."[2] Since the 1960s, the relaxation of censorship and advances in special effects technology have allowed horror movies greater scope in representing the physical side. Thus "the postmodern horror film is obsessed with the wet death, intent on imaging the mutilation and destruction of the body."[3] Isabel Pinedo's evocative term, "wet death," with its violent finality and sexual undertones, suggests an inescapable physicality to the genre. This is compounded by narrative film's insistence on visual evidence—to believe the violence, we must see the blood. Much horror deals with the threat of being overwhelmed by the physical, of being unable to hold onto one's individuality, sanity, or life amid the carnage. On a basic level, for a horror film character to survive, they must transcend the physical and avoid being reduced to anonymous meat.

Alongside the rawness of flesh and blood, then, there always remains an intangible element, even if a film contains nothing strictly supernatural. Often, of course, this element *is* supernatural or takes nature beyond common understanding. The inadequacy of everyday physical explanations is made overt in *Ginger Snaps* (2000). Ginger (Katherine Isabelle) is bitten by a werewolf on the day she starts her first period. The symptoms of her lycanthropy are explained away as menstrual in origin. Only her sister, Brigitte (Emily Perkins), suspects differently, stating, "Something's wrong.

Like, more than you just being female." The threat exists beyond common physicality but remains connected to it in some hazily defined way.

The style of horror movies fosters "uncertainty" about the precise nature of the dangers that the characters face.[4] Monsters and murderers are often unseen until near the end of a film, their motives remaining opaque or poorly explained even then. The ending of *Psycho* (1960) juxtaposes the "easy" explanation of Norman's behavior through the clichés of popular psychoanalysis with the brute physicality of the final shot in which Marion's car is dragged from the swamp, her dead body (itself a horrific unseen element) in it. Horror films show us gruesome and monstrous images but deny us a secure understanding of them. However vast and eloquently articulated Van Helsing's knowledge is, there remains something about Dracula that resists definition. The intangible, it seems, is just as dangerous as that which can be seen and felt. The theme of virginity addresses both of these dangers.

> But first, are you experienced?
> —Jimi Hendrix, *Are You Experienced*

Horror films portray threats that exist simultaneously within and beyond the corporeal. The concept of virginity fits well into this equation. Although supposedly located in the body, it is only ambiguously physical. It is "an abstract idea residing in an anatomical metonym."[5] Virgins enjoy a privileged status within the genre, both as protagonists and as malefactors. They appear as plucky heroines and sacrificial offerings, repressed psychos and misunderstood monsters. The recurrence of virginity relates to the way in which it is able to bridge the gap between the physical and the intangible, acknowledging the former but retaining a connection to the latter. Thus virginity as a theme is often present in vague or oblique ways, informing other themes and tropes or providing sympathetic resonances. Often it is used to give a sense of the strange and the mystical—relating ordinary or narratively specific phenomena back to myth and magic. When virginity is more clearly defined, it is still likely to be somewhat opaque. This is linked to the concept of virginity as physical closure, symbolized by the hymen (historically, female virginity has generally been more culturally significant) but permeating the concept more generally. This can manifest itself in horror films as a perverse form of coherence, distinguishing the identity of the individual virgin against the undifferentiated flesh of bodies forced violently open.

The notion of virgin bodies as closed also implies a separation of interior and exterior. This makes any visual representation of virginity a highly problematic undertaking. Tamar Jeffers identifies this problem in relation to 1950s Hollywood: "Film, as a visual medium, needed to show something, and virginity as an internal, invisible quality was not easily depicted."[6] Without a definite connection to the interior states they purport to represent, outward appearances can be deceiving. Horror exploits this disjunction all the time—monstrosity frequently conceals itself beneath a facade of innocence, beauty, or normality. Monstrous children (*Village of the Damned*, 1960; *The Omen*, 1976), attractive vampires (too many to mention), and murderous clones or doppelgangers (*Invasion of the Body Snatchers*, 1956 and 1978; *The Stepford Wives*, 1975) are all recurring figures. The apparent signifiers of virginity are sometimes used in this way (of which more later), revealing an anxiety about the possibility of verifying apparent "innocence" at all.

> Clowns to the left of me, jokers to the right
> —Stealers Wheel, "Stuck in the Middle"

If the virgin is symbolically individuated by her bounded body, then she is also isolated by it. Perhaps the most isolated virgin in horror cinema is found in *Carrie* (1976). Carrie White (Sissy Spacek) is stuck in the middle (hence the epigraph to this section) of the same tensions between the physical and the intangible that she personifies. From one side, she faces the religious fanaticism of her mother, which manifests itself as a denial of the physical so extreme as to be almost masochistic. Margaret White (Piper Laurie) regards sexual desire as sinful and ordinary physical traits such as breasts and the menstrual cycle as evidence of inner corruption. There remains nonetheless a perverse sensuality to Mrs. White's behavior. The manic intensity with which she slaps herself and tears at her hair suggests the eruption of repressed impulses.

From the other side, Carrie is confronted with the overt and insistent sexuality of high school life, signaled from the start by the slow-motion tracking shot across the girls' locker room in the credit sequence. Here she is just as marginalized—alone in the shower, she is clearly separated from the towel-flicking and cheerful nudity of the rest of the room. It has been claimed that Carrie is masturbating in this scene, but this is based on one ambiguous shot where she could just as easily be washing herself.[7] This interpretation assumes a level of sexual awareness that Carrie just does not have. In the teenage culture she uneasily inhabits, sex is a tradable commodity. Sue Snell (Amy Irving) lends her boyfriend, Tommy Ross (William Katt), to Carrie as a prom date. Chris Hargensen (Nancy Allen) exchanges an unidentified sexual favor (probably fellatio, although she remains able to speak with suspicious clarity throughout) for the cooperation of Billy Nolan (John Travolta) in her vendetta against Carrie. Just as Margaret White's intense austerity has a bodily side, though, high school isn't all brazen physicality. "It is the place of the girl's humiliation, but also of her dreams."[8] Thus Carrie's prom experience (before it all goes horribly wrong) is depicted in a blissful, dreamlike fashion more obliquely linked to sexual desire. Soft focus and diffuse white light creates a benevolent haze in which Carrie can feel momentarily safe. When Carrie and Tommy dance, the camera encircles them repeatedly and closely, as if isolating them from the wider world. Worldly matters, of course, make a gross and irrevocable return when Chris dumps a bucket of pig's blood onto Carrie's head, tarnishing her pristine appearance (even her surname connotes purity) and unleashing her telekinetic rage.

Carrie White is manipulated, discussed, interpreted, and subjected to conspiracies both helpful and malevolent in intent. In short, she is treated as if her identity has yet to be solidly established. This is connected from the start to sex. We first see Carrie sent into a wild panic by the onset of her first period, about which she has been told nothing. This is interpreted in opposite ways by various other characters. Her classmates and gym teacher view it as evidence of excessive innocence and naïveté, her mother as the consequence of sinful thoughts or some other impurity. As a virgin, her character remains unconfirmed and open to interpretation. Her body, having reached sexual maturity, is opening up and revealing its inner workings. Carrie herself, through her shyness and isolation, remains closed. Her virginity is emblematic of the tension between these two states.

This tension manifests itself violently as telekinesis. Carrie's psychic powers emerge out of a combination of personal isolation, repressed sexuality, and an inability to reconcile the physical with the metaphysical. They "project outwards and eliminate the space between herself and those around her."[9] However, through their uniqueness and lack of a distinct physical presence, they also emphasize this space. Like virginity, their basis in the physical is ambiguous. Her powers are associated with blood and the body, and their effects in the physical world are devastating, yet they remain mystical and undefined. This is indicated stylistically through music. Carrie's telekinetic outbursts are accompanied by screeching strings that evoke Bernard Herrmann's score for the shower scene in *Psycho*. To associate Carrie's powers with music that is not only nondiegetic but also carries intertextual connotations places them in some way outside the "physical" world of the film. As a virgin, Carrie stands on the threshold of different worlds, conflicting forces pulling her in opposite directions (like fairy tales, horror films often deal with rites of passage). It is appropriate, then, that her final appearance as a character would be in Sue's disturbed dream. Even in death, the tensions surrounding Carrie White leak into the half-physical, half-abstract domain of the mind.

> Sex is violent
> —Jane's Addiction, "Ted, Just Admit It"

Blade (1998) provides an interesting variation on the highly individuated, semimonstrous virgin protagonist. Like Carrie, Blade (Wesley Snipes) is a walking contradiction. He is a genuine hybrid—half human and half vampire, his human emotions in tension with his vampiric urges. Although more an action film that happens to feature vampires than a horror movie per se, *Blade* makes its debt to the genre clear in a number of ways, from thematic concerns to intertextual references. The source of Blade's supernatural side—his undead "father"—turns out to be his archenemy, Deacon Frost (Stephen Dorff). Thus Blade comes from the kind of abnormal family background common in horror films, from *Cat People* (1942) to *The Texas Chainsaw Massacre* (1974). Blade's mentor, Whistler (Kris Kristofferson), is first seen listening to Creedence Clearwater Revival's "Bad Moon Rising," a song that also features prominently in *An American Werewolf in London* (1981), another film premised on the human and monstrous sides fighting for dominance of the same body.

Blade himself, with his muscular physique, black leather trench coat, and phallic weaponry, may seem an unlikely virgin, but there are many signs within the film that suggest that he is. He has dedicated his life to the killing of vampires at the expense of any personal attachments (except Whistler) and lives in a highly disciplined, almost monastic fashion. His blood is needed as an offering in a ceremony performed by his undead enemies—he is referred to as "the chosen one." The associations between sacrificial victims and virginity are strong enough to carry over into this context. Snipes's appearance and performance are also built around signs of repression and control. He delivers his lines through clenched teeth, constantly reasserting his strict but precarious control over his vampire side. Here the typical curtness of the action hero is recontextualized as severe and painful repression. The prevalence of buckles and clips in his costume also points to this quality—Blade is literally strapped in.

Blade's repression is not primarily of sexual desire but of his hunger for human blood. It is nonetheless fairly standard in vampire films and literature to equate bloodlust with lust of a more everyday variety. Vampires charm their victims into complicity, then revel in penetrating their flesh. *Blade* explicitly engages with this tradition—vampirism is described as a "sexually transmitted disease," and Whistler says that when he first met Blade "his need for blood had taken over at puberty." The second quote renders Blade's vampiric virginity somewhat problematic. As a reformed bloodsucker, he is not without experience but has chosen a life of sanguinary celibacy. It should be clear, though, that virginity as a symbol is not the same as virginity as a fact (which in itself is sufficiently difficult to define as to be sometimes functionally interchangeable with celibacy). Furthermore, Blade's arterial abstinence is also informed by his apparent lack of sexual experience. This parallel culminates near the end when Dr. Karen Jenson (N'Bushe Wright) allows the weakened Blade to drink some of her blood and regain his fighting strength. This sequence is presented as if it were a sex scene. The pair are framed according to the conventions for discreetly simulating missionary intercourse—we see his back and her face over his shoulder. She gasps, convulses, and clutches at his bare torso. When he has finished drinking, he rears up and lets out an animalistic cry.

This scene also makes explicit the connection between sex and violence. Throughout the film, Blade channels his bloodlust into the aggressive destruction of vampires, seeming more at ease doing that than when talking, resting, or otherwise physically disengaged. In this, too, the film owes more generically to horror than action. In noting that "rape is practically nonexistent in the slasher film," Carol Clover suggests that, in this subgenre, "violence and sex are not concomitants but alternatives."[10] Like the psycho killers of the classic slasher, Blade vents his repressed impulses through extreme violence. His apparent motives also bear an interesting resemblance to those of many of cinema's knife-wielding maniacs. "I have spent my whole life searching for that thing that killed my mother, and made me what I am." Screen psychos from Norman Bates to Jason

Voorhees and beyond have been driven to their murderous excesses by maternally based traumas. They remain pseudoinfantile, their repression linked to the continuing pervasive influence of their (often dead) mothers. Blade's mother lingers even more tangibly than these other malevolent matriarchs—late in the film he finds that she did not die, but instead became a vampire. He is reduced to a weakened, childlike state in her presence. Her psychosexual threat is compounded by the fact that, undead, she appears a similar age to her own son. All this emphasizes the state of arrested development that Blade shares with many slasher killers, which in turn contributes to the film's presentation of him as ambiguously virginal.

What sets Blade apart from both the psychopaths of the slasher movie and monstrous victim figures such as Carrie is the dimension of agency he possesses. Unlike either, he is portrayed as generally in control of his actions and impulses (however difficult the film suggests that maintaining this is). Carrie White, by contrast, "seems always on the point of asking, 'did I do that?'"[11] Her absolute isolation extends to a form of alienation from her actions themselves. Despite their potency, her supernatural powers remain invisible, intangible, and often only semivoluntary. Slasher killers are in control of their actions insofar as they are able to kill with ruthless efficiency. This is offset by the amount of times they are described as though they are mystical, unstoppable forces, even in films with no discernible supernatural element. The principal function of Dr. Loomis (Donald Pleasence) in *Halloween* (1978) appears to be to build up this kind of aura around the killer via a series of apocalyptic (and unscientific) remarks. In any case, the subjectivity of psycho killers is of a different order. Blade's presence as a decisive causal agent slants his repressed desires away from the ambiguous territory of virginity toward the more codified domain of celibacy. Nevertheless, the conflation of hero, victim, and monster in one person result in a character who is liminal, undefined, and in conflict. These traits, as *Carrie* demonstrates, can be closely associated with virginity.

> I'm your boyfriend now, Nancy.
> —Freddy Krueger (Robert Englund), *A Nightmare on Elm Street*

The best-known recurring virginal figure in horror movies is the slasher film heroine, dubbed by Carol Cover as the "Final Girl."[12] It is this character type that Randy from *Scream* is referring to. The one character able to escape or defeat the psycho killer, the Final Girl is marked as special and different from other teenage characters, many of whom will end up dead. One of the most frequent ways she is distinguished is through virginity: "Her smartness, gravity, competence in mechanical and other practical matters, and sexual reluctance set her apart from the other girls."[13] Clover continues by suggesting that many of these qualities "ally her, ironically, with the very boys she fears or rejects, not to speak of the killer himself."[14] It is dubious whether the boys do indeed share these traits—in classic slashers such as *Halloween* and *Friday the 13th* (1980) they are generally as ineffectual, highly sexed, and oblivious to danger as their girlfriends, and they die just as gruesomely (Jack Burrell, in *Friday the 13th,* played by a young Kevin Bacon, gets stabbed through the neck with an arrow). The parallels between the Final Girl and the killer, however, run much deeper. Throughout her influential and illuminating study, Clover hints at the configuration of the two characters as a complementary pair (even the title of her chapter, "Her Body, Himself," suggests a structural duality). The heroic side of "the female victim-hero" is "understood as implying some degree of monstrosity."[15]

Virginity is a principal way in which the Final Girl and the psycho killer are presented in parallel to one another. The childlike aspects (see earlier discussion) and solitary, socially peripheral status of many slasher killers suggest sexual inexperience. Many of the major descendents of Norman Bates are presented in this way—Leatherface, Michael Myers, Jason Voorhees. A notable exception is the leering Freddy Krueger, also distinguished by being the only of the well-known slashers to be overtly supernatural from the outset (mystical phenomena are often introduced later in a franchise, perhaps to justify further sequels). The killer is a grotesque reflection of the Final Girl—her sexual hesitance and lack of experience become his "psychosexual fury."[16] Her vigilance becomes his predatory gaze. These elements can be seen in *Halloween*. The Final Girl, Laurie Strode (Jamie Lee Curtis), sees Michael several times during the day leading up to the killings. Her looking is represented as active and informed by fearful curiosity. She stares out of her classroom window, craning her neck when the car she was watching has gone. She scrutinizes suburban hedges, certain that the figure she saw is still somewhere nearby. Michael's vision is represented by the film's famous extended Steadicam shots, eerily drifting through houses as he stalks his prey. Laurie sees the unseen—when she points Michael out to her friends, he disappears. Michael sees and is unseen, either observing from a clandestine position or going unrecognized—

Lynda (P. J. Soles) mistakes him for Bob (John Michael Graham) when he dons Bob's glasses over a ghost costume made from a sheet. The privileged vantage points occupied by both psycho killer and Final Girl are linked to virginity; they view sexual activity from a nonparticipatory distance, allowing them to see things that those more deeply involved might miss. John Carpenter himself makes this point—Laurie's friends are "unaware because they're involved in something else" (i.e., sex), while Laurie is "lonely, she doesn't have a boyfriend, so she's looking around."[17]

The pairing of the figures of killer and Final Girl is complex and contradictory. She may be generically marked for survival, but she is also the killer's most prized victim, the one he spends the longest pursuing, the intended climax of his murderous spree. Kim Newman, again in reference to *Halloween,* observes that "Laurie, the one virgin in the group, escapes, but crucially Michael was after her all the time."[18] The Final Girl's virginity, then, attracts the killer to her as much as it helps protect her from him. Once again, the privileged status of the virgin as sacrificial offering is significant here. The murders in slasher movies are often highly schematic in nature, taking place in a predetermined order or marking the anniversary of a particular disaster or trauma. Consider the number of films from the subgenre with dates in the title—*Halloween, Friday the 13th, Black Christmas* (1974), *I Know What You Did Last Summer* (1997), *Valentine* (2001), and so on. This gives them a ritualistic dimension, in which the figure of the virgin takes a central and precarious position.

The Final Girl survives because she is eventually able to face the killer on his own terms. The parallels between the two characters are intensified in the chase and confrontation scenes that form the "emphatic climax" of many slasher movies.[19] These sequences, through their content, structure, and often protracted length, demonstrate the endurance of both characters. The Final Girl's determination to survive is pitted against the "virtual indestructibility" of the killer.[20] Her ability to repeatedly escape from situations that appear to mean certain death is echoed by his vast capacity to sustain damage without dying, often to the extent that apparently dead killers get back up again. Dr. Loomis empties a revolver into Michael Myers's chest, knocking him out of the window, yet the killer survives into seven sequels. The already-dead but nightmarishly lively Freddy Krueger in *A Nightmare on Elm Street* (1984) endures being hit with a sledgehammer and set on fire. The climactic battle of the slasher film is a fight for bodily integrity between two figures capable of maintaining it in extremely trying circumstances. This is one reason why Final Girls and psycho killers are so often virgins—their bodies are already figured as closed. They are resistant to all forms of penetration.

It is in the last confrontation, too, that the Final Girl's aptitude for violence is made most explicit. Again, John Carpenter's remarks about *Halloween* are relevant here. When Laurie is threatened, "all that repressed sexual energy starts coming out. She uses all those phallic symbols on the guy."[21] It is true that the virginity of the Final Girl is a factor in her ability to summon up sufficient aggression to defend herself, but it is also worth remembering Clover's remarks about the slasher film's substitution of violence for sex. While a prurient Freudian might see a knitting needle and a straightened wire coat hanger as "phallic symbols," the Final Girl sees them as potential weapons. Uninitiated into the world of sex, she belongs, like the killer, to the world of violence. The style of violence she adopts also aligns her closely to her murderous counterpart. Laurie, like Michael, is a stabber. Nancy Thompson (Heather Langenkamp) in *A Nightmare on Elm Street* rigs a series of booby traps in her house, reproducing in the waking world the malevolent ways in which Freddy Krueger manipulates his victims' dreamscapes. In *Hell Night* (1981), the Final Girl's methods of self-defense are opposite, but clearly complementary to, those of the killer. Marti (Linda Blair) finally dispatches her psycho with the aid of a car that she repaired herself using knowledge gained in her father's garage (another trait often shared by killers and Final Girls is a close relationship with one parent—typically mothers for the former and fathers for the latter). Her mobility is juxtaposed with the killer's relative stasis; apart from the final pursuit he remains, as he has for most of his life, within the grounds of the spooky old mansion belonging to his murdered family. Again, both characters are represented as physically bounded—the killer by the house, Marti by the car. The killer loses his physical unity when he is impaled (significantly on the gate marking the edge of the mansion's grounds). Marti survives, virginal and victorious.

> Like a virgin / Touched for the very first time
> —Madonna, "Like a Virgin"

Virginity is prevalent enough in the classic slasher movie that, as the subgenre developed into more baroque and self-conscious forms, it became almost a commonplace. As such, it became more flexible and transposable as a motif, the intertextual weight of previous films informing its continued use. Through this process, characters that are not virgins become virginal through the assumption of the role of Final Girl. Clover notes this in relation to the Final Girl in *The Texas Chainsaw Massacre 2* (1986): "Although Stretch is hardly virginal, she is not available either; early in the film she pointedly turns down a date, and we are given to understand that she is, for the present, unattached and even lonely."[22] Due to the strength and persistence of the Final Girl type, connotations (not even necessarily directly) associated with virginity are able to take the place of virginity itself. This disjunction can be seen in *I Know What You Did Last Summer*. In the first part of the film it is clearly suggested that Final Girl Julie James (Jennifer Love Hewitt) and her boyfriend, Ray (Freddie Prinze Jr.), have sex on the beach. Julie removes her jacket; Ray says, "Are you sure?"; Julie nods; and the camera pans discreetly across to crashing waves. The traditional euphemistic symbolism is not hard to recognize. When the main slasher plot begins, however, a year of narrative time later, Julie is symbolically re-virginized. She returns from college withdrawn and uncommunicative, dressed demurely in a straw hat and cardigan and clutching a teddy bear. These signs combine to represent her as closed, infantile, and sexually inactive. Narratively, this can be explained through the trauma of the incident that sets the plot in motion—"last summer" Julie and her friends hit a man with their car and disposed of his (supposedly) dead body. Generically, however, she takes on a virginal aspect because the role of Final Girl demands it.

That external signifiers can substitute for actual virginity reveals its instability as a concept—there is often little functional difference between being a virgin and looking like one. Its representation is characterized by "metaphors and metonyms—tropes which make visible . . . virginity's constructed character."[23] Outside the slasher tradition, many horror movies explore this tension between external appearance and supposed internal essence, exploiting the illusory capacity of cinema and the reliance of film narratives on readable visual signs. In gothic/occult horror film *The Mask of Satan/La Maschera del demonio* (1960), Barbara Steele plays both a virginal princess and a resurrected vampire witch. The plot hinges on the ease with which the two characters can be confused, which is established early on. When we first see the virtuous Princess Katia, she is framed within a demonic mise-en-scène: "We first glimpse the princess as she silently stands on a crest between gnarled trees, dressed in black and flanked by a pair of wary mastiffs."[24] Ultimately, though, our access to the truth via visual details is reaffirmed—the princess is identified by the cross she wears, while the evil Asa is revealed to have a grotesquely aged body, despite the youthful beauty of her face.

Other films in the gothic tradition, however, opt not to resolve all the ambiguities surrounding virginity. Virginity is central to the mystery plot of *The Wicker Man* (1973) but remains something of an enigma even after all is revealed. Police Sergeant Howie (Edward Woodward) investigates a suspected human sacrifice on a Scottish island, only to be sacrificed himself at the end. A strict Christian and not yet married, Howie's virginity makes him an ideal offering. The beliefs and customs of Summerisle are made apparent quite quickly—their sexual frankness and worship of nature are obvious and explicit (and frequently expressed through bad folk music). Howie, by contrast, unwittingly becomes the object of his own investigation. It is Howie himself who is the mystery, and he remains, by virtue of his virginity, opaque and impenetrable. The denizens of Summerisle strike a successful balance between the physical and the metaphysical, appeasing the latter, that they might continue to enjoy the former. Howie insists on their separation—symbolized by the wall at the inn dividing him from the gleefully promiscuous Willow (Britt Ekland)—and is thus unable to negotiate one of the central dichotomies of horror. In an exemplary case of the return of the repressed, Howie is so utterly estranged from the physical that it finally flares up and consumes him.

> Morality sucks.
> —Glen Lantz (Johnny Depp), *A Nightmare on Elm Street*

Howie's virginity is so divorced from the physical world as to be almost abstract. Such abstraction is unsustainable in a genre preoccupied with the body. This is also the fate of the teenage postmodern slasher movie. Its self-conscious treatment of the conventions of its predecessors, exemplified by Randy's speech in *Scream*, promises an enlightened and implicitly "safe" perspective on the genre. In this context, references to virginity connect to the postmodern slasher's presentation of itself and its characters as knowledgeable and experienced in popular culture—you are a generic virgin if you do not know "the rules." Finally, however, these films usually revert to type. The murders in *Scream* are revealed to be motivated by old-fashioned revenge, and the two killers' undoing begins when they face the physical realities of having to stab one another in order to look like victims who narrowly escaped death. *Cherry Falls* (2000) can be seen as commenting on the inability of postmodern teenage horror to sustain its critical distance from the genre as a whole. The killer initially singles out virgins as victims. In response to this apparently simple logic, the high school students organize an orgy, which takes the form of a grotesque parody of a senior prom. By this point, however, the killer has abandoned his formula, and nobody is safe. Initially assumed to be a woman, he is revealed to be a Hitchcock/De Palma–derived cross-dresser. His motives are subsequently explained via a sins-of-the-fathers backstory reminiscent of *A Nightmare on Elm Street,* mixed with aspects of a rape-revenge narrative. Knowing "the rules" is no adequate protection—the world of the body is irrational and messy, and the slasher tradition guarantees its eventual return. "Tradition," of course, is a contradictory and volatile term, relying as it does on notions of purity and coherence not unlike those related to virginity.

Notes

1. Carol Clover, *Men, Women and Chain Saws: Gender in the Modern Horror Film* (London: British Film Institute, 1992), 41.
2. Noël Carroll, *The Philosophy of Horror or Paradoxes of the Heart* (London: Routledge, 1990), 22.
3. Isabel Cristina Pinedo, *Recreational Terror: Women and the Pleasures of Horror Film Viewing* (Albany, NY: SUNY Press, 1997), 51.
4. Ibid., 53.
5. Kathleen Coyne Kelly, *Performing Virginity and Testing Chastity in the Middle Ages* (London: Routledge, 2000), 7.
6. Tamar Jeffers, "'Should I Surrender?': Performing and Interrogating Female Virginity in Hollywood Films, 1957–64" (PhD thesis, University of Warwick, 2005), 9.
7. Aviva Briefel, "Monster Pains: Masochism, Menstruation and Identification in the Horror Film," *Film Quarterly* 58, no. 3 (2005): 22.
8. David J. Hogan, *Dark Romance: Sex and Death in the Horror Film* (Wellingborough: Equation, 1986), 270.
9. Briefel, "Monster Pains," 23.
10. Clover, *Men, Women and Chain Saws,* 29.
11. Briefel, "Monster Pains," 22.
12. Clover, *Men, Women and Chain Saws,* 35.
13. Ibid., 40.
14. Ibid.
15. Ibid., 4.
16. Ibid., 27.
17. Carpenter, quoted in Todd McCarthy, "Trick and Treat" (interview with John Carpenter), *Film Comment* 16 (1980): 24.

18. Kim Newman, *Nightmare Movies: a Critical Guide to Contemporary Horror Films* (New York: Harmony Books, 1988), 147.
19. Clover, *Men, Women and Chain Saws*, 36.
20. Ibid., 30.
21. Carpenter, quoted in McCarthy, "Trick and Treat," 23.
22. Clover, *Men, Women and Chain Saws*, 39.
23. Kelly, *Performing Virginity*, 11.
24. Hogan, *Dark Romance*, 168.

Nina Martin

Don't Touch Me

Violating Boundaries in Roman Polanski's *Repulsion*

> A virgin body has the freshness of secret springs, the morning sheen of an unopened flower, the orient luster of a pearl on which the sun has never shone. Grotto, temple, sanctuary, secret garden—man, like the child, is fascinated by enclosed and shadowy places not yet animated by any consciousness, which wait to be given a soul: what he alone is to take and to penetrate seems to be in truth created by him. And more, one of the ends sought by all desire is the using up of the desired object, which implies its destruction. In breaking the hymen man takes possession of the feminine body more intimately than by a penetration that leaves it intact; in the irreversible act of defloration he makes that body unequivocally a passive object, he affirms his capture of it.
>
> —Simone de Beauvoir, *The Second Sex*

Grotto, temple, sanctuary—de Beauvoir's description provides the virgin body with an architectural physicality made of boundaries and borders, separating inside from outside. The hymen is the membrane at the threshold to the secret and shadowy place of fascination, a doorway that once opened can never be closed. Likewise, these physical spaces of significance become mentally charged with meaning, as both the body and the spirit of the virgin are rendered passive through the penetration of her defenses. This enclosed place of which de Beauvoir speaks conjures a dramatic Freudian landscape, one vividly depicted in Roman Polanski's harrowing tale of virginal violation and mental deterioration: *Repulsion* (1965).

The settings of *Repulsion* are crucial to understanding the issues regarding insanity and normative femininity that are central to its narrative, for these architectural and urban spaces are manifestations of (and catalysts for) the psychological interior of the film's virginal heroine. In order to comprehend Carole's descent into madness, one must also appreciate the specific settings and circumstances that produce a dynamic and dangerous tension between interior and exterior, inside and outside, and the boundaries that separate them. The film's director was likewise inspired by the settings and specific sociohistorical contexts in which he created this work. Polanski and Gerard Bach wrote the script while holed up in a tenth-floor apartment in Paris and, while ostensibly shut in, "were inspired by the liveliness of what was happening outside," as envisioned through the apartment's windows; simultaneously, the liveliness of urban street culture was frequently interrupted by the regular chiming of convent bells in a nearby backyard.[1] Polanski translates his physical spatial experiences directly onto the screen, as two of the film's primary locations consist of the heroine's dark, upper-floor apartment and the nearby convent as seen through her windows.

The burgeoning tensions of the 1960s were beginning to infiltrate the vibrant urban spaces of Europe, especially London, where Carole's story takes place. As Polanski states, "I was now getting to know, and was falling in love with, the London of the 'swinging sixties.'"[2] In the mid-1960s, the gradual unraveling of rules and conventions, along with a shift in sexual mores and attitudes toward increased sexual freedom and expression—most pronounced in the city's youth culture—created untenable ideals surrounding contemporary heterosexual femininity. In a city that had begun to "swing," the lines separating Madonna and whore, virgin and slut, were becoming increasingly hard to maintain and define. I suggest that these same boundaries, and their blurring, are replicated in the physical boundaries constructed and represented, and in the more mental barriers that the heroine struggles to preserve, in Polanski's film. Carole's desperate battle within her apartment and within her psyche—to protect herself from the outside forces eager to penetrate her—suggests that the changing sexual politics of that era are metaphorically connected to the madness of entering sexual adulthood, and all the anxieties and horrors that the journey entails.

The childlike, golden-haired Carole (Catherine Deneuve) haunts the streets of London like a broken flaneuse, a somnambulist sleepwalking through the city, who only feels safe when sequestered behind the locked doors of the apartment that she shares with her older sister, Helen (Yvonne

Furneaux). When her sister leaves for vacation, this private space becomes increasingly claustrophobic as Carole rapidly loses her ability to distinguish fantasy from reality. Her world increasingly distorts, transforming the space she inhabits into a shadowy lair, where men, real and imagined, attempt to violate her physically and mentally. This violation is rendered visually through spatial penetration, as the gaping fissures and broken doors in her apartment signify the unraveling of young Carole's mind. The apartment (and Carole) continues to transform until violence shatters its once peaceful confines, leaving two men dead and symbolic debris scattered across its surface. Carole, catatonic and feeble, ends the film huddled under Helen's bed, symbolically deflowered and "unequivocally a passive object" as the building's fellow tenants stare down at her with curiosity and disgust. Her "madness" and her beauty appear at odds, but they are one and the same: Carole's desperate clinging to childhood, to virginity and sexual innocence, are ultimately irreconcilable to a culture opening itself to the lustful gazes that her beauty would inspire.

Carole and Her Environment: Inside versus Outside

At the end of the film, in a moment of narrational omniscience similar to the conclusion of *Citizen Kane* (1941), the camera sweeps through the living room, across a mantle covered with toy dogs, past a loudly ticking clock, over a discarded postcard of Pisa, near a crumbled biscuit, to rest on a portrait of Helen and Carole with their family, slowly zooming into a close-up of Carole's face, before fading to black and rolling credits. I begin this discussion of virginal violation and madness in *Repulsion* with the film's final image, for its placement at the film's conclusion serves to burn its significance into the brain, coloring the rest of the film's startling imagery and providing a lens through which to read Carole's unique psyche.

In this portrait, six people are posed outdoors, in front of a modest, nondescript brick building, on what appears to be a warm spring day. In the foreground is a group of five adults sitting in or near lawn chairs—what seem to be Carole and Helen's parents, Helen, the girls' brother, and their grandmother. Helen and the adults all face the camera with slight smiles upon their faces, except for the grandmother, who looks at the others in the picture; still, she is comfortably part of the group. Helen is nestled on the ground, her head on her elbow as she leans on her father's leg. He amiably rests his hand on her shoulder, and their intimacy is apparent. Their brother sits next to the grandmother, and his dog sits nobly beside him.

Violating Boundaries in Roman Polanski's Repulsion

Family portrait: Catherine Deneuve in Roman Polanski's *Repulsion* (1965).

They all appear relaxed and comfortable with each other and within this setting.

To the rear of this family group stands a girl whose presence barely makes an impression, her body partially cut off by her mother seated in the foreground. She stands physically apart, touching nothing and no one, standing stiff and still as a doll. In this gathering of contented adults, she is the only child, isolated and seemingly ignored. Her dress melds perfectly with the brick of the building, almost indistinguishable, and she would simply fade into the background if her hair did not reflect the light. Carole's eyes do not meet the gaze of the camera but determinedly look off in another direction entirely, as absent mentally as she appears to be visually. Those eyes speak of discomfort, as if she would prefer to be somewhere else.

Repulsion's striking visual coda, displayed by the slow zoom-in to the portrait (which is initially shown earlier in the film and later commented on by Carole's lascivious landlord), reiterates the true struggle within this film: Carole's experience of the outside world moves beyond the existential angst popular in Europe at that time and speaks to a far more acute isolation with herself, alienated from her body and its relationship to the world around her. This alienation is especially apparent when Carole is traversing the spaces between her apartment and where she works—an exclusively female beauty salon and spa. Unlike the urban flaneuse, who "joins and becomes a part of the world in which she rambles and observes," Carole stares blankly ahead of her, never interacting with passersby, far more entranced with the cracks in the sidewalk than the liveliness of the city streets.[3] Uninterested in the focused predatory gaze of the men watching her as she passes, she steadfastly ignores the eyes of those around her, even as a prospective suitor frantically bangs on a window to get her attention. In fact, the abrupt and intrusive encounter she has with a workman on a South Kensington street corner triggers her rapid mental deterioration, for she cannot keep her virginal, female-oriented world free from the taint of the men circling around her.

Before Carole decides to lock herself away from these outside influences into the supposed safety of her apartment, her wanderings through the city become increasingly more dreamlike, and her experience of "swinging London" is rendered uncanny; her projected mental state transforms the city into a labyrinth of streets littered with dangerous fissures and cracks in the pavement. As Anthony Vidler outlines in his discussion of an architectural uncanny, "the 'uncanny' is not a property of space itself nor can it be provoked by any particular spatial conformation; it is, in its aesthetic dimension, a representation of a mental state of projection that precisely elides the boundaries of the real and the unreal in order to provoke a disturbing ambiguity, a slippage between waking and dreaming."[4] Carole's vision of London and its environs are ultimately provoked by a violation she feels powerless to dispel, especially when Colin (her persistent suitor) dogs her every move, constantly invading her personal space. She travels the same route again and again, her face shot in close-up, and the camera gradually catches her waxen visage with increasingly canted angles, repeatedly crossing the 180-degree axis of action that maintains spatial orientation in narrative cinema, adding to the film's confusing sense of space. In *Repulsion*, establishing shots that would situate Carole within the city are largely absent, creating an acute sense of both disorientation and isolation, thus replicating within the spectator the heroine's distressed mental state. Indeed, her recurring encounter with the traffic island and its horrendous crack—a crack similar to the one that continually appears on the walls of her apartment—speaks to the consistent "recurrence of the same situations, things, and events" by which Freud defines uncanny experiences, as well as the "sense of helplessness" Carole presents in her wanderings that is "sometimes experienced in dreams."[5] As Ivan Butler points out in his discussion of the film, "Each subsequent journey reflects her growing withdrawal until on her final one, before shutting herself up forever, not even the most attention-drawing of all events, a car accident, has the power to rouse her" from her reverie.[6]

The ragged lack of connection, of isolation, that Carole feels toward the world around her manifests distinctively in the erosion of boundaries between her existence within a universe largely inhabited by women and the men from whom she strives to separate herself. Carole interacts with two primary settings outside her apartment: the feminine spa and the convent attached to the courtyard below. At home, her eyes constantly wander to the adjacent convent, and she appears to be at peace when the convent bell chimes or when she watches nuns playing outside with a ball, their voices joyful and reminiscent of children at recess. At work, Carole surrounds herself with women, and her golden hair and porcelain skin aid her work at this shrine to feminine beauty. Still, from the very first moments of the film, as the credits wander across the vulnerable surface of her moist and fragile eye, she seems disconnected from her place of employment; she stares blankly into space as she performs a manicure on one woman, working on them as if they were dolls she must dress up.[7] The irony here is that the female spa is an impossible space for Carole: she surrounds herself with women, but here they devote themselves to their appearance, styling themselves as passive objects for masculine consumption. Carole may be physically separated from men in this space, but they permeate every discussion, their desires apparent in every beauty treatment she enacts. One client even suggests that her trancelike somnambulism is due to being "in love" or "asleep," never realizing that her distance and lack of affect indicate her inability to function in this sexually charged environment.

Within the feminized spa atmosphere, Carole's coworker, Bridget, stands out as her most significant foil; whereas Carole tries to separate herself from the world of men, Bridget resides comfortably within both spheres. At the entrance to the spa, Colin stiltedly attempts to finagle a date from Carole, and their painfully awkward chitchat mirrors the obvious physical discomfort she feels in his presence. Immediately after Carole clumsily slips away, Bridget is seen bounding out of a Mini Cooper, giving her boyfriend a quick kiss, and then scampering up the stairs next to the clearly disappointed Colin (especially as he watches this pair's comfortable embrace). The contrast Polanski presents in this scene is not accidental—Bridget epitomizes the joie de vivre of the "swinging London" vibe, with her hair in a chic bob, sleek sheath dress, and high-heeled pumps. Yet the darker side of Bridget's carefree sexuality is revealed in a later scene, when Bridget cries over this latest boyfriend who is "just like all the rest"; the following day he has apologized, practically "getting down on his knees." Bridget also comfortably discusses her love life with Carole, and with her female clients. Carole listens closely to these discussions about men, as evidenced by the extreme close-up of one woman's mouth as she ominously verbalizes Carole's virginal fears while simultaneously explicating the double standard that traps these contemporary women within impossible binaries. Carole's point of view is highlighted as the client remarks, "There's only one thing [men] want, and I'll never know why they make such a fuss about it, but they do. And the more you make them beg for it, the happier they are." This frank discussion is enough to send Carole back into catatonia, as she retreats once again into her safe, interior world. Bridget assumes, as do the other women in the film, that Carole's neurasthenia and moodiness are because of a man. This diagnosis is accurate, but only in the sense that Carole's psyche is overwhelmed by her fears of male physical and mental contact. She desires to keep the boundaries between masculine and feminine worlds firmly in place.

The final interaction between these two characters, ostensibly the last time that Carole ventures outside the apartment's confines, represents the only moment of laughter and joy that Carole appears to experience in the entire film. Shortly after Carole cuts a client's finger at the spa and is promptly sent home, Carole and Bridget talk in the spa's employee changing area. Bridget, in an attempt to lift Carole's spirits, tells her she "ought to go out. Go to a movie or something," to which Carole responds, "Oh, I'd love to," clearly wishing to spend time with her female friend. Oblivious to Carole's feelings about men, Bridget recounts the narrative to Chaplin's *The Gold Rush* (1925), and the two tumble into peals of conspiratorial laughter as Bridget mimics Chaplin's characteristic walk and gestures. This moment of shared pleasure is abruptly halted once Bridget mentions her boyfriend's experience of the film, unpleasantly reminding Carole that her friend is not a part of her female-exclusive world. This unwelcome intrusion on the intimacy that Carole feels with Bridget wipes the laughter off her face, only to be replaced by the cold blankness she uses to shield herself from the outside world.

Carole, as a sexually burgeoning and beautiful young woman, cannot possibly maintain the rigid boundaries she tries to establish between feminine and masculine worlds, for men are determined to penetrate these barriers. Michael, her sister's married boyfriend, is the first to seriously invade her space, as his personal (and masculine) grooming tools—a straight razor and shaving brush—find their way into the sisters' shared bathroom. Upon returning home from work, after being verbally accosted by a construction worker and hounded by Colin, she strips off her clothes and washes her feet and legs of street grime. She suddenly spies Michael's

Violating Boundaries in Roman Polanski's Repulsion

"things" throughout the bathroom, the first in a series of spatial violations. She repeatedly demands that her sister explain his presence within their apartment, and why "his toothbrush is in my glass." Their female space has been tainted. Significantly, it is during this discussion with Helen that Carole notices the first crack in the apartment wall, stating, "I must get this crack mended." Too late, the first "crack" in her defenses has appeared, one in a series of penetrations of both her physical and mental spaces. As the film progresses, and Helen and Michael leave Carole, and the apartment, for their Italian vacation, a man's sleeveless T-shirt—which Carole first encounters on Michael when she walks in on him shaving—continues to reappear, symbolizing the simultaneous desire and repulsion she feels toward the men in her world.

Her mental deterioration in the face of trying to keep feminine and masculine spheres separate is exacerbated by her interactions with Colin. This young suitor's tenacious pursuit of Carole, despite her apparent indifference and apathy toward him, typifies the perceptions men had regarding beautiful women during this time of cultural flux. Her youth, her beauty, and her presence within London's urban landscape all suggest her status as an object of desire, styled ideally for Colin's earnest pursuit; he cannot comprehend why she would not be eager and flattered by his attentions. Yet her vapid responses to his wooden attempts at conversation, and her refusal to touch him, point to her repulsion, even as she cannot bring herself to tell him "no" or send him away.

One of the most telling moments in the film occurs when Carole forgets about a date he had previously set with her, stopping at a bench on the ubiquitous South Kensington traffic island, mesmerized by a large pavement crack. When Colin finally finds her hunched on the bench, he furiously accuses her of "playing hard to get," oblivious to her wandering mind. After giving her a ride home, they sit silently in the car in front of her apartment building. At first she avoids his kiss, but then turns to face him, seemingly inviting his attention. When he does touch her, she initially sits unresponsive—a body without a soul. Then, abruptly, she leaps out of the car and runs into the apartment building, viciously scrubbing at her lips with the back of her hand. On entering the apartment, she furiously brushes her teeth, obliterating any remnants of Colin's kiss. At the height of her frenzy, she once again sees Michael's toiletries in the bathroom—his toothbrush in her rinsing glass, his razor by the sink—and tosses them firmly into the trash. Yet this encounter with Colin, and by association, Michael, signifies the initial probing of her virginal innocence by masculine desire. Despite her best efforts, Carole is unable to keep herself unsullied and (mentally) intact.

Eventually, Carole's and Helen's apartment, which originally provided a safe haven from the outside masculine world, transforms into a terrifying trap, as the borders Carole had so firmly erected become porous and permeable. Like Carole's presence in her family portrait, as she fades into the walls of her home, she disappears into her environment, retreating physically and mentally. As architectural scholar Katherine Shonfield explains, "The sane world is one where your personal edges, bodily and architectural, are firmly in place."[8] Yet as illusion and reality begin to dissolve into each other for Carole, growing indistinguishable, so too do the physical boundaries and walls of her home turn out to be less solid and firm. This permeability is strikingly apparent when Carole is sequestered in her tiny bedroom, listening to the sounds of her sister's and Michael's lovemaking through incredibly thin walls; it is as if they are in her bedroom. As Barbara Leaming describes this scene, "Carol is the voyeuristic child witness of furtive embraces, the nocturnal listener to the sounds of lovemaking. Lying in her narrow bed on the other side of the wall, she seems doomed to an endless childhood, from which she escapes only in her fantasies."[9] The film accentuates this aural "primal scene" by augmenting her sister's moans of pleasure, forcing Carole to bury her head in her pillow in order to protect herself from this violation.

If the hymen symbolizes and serves as the threshold between sexual innocence and maturity, the doorways of Carole's London apartment represent a series of thresholds; and as Shonfield points out, "At the threshold of any breach to the membrane of [Carole's] physical security, there is a man, or the threat of one."[10] In *Repulsion*, doors are the gateway into the "enclosed and shadowy places" of the feminine of which de Beauvoir speaks, and the force of heterosexual male desire cannot be stopped by a mere door lock or piece of furniture. When Carole is first accosted by her imaginary attacker—who vaguely resembles one of the construction workers seen earlier and happens to be wearing Michael's sleeveless T-shirt—he effortlessly shoves aside the armoire that bars his entrance into her bedroom. In this scene, the camerawork is handheld and disorienting, the scene utterly silent except for the exaggerated ticking of a nearby clock. While the attack is physically visualized and the man penetrates the space, the scene's accompanying silence suggests that Carole's violation is truly internal, a further crack opening in her fragile mind.

Once this initial hallucination/violation occurs, Carole's struggle to maintain her bodily and mental integrity turns into a life-or-death battle. Any real penetration of her fortress, by Colin or her landlord, must inevitably end in violence. Colin's aggressive breaking down of her front door, essentially destroying the door's deadbolt and rendering it impossible to close, mirrors the irreversibility of innocence lost. In some ways, Carole merely protects herself from his advances by striking him repeatedly with a heavy candleholder. While she attempts to bar further entrance by tearing shelving from the kitchen and clumsily nailing it to the door and its borders, her last-ditch attempt at protection is flimsy at best. Her landlord easily wrenches the door open and crosses the threshold. Like the cracks on the pavement that repeatedly appear on the walls of her apartment, Carole can no longer keep inside and outside separate from each other—the breach has become irreparable.

Carole's family portrait once again haunts this scene, as her landlord actually discusses the photograph, asking where it was taken and commenting on her childlike appearance (in the photo as well as in front of him). As her image dissolves into the walls of her childhood home, by film's end, Carole has become one with her London apartment as well. Not only do the walls form hands that reach out and touch her, but their solidity transforms into a viscous substance, wet and soft, as if they are made of her own flesh. When Carole touches the walls, her handprints remain, the walls molding to her form. The walls are no longer merely permeable and porous but have turned into living and breathing membranes. As Virginia Wright Wexman comments, "The infantile inability to separate the self from its environment also finds expression in the anthropomorphic presentation of the Ledoux apartment. Its increasingly cavernous living room and long, constricting hallways reveal Carol's [sic] vacuous sense of herself."[11] For Carole, just as fantasy has become indistinguishable from reality, so too has the animate become indistinguishable from the inanimate.

Carole's World of Perpetual Childhood: Resisting Adult Femininity

In *Repulsion*, Carole's fraught relationship with her environment, and her unwillingness to interact with the realities of heterosexual life, are all symptoms of her stunted growth and her desire to cling to the childhood represented in the Ledoux family portrait. This childishness is expressed most pointedly through her troubled engagement with her appearance and her virginal body. Carole subconsciously realizes that once she accepts her role

Grabbing walls in *Repulsion*.

as an adult woman and takes on the role of beautiful, passive object for the men around her there is no turning back. As Deanna Holtzman and Nancy Kulish point out in their study on virginity, "The loss of virginity is irreversible. Once lost it can *never* be restored. . . . The loss of virginity is an important developmental milestone that marks the passage to adult sexuality. Thus, on one side of the threshold lies Peter Pan's Never-Never land, a world of perpetual childhood. On the other side lies adult sexuality, procreation and parenthood, and ultimately death."[12] Like the golden-haired child positioned at the borders of the family portrait, Carole's role as an outsider and a virgin are visually demonstrated throughout the film. Her pale blonde hair and equally pale skin contrast sharply with her sister's and her friend Bridget's darker coloring, and her clothes hearken back to an earlier period, before miniskirts or knee-high boots. When Carole first encounters Colin on the street, she wears a floral blouse buttoned tightly to the neck, a skirt that falls decidedly below the knee, and matching white gloves and purse. Furthermore, for the majority of the film she is dressed in a high-necked sleeveless nightgown—a white dress with a hem that falls nearly to her ankles, covered with delicate white dots stitched into the fabric.

Her prim, babyish nightgown and the delicate floral patterns on her largely unflattering clothing signify a girlish desire to hide her body from view, and Carole's subsequent immature and childlike behavior is undeniably enabled by her sister. While Helen is understandably annoyed by Carole's petulant attitude toward Michael and his "things," she also coddles

Violating Boundaries in Roman Polanski's Repulsion

Carole like a child, chiding her for sulking when Helen decides to go out for dinner, trying to comfort her after the soiling kiss she shares with Colin, and soothing Carole's plaintive fears when she leaves for her vacation in Italy. She serves here as both sibling and parental figure. Carole clings to her sister, unraveling whenever she is left on her own, and ultimately suffering from such an acute separation anxiety that she spirals into madness. Yet just as Helen is oblivious to Carole's outsider status, epitomized by their respective positions within their family portrait, she also assiduously closes her eyes to Carole's fragile mental state, demanding to know what Michael is implying when he suggests that her sister needs a doctor. Helen is equally unprepared for the cataclysmic events that occur during her absence, as she fails to recognize Carole's inability to grow up or fit into the contemporary London scene.

Carole's obsessive childlike bond with her sister, and their relationship's eventual dissolution, is epitomized in the symbol of the rabbit and its progressive decay. The rabbit can be seen not only as a child's pet (and now part of Carole and Helen's eventual dinner) but also as a symbol of fertility; rabbits are well known for their prodigious sexual activity, and pregnancy tests were also sometimes called "rabbit tests" at the time this movie was made.[13] While Carole knows that she will be having rabbit for dinner—she in fact tells Colin of this plan in order to avoid a date with him that evening—nothing seemingly prepares her for the creature's fetal appearance when Helen pulls it out of the fridge. Ultimately, Helen ends up leaving the rabbit (and Carole) alone and goes out with Michael instead. The rabbit becomes emblematic of all those aspects of life that Carole obsessively tries to avoid, however unsuccessfully. As her mind disintegrates, the rabbit also decays, eventually drawing flies to its moldering carcass. At the moment of Carole's most severe public breakdown, when she cuts the finger of a client at the spa and is forced to go home to her dark, private lair, Bridget helps to get her things only to find the dead rabbit's head tucked neatly into Carole's purse. When she severs the head from the rabbit's body, Carole definitively indicates her complete disengagement from normative femininity and her forceful retreat into a childish interior world.

The scenes in *Repulsion* that take place in Carole's bedroom are expressively styled to resemble images common to a child's feverish nightmares. The room appears perilously small and claustrophobic, and her narrow single bed, much like a child's bed, seems to dominate the room. The shadows that mark the room make even the most banal objects—tennis rackets perched on the top of an armoire, a bell-shaped lamp hanging from the ceiling, the chasm of a small fireplace grate—appear ominous and threatening. The exaggeration of sounds contributes to the sense of intrusion and violation of this small, safe space, whether these noises are the sounds of laughter and pleasure coming from her sister's bedroom or the echo of ominous footsteps pacing outside her door before her fantasy intruder breaches the space. Once Helen and Michael leave for their trip, Carole's bedroom becomes a place of terror, as even a locked door and a heavy armoire cannot keep out the masculine demons that haunt her day and night. And like a child whose fears overwhelm and distort her views, Carole's perception of the apartment literally transforms as she progressively loses her grip on reality. Almost as if she is regressing day by day, the hallway, once rather short and narrow, becomes looming, dark, and endless. The bathroom's sink and tub are disproportionately small in the now giant room, as are the couch and television in the now cavernous living room. Polanski describes his manipulation of space in *Repulsion* as a significant process:

> My aim was to show Carole's hallucinations through the eye of the camera, augmenting their impact by using wide-angle lenses of progressively increasing scope. But in itself, that wasn't sufficient for my purpose. I also wanted to alter the actual dimensions of the apartment—to expand the rooms and passages and push back the walls so that audiences could experience the full effect of Carole's distorted vision. Accordingly, we designed the walls of the set so they could be moved outward and elongated by the insertion of extra panels. When "stretched" in this way, for example, the narrow passage leading to the bathroom assumed nightmarish proportions.[14]

Thus the transformation of the apartment from a place of safety into a place of terror and fear marks Carole's retreat from a somewhat girlish femininity to increasingly infantile fears of violation and bodily harm. Carole's madness is similarly made evident through a series of childlike actions and gestures that accumulate in the film and signals her continual inability to move toward adult femininity. After Helen and Michael's departure, she sneaks into her sister's room and plunders her closet, holding one of Helen's elegant dresses up against her nightgown-clad form. It is at this moment of girlish dress-up and wish fulfillment that Carole (and the film's spectator) undergoes her first serious hallucination. As she pulls the mirrored closet door closed, in order to admire herself alongside Helen's dress, she, and

Violating Boundaries in Roman Polanski's Repulsion

we, catch our first glimpse, if only momentarily, of Carole's imagined male ravisher. In another instance, after Carole murders Colin, she once again retreats to her childhood realm, humming a quiet little melody as she does a bit of mending, sitting with her knees up to her chin in her white nightgown. Later still, she perches in front of her sister's vanity, messily applying lipstick to her lips in a parody of preparing for a date (which ends up being her final violent encounter with her imaginary ravisher). The next morning she hums another melody, similar to a nursery rhyme, as she irons the ubiquitous man's sleeveless shirt that Michael initially wears; only Carole's behavior is a grotesque mimicry of domestic femininity. The camera pulls back to reveal Carole merely playing pretend, as the iron is shown to be unplugged.

Repulsion's most violent confrontation, between Carole's interior world and the forceful outside presence of male desire and burgeoning sexuality, occurs when these opposite realms jarringly collide during the landlord's impromptu visit. He easily forces the door open (since this threshold has been previously breached) and enters to find Carole standing barefoot and in her nightgown in the doorway to the living room. The landlord shouts, "What's the idea of you barricading the door against me," fully believing in his right to enter the women's apartment at his whim. After handing him the rent and demanding he keep the curtains closed (maintaining a barrier against the outside world), she petulantly flops down on the sofa, knock-kneed, head down, with her nightgown hem riding up around her thighs. The bareness of her silky skin only appeals to his leering perversity, as he eyes her nightgown and asks if she always "runs around like this." He touches her body and strokes her hair, calling her a "poor little girl, all shaking like a frightened little animal." Carole flinches and moves away, further stirring his ardor. Yet not until he literally climbs on top of her, demanding "a little kiss between friends" does she finally retaliate, throwing him off her and slashing him fiercely with Michael's straight razor. She proceeds to hide his body under the couch, like a child who shoves her toys or dirty clothes under the bed instead of putting them away.

Carole fittingly ends up hiding under a bed once she descends into irreversible madness. Yet this image suggests a strange irony. Throughout *Repulsion,* Carole attempts to maintain her childlike existence, assiduously avoiding moving toward a more adult femininity. When her pale arm snakes slowly and haltingly out from under her sister's bed, to Helen's apparent horror, it would appear that Carole has achieved her goal of avoiding adulthood: a neighbor lifts the bed to find her underneath, catatonic, and curled into a fetal position. However, this image is not one of childhood victory but rather is emblematic of Carole's ultimate feminine defeat, as she no longer resists the role assigned to her—that of a beautiful and passive feminine object. All the barriers she had erected, mental and physical, have been destroyed, and her transformation to an "unequivocal passive object" now seems assured.

While Carole's madness is masterfully visualized by Polanski's increased visual distortion of her physical and, by association, her mental world, I suggest that Carole's harrowing journey into insanity could be read as an (understandably) extreme reaction to the social pressures that converged upon women at that particular time. Even though Polanski himself comments on the "liveliness" of "swinging London" through his valorization of Bridget and his representation of London street culture, *Repulsion* also reveals how entrenched the image of the passive, virginal, and virtuous woman was at the same time. These mixed messages regarding appropriate heterosexual female behavior simultaneously encouraged the sexual freedom that allowed for Helen's affair with Michael, while also castigating her through his wife's harassing phone calls and her labeling of Helen as "a filthy bitch." In some senses, Helen is necessary to Carole's world for her ability to draw male sexual attraction and attention away from her sister, as their family portrait indicates through the representation of Helen and her father's physical intimacy (while Carole hovers on the outskirts, far removed from the touch of men). Helen's presence deflects unwanted attention, and only after she leaves for Italy does Carole start to lose her grip on sanity.

These same tensions surrounding mid-1960s femininity allow Carole's lack of interest in men and retreat into her own world to be misread as enigmatic and mysterious, as if she is intent on "playing hard to get," as Colin accuses: For how can a woman so beautiful not be interested in the attentions of men? In fact, this representation of an unknowable womanliness is endlessly reiterated through Polanski's repeated display of a voyeuristic gaze directed at Carole. As Laura Mulvey has pointed out, this visual trope is well established, as "the cinema has, through specific properties, enhanced the image of feminine seductiveness as a surface that conceals."[15] Strikingly, no one in the film, either male or female, can see past Carole's surface beauty to the troubled negotiation of adult female heterosexuality burning within. Indeed, as Albert Johnson points out in his review of the film, "Carol's [sic] physical beauty is so dazzling that one would never think of branding her with the description of homicidal maniac."[16] Her virginal appearance and subsequent objectification by the men interested in uncovering her hidden depths, by taking intimate possession of her feminine body, are seen as tools of seduction.

This dissonance between Carole's seeming indifference and how this behavior is perceived by the men around her is made abundantly clear when the film takes a digressive turn and subjectively follows Colin instead of staying firmly lodged in Carole's subjective world. While the spectator is introduced to Colin and his vulgar bachelor friends in a previous scene, tossing back drinks in a local bar, the audience's second encounter with these men occurs after the camera has been closely following Carole through the city streets, just after she leaves the spa for the last time. On her route, she passes Colin, who is presently in a phone booth, his back turned, once again fruitlessly trying to reach Carole by phone. Instead of following Carole, though, the camera follows Colin into the pub where his pals are waiting. A discussion ensues about virgins, with one man exclaiming, "Don't let her being foreign fool you. They're all the same, these bloody virgins, they're just teasers, that's all." Upon the suggestion that they get her drunk, and *then* she will become receptive to their advances ("at the end of the evening she'll be begging for it"), Colin reacts violently to their joking and storms angrily out of the bar. Nevertheless, despite appearing to be offended by his friends' ribald suggestions, he is eventually influenced by their conversation and ends up breaking down Carole's door, bringing on his own demise. In the end, Colin is a victim on two counts: he proves incapable of curbing his rapacious desire for Carole, and he ends up equally susceptible to confusing notions of mid-1960s femininity that paint her as virginal yet eager, passive yet seductive. Carole's landlord is similarly unable to perceive his attentions as unwanted and ultimately repulsive. As Wexman astutely notes,

The thick-skinned landlord is even more drastically misled by his culturally derived attitudes about female passivity. Though Carol [sic] greets him in a state of semi-catatonia, barely able to function, he reads her behavior as sexual provocation, her carelessness about her person, an invitation, her lack of energy, acquiescence. Because she seems sexually unprotected, she appears sexually available—and therefore sexually conquerable. Her very disintegration constitutes her attractiveness. By comparison, Colin's excitement in the face of her unresponsiveness is different in degree but not in kind.[17]

I am not suggesting that Carole has no recourse other than murder, but rather that these aggressive misreadings of her desires, coupled with her own resistance toward her role as sexual object, provoke her profound acts of violence toward these men. In reacting aggressively to their persistent sexual interest, she attempts to wrest the role of active subject away from them, and the film then proceeds to visually represent *their* victimization at her hands. This victimization is signified by the camerawork used during both murders. At the beginning of Carole's first violent retaliation, the film employs gaze-object-gaze editing to show her point of view as she looks at Colin through the door's peephole. After Colin breaks down Carole's locked apartment door, leaving her open and vulnerable to outside attacks, they stand together for a moment at this threshold, both seemingly stunned by this turn of events. Their further conversation is composed in a masterful two-shot, with their bodies framing the door, which is now ajar. Colin apologizes, claiming he wants "to be with [her] all the time," and in shutting the door in order to give them privacy (away from a neighbor's prying gaze), the image suddenly shifts to Colin's view as he looks through the peephole. Then his gaze falls as he sinks from Carole's first blow with the candleholder, his blood splattering over the door. The rest of the murder is shot from Colin's point of view, floor level, as Carole looks down and strikes him with four more dispassionate blows. The angle is extreme and canted as she looms above him, and then the scene cuts back to her subjective view as the screen shows Colin's final death twitches and a thick trail of blood inching down his skull.

The landlord's subsequent murder also exhibits a decisive visual shift from Carole's point of view to the landlord's, and then back again. As described previously, the man forces her attentions on Carole, pinning her underneath his body on the sofa, and he apparently enjoys her resistance until she successfully throws him off of her. They both stand and face each other in the living room, and the landlord then chuckles, trying to rationalize the previous scene as mere playfulness on Carole's part. Slowly, the camera pulls back to reveal Carole clutching Michael's straight razor behind her; yet the landlord, unaware of the weapon she holds, maintains his role as aggressor and steps ever closer to her. Still, it is only after he attempts to embrace her again that Carole attacks. His leering grin quickly changes to a shocked grimace as she swiftly slashes the blade across the back of his neck. Once he falls bleeding onto the sofa, the scene switches to his cowering vision as Carole viciously slashes at him again and again in a frenzy of action and movement. Again, she is shot from below, appearing to literally attack the camera. Only when he lies passively still does she move away to view the damage, her girlish nightgown now covered in splashes of blood.

This visual shift, from Carole's point of view to that of her helpless victims, highlights Carole's violent opposition to her feminine role as a passive object. Each time men attempt to violate her virginal surface, she momentarily takes on the role of victimizer. Yet this reversal is brief, frenzied, and desperate. What may at first appear in *Repulsion* to be a critique, by Polanski, of the obsessive objectification of beautiful women by men within "swinging sixties" London, ends more as an indictment of those women, Carole in particular, who refuse to follow the accepted path toward appropriate adult femininity. For Carole is not just angry at the outside world that impinges on her personal boundaries; she is "mad," and this madness places her firmly in the position of outsider and outcast—a location visually expressed in the family portrait on which Polanski dwells. While at times the film vigorously aligns the spectator with Carole's fragile point of view, garnering sympathy for her character, this identification is overwhelmed by a visual emphasis on her extreme difference—her otherness—from the other women in the film. In *Repulsion*, Carole's desires cannot be acknowledged, for instead of identifying with the free-spirited Bridget, she finds herself more attracted to the playful, virginal existence of the nuns living in the nearby convent. However, from the film's perspective, her beauty renders her wishes to forgo adult sexual desires, remain in a female-exclusive world, and childishly retain her virginal body impossible to fulfill. Polanski's obsessive focus on Carole's/Denueve's physical beauty, one that is ultimately unaffected by the violence that swirls around her, contributes to the masculine visual fascination that Carole draws toward her. The final moments of the film highlight Carole's own repulsiveness as Helen, the neighbors, and the camera visually recoil from catatonic, fetal Carole. Her presence is aligned with the decayed rabbit that repeatedly haunts the film, a symbol for both Carole's failed adult femininity and her interior unraveling. In the end, Carole is stripped of agency and turned into "an unequivocally passive object," as Michael carries her limp and unresisting body over the threshold a final time, crossing what was once a sacred, physical (and symbolic) barrier—a door that once forced open can never be fully closed.

Notes

1. Paul Cronin, ed., *Roman Polanski: Interviews* (Jackson: University Press of Mississippi, 2005), 9.

2. Roman Polanski, *Roman* (New York: William Morrow and Co., 1984), 211.

3. Janice Mouton, "From Feminine Masquerade to Flaneuse: Agnes Varda's Cleo in the City," *Cinema Journal* 40 (Winter 2001): 9.

4. Anthony Vidler, *The Architectural Uncanny: Essays in the Modern Unhomely* (Cambridge, MA: MIT Press, 1992), 11.

5. Sigmund Freud, "The Uncanny," in *Studies in Parapsychology*, ed. Philip Rieff (New York: Collier Books, 1963), 42–43.

6. Ivan Butler, "The Horror Film: Polanski and *Repulsion*," in *The Horror Film Reader*, ed. Alain Silver and James Ursini (New York: Limelight Editions, 2001), 83.

7. Virginia Wright Wexman points to the connection between *Repulsion*'s opening and Buñuel and Dali's *Un chien andalou* (1928), where a woman's vulnerable eye is slashed with a straight razor. See Virginia Wright Wexman, *Roman Polanski* (Boston: Twayne, 1985), 56.

8. Katherine Shonfield, *Walls Have Feelings: Architecture, Film, and the City* (London: Routledge, 2000), 65.

9. Barbara Leaming, *Polanski: A Biography; The Filmmaker as Voyeur* (New York: Simon and Schuster, 1981), 65.

10. Shonfield, *Walls Have Feelings*, 60.

11. Wexman, *Roman Polanski*, 55.

12. Deanna Holtzman and Nancy Kulish, *Nevermore: The Hymen and the Loss of Virginity* (Northlake, NJ: Jason Aronson, 1997), 1.

13. The "rabbit test" was an early pregnancy test developed in the late 1920s, and the term became a common phrase in the English language in the 1950s. This test involved injecting some of a woman's urine into an unmated female rabbit and later examining the ovaries of the rabbit. The presence of human chorionic gonadotropin (hCG) in the rabbit's ovaries would mean that the woman was pregnant. Thankfully, modern technology now allows us to circumvent this test, which inevitably involved killing the rabbit to examine its ovaries. See http://en.wikipedia.org/wiki/Rabbit_test (accessed October 1, 2007).

14. Roman Polanski, *Roman* (New York: William Morrow and Co., 1984), 210.

15. Laura Mulvey, "Pandora: Topographies of the Mask and Curiosity," in *Sexuality and Space*, ed. Beatriz Colomina (Princeton, NJ: Princeton Architectural Press, 1992), 59.

16. Albert Johnson, "Repulsion," review in *Film Quarterly* (Spring 1966): 45.

17. Wexman, *Roman Polanski*, 53–54.

Greg Tuck

Orgasmic (Teenage) Virgins
Masturbation and Virginity in Contemporary American Cinema

At the center of *American Pie* (1999) lies the hapless Jim (Jason Biggs), a teenage virgin whose desperation for sex is only matched by his carnal ignorance. Indeed, his sexual naïveté is so great that when he is told a vagina feels like a warm apple pie, he believes that this is literally the case. So, on coming home one afternoon and finding such a pie, freshly baked, warm and waiting on the kitchen counter, he cannot but insert two fingers to see what it feels like—and he likes what he feels. However, as is usually the case in the genre, Jim has little time to enjoy this moment in privacy as a cutaway shot through the window shows us his father coming up the path. As he enters the kitchen he discovers Jim gyrating into the corner, trousers round his ankles, and as Jim turns and tries to explain, we see the pie tin stay up without him holding on to it.

While presented as a gross-out sight gag, the contradictions the scene sets up between carnal knowledge and carnal ignorance, innocence and activity, desires felt and those expressed, are of profound relevance to an understanding of teenage sexual identity more generally. There is a desperation here, as with the majority of protagonists in teenage sex comedies, to express an adult sexuality through normative sexual intercourse. However, this scene in *American Pie* is an entirely otherless and nonnormative penetrative act, an event that expresses Jim's obsession with his own state of virginity and sexual being beyond any desire he may have for a particular other. Pies seem a very queer object choice, which suggests that while Jim knows *that* he wants, he doesn't entirely know *what* he wants, let alone *who*. In terms of the demands of mainstream sexual ideology, his sexuality seems to oscillate dangerously between innocence and depravity, knowledge and ignorance, a correct fixation on the other and a solipsistic fixation on himself. This would suggest that the virgin/nonvirgin boundary is not traversed in a single moment through a single act. Instead the transition period produces a far more liminal sexual subjectivity in which, while still "technically" virgins, these teenagers can no longer be thought of as entirely sexually innocent or ignorant. In order to comprehend and discuss such transitional subjectivities, particularly as presented in films where the loss of virginity is a major narrative driver, we therefore need a clearer definition of exactly what is meant by the term *virgin* under such liminal circumstances. The answer is not as straightforward as it might, at first, appear.

Because sexual subjectivity is better thought of as a verb rather than a noun—what (or who) we do rather than what we are—virginity raises a number of specific conceptual problems through being an attribute associated with what we do *not* do. While the obvious definition of the virgin, what could be called the ideal or pure virgin, gets around this problem by defining virginity as simply a person who has not had sex, it needs to be stressed that such a definition implies that the subject has not had *any* sex (pies included). Furthermore, this absolute virginity is usually described in relation to a subject who lacks not merely sexual experience but also sexual knowledge and, most important of all, sexual desire. It is probably in the subjectivity of children, particularly prepubescent children, that this absolute form of virginity still maintains any conceptual and/or representational currency; prohibition against any sexual knowledge or desire is hard to maintain in relation to teenagers, particularly in contemporary cultures in which sexualized teenage imagery and behavior is a commonplace. So against this notion of the absolute virgin there appears to be a range of more culturally negotiated definitions of virginity and virgins in circulation. Usually they are seen as people who have not had a particular form of sex, penetrative sex, and even more specifically, people who have not had heterosexual penetrative sex. This group of people might have engaged in anything from kissing, all the way to genital stimulation and orgasm, but as long as they have not engaged in coitus as such, they are, or can be, still considered virgins. However, once virginity is redefined in these terms, it means that they are, as is the hapless Jim, paradoxically *orgasmic virgins*. Jim is in fact a typical, if extreme, representation of such orgasmic virgins, as it is teenagers who undoubtedly form the bulk of this group. When compared to people who have had normative penetrative sex, two points emerge.

First, according to this model there are actually three potential states, or a double boundary, to consider when discussing virginity. In terms of "stereotypical" definitions, there is pure virginity (mostly of children), semivirginity (typically of sexually active teenagers), and nonvirginity (of heteronormative adults). However, as according to such a definition sexually active gays and lesbians could equally be excluded from the nonvirgin category, it seems that virginity is not simply a sexual category but a specifically heteronormative concept. If coitus is the key to losing one's virginity, the assumption is that virgins are already heterosexual in terms of object choice if not in practice.

Second, the flexibility of the virgin/nonvirgin boundary rests on the fact that virgins are not simply ignorant either psychologically or physiologically of sexual pleasure per se, but they are ignorant of a particular sexual activity—coitus—an activity intimately linked to their understanding of their heteronormative sexual reproductive function. To lose one's virginity seems not simply to learn how to make whoopee but to make babies. Often, however, this link between reproductive knowledge and the loss of virginity is more visible in its negation than in its direct promotion. Hence much of the fear about the sexual advice offered in teenage magazines, particularly to girls, seems precisely centered on the promotion of sexual pleasure, outside or short of full intercourse, thereby promoting its "difference" to "full" or "proper" sex.[1] While "saving" their virginity, there seems to be a fear that such advice potentially negates the need for reproductive sex. Likewise, the historical religious and moral censure attached to both withdrawal and masturbation since the biblical story of Onan onward (Gen. 38:4–10) again suggests deep disquiet over the separation of pleasure from function. Hence I suggest that to lose one's virginity as normatively understood is not simply to *do* something but to *learn* something—a thing that is not simply an objective neutral fact regarding our universal sexual embodiment, our capacity for pleasure, but an evaluation and co-opting of both the pleasure and the fact of our embodied sexual being in terms of purpose. In a move typical of all ideological notions, fact and value merge, and an "is" is mistaken for an "ought." Hence, regardless of whether any particular penetrative act does in fact result in insemination and reproduction, the act of "losing" one's virginity is usually coded by mainstream texts as the moment the subject learns (in principle) how to reproduce. These subjects now have both an intellectual and an embodied knowledge of what sexual acts to engage in should they wish to procreate, within a sexual ideological framework that explains procreation as the underlying point of sex. Therefore it could be argued that the concept of losing one's virginity specifically defines virginity in terms of the value of the subject to heteronormative ideology understood not simply as a gendered system of domination but as an ideology of reproduction. This produces a complex and ambivalent relationship between the subject's embodied knowledge of sexual pleasure and his or her embodied knowledge of sexual function, and the social value placed on the latter as compared with the former. In contemporary representations of teenage sexuality, these ambiguities and anxieties surrounding the status of the orgasmic virgin are particularly visible in the representation of masturbation, an act that, while clearly orgasmic, is not thought to negate the masturbator's virginal status. However, as with *American Pie*'s Jim, while the masturbator may technically remain a virgin, it is an act that affects the subject's virginal status in one of two ways: being perceived as either learner sex or antisex.

First, masturbation can be seen as not proper sex but as a form of infantile/immature sex, merely a stage that must be passed through before one may adopt one's "proper" adult sexuality. This association between teenage virgins and masturbation has a fairly substantial representational history, and mild representation of teenage masturbation can been seen in films as early as *The Apprenticeship of Duddy Kravitz* (1974), *Animal House* (1978), and *Fast Times at Ridgemont High* (1982). A greater number of much more explicit representations of masturbation seemed to enter the mainstream from the late 1990s onward, with *There's Something about Mary* (1998) being a famous example. However, while teenagers seem the obvious subjects to represent masturbating, the second and equally, if not more, common representation in American cinema is the mad masturbator.[2] Rather than an act of learner sex or nonsex, these masturbations are presented as a form of *anti*sex, a perversion of the sex drive negating the subject's desire to enter into any form of partnered sex. Cinematic representations of mad masturbators commonly include both men and women; men such as Miggs (Stuart Rudin) in *The Silence of the Lambs* (1991), Norman Bates (Vince Vaughn) in the remake of *Psycho* (1998), and Carl Stargher (Vincent D'Onofrio) in *The Cell* (2000), and women such as Hedera (Jennifer Jason Leigh) in *Single White Female* (1992), Joanna (Ashley Judd) in *Eye of the Beholder* (1999), and Betty/Diane (Naomi Watts) in *Mulholland Drive* (2001). Even when less psychotic subjects engage in masturbation, they are often represented as deeply neurotic and unbalanced. The police lieutenant (Harvey Keitel) in *Bad Lieutenant* (1992) and the writer Melvin Udall (Jack Nicholson) in *As Good as It Gets* (1997) are both represented as in some way mentally disturbed. While usually "adult" subjects, the solipsistic priorities of these mad masturbators are often presented as linking them both sexually and emotionally to infantile and adolescent sexualities, with the implication, therefore, that they too are antireproductive, orgasmic virgins. This connects them in a number of ways to teenage masturbators, not least the characters involved in teen "caught-masturbating" scenes such as in *American Pie*, who are themselves usually portrayed as anxious and neurotic if not actually mentally ill. Interestingly, while these two attitudes toward orgasmic virginity and their accompanying subject positions might appear quite different, the mad/bad masturbator on the one hand versus the immature masturbator on the other, they are often both present in the same text, interconnecting and conflating concerns regarding the relationship between madness, masturbation, virginity, and reproduction, although with a range of different emphases.

For example, *Slums of Beverly Hills* (1998) provides a representation of teenage masturbation that seems at first to be simply a stage on the way to full adult sexuality and hence an act that is not sex in terms of its negation of virginity. Set in the mid-1970s, the film tells the coming-of-age story of fourteen-year-old Vivian (Natasha Lyonne), who is struggling with her burgeoning sexuality and developing body, while constantly on the move with her divorced father (Alan Arkin) and brothers, moving from cheap motel to cheap motel. In return for financial assistance from his brother, her father agrees to take in Vivian's rehab-fleeing neurotic cousin, Rita (Marisa Tomei), and despite Rita's being in her twenties, she and Vivian strike up a "sisterly" friendship, with Rita acting as a sexual guide for the younger girl. In one scene Rita shows Vivian her vibrator, which she refers to as her "boyfriend," and implies that Vivian may borrow it. This clearly links masturbation with the mentally unstable Rita. In a later scene, we see Vivian rediscover the vibrator, turn it on, and slide it down her body: her facial expressions leave no doubt that she is masturbating. However, to prevent Rita's neurotic coding being passed on to Vivian, at the same time we see Vivian developing a relationship with the young man next door, Elliot (Kevin Corrigan). Furthermore, prior to the masturbation scene, Vivian and Elliot have engaged in partnered sexual activity in which the couple go, in Vivian's words, to "second base," Vivian allowing Elliot to fondle her naked breasts under her jumper. After the masturbation scene, however, she is prepared to lose her virginity to Elliot, the implication being that her newly acquired body knowledge has given her confidence to go further. Interestingly, however, the act of sexual intercourse is not presented as particularly pleasurable for her. Instead, and unlike the masturbatory pleasures of the vibrator scene, it seems more a chore, an event that must be performed in order to move on to the next phase of her sexual development. While Elliot is taken aback to discover she was a virgin, Vivian is far more matter of fact and comments that she wanted "just to get it over with." In addition to the theme of masturbation being coded as potentially both not sexual and/or antisexual, something that can both maintain and pervert virginity, this film also demonstrates a third notion common to such representations. If teenage virgins can be orgasmic, nonvirgins can equally be nonorgasmic. That is, losing one's virginity, particularly for a girl, is not an event necessarily associated with sexual pleasure.

This is made even more explicit in the comedy horror film *Cherry Falls* (2000). In a reverse of a common motif in teenage slasher movies, where the sexually promiscuous get killed, at the start of *Cherry Falls*, it is only virgins who are murdered. The implication is that virginity is a valued state, so by robbing the community of its virgins, the killer is extracting a suitable revenge for the rape of his mother many years previously by men who now run the town. The value of virginity is also suggested by the fact that the "Final Girl" who saves the day maintains her virginity throughout, despite the added danger this brings. For the majority of the town's teenagers, however, the risk entailed in remaining virginal is too great and the chance to engage in sanctioned sexual intercourse too good to ignore. To protect themselves the teenagers of Cherry Falls organize a "pop your cherry ball," at which they can all lose their virginity and so no longer be at risk. Prior to the event, one of the older girls lectures the younger ones on what they are to expect. She is extremely disparaging of the sexual ability of the boys, claiming that they are useless when it comes to sex. Not only do they have difficulty in undoing bras, but they will also need assistance to perform the act of penetration. One of the younger girls asks if she can expect to achieve orgasm; the older is adamant: "Unless we're talking about masturbation—forget it." The fact that the act of coitus needs to be explained while masturbation does not clearly implies that masturbatory orgasm is already known to these girls. Orgasm and coitus are here presented as almost mutually exclusive. This claim about the lack of orgasmic satisfaction for women associated with sexual intercourse was a common theme in the sexual education campaigns of second wave feminists in the early 1970s, such as the Bodysex workshops of Betty Dodson and in the writings of Nancy Friday, and it continues to be discussed in much sexual self-help literature.[3]

Masturbation and Virginity in Contemporary American Cinema

The situation is different for orgasmic virgin teenage boys. In *American Pie*, for example, its four male protagonists, Jim, Oz (Chris Klein), Kevin (Thomas Ian Nicholas), and Finch (Eddie Kaye Thomas) want to lose their virginity before their prom in a few weeks. At the same time, they are clearly represented as already sexually active, both on their own and with partners. Both sexes are represented as experiencing orgasm through masturbation as well as through oral sex. However, even these types of sex, despite offering the intense body knowledge of sexual climax and often being partnered, do not count against the characters' virginal status. While all the boys are shown to be desperate to lose their virginity, the girls are more mixed in terms of experience and attitudes, with some having already lost their virginity and others not. Unlike Vivian in *Beverly Hills*, the emphasis for the girl virgins, particularly Vicky (Tara Reid) and Heather (Mena Suvari), is on finding the right time and the right partner. Vicky's more experienced friend, Jessica (Natasha Lyonne), mocks her desire for the first time to be perfect by reminding her that "you're having sex—you're not launching the space shuttle." However, as we see Vicky both give and receive oral sex, her idealism does not seem to address her hope for sexual pleasure as a thing in itself. For her, it is not enough to engage in partnered orgasmic sex, but coitus. The act must in some sense ape heteronormative partnered (and hence potentially reproductive) sex if it is to be valued. Meanwhile, sexual acts that are not properly partnered and are not potentially reproductive—most notably, but not exclusively, masturbation—are those that attract the most comic opprobrium. The "geek" status of the film's central character, Jim, is confirmed in the opening scene by showing him masturbating while trying to watch scrambled cable television pornography. Unlike his later attempt to pleasure himself with the pie, both parents catch him in the act on this occasion. However, in addition to the sadistic comic potential of Jim's embarrassment, the discovery of his masturbation allows his father (Eugene Levy) to discuss "proper" sex with him. While Dad admits to masturbation himself, the strong implication is that this was confined to his teenage years and therefore allowable as a stage that was passed through before the achievement of "adult" sexuality. The concept of adult masturbation is entirely disavowed: Jim's Dad describes the difference between masturbation and partnered sex in terms of the differential pleasure produced by simply banging a tennis ball against a wall (masturbation) compared with having a match (coitus). However, the text is incapable of balancing the competing ideological implications of its narrative claims, namely that boys only want physical pleasure, girls want emotional commitment, and sexual intercourse is more intensely enjoyable than other forms of sex. This is apparent in the denouement when all four boys finally lose their virginity.

For Kevin and Vicky, the long-term couple of the film, the act is a disappointment, and the implication is that when they go away to college they will go their separate ways. Compared to the obvious physical pleasures they have given each other earlier in the film (both have been brought to climax by the other through oral sex), penetration is a letdown. There is a sense that in their quest for perfect sexual pleasure they have been punished for missing the fundamental point of intercourse, as an act beyond physical pleasure. This seems particularly so when compared to Oz and Heather, who have not simply had sex but have "made love." Oz begins the film as a "jock," but in his pursuit of Heather, his lust slowly evolves into love. Oz actually denies that he and Heather had penetrative sex and is prepared to be seen to have failed by the others in his quest to lose his virginity. He sees the pursuit of a relationship and commitment as more important than either sexual boasting or sexual pleasure. Interestingly, neither of these scenes shows the couples in a particularly comic light. For Finch and Jim, however, not only is the loss of their virginity represented humorously, but both cases are determinedly, if not overdeterminedly, nonreproductive acts. Fitch loses his virginity to the middle-aged mother of one of their fellow students (an unlikely long-term procreative pairing), while Jim is made to wear not one, but two condoms by band geek girl, Michelle (Alyson Hannigan), who is herself a confessed masturbator and who essentially uses Jim for sex. While both these acts involve couples, at an emotional and relational level the people in these couplings remain separate, coding their act in some degree a mutual masturbation as compared with the "lovemaking" of Oz and Heather. However, while nonreproductive, these acts are presented as being sexually pleasurable to various degrees. Hence the film both validates and condemns the pursuit of sexual pleasure while remaining equally conservative and heteronormative in its sexual politics. Though one would expect mainstream teen films to demonstrate such sexual ideology, the anxiety over orgasmic virginity is similarly, although rather more complexly, present in supposedly more sophisticated texts.

For example, there is a moment, toward the end of *American Beauty* (1999), when Lester Burnham (Kevin Spacey) thinks he is finally going to have sex with teenage temptress Angela (Mena Suvari). Lester's infatuation with Angela begins in scopophilic fascination when he sees her performing as a cheerleader, and this develops into Angela's becoming an object of masturbatory fantasy. Before Lester actively rejects his parental/adult status by throwing in his job, beginning to smoke marijuana, and working out, we have already seen him masturbating. The very first time we meet Lester he is masturbating in the shower, his voice-over noting, with both irony and melancholy, that this is "the highlight of my day." There is therefore a sense that if masturbation codes the liminal development of teenagers into adults, the representation of adults masturbating marks a regression back to the sexual status of teenagers. This teenage sexuality is further suggested because Lester's sexual fantasy about Angela does not involve a penetrative act but a masturbatory one: while masturbating in bed Lester fantasizes that Angela, lying in a bath full of rose petals, requests that he wash her because, as she huskily informs him, she is "very dirty." The moment when Lester's hand enters the petals between Angela's thighs is edited as a repetitive montage. Not only is the moment extended and postponed, but the repetitive movements of the film mimic those of masturbation itself. That Lester only fantasizes about manually exciting Angela rather than penetrating her further suggests a semivirginal, nonprocreative level of body knowledge on his part: unlike Jim's act with the pie, Lester's actual masturbatory behavior mimics his fantasized desire as if he doesn't desire adult, but specifically teenage, sex. Lester's movements wake his wife, Carolyn (Annette Bening); she is disgusted by his masturbation and a row ensues. Lester, however, is unrepentant and insists on his right to "jerk off" because no partnered sex is occurring within the marriage, further implying that without regular acts of coitus, male sexuality regresses to an adolescent state. Interestingly, while Lester normalizes his behavior as rational care of the self, the euphemisms he uses to describe masturbation seem particularly adolescent descriptions: "whacking off, choking the bishop, shaving the carrot and saying hi to my monster." While his masturbation involves a certain imaginative richness, his declaration of his right to masturbate in the marriage bed and the terms he uses to describe it renders the behavior as potentially infantile, if not aggressive. Again masturbation is coded as antireproductive and nonadult, despite the fact that it is an adult performing the act.

Eventually the opportunity arises for Lester to have sex with Angela in reality rather than fantasy. Lester and Angela share some beer, Lester declares his desire for her, and she allows him to remove her trousers. Up until this moment Angela has spoken throughout the film as if she was very sexually experienced and not a virgin. Yet at the precise moment that she has the chance to actually have sex with Lester, her confidence eludes her and she confesses her virginal state. The scene reverses one of the most common anxieties over virginity, that it cannot be simply "seen," because the opposite is equally the case: it is likewise impossible to spot a nonvirgin. While it could be argued that Angela is faking her virginity here in order not to have to sleep with Lester, the performance gives little hint of this. Angela's nervousness seems genuine, not least because she allowed herself to go so far before revealing her performance anxiety. While disappointed by Angela's declaration, Lester's erotic desire changes, virtually immediately, into parental concern. Lester, rather than Angela, undergoes a state change here: in forgoing his opportunity to "take" her virginity, he seems to regain full parental status, a status that for much of the film has been in real dispute. Angela declares her epistemological and ontological ignorance; the now parental Lester assures her that everything is OK, but they cannot have a sexual relationship. His understanding of the (ideological) value and status of sexual intercourse respects her virginity over her availability. What seems of particular interest is how the representation of Angela changes from the moment she reveals her virginity. Lester places an oversize jumper around her shoulders and hugs her. Next we see Lester making and feeding Angela a sandwich, actions connoting parental care rather than erotic longing. Hence what seems to be of particular ideological concern is that it is not merely Lester the man but Lester the *father* who has not had sex. Refusing sex for pleasure becomes a—if not *the*—marker of the reproductive status of the individual. Lester's parental, rather than simply masculine, status is regained by his understanding the "proper" value of virginity to patriarchy and the "proper" purpose of sex—heterosexual couple formation and the raising of children.

So, while Lester's masturbations seem to reconnect him with his teenage self, his parental and adult status is reconfirmed by his *not* sleeping with Angela. As with the notion of virginity, it is what is not done that counts. In *Happiness* (1999), however, the essentially masturbatory nature of masculine sexuality as not merely a marker of immaturity but a dangerous form of antisex is even more explicit. Rather than indexing any genuine or valued form of sexual knowledge or pleasure, male masturbation is coded as abject, worthless, and dangerous, particularly as it is linked to pleasures that are specifically antipatriarchal. There are three scenes of male masturbation in *Happiness,* two performed by adults and one by a thirteen-year-old boy, Billy Maplewood (Rufus Reid). The first adult we see masturbating is Billy's father, Bill Maplewood (Dylan Baker), who is struggling to repress growing pedophilic desires. The first time these desires manifest themselves is when he masturbates in the backseat of his car, in broad daylight, in the parking lot at the Quick-Mart, using a children's magazine as a pornographic prop. While himself a psychotherapist, this event occurs after a session with his own therapist in which he unconvincingly states that lack of sexual activity in his marriage is not a problem for either his wife or himself. Rather than providing catharsis, however, this conversation seems merely to stimulate the desires he wishes to deny: on his way home, he stops off to alleviate his sexual tension by masturbating. The link to mental illness and nonprocreation is clear. As he later goes on to commit two child rapes, his masturbations mark the beginning of a distinctively antiprocreative sexuality.

The essentially abusive reading of masturbation is equally present in the second example, undertaken by an obscene telephone caller, Allen (Phillip Seymour Hoffman), whose life seems to be dissolving into a miasma of alcohol, loneliness, pornography, and masturbation. Allen is a deeply unattractive menial office worker whose looks and personality seem stuck in early adolescence. Allen is not muscular or masculine but rather is podgy and pasty and is quite possibly still a virgin. In many ways he looks like an overgrown version of young Billy, which again suggests a fundamental immaturity. A sense of generational leveling seems to operate, such that masculinity outside of patriarchy is always a state of immaturity. It is as if men need to go straight from virginity to fatherhood if they are to avoid Allen's fate as a perpetual desiring yet unsatisfied masturbator.

The film closes with Billy's masturbation, which should be far less negatively coded than the adult acts, as it is the representation of a young boy's first masturbatory ejaculation. Prior to this incident, Billy has explicitly expressed a normative desire to "grow up," to know orgasm in the ontological sense. That such a desire for knowledge and experience of the embodied self comes before knowledge and experience of the other seems a developmental inevitability, suggesting a properly historic interface between the actualities of male bodies and the specific somatic individual prior to the loss of virginity. Likewise, the accidental voyeurism that initiates his masturbation—from a balcony several floors up he spies a bikini-clad young woman sunbathing—is not in itself abusive. Billy is accidentally possessed by the sight of female flesh. However, a number of narrative strategies are employed to refute any potentially celebratory, or even innocent or noncondemnatory, readings of his masturbation, by deploying specifically pornographic tropes to represent Billy's orgasm.

Although the casting of a believable woman who could erotically arouse a young boy offers a wide range of body subjects, the woman cast in *Happiness* clearly partakes of the excessive semiotic of the female pornography performer. In a film in which stereotypical casting is a major narrative strategy (ginger computer geek, brunette femme fatale, obese frustrated spinster, etc.), such a choice cannot be accidental: furthermore, the bikini is particularly small, her very large breasts appear to be surgically augmented, and she is, of course, blonde. The kitsch, nondiegetic music is also reminiscent of that in pornographic movies, and although we see nothing of Billy below the waist, merely seeing him swaying slightly, we are presented with a particularly pornographic trope, the "money shot" that is the realistic image of his ejaculate. This epistemological verification of his masculine embodiment comes at a price, however: not only do we see his ejaculate dripping from the balcony railings, but furthermore the family dog licks it up. So, no sooner has his status as an adult been confirmed than the fundamentally abject nature of male sexual pleasure outside of penetration is suggested. If semen is not seen, if it remains invisible, it stands as that which may confer sublime patriarchal power, but if it is made visible, it cannot inseminate or fertilize and hence negates patriarchy. Semen literally goes from the sublime to the ridiculous. While the generic requirement of the money shot in pornography seems to ally visible semen with masculine pleasure rather than the negation of procreation, the anxiety over its status remains. It can be argued that the presence of a female performer who is made to receive the substance masks the masturbatory status of such acts. Indeed, in this regard the money shot is arguably mimetic of the masturbatory mode of pornographic consumption rather than a representation of partnered sex. Instead of directly indexing pleasure, the transfer of the substance also transfers any sense of abjection from the male to the female performer, which also helps cover up the autoerotic, rather than heterosexual, motivation behind both the mode of consumption and the representational conventions of pornography.[4]

Other mainstream cinematic representations of visible ejaculate, such as in *There's Something about Mary*, *Silence of the Lambs*, and *American Pie*, also represent the transfer of this semen to an other, equally suggesting that the "anxious truth" of male ontology is that at the end of phallic pleasure lies not patriarchal mastery but brute substance, a leftover that cannot be accounted for. Indeed, once he has achieved orgasm, Billy seems far more mesmerized by the sight of his own ejaculate as something that must be urgently accounted for than his experience of sexual pleasure. Furthermore, in choosing to demonstrate a spermatic transfer (the dog wanders back into the apartment where Billy's mother, Trish, insists on a "kiss," letting the animal lick her face) the film clearly suggests, in extreme form, the capacity of ejaculate to make abject. When Billy returns to the dinner table and announces "I came," his family sits in dumb silence and the film ends. While attempting to suggest that nothing can be said of this, the implication being that masculine sexual desire is both inexplicable and inescapable, the sight gag creates meaning beyond this silence. That the narrative ensures a woman, not just any woman, but Billy's mother, choosing in ignorance to accept this substance seems particularly misogynist in intent. Even if unknown to Billy, this transfer in effect places him in the same dominating position over his mother as his father, in threatening to jerk off over him, had claimed to have had over Billy. So while Billy is patently still a virgin, his virginity has undoubtedly lost value due to his knowledge of sexual pleasure outside of any "proper" knowledge of procreation and the misuse of his patriarchal potential.

So, in effect, the two vectors of representation mostly split along gender lines. For male orgasmic virgins, their knowledge and their act is always a negation of their potential patriarchal function, a waste of their procreative power. This validation of spermatic continence, not only the value of semen for procreation, but also the self-denial of masturbatory pleasure as in itself conferring a proper masculine status, has a long heritage.[5] Much of the antimasturbation hysteria of the eighteenth, nineteenth, and twentieth centuries was based precisely on this overvaluation of semen and an equal overvaluation on the effects of its loss. Hence, while still a virgin, the male masturbator offends against the ideology of reproduction, as his behavior is coded as antisex. For the female orgasmic virgin, as her sexual pleasure is seen as outside of or beyond the act of coitus, masturbatory behavior can be more easily coded by patriarchal logic as simply not sexual. However, the split is not a total one, as female masturbation can still be coded as antisex, particularly if masturbatory priorities are seen to take precedent over heteronormative partnered sex, as is the case of the mad female masturbator. Yet it would seem the case that, while less condemnatory and even celebratory representation of female masturbation can be found in mainstream films, no such representation can be found for boys or men, their masturbation instead being presented as at best comic, often pathetic, and at worst a sign of criminal insanity. While masturbation necessarily negates male reproductive potential, hence the male orgasmic virgin always being a figure of ideological concern, it seems that masturbation can either help or hinder women taking up their "proper" sexual function: thus the female orgasmic virgin is a more ambivalent figure. The more pleasure and function are separated, the more permissible the former becomes.

Interestingly, one of the most positive representations of the female orgasmic virgin makes this distinction between masturbatory pleasure and potential motherhood clear by actually making the virgin a "mother." This is only possible because the film in question, *Pleasantville* (1998), is a fantasy that concerns the "magical" appearance of a couple of contemporary teenagers in a 1950s television show set in the small town of Pleasantville. Into this black-and-white world of Eisenhower dullness and conformity, a place without color, sex, or even toilets, they bring the force of embodied passion, represented by the appearance of color in the lives and faces of the previously monochrome inhabitants of Pleasantville. Color is therefore used to index affect. Although the sexless patriarchal authorities who run Pleasantville don't like these new, rather independent colored people, they can do little to stop them. The two teenagers, David (Tobey Maguire) and his older sister, Jennifer (Reese Witherspoon), find themselves the son and daughter of George (William H. Macy) and Betty Parker (Joan Allen). While David, an avid fan of the show, plays along and does nothing to disrupt the "clean living" ideology of the town, Jennifer has other ideas, and it is her seduction of the school basketball champ that begins to change this monochrome world. As more and more of the teenagers suddenly become colored as they experience sex, people become suspicious. Betty, however, is just curious and asks Jennifer what is going on up on lovers lane. When Jennifer tell her "sex," and Betty replies, "What's sex?" the film reverses the usual facts-of-life speech, with the knowledgeable daughter explaining things to the innocent mother. The description Jennifer provides is not heard beyond the opening line ("Well, Mom, when two people love each other very much . . ."); as the speech and scene fade back in, Jennifer asks a rather stunned Betty if she is OK, to which she replies that she is, except, "Your father would never do anything like that." Undeterred, Jennifer smiles and says, "Well, you know, Mom, there are ways of enjoying yourself without Dad." This sets up the masturbation scene to follow.

That evening in the bath, Betty obviously follows Jennifer's instructions.[6] Betty's growing sexual pleasure is indexed by her crying out louder and louder "Oh my goodness!" while objects in the bathroom erupt into color. At the moment of orgasm a tree outside the home bursts into flames, this burning bush clearly indexing her newly found embodied knowledge of orgasmic pleasure. This is not merely a scene of masturbation but of liberation, in which a subject narrowly defined as a dutiful, sexless mother declares herself a woman, with rights and sexual desires no longer narrowly confined by a controlling patriarchy. The literally fantastic use of color and especially fire to materialize the intensity of this experience also demonstrates the divide between our social embodiment of dutiful reproduction and our private experience of embodied sexual consumption. Yet as Betty is clearly a mother, if confusingly a virginal one, her new orgasmic status in no way detracts from her parental status and the fulfillment of her reproductive function. Hence, while in one sense a metaphor for the advances won by feminism with regard to women's right to sexual self-determination, it could equally be argued that the permissibility of female masturbation as compared with male masturbation relies on the fact that it is not in itself a negation of a potential procreative event.

What this reading of orgasmic virginity suggests is that the recent willingness of filmmakers to represent masturbation in mainstream texts is not simply a marker of a more liberated contemporary sexual politics. Instead, it seems permissible for women to be orgasmic virgins only because this body knowledge does not in itself interfere with their normative procreative function. For men, however, orgasmic virginity is at best pathetic and at worst pathological: masculine sexuality is, if anything, under more ideological pressure from patriarchy than is female sexuality, as it has more to "lose." These films reflect this concern as they suggest that the relationship between procreative duty and autoerotic sexual pleasure is inversely proportional. In this regard they perpetuate the underlying ideas of the antimasturbation hysteria of the nineteenth and early-twentieth centuries, where male potency was believed to be under direct threat from masturbation. However, as Laqueur has argued, this fear is further exacerbated by the fact that consumer culture actively promotes our "individual" right to pleasure, creating an anxiety that the "logic" of economic individualism will cross over to the sexual sphere. The criticism of masturbation promoted by these texts can be traced back to the development of the market economy itself, the paradox being that our personal individual pleasure was demanded by economic logic as it was vilified by sexual logic.[7] On the one hand, the market economy is driven by the activities of individuals who seek self-satisfaction, and the masturbatory subject and the commodity consumer are in this regard not antithetical subjects. Hence, if Adam Smith's famous "invisible hand" works to calm the workings of the market in the social sphere, it equally seems to drive it by exciting the individual in the sexual sphere. Yet, on the other hand, masturbation indexes a withdrawal from social interaction, a failure to exchange that profoundly threatens the workings of the market. However, as the demands of capitalism and market exchange come to dominate more and more of our lives, including our sexuality, a new horror presents itself for patriarchy. That is, not the loss or preservation of virginity but something worse—the total loss of male potency itself and hence the risk of extinction. As Nicky Hart has noted, the promotion of individual social and sexual pleasure over collective duties and roles suggests that "procreation is ultimately becoming the Achilles' heel of communities that embrace the capitalist way of life."[8]

However, we must be careful not to distort complex historical realities into simple teleological trends: the model presented earlier does not exist in some timeless fashion. While patriarchy and capitalism are not identical modes of domination and sources of ideology, neither are they quite so contradictory. Interestingly, what seems to link all of these films is precisely their own crisis of historicity in which sexual subjectivity is presented as a universal question rather than a historic materialization. All of these films present white, suburban settings, which (explicitly in *Pleasantville*) are not timeless expressions of the human condition but are deeply nostalgic for the 1950s or early 1960s of white America, a time when patriarchy and capital got on extremely well.

The anxieties over orgasmic virgins played out in these films reflect the continuing influence and appeal to the sexual ideology of these times and communities. Unlike then, however, these films are aware of how different the current circumstances seem to the postwar and "baby boom" periods of the 1950s and 1960s: a time of larger families, early marriage, and little divorce. While, as Göran Therbon has argued, we must remember that this period was itself an exception rather than the rule in the antipathy between sexual function and pleasure, these films suggest that much of its fundamental sexual ideology still persists.[9] The melancholia and nostalgia for more patriarchal and less liberated times suggest that the sexual revolution of the late 1960s and the 1970s achieved rather less than is often assumed, and perhaps the gains are in danger of reversal. The neoliberal ideological combination of free markets and family values suggest that patriarchal restraint and capitalist consumption may be finding a new and troubling rapprochement. With the figure of the orgasmic virgin, contemporary sexual ideology attempts to reveal and negate what troubles it, to value virginity and pleasure, sexual continence and consumption, but it is not a very convincing combination. Until such time as the value we place on sexual pleasure is truly liberated from sexual function, these paradoxes and anxieties will undoubtedly remain.

Notes

1. Mary Jane Kehily, "More Sugar? Teenage Magazines, Gender Displays and Sexual Learning," *European Journal of Cultural Studies* 2, no. 1 (1999): 65–89.

2. Greg Tuck, "Of Monsters, Masturbators and Markets: Autoerotic Desire, Sexual Exchange and the Cinematic Serial Killer," in *Monsters and the Monstrous: Myths and Metaphors of Enduring Evil* 3, edited by Niall Scot (Amsterdam: At the Interface Publications/Rodopi, 2006).

3. Anthony Giddens, *The Transformation of Intimacy: Sexuality, Love and Eroticisms in Modern Societies* (Cambridge: Polity Press, 1992). See also Nancy Friday, *Sex for One: The Joy of Self Loving*, 25th ed. (New York: Crown, 1996).

4. Greg Tuck, "Mainstreaming the Money Shot: Representations of Ejaculation in Mainstream American Cinema," *Paragraph* 2 (August–September 2003): 263–80.

5. Laurence Goldstein, ed., *The Male Body: Features, Destinies, Exposures* (Ann Arbor: University of Michigan Press, 1994); Thomas Laqueur, "The Social Evil, the Solitary Vice and Pouring Tea," in *Solitary Sex: A Cultural History of Masturbation*, ed. Paula Bennett and Thomas Laqueur (New York: Zone Books), 155–62.

6. As with Vivian in *Slums of Beverly Hills*, we see nothing of her from the shoulders down: one of the things that seems to code whether a female masturbation is a potentially liberatory or perverting act is the level of explicitness with which it is shown. The more obvious the manipulation, the more similarity it shares with the representations of arm or hand movements in scenes of male masturbation, the more likely the masturbation will be seen as anti sex rather than simply not sex.

7. Laqueur, "Social Evil," 157.

8. Nicky Hart, "Of Procreation and Power," *New Left Review* 35 (September–October 2005): 91.

9. Göran Therbon, *Between Sex and Power: Family in the World, 1900–2000* (London: Routledge, 2004).

Lisa M. Dresner

Love's Labor's Lost?
Early 1980s Representations of Girls' Sexual Decision Making in *Fast Times at Ridgemont High* and *Little Darlings*

Ironically, the two films primarily responsible for keeping me a virgin until I was in my early twenties were both films about teenage girls who chose not to wait for true love—or even college—before they had sex: *Fast Times at Ridgemont High* (1982) and *Little Darlings* (1980). These films of the early 1980s, coming, as Chuck Kleinhans puts it, "on the [e]dge of the Reagan Era" reflect an all too brief period in American film history between the sexual empowerment of the 1970s women's movement and the "just say no" sexual abstinence campaigns of the mid-1980s and beyond.[1] In this brief era, girls' sexual decision making is represented as intelligent, responsible, and important, and the films make their points about not rushing into sex in a way that respects and empowers teenage girls instead of romanticizing or infantilizing them.

Audiences, Critical Responses, and the Historical Moment

Both films are somewhat problematic in terms of their audiences, *Little Darlings* perhaps more so than *Fast Times at Ridgemont High*. Jim Craddock and the other editors of *VideoHound's Golden Movie Retriever* muse, "Just who is meant to be the market for this movie, anyway?" and their point is well taken.[2] These films seem really aimed at a youth market, but both were rated "R," which means that teens under seventeen theoretically had to have a parent accompany them to the theater. In practice, that meant that most teens who wanted to see these films had to sneak in by themselves.[3] Therefore the films straddle an uneasy line—they are a bit racy for (and, indeed, forbidden to) their natural audience, yet they are a bit tame for the adults and older teens who can see them legally.

Adult critics generally enjoyed *Fast Times at Ridgemont High*. Jack Kroll gives an enthusiastic review of *Fast Times* in *Newsweek*, comparing the film favorably with *Porky's* and noting with approval that "Heckerling's treatment of kid sex . . . is really sexy, friendly[,] and funny."[4] David Denby also compares *Fast Times* favorably with *Porky's* and lauds "the overall tenderness of the movie—the curiosity combined with delicacy [and] the emotionally specific responses to sex."[5] Even the terminally grouchy *New Yorker* film reviewer, Pauline Kael, starts her *Fast Times* review positively (for her): "Watching 'Fast Times at Ridgemont High,' I was surprised at how not-bad it is."[6] Only the *New York Times'* Janet Maslin seems to dislike the film, though not on the grounds that it deals with teen sex—on the contrary, her criticism is that the film is "too fluffy" and does not include enough of the "deaths, drug problems and other bleak moments" that populate the book upon which the film was based.[7] Maslin does call the film "appealing," however.

Critical reaction to *Little Darlings* was considerably more mixed, perhaps depending on the reviewer's opinion of teen sex. "What began as a racy farce grows wearily moralistic," complains a disappointed David Ansen in *Newsweek*.[8] The *New Yorker* review by "B.G." has the opposite quarrel with the film, however, sniffily calling its premise of a teen virginity-loss contest "a disgusting idea for a movie."[9] In turn, Frank Rich's *Time* magazine review calls it "an amusing premise."[10] On the one hand, Lawrence O'Toole mildly calls it "a pleasant enough diversion," while on the other hand, Janet Maslin complains that if only *Little Darlings* "were funnier about other things, it might have the wherewithal to keep the plot's sexual undertones from becoming *un*pleasant."[11] Only David Denby seems to appreciate the film's turns from silly to soulful, calling it "a slick, whory, irresistibly entertaining movie with some scenes of surprising power at the end" and lauding its "sensitive, almost exquisite rendering of the adolescent dilemmas, the uncertainty and suffering, that even the most self-confident kids must go through."[12]

The markedly schizophrenic reaction of the critics to *Little Darlings* noted here is perhaps reflective of conflicted North American attitudes toward sex during this period. Even in the brief period between the sexually liberated 1970s and the "just say no" era of the mid-1980s, American society seems to have been deeply ambivalent about the concept of teen sexuality. For instance, on the one hand, the March 31, 1980, issue of *Peo-*

ple magazine features a picture on its cover of *Little Darlings* stars Tatum O'Neal and Kristy McNichol in bikini tops, with O'Neal leaning into McNichol so that their breasts touch suggestively; on the other hand, the accompanying article primly decries the "lurid ad campaign" accompanying the film.[13]

Perhaps this anxiety was caused by a very real increase in teen sexual behavior that had developed in North America due to the sexual revolution and to teenagers' improved access to birth control. Indeed, in the same issue containing its review of *Little Darlings*, the Canadian magazine *Maclean's* featured an article on "Teen Sex" that includes this American statistic: "55 per cent of teen-agers between the ages of 15 and 19 are having sexual intercourse."[14] The article further proclaims that "the idea that premarital sex for teen-agers is a no-no has disappeared" and cites Canadian sex lecturer Sue Johanson, who noted that teens of the time were starting to have sex at younger and younger ages: "Eight years ago, the common age for starting to have sexual intercourse was 18; now [in 1980] it is more common at 16 and not uncommon at 14."[15] No wonder, then, that this subject promptly made its way into popular film.

The Virginity-Loss Plots

Fast Times at Ridgemont High, based on an actual undercover journalistic exercise that young writer Cameron Crowe turned into a book (he also wrote the screenplay), interweaves several plots about the lives of high school students.[16] The one relevant for our purposes reflects what Gayle Wald aptly describes as "sexual turmoil" and concerns Stacy Hamilton (Jennifer Jason Leigh), a fifteen-year-old high school freshman who deliberately sets out to have sex.[17] Stacy decides to have sex with an older man she meets at the mall, who drops her a few months later, and with one of the "cool" kids at her school, Mike Damone (Robert Romanus), who drops her immediately after they have sex. She also tries to have sex with the adorably nerdy Mark Ratner (Brian Backer), nicknamed "Rat," who has a crush on her and who asks her out, but when she tries to seduce him, he panics and leaves. She eventually discovers that she is pregnant by Damone and has an abortion. She and Rat continue to flirt, however, and by the film's end, she has learned that she really wants love instead of sex: "I finally figured it out," she says. "I don't want sex. Anyone can have sex. . . . I want a relationship. I want romance." The film's final update lets us know that Stacy has remained true to her new insight as it informs us that she and Rat are now "having a passionate love affair [b]ut still haven't gone all the way."

In *Little Darlings*, poor girl Angel Bright (Kristy McNichol) and rich girl Ferris Whitney (Tatum O'Neal) develop an instant dislike for each other on the way to a summer camp full of girls obsessed with sex.[18] Bitchy model Cinder (Krista Errickson) discovers that they are both virgins, exploits their mutual antagonism, and bullies them into engaging in a virginity-loss contest on which all of the other campers bet cash. With the support of their bunkmates, the girls secure birth control and select their intended deflowerers: Angel picks the suggestively named Randy (Matt Dillon), a camper at a neighboring boys' camp (the phallically named Camp Tomahawk), while Ferris picks Gary Callahan (Armand Assante), a hunky teacher who is moonlighting as a sports counselor at the girls' camp.

After some failed attempts, Angel and Randy eventually have sex, but it is "not like [she] thought it would be." In what David M. Considine notes is "a rare post-coital scene" for the time, Angel winds up crying, confessing that she had been a virgin, and telling Randy, "Making love is . . . different than what I thought it would be like."[19] Touched, Randy comforts her and expresses love for her, but Angel still looks miserable. When she returns to camp, Angel lies, tells the girls that she hasn't had sex with Randy, and offers both her hand and her congratulations to Ferris.

Ferris, on the other hand, throws herself at Mr. Callahan, who rejects her advances as kindly as possible, assures her that if she were older, he would "fall madly in love with [her]," and leaves her feeling exceedingly good about herself. Indeed, Ferris is so visibly ecstatic when she returns to the cabin that her bunkmates all assume that she has had sex. (Although the audience does not know it at this point in the film, all of the girls except for Cinder are virgins themselves. In a naïve display of their expectations about the bliss of first-time sex, the girls decide that they will know when Angel and Ferris have had sex because, as Dana puts it, "their faces'll get all shiny and radiant-looking.")[20] Far from disabusing her bunkmates of the notion that her tryst has been successful, Ferris lies and regales them with a romantic tale about her encounter with Mr. Callahan. Accordingly, the others mistakenly believe that Ferris has lost her virginity while Angel has not.

Due to the contest, both girls come to grief. Randy temporarily drops Angel for Cinder when Cinder describes the contest—though apparently not her own role as its instigator—to him. Although Randy later wants to continue their relationship when he discovers that Angel has never revealed their tryst, Angel tells him: "It's too late. We started in the middle. We never even had a beginning." When he offers to continue even a nonsexual relationship with her, she rejects that option as well.

Meanwhile, because the other campers mistakenly believe that Ferris has slept with Mr. Callahan, rumors come to the attention of the camp authorities, Mr. Callahan's job is jeopardized, and he angrily calls Ferris "a God-damned trollop." Angel and Ferris eventually reveal the truth to each other and ask the other girls to support them in telling the camp authorities about the bet. Cinder claims no one will believe them, taunts them for being virgins, and attempts to rally the other girls against them. Instead, one by one, the other girls all start admitting that they themselves are virgins, and the peaceful hippie Sunshine symbolizes their rejection of Cinder's heterosexist tyranny by punching Cinder in the face. Ferris and Angel's plan works: Mr. Callahan's job is saved, and Ferris and Angel leave camp as fast friends.[21]

Virgins and Sexual Curiosity

Both films represent their protagonists as thinking almost constantly about sex and virginity loss. Indeed, *Fast Times at Ridgemont High* starts with teen waitresses at the mall admiring an older customer's "cute little butt," and Stacy is continually portrayed as seeking sexual advice from her older friend, Linda Barrett (Phoebe Cates). Stacy is also represented as actively seeking to lose her virginity, as seeing it as a normal rite of passage of adolescence. Moreover, even though her first experience with intercourse proves underwhelming, she still considers sex to be a goal worth pursuing, as her later advances toward Damone and Rat suggest. Indeed, even her repeated unfulfilling sexual experiences don't dissuade her from thinking that sex is bound to be pleasurable eventually. Only the end of the film's "Where are they now?" sequence shows that she has finally given up on rushing into sex.

The girls of *Little Darlings* are similarly portrayed as obsessed with sex. Their rowdy bus trip up to Camp Little Wolf (perhaps the writers thought Camp Little Fox sounded too suggestive!) demonstrates that sex is their favorite topic of conversation. One girl confides, "You know what my favorite movie was? *Last Tango in Paris*. I saw it ten times." Others express their appreciation of matinee idols such as John Travolta and Andy Gibb, one enthusing (much like the girls in *Fast Times*) that she "love[s Gibbs's] ass. . . . It's so small and cute." Another muses, "I knew this one girl—she did it on a roller coaster." While the girls have different approaches to sex—from the romantic to the pornographic—they are clearly all fascinated by it. Indeed, they are so interested in it, and so certain that it defines who they are as teenagers, that none of the girls—except for Angel and Ferris—is willing to admit that she's a virgin. The girls' mistaken perception that everyone *else* is sexually experienced is highlighted by Ferris's assertion that she is "almost the only virgin in camp" and by her plaintive lament to Mr. Callahan: "Every girl knows this secret life except me."

Admittedly, there is another, more insidious subtext at work here: virginity loss is portrayed in this film as proof of heterosexuality, and accordingly, homophobia is the club used to bully Angel and Ferris into the virginity-loss contest. The insidious Cinder gives this homophobic analysis of the tension between Angel and Ferris: "Two little virgins. Quaint. No wonder you're always fighting. It's all that unreleased energy. You're probably lezzies." In a classic portrayal of scapegoating, Ferris responds, "Maybe *she* is, but I'm straight." Angel simply responds physically by attacking Cinder when Cinder suggests that Angel is "into girls." Again playing on the girls' terror of being labeled as lesbians to push them toward virginity loss, Cinder moves in for the kill, saying, "Ferris probably isn't gay, just sexually immature. . . . I think she'd go all the way if she had the chance." This homophobia as plot device is particularly interesting given the actual lesbian subtext of the eventual flowering of the friendship between Angel and Ferris, a subtext that has been nicely elucidated by Kristen Hatch and Chuck Kleinhans.[22] The homophobia is perhaps also countered by two scenes reaffirming female solidarity at the film's end—both the scene in which Sunshine punches the malevolent Cinder and the final scene, where Angel warmly introduces Ferris as her "best friend."

Virgins and Sexual Assertion

All three protagonists—Stacy, Angel, and Ferris—act in some measure as sexual initiators/aggressors toward the male objects of their desires in these films. Stacy displays a mixture of "masculine" and "feminine" approaches to initiating sex with different potential partners, whereas Angel and Ferris respectively display more rigidly fixed "masculine" and "feminine" ways of initiating sex.

Stacy's approach to initiating sex is either "masculine," "feminine," or "mixed," depending on her potential partner. Stacy is clearly more of the masculine aggressor in her initial sexual encounter with the shy Rat, as she invites him into her house, changes into her bathrobe, has him sit on her bed, and then kisses him. In contrast, she takes a more feminine approach when she tries to "go for it" in her earliest meeting with her eventual deflowerer, Ron Johnson, by following Linda's advice to laugh at anything he says that is "remotely funny." She does, however, apparently call him (also on Linda's advice) and sneak out to see him. With Mike Damone, the initiation of sex seems to be a fairly equal affair. Stacy tells Damone that she likes him, but she asks Damone into her house only after he asks her whether she has some iced tea. She then invites him to go swimming, but their kissing in the pool house that leads to sex seems mutually initiated. When a panicked Damone later tells the pregnant Stacy, "You wanted it more than I did," she rejects that idea firmly: "No. You take that back," she insists, emphasizing that their decision to have sex was a mutual one.

By contrast, *Little Darlings* splits its representation of the masculine and feminine approaches to pursuing sex between its two protagonists: Angel's approach to sex, at least initially, is coded as masculine. Angel picks Randy out as her sexual prey when the girls are in the middle of their condom-stealing escapade. She looks at him and speaks to him first, before he sees or hears her, emphasizing her role as a powerful sexual initiator and spectator. Indeed, the camera aligns the film's spectators with Angel as an appreciative viewing subject of Randy as a male viewed object: the camera pans up the back of Randy's jeans until it reaches his behind, then cuts to a shot of Angel looking appreciative and raising a speculative eyebrow. Angel's masculine position in their relationship is also underlined by the fact that she provides all of the transportation for her dates with Randy: she rows a canoe over to the boys' camp three times to pick him up. She also (unsuccessfully) follows the traditionally masculine-coded strategy of trying to get her potential sexual partner drunk. She gets Randy a six-pack of beer and pushes the drinks on him so quickly that he asks her to slow down. She gets him so drunk, however, that he falls asleep!

In contrast, Ferris's approach to seduction is coded as decidedly feminine. Having selected counselor Gary Callahan as her intended prey, Ferris then produces a carefully orchestrated display of feminine helplessness designed to win his heart—she pretends that she cannot swim and gets him to give her private swimming lessons; then she shows up at his private cabin clad only in her virginal nightdress, blatantly lies to him about only having six weeks to live, pulls his arm around her, and closes her eyes and purses her lips in anticipation of the kiss that she thinks is sure to follow. In whichever way they approach it, however, the girls in these films all view the initiation of sex as an appropriate female activity.

Early 1980s Representations of Girls' Sexual Decision Making

Virgins and Nudity

Both films portray girls as being shy about their own nudity but fascinated by the nude male body. Certainly, the politics of disrobing proves to be a touchy issue for the protagonists of both films. In *Fast Times at Ridgemont High*, Stacy eventually resolves the issue in an egalitarian way with Damone:

> STACY: You wanna take off your clothes, Mike?
>
> DAMONE: You first.
>
> STACY: Both of us at the same time.
>
> DAMONE: OK.

It is telling that while Stacy initially tries to take control of the disrobing process here, she at least claims to espouse a more egalitarian approach. In point of fact, however, Stacy actually waits until Damone has disrobed before she does the same—perhaps suggesting that it is easier to champion egalitarian sexual politics than to conform one's actions to them.

In *Little Darlings*, Angel and Randy's first attempt at sex involves a similar power struggle over nudity. During this abortive first try, Angel clearly becomes uncomfortable when Randy starts to unbutton her shirt: in response, she steps back and rebuttons it. When she does decide to get undressed, she makes it clear that she does not want Randy either looking at her or touching her: she orders Randy to turn around and refuses his offer to help her undress. Moreover, it is clearly important to her to control the circumstances of Randy's disrobing as well:

> ANGEL: So, you gonna get undressed or what?
>
> RANDY: Yeah, sure.
>
> ANGEL: Go ahead. . . . Not here—over there.
>
> RANDY: You're kinky.

There is, in fact, nothing particularly kinky about Angel's request here, but Randy correctly interprets it as reflecting Angel's desire to control him and all of the circumstances of their lovemaking and thus makes this veiled joke highlighting the fact that the woman is taking the socially unexpected dominant role here. The issue of nudity actually proves to be a deal breaker during this attempt at sex: having stripped down to his underwear, a potentially vulnerable Randy pressures Angel to hurry up and get undressed, even though she looks ill. They argue, and Randy then rejects Angel by saying that she talks too much and that she is a tease. On the verge of tears, Angel confesses, "I like you." She then says that she is indeed ready to have sex, but on this occasion, Randy will have none of it.

Admittedly, Ferris never gets to the stage of disrobing with Gary Callahan, but her costume choice is interesting. As the "good girl" who will wind up not having sex, she wears a virginal white nightgown whose effect is perhaps more romantic than sexual. Moreover, she rejects both male and female nudity in her fabricated account of her supposed lovemaking with Gary: when little Penelope asks, "Did you see him naked?" Ferris's answer is a shocked "No!" and in the rest of her fabricated account, they make love in the dark so that *her* fictional nudity also remains unseen.

Despite their own shyness, however, the girls in *Little Darlings* are generally portrayed as enthusiastic voyeurs who are fascinated by the male body and male nudity. Most of them spy on the boys skinny-dipping at the neighboring boys' camp as a female-bonding activity.[23] Later, Cinder and Sunshine similarly spy on Ferris's swimming lesson with the bare-chested Gary Callahan, while Dana and Angel surreptitiously observe Randy's inept dirt-bike riding. Even Angel's mom (Maggie Blye) admires a bare-chested archery counselor she spots on visiting day, commenting, "Not bad. Not bad at all!" as she gives him the once-over. In general, the girls seem to derive copious pleasure from looking at the nude or partially clad male form. When they watch the male skinny-dippers, Dana (Alexa Kenin) quotes some appreciative lines from Shakespeare; Cinder defends their spying by saying, "You can't get pregnant from looking!"; and Carrots (Simone Schachter) chuckles and responds: "God, I hope not!" While their remarks here emphasize the fact that long-distance voyeurism is safer for teen girls than actually having sex would be, these comments also suggest that teen female desire is simultaneously both normal and overwhelming. The female viewing pleasure in the male form depicted here is also emphasized by the camerawork of the film, which lingers on bare male chests rather often given that the film is set in a camp for girls.

Virgins and Sexual Pleasure, or the Lack Thereof

Interestingly, neither film represents female orgasm as achievable by its protagonists. This is somewhat surprising given that these films of the early

Early 1980s Representations of Girls' Sexual Decision Making

1980s immediately follow the 1970s era of female sexual empowerment. Progressive feminist medical texts of the 1970s such as *Our Bodies, Ourselves* encouraged women to become aware of their sexual fantasies and to masturbate.[24] The 1979 edition, for instance, cheers on the gentle reader thus: "If you have never masturbated, we invite you to try," and then advocates seducing oneself with "cream, lotion, oil, or anything else that feels good," "a favorite record," and "a glass of wine."[25]

Perhaps the pendulum never swung as far toward female sexual pleasure in the early 1980s as the authors of *Our Bodies, Ourselves* had hoped it might. In her 1982 self-help guide, *Having It All*, then *Cosmopolitan* magazine editor Helen Gurley Brown seems to focus a great deal more on male sexual pleasure than on its female counterpart. Indeed, she devotes nearly ten pages to the specifics of pleasuring men, while providing fewer details about how women are supposed to achieve pleasure for themselves.[26] Furthermore, while Brown does encourage female masturbation and encourages women to tell men what they like in bed, she urges women never to tell men that they masturbate: "Men usually don't like to *think* about your masturbating—like you should save everything for *them*. Don't tell!"[27] This seems to suggest that women need almost to be ashamed of their own sexual pleasure or that they need to hide it if it is in any way unpleasant for—or threatening to—men.

Brown's privileging of men's sexual pleasure over women's sexual pleasure continues throughout her self-help tome. Indeed, Brown urges women to "do it anyway" if approached by their partner when they're not in the mood and gives them this cold comfort: "You don't have to rev up and have an orgasm."[28] She even goes so far in her chapter on marriage as to command, "Never refuse to make love, even if you don't feel like it."[29] Moreover, as the flip side of pretending that one doesn't masturbate to protect a man's ego, Brown also advocates faking orgasm "sometimes" in order to protect a man's ego: "After someone has made love to you with skill and grace, a [faked] orgasm is a way of saying you enjoyed yourself, even as you compliment a host on a wonderful spinach quiche."[30] She even urges women to sleep with men they don't particularly feel like sleeping with: "Perhaps a man you adore as a friend, or someone you owe a lot to, is simply terrible in bed . . . that doesn't mean you *shouldn't* sleep with him," she admonishes.[31]

In any case, despite their explicitly sexual subject matter, neither *Fast Times* nor *Little Darlings* represents any women who have achieved sexual pleasure. On the contrary, it appears that sex has caused Stacy pain, while her sexually experienced friend, Linda, winds up implying that *she* hasn't experienced sexual pleasure either; we don't see Angel having sex, but she looks pretty shell-shocked afterward, and it seems apparent that she has not had an orgasm (although the novelization of the film implies that she has); and Ferris, of course, never has sex at all.[32]

Certainly, *Fast Times at Ridgemont High* is remarkable for the unromanticized way it portrays the potential pain of virginity loss and of sex with insufficient foreplay for women. First of all, in a brilliantly shot scene, Stacy's virginity loss to Ron Johnson is reflected by a look of desperate pain crossing her face. The film reinforces the unpleasant nature of their encounter through Stacy's next conversation with Linda:

STACY: It hurt so bad.

LINDA: Don't worry. Keep doing it. It gets a lot better. I swear.

STACY: It'd better.

Stacy's physically disappointing sex with Ron Johnson here (which we never see mitigated by her having any better sex with him) is mirrored by the similarly unfulfilling sex she has with Mike Damone later in the film. After Stacy and Damone disrobe, he jumps on her, comes immediately, and departs promptly afterward, leaving Stacy lying on the couch naked, looking frustrated.

Moreover, the girls don't always seem to expect to have an orgasm or to know exactly what that would feel like. While Stacy and Linda are taking a *Cosmopolitan* magazine quiz on orgasms, Stacy asks Linda, "Do you always climax with Rick [Linda's fiancé]?" Stacy clearly is wondering here whether she herself will ever get to have an orgasm. Linda's reply is even more telling, "Yes. I think so. He's no high school boy." The tentative, naïve nature of Linda's reply here suggests that, in fact, she *never* has had an orgasm, with Rick or with anyone else. Similarly, when Damone asks Stacy, "Didn't you feel it?" after their spectacularly brief sexual encounter, her "Yeah, I guess I did" rings patently false.

Instead of focusing on their own sexual pleasure, the protagonists in both films focus on doing things "correctly" to maximize the pleasure of the men they're with. For instance, with the assistance of a carrot, Stacy gets an amusingly public lesson on giving a blow job from Linda in the high school cafeteria, but their emphasis is completely on what to do to please a man.[33] In contrast, no mention is ever made in either film of women *receiv-*

ing oral sex. Moreover, while male masturbation is explicitly represented in *Fast Times at Ridgemont High* (Brad is interrupted in the bathroom by Linda, the object of the sexual fantasy he is having), female masturbation is never represented or even mentioned in that film or in *Little Darlings*. The girls' low expectations in these films may reflect women's still-emerging expectations of the sex act for themselves.

To be fair, male orgasm is not reflected particularly positively in either film either, though it happens. For instance, as Jon Lewis has noted, when Ron Johnson, the first man Stacy sleeps with, is having his orgasm, we focus mainly on her face, not his.[34] A brief shot of the triumphant, solipsistic look on Johnson's face simply serves to provide a contrast to the pained look on Stacy's face. Director Amy Heckerling highlights a similar contrast when Stacy and Damone have sex. The focus is more on the discomfort that she has than on the pleasure he has. Actually, although he clearly does have an—apparently premature—orgasm, Damone doesn't look like he's having a very good time either. He even seems a bit unsure about his own orgasm, announcing, "I think I came."[35]

Moreover, in *Little Darlings*, Randy's orgasm isn't shown at all. Indeed, none of the "successful" sex between Angel and Randy is shown, perhaps emphasizing the fact that the sex act has not been successful from Angel's point of view.

It is also true that neither film explicitly presents itself as having a feminist agenda—indeed, quite the contrary—so perhaps we should not be surprised that female sexual pleasure is not represented in them. Yet I suggest that both films are strongly feminist in effect and that the lack of female sexual pleasure in them paradoxically enhances that effect: while girls are not represented as obtaining fulfillment through sex, they are alternately represented as obtaining fulfillment through female friendships, caring relationships with men that don't include sex, work, and honorable behavior. Oddly, then, the removal of the woman from the realm of satisfied sexual subjecthood appears also to remove her from the dangerous, distracting realm of sexual objecthood and to free her to pursue avenues of fulfillment that are arguably ultimately more useful to her.

This explicit rejection of sex in favor of friendship and self-actualization is an interesting early manifestation of the social phenomenon chronicled by journalist Wendy Keller in the late 1990s in her well-documented self-help book *The Cult of the Born-Again Virgin: How Single Women Can Reclaim Their Sexual Power*. In her book, Keller both describes and encourages women who have decided to experiment with a period of celibacy to foster personal growth (which might or might not include finding a good life partner). Among the many nonromantic potential reasons Keller proposes for eschewing sex, at least temporarily, are "to think about what you really want[,] . . . [t]o cultivate a sense of personal dignity[,] . . . [t]o enhance self-esteem[,] . . . [t]o break an addiction[,] . . . [t]o finish college or get an advanced degree[,] . . . [t]o develop relationships with women friends[,]. . . [t]o explore a change in sexual orientation[,] . . . [t]o get finances in order[,] . . . [t]o change religions[,] . . . [and t]o get in shape."[36] By focusing on their female friendships and on their sense of honor in righting an injustice instead of on sex, the young women of *Little Darlings* anticipate this "born-again virgin" movement described by Keller by almost two decades, but they seem to find some of the same empowerment through their chosen celibacy that Keller touts.

Virgins and Birth Control (or the Lack Thereof)

One of the most striking ways in which these films treat their teen girl protagonists (and their teen girl audiences) as intelligent adults is in their portrayal of the consequences of not using birth control and of responsible teen girls making the informed choice to obtain and use it. *Fast Times at Ridgemont High* emphasizes the importance of using birth control by stressing the perils of not using it: Stacy eschews birth control when she has sex with Ron Johnson and with Mike Damone, and consequently she becomes pregnant by Damone. The film is remarkable in its difference from later films such as *Just Another Girl on the I.R.T.* (1992) (and especially from later television series), however, in that neither Stacy nor Damone ever even considers keeping their baby and that both sexual partners seem certain that an abortion is the correct solution to their problem. To see how very rare such a reaction by characters to an unplanned pregnancy became in the 1980s and beyond for women of any age, one need only list the responses of major characters on American television series who became pregnant during those years. Tough, middle-aged news anchor Murphy Brown on the eponymous sitcom *Murphy Brown* became pregnant accidentally and decided to keep her baby. The married, working-class Roseanne and her single sister, Jackie, on the sitcom *Roseanne* (both self-made businesswomen) became pregnant accidentally and decided to keep their babies. Teen genius Andrea on the teenage nighttime soap opera *Beverly Hills, 90210* became pregnant accidentally and, after briefly considering an abortion, decided to keep her baby, marry the baby's father, and temporarily put her career plans on hold. Proprietor of her own detective agency, Maddie Hayes on the series *Moonlighting* got pregnant accidentally, decided to keep her baby, briefly married a man who was not the baby's father, and eventually had a convenient miscarriage. Divorced career woman Molly Dodd on *The Days and Nights of Molly Dodd* got pregnant accidentally and decided to keep her baby. Fashion buyer Rachel on the vastly popular 1990s sitcom *Friends* got pregnant accidentally, decided to keep her baby, and (eventually) married the baby's father. The trend continues: Aspiring teen author Donna on the twenty-first-century sitcom *That '70s Show* mistakenly thought she was pregnant but at no point considered having an abortion or even putting the expected baby up for adoption. This epidemic of unplanned pregnancies is striking not simply because of the pregnancies' unplanned nature—what kind of an idiot wouldn't use condoms during the AIDS epidemic?—but also because of the kind of women who become pregnant. All of these accidental pregnancies happen not to aspiring homemakers who long to stay home with large families but to vital career women who have meaningful work (or studies) outside of the home and who are presumably intelligent and informed enough to use birth control. The uniformity of the reaction to these pregnancies is also quite striking: I was hard-pressed to recall *any* American prime-time television series of the 1980s or beyond (I cannot speak as to daytime soap operas)[37] where any pregnant woman decided upon—and went through with—an abortion.[38]

Stacy, who has already researched the issue like the intelligent and capable teenage girl that she is, asks Damone to split the costs of the abortion equally, another attitude that reflects the feminism of the times—she wants to go Dutch. She also asks him for a ride to the clinic, which underlines her extreme youth, for she is too young to drive. Unable to come up with his half of the money, however, an embarrassed Damone skips out of picking her up to drive her to the clinic. The resourceful Stacy is forced instead to ask her big brother, Brad (Judge Reinhold), for a ride downtown. What follows is one of the most positive, moving abortion scenes portrayed in film.[39] After her abortion, which does not seem to have caused her much physical discomfort (certainly, she looks more at peace after the abortion than after either time she has had sex), a subdued Stacy is cared for by kind clinic workers who tell her that they cannot allow her to leave unless she has a ride home. Stacy lies and tells them that her boyfriend is picking her up downstairs, but when she forlornly emerges from the clinic, her big brother, having guessed all, is waiting to pick her up. Instead of berating her, he reassures her that he will keep her secret, asks if she's OK, and takes her to get some food. Strikingly, the abortion, which in earlier or later eras might be portrayed as a negative, family-harming choice, here leads to a scene that affirms love, nurturing, and solidarity between siblings and that highlights their family bond.[40] It is interesting that Stacy does not call on her friend Linda for help with her abortion problem; instead, this brother-assisted abortion is portrayed as an affirmation of possible familial bonding across gender lines.[41] The unwanted pregnancy and subsequent abortion here not only underline the consequences of not using birth control but also suggest that sexually active teenage girls are intelligent enough and morally responsible enough to deal with the consequences of their sexual activity without the input and assistance of their parents or their sexual partners.

I imagine that the positive view of abortion at this moment in time resulted from several factors: the legalization of abortion throughout the United States after the *Roe v. Wade* U.S. Supreme Court decision of 1973, the ideology of the women's movement of the 1970s generally, and specifically, the accompanying feminist medical literature that presented abortion as a safe, rational, positive choice for women. The 1979 edition of *Our Bodies, Ourselves*, for example, is overwhelmingly pro-choice, contains detailed information about abortion procedures, and enthusiastically informs the reader: "*The earlier an abortion is done, the safer it is!*"[42]

Little Darlings takes the opposite approach to the issue of birth control by emphasizing the importance of using it as a matter of course. Indeed, birth control becomes the topic of an explicit group planning session:

> DANA: Hey, what are they going to do about protection?
>
> PENNY: Protection?
>
> SUNSHINE: Birth control.
>
> UNIDENTIFIED VOICE-OFF: Oh, the guy takes care of that.
>
> CINDER: Not since the pill . . .
>
> DANA: You know, guys, this is serious.

Interestingly, in this post-Pill, pre-AIDS era, the girls eventually pick the condom as their method of choice, certainly a feminist selection, given that it is still the only method of birth control that makes men participate in pregnancy protection. Of course, it is also the form of birth control most accessible to underage girls, for at summer camp, they have no access to the birth control pill or to other methods that might be available at a free clinic.

Obtaining birth control is portrayed as a fun, though decidedly illicit, female-bonding activity in *Little Darlings,* one in which even the littlest camper, ten-year-old Penny (Jenn Thompson), participates. The girls sneak out of church services, steal the camp bus (fortunately, budding juvenile delinquent Angel knows how to hot-wire it), head to the nearest gas station, try to break down a locked men's room door, stuff Penny through a transom, steal an entire vending machine full of condoms (determined little Penny kicks it off the wall), and bring it back to camp. In a phallically cathected scene, the girls then use the penis substitutes of a sledgehammer and a crowbar to break open the machine. The girls' effective use of these phallic substitutes both highlights their sexual power and undercuts that power by aligning it with masculinity and its symbols rather than with symbols of femininity.

The condom theme is reinforced throughout the film: on parents' visiting day, one shocked mother opens her daughter's drawer to find it full of the stolen condoms. Tellingly, however, she says nothing to the girl of her discovery, perhaps reflecting the "at least she's using birth control" attitude that was a staple of 1970s and 1980s American television series.[43] She also says nothing to her husband about her find, perhaps also reflecting the retro notion that birth control is a concern for women, not men.

More significantly, when Angel and Randy are first planning to have sex, Angel is extremely insistent upon—and unapologetic for—the use of condoms: "Oh, this is for you," she says as she hands Randy a condom. Randy looks nonplussed. "It's so I don't get pregnant, stupid," she continues. In the same vein, when she later sends Randy off to disrobe, she reminds him to come back wearing the condom she has provided: "Just don't forget the stuff in the package, OK?" Then, when Randy starts pressuring her to speed things along, Angel's impassioned rejoinder reinforces the importance of using condoms and the consequences of not doing so: "Don't yell at me! And if you forget to put that thing on, I swear I'll kill you. I'm not getting myself pregnant. I'm not ready to take care of some guy's brat. I don't know what's with men—they never come prepared. They think it's the woman's responsibility or something." Angel's matter-of-fact attitude toward condom use here suggests that girls are intelligent enough to know the facts of life and to take steps to prevent unwanted pregnancies. Moreover, Angel's extreme sensitivity toward the possibility of unplanned teen pregnancy suggests that she herself may have been an unplanned child. While that is not made explicit in the film (in fact, we learn that her mother is forty and hence must have been a respectable twenty-five when she had Angel), there is no mention of Angel's father in the film, and we learn that Angel's single mother has been seeing a series of unsuitable men.

In contrast, Ferris, the romantic who doesn't wind up having sex, is somewhat disassociated from the condoms in *Little Darlings*. While she does go on the condom-collecting run with the other girls, and while she does help gather up the condoms from the broken machine, we don't see her bringing any condoms to her planned tryst with Mr. Callahan. This "forgetfulness" may imply a subconscious desire on Ferris's part not to have sex, but more likely it reflects her overly romanticized view of the sex act: while Angel, the realist, baldly acknowledges the probable consequences of unprotected sex, Ferris, the romantic, resolutely ignores them. This second interpretation of Ferris's "forgetfulness" is supported by the fact that her fictional account of her sexual initiation by Mr. Callahan also neglects any mention of birth control.

Virginity Loss and Guidance from Older Teens and Adults

The protagonists of these films get little effective guidance about sex from the adults in their lives and are thus forced to consult older teens, who prove just as unreliable. In *Fast Times at Ridgemont High*, Stacy's parents exist mainly as taskmasters from afar (the ones who send messages to clean the pool), and their absence means there are few obstacles to Stacy's romantic life—Stacy is able to try to seduce Rat because her parents are out of town, and they are likewise absent when Ron Johnson sends her flowers, when Rat and Damone drop by, when she and Damone have sex, and when she needs a ride to the clinic for her abortion. Stacy's clueless mother is briefly shown kissing her goodnight—just before Stacy sneaks out her bedroom window to lose her virginity to Ron Johnson. Instead of her parents, Stacy uses Linda, her older, engaged friend and coworker, as her main source of sexual information, but this information is clearly marked as suspect as well. As noted earlier, Linda doesn't even seem to know if she has had orgasms. Moreover, in a scene in which the girls are both slicing an enormous salami (offering a striking visual parallel to the way in which their commentary cuts male sexual prowess down to size), Linda gives contradictory answers when Stacy asks her how long it takes for Linda and her fiancé to have sex, indicating that Linda has been exaggerating considerably about her partner's sexual stamina.

In *Little Darlings*, however, the girls do ask for virginity-loss advice from adults, but the advice they receive isn't particularly helpful. For instance, in a scene that is oddly reminiscent of a Tampax commercial of the time (with girls dressed in white picking flowers in a field), Ferris asks trusted female counselor Diane (Troas Hayes) whether she "would . . . be different afterwards" and gets the advice: "Just don't do it until you're in love." The message she takes from this is: "So, if I'm in love, you think it'll be all right?" Given Ferris's romantic nature, however, it is hard for one to imagine her having sex with anyone with whom she doesn't think she's in love; therefore, paradoxically, the practical effect of this advice is to encourage Ferris to have sex with anyone she fancies.

Paradoxically, tough girl Angel is the only character in these films who asks her mother about sex, but the advice she receives is hardly what one might wish:

ANGEL: When did . . . you lose your virginity? I just want to know.

ANGEL'S MOM: I know I must have been at least nineteen.

ANGEL: Nineteen?

ANGEL'S MOM: It was nothing. It still is . . . nothing.

ANGEL: Then what's everybody making such a big deal about it for?

ANGEL'S MOM: [Sound indicating "I don't know."]

Although Angel seems to accept this advice when it is given, after she has experienced the intimacy of sex for herself, she explicitly rejects her mother's advice and sagely challenges her mother to start dating nicer men. The switch in advisor/advisee roles here suggests that Angel's perspective is the correct one: the film posits that sex *is* a big deal for women of any age and that women would be wise to remember that.

Virgins, "Born-Again Virgins," and the Empowering Decision Not to Have Sex (or Not to Have Sex Anymore)

Both of these films feature girls who eventually decide not to have sex or not to keep on having sex: Ferris is persuaded by Gary that it's fine to wait; Stacy decides she doesn't want to have sex with Rat after all; and Angel decides that she doesn't want to continue having sex or even a relationship with Randy, even after their misunderstanding about the contest is cleared up. Stacy's and Angel's decisions to stop having sex are particularly interesting in light of the popular view of virginity as a sort of irreversible process. Once you've had sex once, one theory goes, what's the point in not having it some more? It's not like you have any virginity left to preserve. Yet these texts, while they come almost two full decades before the "born-again virgin" movement described earlier and chronicled by Wendy Keller in 1999, espouse its most important tenet—making "the choice to *make sex a choice again* instead of" something that is done simply because it is expected.[44] The decision to stop having sex (or not to have it in the first place) seems to act as a tool of feminist empowerment for the protagonists of these films. Stacy hardly gives up the role of romantic initiator—she just tones things down a bit. As they start their summer jobs again, she motions Rat over from across the mall, gives him a pretty (but not overtly sexual) picture of herself, tells him to call her over the summer, and gives him a kiss. He tries to play it cool, but his expression after she turns away is one of pure delight, and as the film's epilogue makes clear, Stacy's flirtation with him proves entirely successful. On the one hand, the film's approbation of women's making the first move here stands in stark contrast to later, less feminist dating-advice trends, such as the "don't call him and rarely return his calls" strategy advocated in Ellen Fein and Sherri Schneider's 1995 best-selling tome *The Rules: Time-Tested Secrets for Capturing the Heart of Mr. Right*, advice that has apparently now carried Fein right past her notorious divorce and into a recent second marriage.[45] On the other hand, Fein and Schneider do advocate that "*Rules* girls" hold off on having sex with potential romantic partners for a while—Rule 15 is "Don't rush into sex"—which dovetails with Stacy's decision to take her time.[46]

As a counterexample to the happiness that Stacy finds due to her eventual sexual restraint, Stacy's "experienced" friend, Linda, who has a much older boyfriend and whom the film generally constructs as "oversexed," as Timothy Shary notes, comes to grief.[47] We find out near the end of the film that her boyfriend has refused to attend her high school graduation, which clearly pains her. Although the "where-are-they-now?" sequence assures us that Linda is attending college, it also informs us that she is "living with her abnormal psych professor," a life choice that one suspects will not lead her to permanent happiness.

Early 1980s Representations of Girls' Sexual Decision Making

In *Little Darlings,* giving up on sex for the moment allows all the girls in the film (except for Cinder) to gain access to female solidarity and close female friendships. Indeed, their rejection of sex and its commodification as the object of female competition is what allows Angel and Ferris to communicate honestly and to overcome their enmity. It is also what allows all of the rest of the girls to resist Cinder, who is portrayed as the representative of a patriarchal system that plays women against each other. The implication of this dynamic is that homosocial and heterosexual relationships are fundamentally incompatible and that homosocial relationships are the more important ones.

Conclusions: Films of Their Era

In their portrayal of empowered, reasoning, sexually curious girls who decide to lose their virginity and who then decide to stop having sex, these two films show a respect for their characters and their audiences that is sadly lacking in many films and television programs of the later 1980s, 1990s, and beyond. As such, these films reflect a fleeting moment in history between the sexual liberation movement of the 1970s and the advent of the AIDS crisis in the 1980s, a moment when young women had perhaps their greatest taste of sexual freedom.

Certainly, Stacy's determination not to have the baby resulting from her casual sex with Damone contrasts enormously with protagonists' decisions in two 2007 films, *Knocked Up* and *Juno,* which feature similar situations. In *Knocked Up,* young career woman Alison (Katherine Heigl) gets pregnant after a one-night stand with slacker Ben (Seth Rogen); she decides to keep her baby despite the probable negative effects this choice will have on her career.[48] While abortion is never seriously considered in the film, it is raised as a possibility, if only so it can be rejected as an option. The heroine's mother, who is presented as an obnoxious woman, vehemently urges the heroine to "take care of it," speaks well of a relative's earlier decision to have an abortion, and praises the fact that this relative now has "real children" as opposed to illegitimate progeny. One of the hero's loser buddies is also in favor of termination but acknowledges his listeners' delicacy by not saying the word aloud, instead suggesting a "schmaschmortion." The net effect of these suggestions is that, although the film appears to give the option of abortion fair play, it is overdetermined as an unappealing option, espoused only by a status-conscious harpy and a clueless man-child.

This lack of abortion as a potential option in contemporary film and on television programs has been recently addressed by Mireya Navarro in a *New York Times* article inspired by the unwanted but kept pregnancies in *Waitress* (2007) and in *Knocked Up*. Navarro points out that the dearth of abortion on the big and small screens may be due to market pressures—fear of losing audiences and fear of losing advertisers.[49] Even more interesting is the letter from Laura Meyers, who identifies herself as "the C.E.O. of a Planned Parenthood affiliate," that appears in the *New York Times Magazine* on the same date as Navarro's article. While her letter bemoans the "agonizing decisions" faced by women who have "an unwanted pregnancy," Meyers, just like the young man in *Knocked Up*, won't say the "A-word" or even specify further what those "agonizing decisions" might be. Instead of touting the availability of abortion, Meyers's letter simply reminds readers of, as she puts it, "ways to prevent . . . pregnancy: everything from abstinence, condom use and birth-control methods to emergency contraception after unprotected sex."[50] It is a telling statement about the social acceptability of presenting abortion as an option in public discourse these days when even the head of a Planned Parenthood affiliate won't mention it directly.

Clearly, there is a powerful chilling effect on all members of a society, both anti-abortion and pro-choice, when abortion generally cannot be shown on film or on television. (The opposing view—that the current lack of abortion in film is simply an artistic choice and not reflective of any societal anxieties or self-censorship—was represented by a letter to the editor in the *New York Times* one week later, in which Eva Nyqvist rather disingenuously writes, "I don't think Hollywood shuns the topic of abortion in fear of anything but boredom. Abortion is not—as a plot point—interesting or dramatic enough, and certainly not funny.")[51] Finally, the particular way in which the heroine of *Knocked Up* gets pregnant is as problematic as the fact that abortion is not presented as a real choice in the film. On the one hand, *Knocked Up* sets up the fact of the pregnancy as both partners' fault equally and as the result of a misunderstanding. Dead drunk, Ben fumbles awkwardly with a condom wrapper, causing the equally dead drunk Alison to yell, "Just do it already!" He misunderstands and has sex with her without a condom, drunkenly thinking that is what she is requesting, whereas she simply means that he should open the condom wrapper more quickly. Yet on the other hand, Ben's decision to forge ahead without using birth control or protection against sexually transmitted diseases with a partner he's just met (no matter what he thinks Alison has said) is stunningly irresponsible and suggests that even grown men are sometimes incapable of the thoughtful sexual decision making that the young women of *Fast Times* and *Little Darlings* are eventually able to manage.

Likewise, the recent popular and critically acclaimed film *Juno* is similarly problematic in its portrayal of teen sexual decision making about intercourse, birth control, and abortion. In that film, the title character, sixteen-year-old Juno (Ellen Page), is generally presented as a witty, intelligent, extremely self-actualized teen. The film repeatedly makes clear that the single act of unprotected sex with her nebbishy friend Paulie (Michael Cera) that gets Juno pregnant is her idea, ostensibly her way to cure boredom on a dull afternoon. Juno's uncharacteristic lapse of common sense in not using birth control seems entirely unmotivated and is never sufficiently explained in the film (which is admittedly more concerned with the aftermath of the pregnancy than with exactly how it occurred). Because we never quite see what has led up to Juno's decision to have sex (and because the sex itself is only briefly shown in flashbacks consisting of fragmented, de-sexualized shots), the audience is left with the impression that the otherwise capable Juno (who is portrayed as extremely efficient in obtaining pregnancy tests and in planning an adoptive placement for her baby before she even tells her parents that she's pregnant) has simply had an attack of stupidity in her decision to have sex without protection.[52] This seems particularly odd, as she claims to have planned her seduction of Paulie up to a year earlier—did she not once during that year think about procuring some birth control?

Juno and her best friend initially assume that she will obtain an abortion, and with Paulie's blessing to do whatever she thinks best, she visits the local clinic. Outside, however, she runs into her abortion-protester classmate Su-Chin (Valerie Tian), who tells her that the fetus "probably has a beating heart . . . and [that] it has fingernails." Then, when the vapid clinic receptionist flippantly offers Juno some flavored condoms (a little late!) and doesn't make Juno feel welcome, based on Su-Chin's "fingernails" argument, Juno decides against the abortion. While Su-Chin is portrayed as grammatically challenged and as rather vapid herself, she wins the battle over Juno's uterus here. Interestingly, Juno later entirely disavows her initial impulse to get an abortion. When her stepmother gently asks, "Honey, had you considered, you know, the alternative?" Juno lies and says she hasn't; the implication is that she is ashamed of having ever even considered having an abortion. The change from the abortion clinic scene in *Fast Times* is palpable: instead of kind, capable clinic workers and a successful abortion that brings the family unit closer together, we see in *Juno* an incompetent clinic worker and Juno's shame at admitting even the possibility of abortion to her family.

Juno does resemble the protagonists of *Little Darlings* and *Fast Times at Ridgemont High* in one significant way, however. After her one sexual encounter with Paulie, she decides not to have sex with him (or anyone) anymore, apparently even before she finds out that she's pregnant. Even after Juno and Paulie reconnect after a period of estrangement (she holds him at arm's length during most of the pregnancy, even though he tries to be supportive), and even though she decides that she's in love with him, the film's end implies that they still aren't necessarily having sex—their romance seems to consist more of kissing and playing their guitars together. In this respect, Paulie and Juno's position at the film's end seems quite similar to Rat and Stacy's position at the end of *Fast Times at Ridgemont High:* both films postulate that teens can have healthy, fulfilling romantic relationships without necessarily rushing into having sex.

It is ironic, though perhaps appropriate, that the brief age of sexual freedom without fear in the early 1980s produced some of the best rationales for not rushing into sex. Perhaps we should not be surprised at this apparent irony, however, as it may simply reflect the aims of real-life health-care educators trying to help teens who were making decisions about becoming sexually active in those heady times. The *Maclean's* story on teen sex in 1980, for instance, details many cases where sex educators' duties included counseling teens (and sometimes preteens) on their right not to have sex.[53] The women's movement, after all, while sometimes portrayed by its detractors as an attack on motherhood, really encompasses the right for mothers to choose to work or to stay home, as they think is best. Accordingly, rather than deriding *Little Darlings* and *Fast Times at Ridgemont High* as merely exploitative, one can value them as two of the most truly feminist teen films.

Notes

1. Chuck Kleinhans, "Girls on the Edge of the Reagan Era," in *Sugar, Spice and Everything Nice: Cinemas of Girlhood*, ed. Frances Gateward and Murray Pomerance (Detroit: Wayne State University Press, 2002), 73. "Just say no" was a phrase originally used to kick off the Reagan administration's slogan for Nancy Reagan's advertising campaign against teenage drug use in 1983. Philip H. Dougherty, "Drug Drive Outlined to First Lady," *New York Times*, October 12, 1983, D22. By the

Early 1980s Representations of Girls' Sexual Decision Making

late 1980s, however, the phrase had been adapted to describe both governmental campaigns and societal expectations promoting teenage sexual abstinence. Susan N. Wilson, "Teen-Agers and AIDS: Protection, Yes, But How?" *New York Times,* January 8, 1989, NJ24; Ronnie Wacker, "Suffolk Teen-Agers Find Responsibility Begins with an Egg," *New York Times,* February 14, 1988, A1.

2. Jim Craddock, review of *Little Darlings, VideoHound's Golden Movie Retriever: The Complete Guide to Movies on Videocassette and DVD* (Detroit, MI: Gale Group/Thomson Learning, 2002), 431.

3. I was probably one of the only thirteen-year-olds in America who saw *Little Darlings* legally when it first came out—my older cousins persuaded my Dad to take me after a huge family fight at a Passover seder. I can't imagine many other parents taking their children—a friend's mother refused to let her go with us when she found out what film we were seeing.

4. Jack Kroll, review of *Fast Times at Ridgemont High, Newsweek,* September 20, 1982, 96.

5. David Denby, "Growing Up Absurd," review of *Fast Times at Ridgemont High,* New York, September 27, 1982, 50.

6. Pauline Kael, review of *Fast Times at Ridgemont High, New Yorker,* November 1, 1982, 146.

7. Janet Maslin, review of *Fast Times at Ridgemont High, New York Times,* September 3, 1982, C6.

8. David Ansen, review of *Little Darlings, Newsweek,* March 24, 1980, 79.

9. "B.G.," review of *Little Darlings, New Yorker,* March 31, 1980, 108.

10. Frank Rich, review of *Little Darlings, Time,* March 31, 1980, 84.

11. Lawrence O'Toole, review of *Little Darlings, Maclean's,* March 31, 1980, 50; Janet Maslin, review of *Little Darlings, New York Times,* March 28, 1980, C15 (italics mine).

12. David Denby, review of *Little Darlings, New York,* April 7, 1980, 86–87.

13. Karen G. Jackovich, "Kristy McNichol Leaves the 'Family' Hour Behind for a Pad of Her Own and an 'R' Rating," *People,* March 31, 1980, 90.

14. Judith Timson, "Teen Sex," *Maclean's,* March 31, 1980, 39.

15. Ibid.; Johanson quoted in ibid.

16. Timothy Shary, *Generation Multiplex: The Image of Youth in Contemporary American Cinema* (Austin: University of Texas Press, 2002), 30–31.

17. Gayle Wald, "Clueless in the Neocolonial World Order," in *Sugar, Spice and Everything Nice: Cinemas of Girlhood,* ed. Frances Gateward and Murray Pomerance (Detroit: Wayne State University Press, 2002), 103.

18. It is perhaps due to their extreme positions on the class ladder that both Angel and Ferris are excluded from the otherwise solidly middle-class world of the camp. Both girls arrive late to the camp bus in aberrant cars (Angel in a battered Chevy convertible; Ferris in a Rolls Royce), and both girls are teased by the other girls for their clothing: Angel wears a denim jacket and black tank top, while Ferris wears a precious white outfit with matching beret. Cinder also later teases Ferris for the "pure" nightgown her mother picked out and Angel for not having many clothes to put away—two further stabs at the girls' class status.

19. David M. Considine, *The Cinema of Adolescence* (Jefferson, NC: McFarland, 1985), 269.

20. In response to Cinder's implication that sexually experienced women somehow magically know when another woman has had sex, Sunshine also tells a fib that showcases her sexual naïveté: "When *I* became a woman, my eyes tilted."

21. While it reflects well on Ferris and Angel as moral beings that they do not want the mostly innocent Mr. Callahan (he is a bit of a flirt) to suffer unfairly, it is interesting that their main concern is the protection of a *man's* job.

22. Kristen Hatch, "Little Butches: The Tomboy Film in the 1970s" (Paper presented at the Society for Cinema and Media Studies Annual Conference, Atlanta, GA, March 4, 2004); Kleinhans, "Girls on the Edge of the Reagan Era," 80.

23. The only girls who reject watching the boys skinny-dipping are ten-year-old Penny and Angel, both of whom look disgusted.

24. Boston Women's Health Book Collective, *Our Bodies, Ourselves: A Book by and for Women*, 2nd ed. (New York: Simon and Schuster, 1979), 41–43, 47–48.

25. Ibid., 47.

26. Helen Gurley Brown, *Having It All: Love—Success—Sex—Money, Even If You're Starting with Nothing* (New York: Simon and Schuster, 1982), 219–27.

27. Ibid., 210–11, and 211 (italics in original).

28. Ibid., 245.

29. Ibid., 362.

30. Ibid., 214.

31. Ibid., 246.

32. Sonia Pilcer, *Little Darlings*, based on the screenplay by Kimi Peck and Dalene [*sic*] Young, story by Kimi Peck (New York: Ballantine, 1980), 157.

33. The girls in *Little Darlings* are similarly focused on pleasing boys at all costs. Angel, for example, receives a great deal of suspect advice: "Don't talk about your past; that turns men off. . . . Don't get personal with him." She's also told to watch her cake consumption so that she doesn't get fat. This provides an eerie echo of Helen Gurley Brown's advice to women in *Having It All:* "It is unthinkable that a woman bent on having it all would want to be fat, or even plump" (96).

34. Jon Lewis, *The Road to Romance and Ruin: Teen Films and Youth Culture* (New York: Routledge, 1992), 73; Kleinhans, "Girls on the Edge of the Reagan Era," 75.

35. Interestingly, the graphic sex scene with Damone was apparently cut considerably because it "made the young women in the preview audiences uncomfortable." Chris Chase, "At the Movies: Jennifer Leigh [*sic*] and Her Trip from X to R," *New York Times*, September 3, 1982, C6. According to Jennifer Jason Leigh's description of the original scene, "[Damone] is a virgin, which no one in the movie is supposed to know, and it's his first attempt at love making, and it's very awkward, shallow, awful. But funny, too." Quoted in Chase, "At the Movies," C6. Although the film might have been even better with that scene left intact, cutting it may have helped the film's box office considerably, since it allowed the film to avoid a hardcore "X" rating (no one under 18 admitted) for the more inclusive "R" rating, opening the film up to older teens and mainstream movie theaters. Chase, "At the Movies," C6.

36. Wendy Keller, *The Cult of the Born-Again Virgin: How Single Women Can*

Reclaim Their Sexual Power (Deerfield Beach, FL: Health Communications, 1999), 11–15.

37. Mireya Navarro's *New York Times* article notes that a character on the American soap opera *General Hospital* did actually have an abortion in 2006, but that seems to have been a special case: Navarro describes Nancy Lee Grahn, the actress who played that character, as "a longtime abortion rights advocate . . . who said she had an abortion in her 20s." Navarro, "On Abortion, Hollywood Is No-Choice," *New York Times,* sec. 9, June 10, 2007, 8. One imagines that the actress's personal stake in this plot arc contributed to its airing. Navarro also mentions that the American television programs *Everwood* and *Six Feet Under* have "presented the subject," but she gives no details as to how. Ibid.

38. The obvious counterexample is the famous 1972 episode of the feminist sitcom *Maude* in which the middle-aged Maude, mother of a grown-up daughter, finds herself unexpectedly pregnant and does have an abortion. What was possible to show on the air in 1972, however, does not seem to have been possible to show on the air in the 1980s. For more on the shift in the mid to late 1980s to films where teens keep their babies and reject abortion, see Shary, *Generation Multiplex*, 247–54. Indeed, Shary notes only three films of the early 1980s that feature teen abortions, and one of those is *Fast Times* (the others are *The Last American Virgin* [dir. Boaz Davidson, 1982] and *Teachers* [dir. Arthur Hiller, 1984]). Shary, *Generation Multiplex*, 247–48.

39. According to Shary, it is also "the *first* positive depiction of teen abortion in American youth cinema." Shary, *Generation Multiplex,* 247 (italics mine).

40. As both Nina Leibman and Timothy Shary discuss, earlier films such as *Blue Denim* (dir. Philip Dunne, 1959) portray abortion as quite a negative choice. Nina Leibman, "The Way We Weren't: Abortion 1950s Style in *Blue Denim* and *Our Time,*" *Velvet Light Trap* 29 (Spring 1992): 33–34; Shary, *Generation Multiplex,* 246–47. Indeed, Leibman notes that *Blue Denim* ultimately makes the decision for or against abortion the *man's* choice (33–34).

41. On the one hand, we might think that Stacy does not call upon Linda for a ride to the clinic because Linda is too young to drive as well, but this is unlikely: we learn later in the film that Linda is about to graduate from high school this year. On the other hand, Linda does provide solidarity in female vengeance—she apparently spray-paints Damone's car with the word *prick* and his locker with *little prick* in retaliation for his not giving Stacy a ride to the clinic.

42. Boston Women's Health Book Collective, *Our Bodies, Ourselves,* 216–21, 223–34, and 221 (italics and exclamation point in original).

43. The sitcom *One Day at a Time* and the family drama *Eight Is Enough,* for instance, both portrayed teenage girls' obtaining birth control with their parents' knowledge and ambivalent consent. That became rarer in later years, although the feminist sitcom *Roseanne* boasted a similar episode.

44. Keller, *Cult of the Born-Again Virgin,* xxi–xxii (italics in original).

45. Lois Smith Brady, "Vows: Ellen Fein and Lance Houpt," *New York Times,* Weddings/Celebrations, August 10, 2008, 13; Ellen Fein and Sherrie Schneider, *All the Rules: Time-Tested Secrets for Capturing the Heart of Mr. Right* [*The Rules* and *The Rules II* combined ed.] (New York: Grand Central, 1995, 1997), 42.

46. Fein and Schneider have a much less feminist agenda than Wendy Keller does, however, when they advise women not to rush into sex. Their advice is predicated on the idea that it is a means to one particular end—marriage: "We know it can be excruciating to put sex off with someone you're attracted to, but you must think long term here. If you play your cards right, you can have sex with him every night for the rest of your life when you're married!" they crow. Fein and Schneider, *All the Rules*, 79.

47. Shary, *Generation Multiplex*, 228.

48. Ironically, the kept pregnancy actually helps Alison's broadcasting career, signifying to the film's viewers that keeping one's initially unwanted pregnancy is a sound career move.

49. Navarro, "On Abortion, Hollywood Is No-Choice," 8.

50. Laura Meyers, letter, *New York Times Magazine*, June 10, 2007, 8.

51. Eva Nyqvist, letter, *New York Times Magazine*, sec. 9, June 17, 2007, 11.

52. The flashback shots do underscore the fact that Juno is entirely in control of the sex act: she drops her underwear across the room from Paulie, keeps her shirt on, and straddles him in a chair, while he seems not to move at all other than to pop some orange Tic Tacs. (This woman-on-top position is an interesting signifier of Juno's position of control, though it seems to pose some practical difficulties for hymen breaking.) In this respect, on the one hand, Juno differs from the women of *Fast Times* and *Little Darlings*, who lose their virginity willingly but with men taking the lead in the sex act. On the other hand, Juno resembles the protagonists of these earlier films in her lack of sexual pleasure: Juno claims that Paulie is good "in chair," but the viewer never sees anything to suggest that he gives her an orgasm or anything approaching one.

53. Timson, "Teen Sex," 39, 41, 43, 46. Notes Timson, "What is puzzling and ultimately disappointing to many female birth control counselors is that the past decade of feminism has not resulted in more assertive young females" (43).

Shelley Cobb

Was She or Wasn't She?

Virginity and Identity in the Critical Reception of *Elizabeth* (1998)

On a first viewing, Shekhar Kapur's *Elizabeth* (1998) is a film about the Virgin Queen in which virginity makes an appearance only in the final ten minutes. Up to that point, Elizabeth as both princess and queen engages in a passionate affair with Sir Robert Dudley, earl of Leicester, its romantic height presented through a sex scene on what appears to be the night of her coronation. Having rejected Dudley (upon learning he has a wife) and all other suitors and having executed all conspirators in the Norfolk rebellion (except Dudley), the queen's advisor, Walsingham, finds her in church, under a statue of the Virgin Mary, and she asks, "Am I to be made of stone? Must I be touched by nothing?" He answers, "Yes, to reign supreme. All men need something greater than themselves. They need to be able to touch the divine, here on earth." It is then that she transforms herself from the youthful, lively, and passionate young queen into the ornate, stiff, and imperious Virgin Queen—her whitened skin, painted face, stiff red wig, and her heavily elaborate dress, ruff, and jewels constructing her into the familiar icon presented in the famous Ditchley Armada portrait of 1592[1]—and declares to her former advisor, Lord Burghley, "I am married. To England." The preceding transformation scene lasts only a few minutes, but it is presented as the climax of the film, with its extreme close-ups, quick crosscutting, dramatic music, and emotionalism: it begins with Elizabeth's head bent forward, her neck exposed as if for execution, and her hair flowing freely. She lifts up her head, her face stoic, and her lady-in-waiting Kat cuts Elizabeth's hair till it is shorn short (a process that parallels the shearing of the female protestant martyr's hair before her burning in the opening credit sequence). Kat does her job with tears streaming down her face. The cutting of Elizabeth's hair is crosscut with various scenes from throughout her reign, ending with images from the first moments that she is introduced in the film: Elizabeth and Dudley dancing, smiling, laughing, and romancing in the open fields. At the end of this sequence, we see Elizabeth in a medium shot, her hair shorn, her makeup white, wearing a smocklike garment with no jewelry or other adornments. Her eyes are rimmed red with tears. She speaks the infamous line, "I have become a virgin."

The contrast from the images of Elizabeth's youthful sexuality with Dudley, when she still wore her long hair down, wore less ornate dresses, and was pale but flushed naturally, to her presentation at court as the icon, the Virgin Queen, inverts our expectations of the narrative of female sexual maturity. In the film, sexual activity is associated with youth; virginity with age. The film presents virginity, not as a biological state existing at birth that can be lost, but as a life choice, an image that can be acquired through an act of self-presentation, defying our traditional ideas of what virginity is. Of course, women have always found ways to subvert the patriarchal value of virginity by "faking" its supposed signs (timing wedding nights with periods, cutting labia to create scabs that will bleed with intercourse.[2] Despite ongoing myths about the hymen, virginity is not and never has been an easily verifiable physical fact, even in eras and places where its value is rated much higher than it is in present-day Western society.[3] However, in contemporary Western society, where virginity as a state of being is no longer the cultural necessity it once was and where those women (with enough money) who see it as an individual necessity can choose "hymen-rejuvenation" surgery, the film's portrayal of Elizabeth's adoption of virginity did not instigate questions about the nature of virginity and how one might "become a virgin." Instead, as this chapter will discuss, the declaration of virginity and transformation from sexually active Elizabeth to Virgin Queen became metonymic in the reception discourse of various concerns for cultural identity raised by the film's presentation of history, spectacle/heritage, and women. First, and most predictably, it raised the "was she or wasn't she" question of Queen Elizabeth's lifelong virginity, and the dislocation of the Virgin Queen from virginity per se was where "the tension between official history and filmic narrative came into sharpest focus."[4] The defense of her honor as a representative of English history was ardent in some quarters, but in others the film was deemed all the better for its dismissal of official history. Second, as one of the most spectacular moments in a film with many, critics presented it as emblematic of the

The carefree, younger *Elizabeth:* Cate Blanchett as the queen in Shekhar Kapur's 1998 film.

The older Elizabeth realizes the political power of chastity: "I have become a virgin."

changes in what was successfully exportable English cinema: from the slow, reverential, literary films of the 1980s (represented by the successful Merchant Ivory adaptations) to the films of "Cool Britannia" associated with Tony Blair's New Labour government (such as *Trainspotting,* 1996). Third and most vociferous was the discourse the film generated about contemporary women. *Elizabeth*'s refashioning of herself as virgin raised questions about the feminist benefits of gender performativity for women's power in our highly mediated culture as well as the postfeminist debates about "having it all." Blanchett's queen was compared to varying female media figures, but she was most often compared to two English icons who have been considered both feminist and antifeminist: Princess Diana and Margaret Thatcher.

Virginity and History

Debate over the historical accuracy of *Elizabeth* (or rather its pointed lack of accuracy) was a starting point or centerpiece for many reviews of the film. The director, Kapur, said, "People are saying I have sullied her reputation. . . . I read it in the press all the time."[5] And in many reviews "prominent Tudor historians . . . were duly trotted out" in order to contest the film's authenticity and defend the Virgin Queen's honor.[6] One of the historians quoted was Alison Weir, author of many biographies of Tudor royalty, including one on the life of Elizabeth I published near the film's release date. When asked about the love scenes in the film, she responded, "It's rubbish! . . . The queen would have been scandalized by such behavior."[7] Some of the more frustrated were American historians quoted in American newspaper reviews. The *Washington Post* quotes Marvin Breslow of the University of Maryland, who says, "There's just so much gratuitous inaccuracy . . . none of it to any purpose. . . . Elizabeth is interesting and compelling herself. You don't need to screw it up this badly."[8]

Elizabeth begins with the future queen's life as a protestant princess under her Catholic sister (Bloody) Mary's reign. The film opens dramatically with the burning of protestant heretics. Princess Elizabeth survives imprisonment at her sister's command to inherit the crown at the age of twenty-five upon Mary's death. As queen she endures the pressures of her councilors and foreign ambassadors to marry; the power of the Catholic clergy as she passes the Act of Uniformity; a lost war with Scotland to which her military sent young boys to fight; multiple assassination attempts (at least one approved by the pope); the duke of Norfolk's plot to overthrow her, in which her beloved Dudley is implicated; and her decision to kill all those involved in the plot, except Dudley, whom she keeps around to remind herself how close she came to losing the throne. When compared with histories of Queen Elizabeth I's life and reign, the film compresses timelines and chronologies, moving events that happened after the film's end (approximately 1563) into the narrative, such as the Norfolk rebellion; retiring William Cecil into Lord Burghley early; conflating characters and events (the Duc d'Anjou with his brother Henry III and Mary of Guise with her daughter Mary Queen of Scots); and including Dudley in the Norfolk rebellion when there is no evidence that he was part of this.[9]

There are a myriad of historical inaccuracies for the reviews to pick on, but they always mention the problem of the queen's virginity, even when it appears that they do not mean to. In Michael Farquhar's piece on history, he takes on the film's lack of veracity and declares, "Start with the entire premise of the film: The formerly lusty young Elizabeth was stunned into becoming a frigid, born-again virgin because of a hideous conspiracy involving her lover, Robert Dudley. Never happened. Professor Mack Holt of George Mason University calls the very idea of Dudley being involved in any plot to kill the queen 'ludicrous.'"[10] The structure of this sentence leads us to think that it is her "born-again" virginity and Dudley's role as the queen's lover that "never happened," but the historian's comments are directed toward Dudley's involvement in a treasonous plot. This displacement of the truth of her virginity onto the multiple "untruths" of the film seems to be an admission to the ultimate answer to the question of "was she or wasn't she," which, as Kathryn Schwarz simply puts it, is "how, after all, could we know?"[11]

In this respect, many other reviewers agreed with Tom Shone of the *Sunday Times*, who pronounced that "no historical drama can be said to have done its job, I think, unless it causes at least a dozen historians to tear their hair out."[12] Kapur suggests that they kept this view of history and historians in mind during the making of the film: "Whether she was or wasn't a virgin I think is unimportant. . . . She had at least three very well documented relationships. No reason has ever been given for her not having consummated her virginity. . . . History has not proved she was not a virgin."[13] A few well-known historians reject Shone's hopes; Weir, quoted earlier, was presented by the article as being a fan of the film: "In reviewing the cinematic Elizabeths, Weir counts Blanchett's among the best. 'She does a superb job,' said the author. . . .' She obviously studied the character.'"[14] Even David Starkey, whom the "incensed" *Daily Telegraph* quoted to refute the love scenes, writes in a piece for the *Sunday Times,* "The film shows Cate Blanchett's Elizabeth having sex with Robert Dudley. Something like this almost certainly happened. Or perhaps it was just, in the Clintonesque formulation, that Dudley had sex with her even though she didn't have it with him."[15] The reference to the Clinton-Lewinsky affair is not unique. President Clinton's public dissembling over how to define sexual relations strikes multiple reviewers as a contemporary parallel to the film's portrayal of Elizabeth I's fabrication of virginity. Kapur mentions it in an interview: "Even the President of the United States cannot be human anymore."[16]

Legal definitions of sexual relations and physical evidence of virginity share the problem of being extremely subjective. And in the late twentieth century there is much debate about how much personal sexual morality is important for public life. The question of "does it or doesn't it matter" regarding personal sexual morality in a way parallels some of the debates about how important, and even how possible, detailed historical accuracy is for a historical film. For the critical reception of *Elizabeth,* the question of whether the queen was a virgin transmutes into the question of whether it *matters* if she was or wasn't, which for the film reflects the perennial debate among historians, cultural commentators, and film scholars over the question of whether it matters if historical films get their history "right."

Virginity and Heritage

For several film academics, *Elizabeth* came to be emblematic of "a new stage in the development of the quality 'British' costume drama of the 1980s and 1990s" that was linked to other films such as *The Madness of King George* (1994) and *Mrs. Brown* (1997).[17] Still, there is much debate about what does and does not constitute the characteristics of British cinema and heritage cinema, as well as which films should and should not be included in those designations, or even the usefulness of those designations in regard to production, distribution, and content.[18] *Elizabeth*'s place in those debates was not always unreservedly accepted. In his book *English Heritage, English Cinema: Costume Drama since 1980,* Andrew Higson writes, "The film-makers hoped to attract . . . a street-wise youthful audience and a politically aware feminist audience—neither of which are conventionally thought of as the core audience for romantic costume dramas or historical period pieces. Is this then really the sort of film I should be addressing at length in this book?"[19] The disconcerted tone of Higson's comments suggests that the film had a potential shock value for adherents to a certain view on heritage cinema. This view of (English) heritage cinema includes an emphasis on "manners and proprieties" of the upper middle class, particularly of the Victorian era, using the slow pacing of European art cinema, the luxurious landscapes of the epic, and the conventional narrative structure of mainstream drama. In many ways, *Elizabeth* broke with the expectations of English heritage cinema and more than one scholar, and several reviewers directly compared its differences to the Merchant Ivory films of the 1980s, as James Chapman does:

[*Elizabeth*] was far less bound by the discourse of historical authenticity than most biopics . . . [and] is a film of remarkable cultural confidence and visual power—characteristics widely attributed to its Indian director, making his first English-language film—that represents a departure from the restrained and sober style of the heritage cinema of the previous decade. In contrast to what is often referred to as the Merchant-Ivory style of film-making, with its literary pedigree and overriding theme of emotional repression, *Elizabeth* is notable for its highly "filmic" style and for its daring representation of Elizabethan England as a hotbed of political intrigue and sexual passion.[20]

Stella Bruzzi, in her *Sight and Sound* review, suggests that the film's differences destabilize one of the main qualities of heritage cinema: reverence for England and Englishness. She argues, "[The film] is marked by its distance rather than veneration for its subject."[21] This sets the film in distinct opposition to a generally accepted idea of English heritage films (as exemplified by the Merchant Ivory productions) as promoting the preservation of English history and national identity. For many critics, the film seemed to explicitly and intently reject that mode of cinema: "*Elizabeth*, unlike its predecessors, shows us the realities of political power and its ability to corrupt everything and everyone. No heritage film operates quite like this, just as no heritage film would begin with the visceral spectacle of heretics burning at the stake and close with a triple beheading."[22] Higson, in the end, tries to contain the film's differences and argues, "If [it] is not a *celebration* of Englishness, it can certainly be read as an *exploration* of Englishness, a historical meditation on the making of modern England and the construction of a central icon of the national heritage, the image of the Virgin Queen."[23]

Whatever their differences and similarities on the film's relationship to heritage cinema, Chapman, Higson, and Pamela Church Gibson all note the film's representation of history as a key element. Chapman writes about its "irreverential attitude to period authenticity"; Higson says that "the film-makers were not overly concerned to establish historical accuracy"; and Church Gibson refers to its "move away from the fetishisation of 'authenticity' and desire for painstaking re-creation."[24] As film scholars they are mostly interested in the style and look of *Elizabeth* and the fact that it does not use "authentic" Elizabethan costume, settings, and music, and they are disinclined to be concerned that it does not carefully represent historical fact. Still, they do mention the film's "attitude" toward history, but the only example given by each is the fact of Queen Elizabeth I's debated virginity. Each depicts "the controversy that erupted over *Elizabeth's*" version of history by referencing the film's presentation of the queen's sexual activity that defied "official history."[25] None mention in any detail the timeline changes, character changes, or fictionalized events. This does not necessarily discredit their analyses of the film; however, it does show how Queen Elizabeth's performance of virginity at the end of the film represented more than just itself in the criticism. In part, for Chapman and Higson, this is the case, because they also focus on the reception of the film and how the press received the film. However, as all three try to situate the film in relationship to academic debates of English heritage cinema and to reference its historical inaccuracy as a difference from previous heritage cinema, the question of "was she or wasn't she" a virgin gets tied up into the question of "is it or isn't it heritage cinema?"

Virginity as Image

While situating *Elizabeth* within a tradition of heritage cinema, Chapman, Higson, and Church Gibson also link it to its contemporaries. The film's fast pace, thriller elements, and "irreverent attitude" are the qualities that both distance it from the expectations of heritage cinema as mentioned earlier and associate it with a new kind of successful British cinema, typified by such films as *The Full Monty* (1997) and *Trainspotting*.[26] These films, along with others like *Austin Powers* (1997); the trans-Atlantic success of Britpop, such as Oasis and Blur (and even the brief success of the Spice Girls); and the new high profile of other British art and cultural productions (through figures such as Alexander McQueen and Damien Hirst) embodied the notion of Cool Britannia, "a label applied by the press to the sense of cultural renewal that seemed to feed off the election of the New Labour government in 1997."[27] On the face of it, Cool Britannia and

Virginity and Identity in the Critical Reception of Elizabeth

English heritage would seem to be opposing ideas; however, in reference to *Elizabeth*'s connections to both heritage cinema and Cool Britannia, Higson suggests, "[It should be] no surprise, perhaps, that such a film should have emerged in a period when New Labour were seeking to rebrand Britain, to give it a more modern face while not ignoring established traditions."[28] However, from early on Cool Britannia came under suspicion for being an exercise in image management for the new government, epitomized by Tony Blair's photo opportunities with the likes of Noel Gallagher of Oasis. The image managers of the government, including Blair, who orchestrated Cool Britannia, also managed the aftermath of Princess Diana's death, and Higson implicitly makes a link between the two and the film. He notes that it is no wonder "that such a film should prove successful so shortly after the death of that modern 'Virgin Queen,' Princess Diana."[29] Higson makes no further mention of Diana, but his allusion to her as "that modern 'Virgin Queen'" encapsulates readings by both Chapman and Church Gibson of the film and its popular reception in relationship to the princess. Chapman notes that many reviewers of Kapur's *Elizabeth* accepted the historical liberties that the film took, but he points to the UK newspaper the *Daily Telegraph*, as mentioned earlier, as an example of some of the reception discourse that took issue with the portrayal in the film of a sexually active Virgin Queen and led the defense of her honor against the ravages of popular culture. For contrast, Chapman notes that the 1972 film *Mary, Queen of Scots* puts Elizabeth and Dudley in bed together; as this, at the time, "passed without censure," he wonders why *Elizabeth* came under disapprobation. He offers a question/answer to his question: "Is it entirely too fanciful to suggest that the defence of Elizabeth's reputation in response to the film was also, in some way, a defence of the memory of Princess Diana?"[30]

The connection is indeed not too fanciful, as several reviews of the film mention Princess Diana. David Starkey praises Cate Blanchett's performance, commenting that "there's no doubting the effectiveness of her impersonation of the woman who ruled England for 45 years with an improbable fusion of the more histrionic qualities of Lady Thatcher and Princess Diana."[31] And Philip French of the *Observer* asserts that "comparisons with Princess Diana are encouraged by the casting of her mentor, Richard Attenborough, as Elizabeth's wise adviser, Sir William Cecil."[32] In addition, the timing of *Elizabeth*'s filming and release in the year and a half after the princess' death became a part of the film's production and distribution narratives. Upon the film's release, Blanchett remarked, "Last summer on the first day of filming, the first lines that were spoken were, 'The Queen is dead, long live the Queen!' Princess Diana had died two days before. It was very eerie."[33] Director Shekhar Kapur also commented, "I was at a cinema in London where the film was playing, and I saw young girls come out with tears in their eyes. One of them said this was Princess Diana. After all, Diana's greatest fear was if she continued to live in the Palace, she'd become a shell of a human being. And this is what happened to Elizabeth."[34] A few feminist writers, such as Beatrix Campbell, have situated the princess in a feminist analysis of a female victim of the patriarchal monarchy who fought back and made a new independent version of herself, and Diana's apparent resistance to marriage and monarchy's making her into a "shell of a human being" seems to be the reason some "feminist Socialists briefly and bizarrely champion[ed] the dead Diana as republican martyr and sisterly fellow-traveller."[35]

In her article "No Man's Elizabeth: The Virgin Queen in Recent Films," Renée Pigeon sums up the seeming connections between Elizabeth and Diana: "[The depiction of Elizabeth] seems indebted to the widespread public perception of the late Princess of Wales as an initially innocent young woman destroyed by the role she was required to play, the rigid orthodoxy of the Royal Family, and her husband's betrayal of her."[36] The significant word here is *perception*. Since at least the first anniversary of her death, Princess Diana's popularity and her image as the "People's Princess" has been reread in light of knowledge about her proactive engagement with the press[37]—tipping them off to her whereabouts and, more important, using a confessional mode in her interviews to gain sympathy.[38] It is not only Diana's married life—before she gained her freedom and independence and became a feminist icon for some—that parallels the narrative of *Elizabeth*. Elizabeth's performance of virginity and her self-fashioning into the icon of the Virgin Queen evokes Princess Diana's relentless self-(re)fashioning after her divorce. In Joan Bridgman's article "Diana's Country," published in 1999, she reflects back on the mass mediation of the princess's death and funeral and the expression of "national" grief and mourning as well as on Diana's own mediation. She writes,

[Diana's] own favourite image of herself was that of her holding a dying black child on which she gazes raptly. It conveys devoted motherhood, but more importantly it appropriates the schemata of the Virgin and Christ child—a holy face symbolising motherhood yet contradictorily also the image of virginity and purity. With the English Reformation there was a suppression of the worship of

Mary, leaving a gap in our culture of the Great Mother figure. It is perhaps to this lost image the crowds were responding with their votive gifts, flowers and candles.[39]

Elizabeth presents the "gap in our culture of the Great Mother figure" as the same reason Queen Elizabeth I made herself into the Virgin Queen. In the scene mentioned at the beginning of this chapter when Elizabeth asks Walsingham if she is to be made of stone, and he responds that people need to touch the divine on earth, Elizabeth looks up at the statue of the Virgin Mary and says, "She had such power over men's hearts. They died for her." And, Walsingham suggestively adds, "They have found nothing to replace her." Elizabeth puts her head in her hands, but the moment ends on the beatific face of the statue, and then the film cuts to the transformation scene—Elizabeth's head bent forward for her hair to be cut. David Grant Moss argues that the film's final emphasis on the iconicity of the Virgin Queen as Elizabeth's ultimate triumph is a problem because "the film thus embraces the view that the popularity and success of Elizabeth's Virgin Queen persona are simply due to her filling the post-Reformation void left by the now absent Virgin Mary."[40] The instinctive comparison of Elizabeth to Princess Diana by various reviewers and critics seems even more suggestive now, tied together as they are by some cultural need for a female icon that is both of this world and exception to it.

However, icons need a sustained image. Queen Elizabeth I had hers regulated by law; Princess Diana also put enormous time, effort, and planning into hers. In her article "From Dancing Queen to Plaster Virgin: *Elizabeth* and the End of English Heritage?" Pamela Church Gibson situates her reading of the film's new version of spectacle compared with previous heritage films, and she situates her analysis in the context of a reading of the Windsors as spectacle. She focuses on Charles and Diana, from their wedding to their divorce, and particularly develops Diana's interview with Martin Bashir on the BBC. She describes it in detail:

Diana chose to dress in a severe black suit with black tights, suggesting . . . a lifelong mourning. Her performance was carefully rehearsed, her posture composed and calculated, her eye make-up as thick and black as that of any Hollywood star—all in sharp contrast to her normal make-up and manner. The interview was an extremely effective performance, and Diana was judged to have scored victory and further increased her vast popularity at the expense of the flinty-hearted Windsors.[41]

Although Church Gibson does not explicitly compare her version of the interview to the final scene in *Elizabeth,* the above account functions like a displaced description of Queen Elizabeth's presentation of herself as the Virgin Queen in the denouement of the film: the monochromatic dress, calculated composure, thick makeup, all in contrast to her previous appearance. The film also suggests that the Queen's performance secured her popularity, as it ends with the statement, "Elizabeth reigned for another 40 years." The problem is that the performance could potentially be an act, a playing of a part that is disconnected from any kind of genuineness or, for that matter, authenticity. For Church Gibson, then, the performance of the Virgin Queen reflects the performance of the People's Princess, and the potential lack of truthfulness in both cases highlights, for her, the film's irreverence for historical authenticity and heritage. The "was she or wasn't she" question about Elizabeth's virginity parallels questions about Princess Diana: "Was she 'the people's princess,' who electrified the world with her beauty and humanitarian missions? Or was she a manipulative, media-savvy neurotic who nearly brought down the monarchy?"[42]

Sex, Power, and Performance

For Moss, Elizabeth's self-fashioning and declaration, "I have become a virgin," reduces her power and iconicity to "a public-relations decision."[43] He further criticizes the film, adding, "While this tactic is in some ways postmodern given its gleeful anachronism and its self-referential nature, it is also reactionary, for this Elizabeth is concerned solely with love and appearances."[44] Moss is not the only critic to argue that the film is relatively conservative in its gender politics. Pigeon notes that "part of the conventional popular image of Elizabeth has been that she achieved that ultimate power by giving up her 'natural' destiny as a woman . . . and turns herself into an icon for her people to adore" and that *Elizabeth* promotes this view particularly vehemently.[45] Characterized as an anachronistic "public-relations decision" to become "an icon for her people," Elizabeth's transformation into the Virgin Queen offers us nothing more than a young woman caught between love and duty, both Moss and Pigeon argue. This is particularly the case as they focus on comparing the film to the "real" Queen Elizabeth in all her complexity; within this paradigm the film cannot help but appear shallow and enthralled with surface and image.

In order to contrast these views of the film's climax, I want to quote somewhat extensively from Kathryn Schwartz's perceptive reading of *Eliza-*

beth in her article "The Wrong Question: Thinking through Virginity." She writes,

> Anyone with a decent sense of story lines knows that they start with a virgin in order to construct a seduction, and not the other way around. In reversing this seemingly natural teleology, *Elizabeth* presents virginity as an aggressive fiction which, projected backward, becomes history. . . . Virginity here is a makeover, a cosmetic effect that changes what the body means. The process does not insert recuperated femininity into its appropriate space; instead of guaranteeing a bodily condition or imposing a social value, Elizabeth's virginity proves her mastery both of signification and of monarchical authority.[46]

Schwarz is concerned with larger discourses and ideas about virginity and Queen Elizabeth than just the film and attempts to "get at some of the meanings of early modern virginity not so much by analyzing what early modern authors said about Elizabeth I as by looking at what we ourselves have done with her."[47] What we ourselves have done with her in relation to the film's critical reception is to use her virginity to reference contemporary concerns other than itself. I have suggested that this is in large part because of the unanswerable nature of the "was she or wasn't she" question, but it is also, as I argued in the last section, because of the nature of virginity in the film as a performance, an image rather than a "truth." Schwarz reads Elizabeth's transformation scene as "a makeover, a cosmetic effect that changes what the body means" and situates the performance of virginity by the queen at the end of the film through Judith Butler's work on drag and gender performativity.[48] Performativity has been, and was particularly in the 1990s, a central term for feminist and queer readings of gender and sexual identity that resist hegemonic identity constructions, which largely confine gender to biology. Performativity allows a separation between body and identity. Elizabeth's performance as the Virgin Queen, her declaration that "I have become a virgin," discounts her bodily experience of having had sexual intercourse with Dudley for her own self-made identification.

In the transformation scene, Elizabeth's body is remade so that it references identities that separate Elizabeth's sexual experience from her new self. For instance, the hair cutting, with its submissive imagery and severity of excision, recalls many scenes of a nun's initiation, evoking the renunciation of vanity and sexuality.[49] Despite the fact that throughout Christian history female monasteries have welcomed both never-married virgins and previously married women to take vows of chastity, a consecrated virgin who never experiences sexual intercourse is a common Western cultural idea(l) of the nun who has wed herself to Christ.[50] The nun's haircut, as an image, creates an outward sign of an inward state. As an image in *Elizabeth*, it performs "a version of cross-dressing that transforms not gender but the legibility of sex, constructing an unexpected relationship between identity and act."[51] Virginity as the state of inexperience (a non-act) by an individual can be attested to only by the individual. This creates a contradiction for women for whom virginity, historically, has been more insistently required and who have not been allowed the right of testimony. Virginity, then, as a commodity of patriarchy, the value of daughter to a father and the value of a prospective wife to a husband, had to be verifiable by men. Despite ongoing myths about the hymen, virginity is not and never has been an easily verifiable physical fact. Both the tests of virginity and its fakes participate in the ideology of female virtue required for patrilineal legitimacy. As Schwarz argues, virginity's "elusiveness of somatic certainty . . . requires its object to speak it."[52] The ideology of virginity requires women to testify to their participation in the rules of patriarchy, to willfully speak their submission:

For a virtuous woman to be taken as a commodity she must also be taken at her word, forcing the collaborative work between coercion and intention into view. Virginity is a speech act that masquerades as a bodily state, a male fantasy that locates feminine will at the heart of heterosocial production, a licensed performance that incorporates, co-opts and conspires with the body beneath.[53]

Queen Elizabeth's virginity, which both fulfills male ideals of femininity and asserts her individual and political will, simultaneously affirms and subverts patriarchal order. In this, as Schwarz notes, the film does nothing new with the myth of Queen Elizabeth. The significance of a performative reading of the transformation scene in *Elizabeth* is the separation of body and identity—it presents an answer to the perpetual question of "was she or wasn't she?" (an answer that, as I noted earlier, upset some reviewers of the film). To repeat Schwarz's answer to the question: "How, after all, could we know?"

And yet the simultaneous affirmation and subversion of patriarchal order remains an aporia for critics of the film. Julianne Pidduck suggests that "the film's framing of *Elizabeth* aligns adroitly with certain contemporary feminist dilemmas: How can a woman navigate the conflicting pressures of social decorum, sexual desire, power?"[54] One answer to that question was offered in the critical reception through the comparisons that reviewers made between Elizabeth as a young princess and queen to the contemporary rhetoric of "girl power," a postfeminist discourse that promotes the power of self-(re)presentation. In a few reviews, the young Elizabeth of the film was directly compared to the Spice Girls and their representation of girl power. Higson thoroughly records the various references that culminate in the example of the magazine *19* that "charted some of the problems 'Liz' faced, concluding that 'Worst of all, her childhood sweetheart Robert Dudley (the not altogether unattractive Joseph Fiennes) has been lying to her. . . . Despite it all, Elizabeth's courage and tenacity help her emerge a winner—now *that's* Girl Power.'"[55] Within feminist criticism, girl power has both positive connotations, as it has been read, and practiced, by third wave feminists, and negative connotations, as it has been read by feminist critics of a popular postfeminist culture.[56]

For some third wave feminists, girl power, when it is a performance of girlish femininity by independent and confident women in their twenties and thirties, can expose the ways that images of girlishness (pigtails, school outfits, rosy cheeks) can be easily appropriated and therefore undermined, effecting a feminist critique of feminine stereotypes. And Rebecca Munford argues that "insofar as [its] playful recognition of the signifiers of 'femininity' and 'girlhood' destabilises traditional categories of gender it . . . [resonates] with Judith Butler's conceptualisation of the performativity of gender."[57] However, Munford makes it clear that girl power can be easily (re)appropriated by hegemonic capitalism: "The positioning of the individual members of the Spice Girls into five clearly delineated and marketable categories of femininity—Baby, Scary, Posh, Sporty and Ginger—demonstrates the extent to which this 'brand' of girl power represents the commodification and containment of feminism—the triumph of 'image power' over 'political power.'"[58]

Feminine "image power," both fulfilling and subverting patriarchal norms, is exactly what these critics argue is the problem with the ending of *Elizabeth*. They argue that the film suggests the only power Queen Elizabeth I had was to sell herself as the Virgin Queen as an idea and an identity that had very little to do with her "real" political powers. The film's presentation of the Virgin Queen's performance references nothing beyond itself and therefore does not actually signify any individual female power. From the very beginning, the Spice Girls were accused of being packaged and managed by their Svengali-like manager, Simon Fuller. Critics have charged *Elizabeth* with promoting the same view of the final transformation into the Virgin Queen, "encouraged by the Svengali-like influence of Walsingham."[59] The rhetoric of girl power in the reception of the film seems to have little to do with virginity because it more obviously applies to her pretransformation narrative, when Elizabeth is youthful, playful, feminine, flirty, energetic, and sexually active. Viewing the film through girl power largely requires ignoring Elizabeth's transformation into the Virgin Queen icon and how that transformation turns her into a kind of "freak"—unmarried and sexless for the rest of her life, made up to look nearly inhuman.[60] The visuals, framing, and narrative of the film create her freakishness as the Virgin Queen in opposition to the youthful, attractive Elizabeth who is the subject of the previous 150 minutes.

However, the transfiguration of Elizabeth from girly queen to Virgin icon is the moment for some when she changes from Princess Diana into Margaret Thatcher.[61] Cate Blanchett said, "To become queen means to erase your past in a lot of ways—look at Diana, her past haunted her, and people wanted to know all about her. But how can you actually rule without a personal self and a personal history? Elizabeth was as much a Maggie Thatcher as a popular Diana. She was able to meld those two things."[62] Pigeon argues that "the attempt to meld 'those two things' . . . is inevitably construed as a loss of humanity for Elizabeth in the film."[63]

I agree that the film's final image of Elizabeth as Virgin Queen frames the iconic image so that it presents a loss of humanity in the name of leadership and duty to country. However, I argue that there is no melding here; she does not become a Diana-Thatcher hybrid but changes her image from sexy girlish Diana into the sexless imperial Thatcher. Kapur sees it as the corruption of power: "It's this whole success and love and ruthlessness and innocence thing. . . . We looked at the film at the end and said, 'God, this is the greatest career woman ever.' She's devoid of emotion, omnipresent, just standing there. . . . That is the ultimate tragedy of having to be the ultimate power."[64]

As I have argued, the film structures an opposition between the two images of Elizabeth through the contrast of "natural" sex and "chosen" virginity that frames the queen's narrative as a choice between humanity and power, love and duty, individuality and iconicity. Pigeon argues that, in *Elizabeth*, "her choice is not an astute political strategy but a sacrifice that arises from her own emotional pain, and one that can hardly even be characterised *as* a choice, given her limited alternatives as the film presents them."[65] She becomes, in the end, a freak, "no longer a living, mortal woman but a stiff, statuesque demigoddess, no longer appearing human."[66]

Virginity and Identity in the Critical Reception of Elizabeth

This is a description that many might make of Margaret Thatcher. As Moss argues of her, in comparison to the film's presentation of female power, "[Despite her marriage,] Thatcher's imagery was primarily that of someone who ruled alone. She presented herself not as a wife and mother like other women, but as a stronger, iron woman who rose above such banalities to achieve greater things."[67] At the turn of the century, feminists such as Elaine Showalter and Natasha Walter have argued for rereading Thatcher as the "great unsung heroine of British feminism," attempting to counteract the usual feminist criticisms of her conservative policies toward gender and women and her self-presentation, alluded to above, as the exception that proved the rule. Walter argues, "[Feminism's] inability to accept worldly female power is most clearly shown in the way that the women's movement disowned Margaret Thatcher. . . . Thatcher displayed no problems about dealing with hierarchies and structures, displaying ego and opportunism. She showed her pleasure in power and her misery when she was ousted from it."[68] This reading of Thatcher is indicative of the postfeminist discourse of the 1990s (and ongoing) that emphasizes individual female choice and success over collective feminist action and success.[69] Postfeminist culture is constantly questioning what feminism is and reevaluating who the "real" feminists are, especially as these debates are concerned with female power, that is, girl power. Thatcher has, in Britain, become symbolic of these debates, especially because her acquisition of power has been critiqued for being predicated on a performance of femininity that secured her own individual power while upholding the patriarchal system:

> To discuss Mrs. Thatcher in terms of a positive meaning for women is a mistake. . . . Her success lay in her ability to perform a trick . . . to all intents and purposes, Mrs. Thatcher disguised herself as a man. . . . But, and it is an important but, she never renounced her right to claim the privileges of a woman. Hence, her handbag, symbol that, no matter how tough and ambitious a political animal she might be . . . there was always something that differentiated her from them. . . . Her covert adherence to a traditional model of femininity was most marked when it came to her attitude to the rest of her sex, an attitude which was competitive and owed nothing to any notion of female solidarity. She insisted: "I owe nothing to women's lib."[70]

It may be a stretch to compare Thatcher's handbag to Elizabeth's virginity, but Elizabeth's performance of the Virgin Queen at the end of the film, which draws on the power of a hyperfeminine image, evokes Thatcher's insistence on foregrounding her femininity and womanhood to secure her unique claim to power. Thatcher's evocation in the critical reception of the film with regard to girl power suggests that the "was she or wasn't she" question of Elizabeth's virginity parallels contemporary cultural debates about whether Thatcher is or isn't a feminist icon and draws on the larger cultural debates about women and feminist identity from the postfeminist 1990s.

In her article "The Wrong Question: Thinking through Virginity," Schwarz argues that virginity is "a series of questions."[71] For the critical reception of Elizabeth, virginity not only is a series of questions, but it generates a series of questions about identity, suggesting that our national and gendered identities are as much about image and spectacle as Elizabeth's transformation into the Virgin Queen.

Notes

1. A copy of the portrait can be found at www.marileecody.com/gloriana/elizabethditchley.jpg (accessed July 17, 2007).

2. Hanne Blank, *Virgin: The Untouched History* (New York: Bloomsbury, 2007).

3. Marie H. Loughlin, *Hymeneutics: Interpreting Virginity on the Early Modern Stage* (Lewisburg, PA: Bucknell University Press, 1997).

4. Andrew Higson, *English Heritage, English Cinema: Costume Drama since 1980* (Oxford: Oxford University Press, 2003), 243.

5. Rosanna de Lisle, "The Original Elizabethan: What Was It Like Being Elizabeth I?" *Independent* (London), September 27, 1998, 308.

6. James Chapman, *National Identity and the British Historical Film* (London: I. B. Tauris, 2005), 308.

7. Quoted in Alicia Potter, "Her Royal Slyness—Colorful Virgin Queen Ascends to the Screen Again in *Elizabeth*," *Boston Herald*, November 22, 1998, 60.

8. Michael Farquhar, "As a Matter of Fact, Elizabeth Is a Pretender to the Throne," *Washington Post*, December 20, 1998, 4.

9. Ian McAdam, "Fiction and Projection: The Construction of Early Modern Sexuality in *Elizabeth* and *Shakespeare in Love*," *Pacific Coast Philology* 35, no. 1 (2000): 149–60; David Grant Moss, "A Queen for Whose Time? Elizabeth I as Icon for the Twentieth Century," *Journal of Popular Culture* 39, no. 5 (2006): 796–816.

10. Farquhar, "As a Matter of Fact," 4.

11. Kathryn Schwarz, "The Wrong Question: Thinking through Virginity," *differences: A Journal of Feminist Cultural Studies* 13, no. 2 (2002): 5.

12. Tom Shone, "Romp without Pomp," *Sunday Times* (London), October 4, 1998, 6.

13. de Lisle, "Original Elizabethan," 2.

14. Quoted in Potter, "Her Royal Slyness," 60.

15. Chapman, *National Identity*, 308; David Starkey, "The Drama Queen," *Sunday Times* (London), September 20, 1998, 5.
16. Quoted in Michael O'Sullivan, "Elizabeth: The Godmother," *Washington Post*, November 27, 1998, 59.
17. Higson, *English Heritage*, 194.
18. See Higson, *English Heritage*; Claire Monk, "Sexuality and Heritage," in *Film/Literature/Heritage: A Sight and Sound Reader*, ed. Ginette Vincendeau (London: BFI, 2001), 6–11; Richard Dyer, "Heritage Cinema in Europe," in *Encyclopedia of European Cinema*, ed. Ginette Vincendeau (London: Facts on File, 1995), 204–5; Paul Willeman, "The National," in *Looks and Frictions: Essays in Cultural Studies and Film Theory* (London: BFI, 1994), 206–19.
19. Higson, *English Heritage*, 195.
20. Chapman, *National Identity*, 299.
21. Stella Bruzzi, "Elizabeth," *Sight and Sound* 8, no. 11 (1998): 48.
22. Pamela Church Gibson, "From Dancing Queen to Plaster Virgin: Elizabeth and the End of the English Heritage?" *Journal of British Popular Culture* 4 (2002): 139.
23. Higson, *English Heritage*, 198.
24. Chapman, *National Identity*, 308; Higson, *English Heritage*, 241; Church Gibson, "From Dancing Queen to Plaster Virgin," 135.
25. Chapman, *National Identity*, 308.
26. It would be difficult to define any consistent quality (or qualities) of the films of Cool Britannia. It seems that collectively they largely rely on their differences from the English heritage films. In this way, films as disparate as *Trainspotting*, *The Full Monty*, *Ratcatcher* (dir. Lynne Ramsay, 1999), and *Notting Hill* (dir. Roger Michell, 1999) can come under the same banner via national identity (Scottishness vs. Englishness), genre (comedy vs. drama), class (working vs. upper), time period (present vs. past). Of course, my description here is in no way exhaustive or definitive, as the idea of Cool Britannia is inherently vague and its popularity brief.
27. Chapman, *National Identity*, 312.
28. Higson, *English Heritage*, 198.
29. Tom Nairn, *After Britain: New Labour and the Return of Scotland* (London: Granta, 2000); Higson, *English Heritage*, 198.
30. Chapman, *National Identity*, 309.
31. Starkey, "Drama Queen," 5.
32. Philip French, "Film of the Week: Another Fine Bess," *Observer* (London), October 4, 1998, 6.
33. de Lisle, "Original Elizabethan," 2.
34. Bernard Weinraub, "At the Movies: A Goofball Guy's Guy," *New York Times*, November 13, 1998, http://query.nytimes.com/gst/fullpage.html?res=9E04E1DD1431F930A25752C1A96E958260&sec=&spon=&pagewanted=1 (accessed July 5, 2007).
35. See Beatrix Campbell, *Diana, Princess of Wales: How Sexual Politics Shook the Monarchy* (London: Women's Press, 1998). Church Gibson, "From Dancing Queen to Plaster Virgin," 140.

36. Renée Pigeon, "'No Man's Elizabeth': The Virgin Queen in Recent Films," in *Retrovisions: Reinventing the Past in Film and Fiction,* ed. Deborah Cartmell, I. Q. Hunter, and Imelda Whelehan (London: Pluto Press, 2001), 19.

37. The moniker was put into public circulation by then Prime Minister Tony Blair who used it to describe her in a televised speech only a few hours after her death. That speech has since been evaluated as another image management moment for the new government, provocatively portrayed in the 2006 film *The Queen.*

38. Tina Brown, *The Diana Chronicles* (New York: Random House, 2007).

39. Joan Bridgman, "Diana's Country," *Contemporary Review,* January 1999, 20.

40. Moss, "A Queen for Whose Time?" 801.

41. Church Gibson, "From Dancing Queen to Plaster Virgin," 234.

42. These rhetorical questions are taken from the Random House promotional Web page for *The Diana Chronicles* by Tina Brown. www.randomhouse.com/doubleday/dianachronicles/ (accessed August 20, 2007).

43. Moss, "A Queen for Whose Time?" 801.

44. Ibid., 802.

45. Pigeon, "'No Man's Elizabeth,'" 18; Moss, "A Queen for Whose Time?"; Thomas Betteridge, "A Queen for All Seasons: Elizabeth I on Film," in *The Myth of Elizabeth,* ed. Susan Doran and Thomas S. Freeman (Basingstoke: Palgrave Macmillan, 2003), 242–60.

46. Schwarz, "Wrong Question," 9.

47. Ibid., 5.

48. Ibid., 9; Betteridge, "Queen for All Seasons," 254.

49. A few examples of films with the shearing of an initiate's hair include *The Nun's Story* (dir. Fred Zinneman, 1959), *Brother Sun, Sister Moon* (dir. Franco Zeffirelli, 1972), and *Thérèse* (dir. Alain Cavalier, 1986).

50. Blank, *Virgin.*

51. Schwarz, "Wrong Question," 9.

52. Ibid., 15.

53. Ibid.

54. Julianne Pidduck, "*Elizabeth* and *Shakespeare in Love*: Screening the Elizabethans," in *Encyclopedia of European Cinema,* ed. Ginette Vincendeau (London: Facts on File, 1995), 130–35.

55. Higson, *English Heritage,* 218. Other quotes include the following from the *Times* review of the film: "'I am not your Elizabeth,' she cries, 'I am no man's Elizabeth.' Talk about Girl Power." Several others are online reviews, such as the following from *This Is London* and Mr. Showbiz Movie Guide, respectively: "The appeal of the Tudor boss-lady is undiminished as Girl Power takes hold," and "Elizabeth breathlessly exemplifies the double-edged sword that is true girl power." For full references and other review quotes that indirectly reference girl power see Higson, *English Heritage,* 217–20.

56. "Third wave feminism" and "postfeminism" are highly contested terms that have been both differentiated from each other and shown to cross over. I use them with the weight on their differences, summed up by the third wave, while differentiating itself from second wave feminism, as distinguished by its call for a continued

and developing feminist movement and by postfeminism as distinguished by its declaration of feminism's end occasioned by an apparent contemporary state of political and cultural equality for women. Third wave feminism is generally understood to operate on the edges of mainstream culture, often critiquing it but also co-opting it for political use. Postfeminism is generally understood to be a product of mainstream media culture and discourse. I am highly aware of the simplification of these definitions and do not intend them to be conclusive but rather more suggestive of popular perceptions of these terms. See also Stacy Gillis, Gillian Howie, and Rebecca Munford, eds., *Third Wave Feminism: A Critical Exploration* (Houndmills, UK: Palgrave Macmillan, 2007); and Yvonne Tasker and Diane Negra, eds., *Interrogating Postfeminism: Gender and the Politics of Popular Culture* (Durham, NC: Duke University Press, 2007).

57. Rebecca Munford, "'Wake Up and Smell the Lipgloss': Gender, Generation and the (A)politics of Girl Power," in *Third Wave Feminism*, ed. Gillis, Howie, and Munford, 266–79.

58. Ibid., 274.

59. Pigeon, "'No Man's Elizabeth,'" 18.

60. In contrast, in an Elizabethan historical context, white makeup and overly rouged cheeks were used commonly by older women to approximate youthfulness.

61. The connection between the princess and the former prime minister might seem vaguely ludicrous, unless we consider the role of Ginger Spice (a.k.a. Geri Halliwell) in the promotion of the girl power discourse. In an interview in the run-up to the 1997 UK general election that New Labour won, Ginger declared her support for the conservatives, saying, "I saw a lot of what Mrs Thatcher did. She was definitely the original Spice Girl rising from the greengrocer's daughter to Prime Minister. She was a real role model of a strong woman." One of the most famous images of the Spice Girls is from their concert when Ginger wore a micro-mini dress in a Union Jack pattern. Her implied promotion of Britishness seemed to sit easily with Thatcher's conservative cultural rhetoric. Infamously, though, Ginger changed her political affiliations by the 2001 election and came out in support of Labour and Tony Blair. By then, the Spice Girls had broken up, but their place in the fleeting high profile of Cool Britannia had been solidified. Their ability to project an image of both familiar Britishness (particularly through Ginger's whiteness and her wearing of the flag) and modernity (through pop music and girl power) fit easily into Blair's political image of Labour—an image that Princess Diana also fit into and promoted easily (however briefly).

62. Harvey Feinstein, "The Queen and I," *Guardian* (London), November 28, 1998, 12.

63. Pigeon, "'No Man's Elizabeth,'" 19.

64. O'Sullivan, "Elizabeth," 59.

65. Pigeon, "'No Man's Elizabeth,'" 18.

66. Ibid.; Moss, "A Queen for Whose Time?"; Betteridge, "Queen for All Seasons."

67. Moss, "A Queen for Whose Time?" 813.

68. Natasha Walter, *The New Feminism* (London: Little Brown and Co., 1998),

172–73.

69. My own feminist politics are highly critical of the individualism of postfeminist culture, but I am interested in foregrounding the discourse of "unknowability."

70. Joan Smith, *Misogynies* (London: Vintage, 1989), 158–59.

71. Schwartz, "Wrong Question," 2.

Andrea Sabbadini

The Window and the Door

> Virginity's proliferation of meanings and desires ensures its ongoing presence in Western culture. Virginity is never lost.
> —Anke Bernau, *Virgins: A Cultural History*

The theme of virginity—with its complex anatomicophysiological, emotional, interpersonal, social, moral, and religious implications—can be approached from a variety of perspectives. Here I intend to review, introduce, and discuss some relevant psychoanalytic concepts in the hope that they may cast some new light on certain important aspects of the intrapsychic, conscious, as well as unconscious meanings of this phenomenon.

As illustration, instead of using clinical material from patients in analysis, I shall refer to instances of virginity as represented in two films: Krzysztof Kieślowski's *A Short Film about Love* [*Krotki Film O Milosci*] (1988) and Bernardo Bertolucci's *Stealing Beauty* (1996). Of course, virginity has been represented throughout the history of cinema, in films from all genres, whether light comedies, intense dramas, or horror. In this respect, cinema follows, not surprisingly, the example of literature and theater, where the character type of the virgin—an individual either unwilling or unable to engage in a sexual relationship—is also frequently met. My choice of these two particular films, arbitrary as it may seem, can be justified on several grounds. Released only a few years apart, both were directed by prominent European auteurs using a narrative style based on intelligent screenplays and formal elegance. In both movies it is the main characters—a boy, Tomek, in the Polish one, and a girl, Lucy, in the Italian one—rather than secondary characters who struggle with their conflict-ridden issues about virginity; and both Tomek and Lucy happen to be nineteen-year-olds and explicitly declare never to have had sexual intercourse.[1]

● ● ●

What is virginity? To avoid misunderstandings, frequent whenever the phenomenon under observation is as ambiguous, overdetermined, and anxiety-provoking as this one, I propose to define virginity in the most general of terms as "the absence of the experience of genital intercourse."

Such a definition has a number of features. It applies to all individuals, regardless of age, gender, or sexual orientation. It emphasizes the primacy of the genital apparatus over other erogenous zones insofar as it does not take into account other sexual activities, such as oral sex. It classifies a victim of abuse or rape through genital penetration as no longer a virgin. It leaves room to consider both psychological and physical factors (virginity as a state of mind as well as a physiological feature of the body). Last, by referring to an "absence" it implies that the phenomenon is as such unrepresentable.

This final consideration, which seems to contradict what I said earlier in this chapter, is a serious one in the context of this discussion. It suggests that films can show virginity only indirectly, either through its contrast with the presence of other related phenomena (for instance, the character's sexual activities other than genital intercourse, or his or her feelings about virginity such as desire, fear, guilt, or shame) or, and more emphatically, by representing the very act of genital penetration that puts an end to it. Indeed, as Bernau points out, "much literature on virginity is about its loss: either through rape, unscrupulous seduction, love, marriage or death."[2]

● ● ●

In Western societies the discourse about virginity has not disappeared in the course of the past several decades, but it has undergone radical transformations.

On the one hand, and in particular with the gradual dissolution of Victorian morality, partly also thanks to psychoanalysis, culminating with the sexual revolution of the 1960s, virginity has lost much of that religious high ground of sanctity, purity, and innocence boasted by those who claimed to have remained chaste, at least until their wedding night. We could mention here, incidentally, that the Christian emphasis on Mary's virginity, so prevalent in our popular culture and iconology, is also reflected in a myriad of other mythologies—from the classical Greek legend of the Minotaur's demanding a regular supply of "seven youths and seven maidens" from Athens to be devoured by him, to the modern one, much exploited in literature and cinema, of Count Dracula nightly sinking his teeth into the necks of young virgins to satisfy his thirst for fresh blood.

On the other hand, virginity has also attracted the attention of new fundamentalist groups, such as the American prochastity organization Silver Ring Thing, that claim, among other social and spiritual advantages, a healthier mental life for their sexually abstinent adherents. Hundreds of thousands of young people, it claims, wear with pride on their left-hand third fingers their symbolic rings, inscribed with Bible verses. I understand these rings to be the latter-day, self-imposed, mini versions of medieval chastity belts.

Is virginity, we may then ask, to be understood as a form of self-discipline or as the evidence of sexual repression—or even, at least in some instances, of neurotic psychopathology? Is it an expression of individual freedom to be treasured or a prison from which to escape as soon as possible? In our postfeminist era, a girl may well feel that she does own her body, but that still leaves her with the problem of whether that means renouncing her sexual innocence or holding on to it—a personal dilemma that, in the past, tended to be resolved for the individual within the social community to which he or she belonged and who shared similar moral values.

According to Bernau, virginity can be represented "as a radical choice, a reaction against a world in which sex is just another commodity. . . . But virginity can equally be understood as a consumer choice. . . . It may be less fiercely guarded by most than in previous centuries, but losing one's virginity is still perceived as a threshold moment."[3] This emphasis on "a threshold moment"—between childhood innocence and adulthood experience—is of particular importance, as at least some of the anxieties associated with the loss of virginity, for both boys and girls, belong to the ambiguous border territory of bodily sensations, interpersonal relationships, emotional commitments, and sexual morality and might relate to conflictual wishes and fears of engaging for the first time with a new experience.

● ● ●

People are likely to use a combination of psychological mechanisms, in particular denial and rationalization, to help them deal—or, more accurately, avoid dealing—with the anxieties that the issue of virginity may evoke for them, such as the insecurity they may feel in relation to their bodies, to their sense of identity, and to getting involved in intimate relationships.

On the one hand, as to the defensive use of denial, we are all prone to unconsciously deny the existence of realities we find physically, psychologically, morally, or socially unacceptable, or even just too unpleasant; so-called magical thinking allows us to make whatever we dislike disappear (from our perception, sensation, knowledge, or memory) and thus pretend it had never existed in the first place. This mechanism, however, can also be used consciously and deliberately to deceive others and, in the process, oneself—a far from uncommon situation in relation to virginity. Rationalization, on the other hand, consists of finding a pseudorational explanation for a fact otherwise experienced as intolerable—the way the fox in Aesop's fable describes the grapes he cannot reach as "sour." Examples of denials and rationalizations in relation to virginity are plentiful, and I shall mention here a few:

—Some people may explain away their wish to remain chaste, or rather their fear of genital intercourse, in terms of their conscious concerns about sexually transmitted diseases or unwanted pregnancies—a possible but by no means inevitable consequence of becoming sexually active.[4]
—Alternatively, others may dismiss the ease with which they engage in their first sexual relationship, often at an extremely young age, by attributing the entire responsibility of it to their partner's insistence, to peer-group pressures, or to excessive drinking, all the while claiming indifference to its consequences for themselves.
—Some no longer chaste girls rewrite their sexual history by buying themselves plastic surgical "re-hymenization," much as they could get themselves a new nose.
—So-called technical virgins, corresponding to the demi-vierges of some decades ago, would do "everything but" in order to maintain their virginal status.

Such denials, rationalizations, and other defensive strategies, I suggest, function to replace the more arduous psychological task of coming to terms with deep-rooted preoccupations that, as I will show, are mostly unconscious and stem from the subjects' early relationship with their parents, and more specifically with unresolved oedipal scenarios.

● ● ●

In recent times, sexuality seems to have lost the privileged place it once occupied in classical psychoanalytic theories and debates. Even in earlier analytic literature, however, the theme of virginity—how it should be defined, how it relates to other aspects of psychosexual development, which unconscious fantasies are associated with it, how its impact on male and female individuals differs—has been largely neglected. This is in contrast to such other disciplines as anthropology, ethnology, sociology, cultural studies, and feminist theory, a review of whose valuable works on this subject is, however, beyond the scope of this chapter.

Indeed, even Freud's study on this topic—the last of his three "contributions to the psychology of love," with the suggestive title *The Taboo of Virginity* (1918)—is, in line with his earlier essays on *Totem and Taboo* (1913), a mostly anthropological account of virginity as "a logical continuation of the right to exclusive possession of a woman, which forms the essence of monogamy, the extension of this monopoly to cover the past."[5] According to Freud, even for "primitive people," defloration, often performed ritually before the first act of marital intercourse, "is a significant act . . . the subject of a taboo—of a prohibition which may be described as religious."[6] Yates, another psychoanalytic author, believes that the woman values her chastity mostly because "she wishes to preserve her virginity for God. And I think," she adds, "that we will have no great difficulty in seeing that God here is largely a father substitute. . . . The husband in insisting on virginity in his bride is seeking reassurance of his wish that she should not have belonged to his father."[7] I would add here "or to *her* father."

Summarizing the anthropological literature on the subject, Freud concludes that explanations of the taboo of virginity include an apprehension for anything that, like the first intercourse, is new and uncanny; the suggestion that this taboo is an aspect of a wider one that embraces the whole of sexual life; and man's fear of women, experienced as dangerous, whereby their defloration would draw their hostility upon the man responsible for it because of "the pain which defloration causes a virgin" or rather "the narcissistic injury which proceeds from the destruction of an organ."[8] Finally, most early psychoanalysts who have written about virginity point out that defloration, like menstruation, is connected with the idea of a wound and bleeding, and in turn with castration anxieties and death.[9]

These texts, however, do little to enlighten us on what should be of central interest to analysts: the unconscious significance of the first sexual intercourse for young men and women and the complex psychodynamic interplay of attachments, separations, identifications, and projections involved. An exception is Weissman's detailed case history of "neurotic virginity and old maidenhood," a condition he describes as "a psychological state in which sexual intercourse is warded off unconsciously rather than consciously" and characterized by "the inability to finalize a heterosexual object relationship."[10] This author explains "neurotic virginity" in terms of early psychosexual maturation: "The intense fixation on the Oedipal father was devoid of the typical Oedipal wishes present in normal development. The father fixation represented an extension of the strong fixation on the preoedipal mother . . . and more regressive oral and sadistic wishes for and fears of the mother."[11] Weissman's explanation constitutes an extension and elaboration of the classical psychoanalytic theory according to which prolonged virginity is attributed to an unresolved oedipal conflict, as "the little girl remains unconsciously erotically fixated on her father, whom she cannot give up, and thus is unable to extend her affectionate and sexual feelings to another and suitable male."[12] Analogous considerations, of course, are valid mutatis mutandis also for "the little boy."

Two other psychoanalytic authors, Holtzman and Kulish, systematically analyze clinical material on the topic of defloration by relating it to such themes as oedipal conflicts, castration anxieties, sadomasochistic fantasies, blood and menstruation, guilt about masturbation, childbirth, and so on. In particular, they insist on "the importance and the reality of the hymen as the representation of the entry into adult female genital sexuality. The representation of the hymen is frequently repressed and often suppressed, and serves as an organizing image around which fantasies and conflicts are elaborated."[13]

● ● ●

The hymen surrounding the entrance to a girl's vagina may be experienced by her as a kind of closed door (but all closed doors, of course, invite opening).[14] One could speculate about the complex of fantasies of what, when opened, would come through it: Pleasure? Pain? Disease? Madness? Or indeed the complex of fantasies of what would flow out: Blood? Babies? The infantile part of the self? The virginal vagina could then be conceptualized as a more or less safe container of the sexual self—or, in more general terms, as both a potential link with the external world and as an ambivalently experienced barrier to it. As the latter, it could operate as a protection, or as an obstacle, or—more likely—as both things at once.

In particular I would suggest that the hymen constitutes for a girl the anatomical representative of essentially a severe superego, a kind of guardian of her bodily self, interpersonal relationships, and sexual morality, to be either complied with or rebelled against. On the one hand, girls may experience a conflict between a cultural view of virginity as a virtue, and therefore its loss as a sin, constructed on the religious Manichean opposition between celibate madonnas and nymphomaniac whores, whereby they should hold on to it at least until their wedding night, if not forever. On the other hand, never having experienced a sexual relationship may make them feel like immature children still emotionally dependent on their families, and they may therefore indulge in the illusion that the renunciation of their virginal status would by itself allow them access to the world of adulthood—girls would then be magically transformed overnight into women and daughters into (potential) mothers.

At the same time, a girl's ambivalence toward sexual innocence is closely linked, as we have seen, to her relationship to her own mother and to unresolved (or only partially resolved) oedipal conflicts. A girl may want to treasure her virginity—as a part of her anatomy but also as its mental representation—insofar as she experiences it as a precious gift from her mother who, in the daughter's unconscious fantasy, sacrificed her own in order to conceive and give birth. At the opposite extreme, a girl may want to dispense with it at all costs, and as soon as possible, hating it because she may feel that her mother only provided her with it out of jealousy, to prevent her from enacting her oedipal desires toward her father—and, later, toward any other man representing him.

Boys, conversely, would tend to find themselves in a less conflictual position, partly because in their case the loss of virginity does not in itself have direct physical consequences for their bodies. It could be argued, in this respect, that the presence of the anatomical membrane of the hymen is a psychologically more important difference between men and women than is usually recognized. Furthermore, the cultural view of virginity as a virtue has never applied to the same degree to boys as to girls. For pubescent boys, as many anthropological studies have demonstrated, losing virginity is mainly experienced as a straightforward rite of passage from boyhood into adulthood, to be performed, depending on the specific culture, ritually or even quite casually. However, boys who have not resolved their oedipal issues may be unable to renounce their virginity insofar as they may identify every potential sexual partner with their own mother, and engaging in a sexual relationship would therefore be experienced by them as either betrayal or the enactment of an incestuous fantasy. For such men, genital intercourse with a woman is then likely to be replaced by masturbatory, pregenital, and preoedipal activities, inasmuch as these, being linked to the "polymorphous perversity" of the child, have a regressive quality.

The characters of the two films discussed in this chapter will illustrate some of the features I have presented so far.

● ● ●

Krzysztof Kieślowski's *A Short Film about Love* centers on the unusual erotic relationship that develops between an adolescent man, Tomek (Olaf Lubaszenko), and an older woman, Magda (Grazina Szapolowska).[15] Following in the footsteps of the main characters of other famous films on voyeurism, such as Jefferies (James Stewart) in Hitchcock's *Rear Window* (1954) and Mark (Karl Boehm) in Powell's *Peeping Tom* (1960), Tomek mostly relates to Magda, the beautiful girl who has become the obsessional obscure object of his desire, by spying on her from a distance.

Brought up in an orphanage and now living with the mother of an absent friend, Tomek is a shy nineteen-year-old with delinquent tendencies: we see him stealing the telescope that allows him to zoom in on Magda at night from his bedroom window; we know that he does such things as withhold her mail, send her forged notices of payments, and tell her lies. We also become aware of his self-destructiveness as we watch him play a game of stabbing his hand with a pair of scissors and, after Magda rejects him, climb on top of her building, most likely with suicidal intentions. His deep depression is best expressed in a scene where he regresses to sucking on a piece of ice, indicating perhaps his experiences of deprivation as an abandoned child.

For Tomek, who has no experience of sexual closeness, the problem is how to approach a woman without letting her become either too intimate or too rejecting. With some prosthetic help from a powerful optical instrument, his eyes let him travel the distance that separates him from Magda and penetrate her space with the same clumsy intrusiveness of the false notices he puts through her letter box and of his wordless or apologetic telephone messages—his only available means of relating to her.

Magda, under a veneer of self-confidence that manifests itself, in Tomek's eyes, through her promiscuous sexual activities, is herself insecure and emotionally troubled. Her disappointment in the affairs of the heart is expressed in a scene where we, and Tomek, watch her cry after spilling milk on the kitchen table and doing nothing to pick up the bottle. Tomek, who cannot himself cry, is moved by her despair. His initial autoerotic interest in her as an object of instinctual gratification is now replaced by a new feeling—genuine as it is perverted, innocent as it is intrusive, passionate as it is immature—and for a moment Magda stops being for him just a body to watch and becomes a three-dimensional person he could relate to.

But as soon as the gap between them begins to be bridged, as soon as he accepts her seductive invitation to step through the threshold of her life and he finds himself in physical intimacy with her, he is overcome by panic.

At the dramatic climax of their encounter, when he is faced with the opportunity to make love with her, he ends up instead ejaculating in his trousers, and she cannot help but cruelly dismiss his feelings: "That's all there is to love," she tells him. Tomek, still a virgin, rejected by Magda, and overwhelmed by shameful confusion—will now run back home and slash his wrists with a razor blade.

With the critical help of our psychoanalytic tools, we may consider this film from the perspective of its search for an elusive meeting point, for a new interpersonal focus. Kieślowski's message concerns the existential dangers of prying into other people's private spaces (with telescopes, binoculars, telephones), rupturing or invading the containers' boundaries (we watch Tomek shatter a window to burgle the school, force false notices into Magda's letter box, slit his wrists), or indeed spilling out the content (milk, semen, blood, tears). Yet these elements are only the background to Kieślowski's representation of his two characters' struggles to find the optimal distance from—or perhaps the optimal closeness to— one another. But the point of convergence, somewhere in the trajectory of their lives, seems to be an illusory wish never to be realized.

● ● ●

After his exotic trilogy, Bernardo Bertolucci came back home to a more familiar setting and reflective mood to explore in *Stealing Beauty* the inner turmoil of a girl having to negotiate an adult world she is not quite ready to engage with.[16]

Lucy (Liv Tyler), a beautiful American young woman, returns after four years for a summer holiday to the villa in the countryside where her late mother, Sara, also used to spend her vacations. Here, in the luxury of lazy afternoons under the Tuscan sun and in the company of a bunch of late-day hippylike friends, Lucy can indulge in the pleasures and pains of experiencing her adolescent angst and trying to resolve some of her existential dilemmas. In reality, much of Lucy's holiday is spent smoking cannabis, crying self-indulgent tears, masturbating, and writing in her diary.

Noemi, one of Sara's friends, tells Lucy that "nineteen is all about boys!"—but by now we know that Lucy has never had a sexual relationship with any of them. "Hi! I'm Lucy. I'm 19. I'm a virgin," is the laconic self-descriptive and profoundly sad message she leaves in an Internet chat room. Elsewhere, Lucy reluctantly talks about it with Alex (Jeremy Irons), a terminally ill writer who had already been close to Sara and who now takes Lucy under his wing, like the father she has never met might have done. When one evening they share a joint and an intimate chat in the garden, Alex can hardly believe she is still sexually innocent.

> ALEX: You mean you never slept with anyone?
>
> LUCY: No.
>
> ALEX (incredulous): A beautiful girl like you? . . . Why? . . . You're in need of a ravisher.
>
> LUCY: I'm waiting.
>
> ALEX: You're scared. . . . What is it you're scared of?

But Lucy has no answers to such a question, her fears being buried inside the deepest recesses of her unconscious mind.

Another message, this time written on some notepaper while taking a bath and casually dropped out of the window, reads: "I wait, I wait, so patiently. . . . I'm quiet as a cup—I hope you'll come and rattle me—Quick! Come! Wake me up!" Freely associating to the English title of the film, *Stealing Beauty*, we think here of another fairy-tale beauty, (sexually) asleep for a hundred years and waiting for a handsome prince, a ravisher, to come and rattle her quiet cup with a kiss.

Lucy, who must somehow negotiate the similar biological needs, psychological pressures, and social expectations of most other contemporary nineteen-year-olds in her condition, is desperate—that is, as keen as she is fearful—to lose her virginity. Opportunities are plentiful for her, many suitable men of all ages being only too eager to receive an encouraging sign from her. Yet even when her inviting messages are dropped from a bathroom window, her door is kept sealed by some internal glue, the nature of which Lucy is herself hardly aware of.

We understand this as her need to first come to terms with her confused relationship to Sara, her dead mother, whom Lucy appears to have been unable to mourn. To do so, Lucy must first overcome what Costantini describes as her "narcissistic idealization and pseudo-identity."[17]

These are the defensive modalities Lucy has adopted to avoid having to deal with her traumatic loss by experiencing the appropriate sense of rage, and the inevitable guilt that goes with it, for having been abandoned by Sara. "Lucy does not just identify with her mother, but she becomes her, wears the same clothes, re-writes her poems, and wishes to re-live her own conception by trying to make her first sexual encounter identical to the one experienced, nineteen years earlier, by her mother."[18]

Lucy's confusion is compounded by a posthumous letter from Sara, in which she reveals that Lucy's father is a different man from the one she had always believed him to be, for Lucy was conceived from Sara's brief encounter with another man in the very location where Lucy is now spending her summer. In that letter, Sara describes in detail the sexual scene of Lucy's conception under an olive tree but tantalizingly withholds the name of her lover. This leaves Lucy with the painful yet also exciting task of discovering her father's identity. At first she (and we, the voyeuristic spectators of her inner turmoil) suspect him to be a fortysomething war correspondent whom she fancies, or perhaps Alex, the dying writer who fancies her. Then she discovers it was Noemi's husband, Ian (Donal McCann), a talented but currently unproductive Irish sculptor who was doing Sara's portrait at the time of Lucy's conception and has now taken Lucy herself as his new model.

It is finding the identity of her own father, combined with "the collapse of her idealization of the mother," that will allow Lucy access to her sexuality.[19] It will be with a shy young boyfriend, himself experiencing his first sexual encounter, that Lucy can now finally let herself be genitally penetrated.

It could, however, be suggested that by then Lucy had already lost, a few days earlier, her psychological chastity, when she had not too innocently exposed her breast when posing for her father. He, in turn, by doing her portrait, was beginning to emerge from his own unproductive artistic phase in a new spurt of creative inspiration. Thus the oedipal dream is at long last fulfilled. Lucy can now let herself compete with her dead mother for Ian's love, thus turning her closed door into a window of opportunity to become a grown-up woman.

● ● ●

A Short Film about Love and *Stealing Beauty* present us with sophisticated scenarios and convincing characters who struggle, both within themselves and in their relationships, with complex emotional issues. These, it is safe to suggest, are rooted in their earlier experiences as children, even if the films give us viewers only minimal information about their past.

Both Kieślowski and Bertolucci show us young people being drawn toward their first sexual experiences, yet having to negotiate personal issues before being able to break through that psychological and physical boundary referred to as "virginity." As their characters develop in the course of the film narratives, we observe one of them, Tomek, fail in his attempt to engage in an adult sexual relation, while the other, Lucy, appears to succeed. But we can only guess at how each of their histories of sexual relations may later unfold as they grow older.

As expected, the limitation intrinsic in our definition of virginity as the absence of an experience means that virginity itself could never be directly represented in our films. In Kieślowski's, we are spectators to Tomek's regressive, delinquent, self-destructive, and perverse (voyeuristic) activities and to a failed attempt at intercourse; in Bertolucci's, virginity is being much fantasized, talked, and written about but only represented indirectly through Lucy's encounter with her father and through virginity's very opposite—her first intercourse with a boyfriend.

We cannot, of course, ignore that, within their respective fictional film worlds, Tomek and Lucy, while struggling with similar problems in their personal lives, belong to different social classes and cultures—a morally rather austere one in Kieślowski's film, set in the gloomy housing estate in the outskirts of Warsaw; an affluent and decadent one in Bertolucci's, set in a sunlit villa in the Siena countryside—and are therefore conditioned by different sets of values. However, here I mainly focus on some of the similarities between the two characters. Not only, as already pointed out, are they both nineteen-year-olds—perhaps a significant age to question one's sexuality, on the threshold of life's third decade and of adulthood, much as the ages of twenty-nine and thirty-nine are significant for many women struggling with ambivalent wishes to have a child. But Tomek and Lucy also share important aspects of their personal histories. Prominent among these is the absence for both adolescents of parents, if not of substitute parental figures (the mother of Tomek's friend, in Kieślowski's film; Alex, Noemi, and other friends of Sara's, in Bertolucci's). I believe that this absence, and the loss that had caused it, must have played a significant role in the development of Tomek's and Lucy's personalities (different as these may have turned out to be due to other external or internal factors) and of their sexuality—with obvious implications concerning their attitudes to virginity.

The case of Tomek is one in which the overcoming of the "taboo" of virginity will prove—for reasons we can only guess at, knowing too little about his family background—tragically impossible. Tomek's scopophilia (pregenital, autoerotic, and linked to regressive "primal scene" fantasies) cannot evolve to an adult relationship that would include genital intercourse. In his virginal imagination, Magda's hymen is replaced by the layers of glass—optical lenses and window panes—separating him from her apartment: Tomek can look through his telescope and penetrate her "window" but cannot go through her "door," as physical contact would be experienced by him as terrifying. Because of what we assume to be his unresolved unconscious associations between the older woman with whom he is convinced he is in love and his lost mother, the move from voyeuristic sexuality to genital penetration would bring him dangerously close to his repressed incestuous fantasies. Spilling semen at the threshold of adult sexuality and drawing suicidal blood from his wrists are the only options available to him.

Lucy's trajectory to adult sexuality, conversely, seems to be more successful. When she is still pathologically identified with her mother and has not yet found out who her father is, she cannot let anybody get physically near her, for in her unconscious mind she fears (or wishes) to end up making love with her own father—who, indeed, could have been any old-enough man. However, the overcoming of the narcissistic idealization of her mother and the eventual discovery of her father's identity finally allows her to let go of the bond that virginity represents for her. It may be noticed here that, even before finding out the identity of her father and letting her chosen boyfriend deflower her, she had offered Ian a bunch of flowers—a symbolic gesture revealing the oedipal significance of her struggles with sexuality.

* * *

In this chapter I have presented some psychoanalytic ideas relevant to the understanding of virginity and illustrated them with reference to the experiences of two young people only existing on the cinema screen.

Virginity, as I have shown here, occupies an emotionally ambiguous place in the moral landscape of our relationship to our own and other people's bodies. It can be invested with either positive connotations ("It's a precious part of me, and I should hold on to it until I find true love") or negative ones ("It's a useless impediment to my sexual freedom, and I should get rid of it as soon as I can"), or both. Therefore virginity, alongside adolescence itself with which it is often associated, placed as they are in a "border space," can symbolically represent a number of other ambivalently invested aspects of our lives, such as the need to grow up and the wish to remain dependent on our families. All of this is rich in the kind of unconscious significance, stemming from our earliest experiences, that psychoanalytic concepts are particularly well suited to interpret.

I have felt justified in making extensive reference here to films, believing that the dramatic experiences of their adolescent and still-virgin leading characters can provide us with relevant illustration to our thoughts on these matters. Psychoanalysis and cinema are involved in a mutually rewarding interdisciplinary dialogue: not only do psychoanalytic concepts lend themselves to the interpretation of films (and indeed there exists a vast literature of analytically oriented film criticism), but films themselves, as well as other artistic products, can also offer an important contribution to our psychoanalytic knowledge of peoples' minds by projecting on a flat screen three-dimensional fictional characters—such as Tomek and Lucy—whose features, vicissitudes, and dilemmas we can identify with or recognize in others.

Notes

1. Just to give an example of a secondary character in a film from the same period as those considered here, there is sexy cheerleader Angela (Mena Suvari) in Sam Mendes's *American Beauty* (1999). Angela boasts about her extensive erotic experiences until the opportunity comes to have sex with Lester (Kevin Spacey), when she has to confess that she is still a virgin.

2. Anke Bernau, *Virgins: A Cultural History* (London: Granta, 2007), 80.

3. Anke Bernau, "Eternally Virginal," *Guardian*, July 18, 2007, 28.

4. It seems ironic, in this respect, that throughout the history of Western art the image of the Virgin should be associated with the presence of her Child.

5. Sigmund Freud, *The Taboo of Virginity*, vol. 11 in *Standard Edition* (London: Hogarth Press, 1918), 193.

6. Ibid., 194.

7. Sybille Yates, "An Investigation of the Psychological Factors in Virginity and Ritual Defloration," *International Journal of Psychoanalysis* 11 (1930): 173, 182–83.

8. Freud, *Taboo of Virginity*, 202.

9. Karl Abraham, "Manifestations of the Female Castration Complex," *International Journal of Psychoanalysis* 3, no.1 (1922): 1–28; Yates, "Investigation of the Psychological Factors in Virginity"; Karen Horney, "The Denial of the Vagina," *International Journal of Psychoanalysis* 14 (1933): 57–70; Helen Deutsch, *The Psychology of Women: A Psychoanalytic Interpretation*, vols. 1 and 2 (New York: Grune and Stratton, 1944–45).

10. Philip Weissman, "Psychosexual Development in a Case of Neurotic Virginity and Old Maidenhood," *International Journal of Psychoanalysis* 45 (1964): 110.

11. Ibid., 119.

12. Ibid., 111.

13. Deanna Holtzman and Nancy Kulish, "Nevermore: The Hymen and the Loss of Virginity," *Journal of the American Psychoanalytic Association* 44 (1996): 325.

14. See, for instance, in this respect, the frightening folktale of Bluebeard's castle.

15. The film is the expanded, feature-length version of the sixth of ten one-hour-long episodes from *Dekalog* (1988) which Kieślowski directed for television.

16. Bertolucci's previous three films were *The Last Emperor* (1987), *Sheltering Sky* (1990), and *Little Buddha* (1993).

17. Maria Vittoria Costantini, "La rabbia impossibile" (unpublished paper, 1996).

18. Ibid.

19. Ibid.

Carol Siegel

Irreconcilable Feminisms and the Construction of a Cultural Memory of Virginity's Loss
À ma soeur! and Thirteen

In this chapter, I examine two films that represent opposed views of girls' first sexual experiences, Catherine Breillat's *À ma soeur!* (2001) and Catherine Hardwicke's *Thirteen* (2003). The films are ideal for such a comparison because each focuses on a girl just entering puberty (Breillat's protagonist is twelve, Hardwicke's a year older) and her relationship with a slightly older female mentor, as well as depicting the younger girl's movement toward womanhood in terms of her loss or preservation of virginity. In the promotion of each film, the director emphasized its grounding in reality, Hardwicke through discussion of her collaboration on the script with fourteen-year-old Nikki Reed, who plays Evie Zamora in the film, and Breillat through revealing her film's inspiration by her relationship with her actress-model twin sister. In keeping with each film's focus on the figure of "a true young girl" (the title of Breillat's first film), each implicitly responds to various discourses that universalize certain desires as natural or unnatural to girls. Analysis of the mechanisms of the two films' separate treatments of universalization/naturalization will uncover foundational assumptions of the two feminist philosophies whose opposition has resulted in an ongoing division between feminists, and it will also raise some questions about the ways film works to construct collective cultural memories.

Since the first wave of feminism as a political movement in the nineteenth century, women's narratives of girls' sexual initiation have been taken increasingly seriously as authoritative sources for creating generalized concepts of female sexuality. While such narratives almost always receive respectful attention from feminist critics as correctives to traditional, masculinist perspectives on female sexuality, they are also usually stripped of their particularity and incorporated into feminist theories as evidence for some posited areas of commonality among women. The construction of an agreed-upon account of female sexual development is necessary to psychoanalytic theory, which provides our primary approach to understanding sexuality, because the emphasis on the unconscious in the putative science of the mind calls into question the accuracy of individual women's memories of our own sexual awakening. However, construction of a consensus is also necessary to women's collective contestation of the misogynistic view of female sexuality central to traditional Western culture. Truth claims about women generated through narrative determine much in therapeutic practice, functioning as touchstones for the diagnosis of delusions reflecting neuroses, whether or not the therapy in question is informed by feminism. Consequently narratives of girls' loss of virginity heavily influence official policies and laws regulating adolescent sexuality, from age-of-consent statutes to film rating systems. The increase in the influence of female-authored narratives in such power-knowledge formations is a triumph for feminism. But changes in the officially accepted story of the import of virginity's loss also disturbingly reflect extreme differences between feminisms as they pertain to sexuality.

The two films examined here make a useful contrast because they can be seen as arising from these different feminisms. To review, briefly, French feminisms developed out of Lacanian discussion of jouissance as a force that disrupts normative configuration of identity through a culturally shared symbolic register and Foucauldian discussion of sexuality/gender as linguistically situated constructs that could be disrupted through the development of new pleasures not yet contained within master discourses. French feminist theories focused on bodily pleasure as a positive mode of self- and cultural transformation. Leading figures such as Catherine Clément, Hélène Cixous, Julia Kristeva, and Luce Irigaray developed psycholinguistically based theories to provide an approach to the problem of female subjectivity within phallocentric systems of signification. In contrast, most early influential American feminist academics rejected high theory as masculinist and instead adopted sociological and historical approaches to reveal effects of cultural concepts of gender and sexuality on relationships between partners and within social groups. For the French, sexual pleasure was assumed to exist meaningfully outside relationships between lovers, the two vaginal lips touching each other, for instance.[1] And meanings were made through the interplay of cultural discourses, not through an individual's consciously adopted gender politics.

Debates over the relative importance of focus on the linguistically and/ or culturally constructed body or on the socius were superseded in the United States in the late 1980s by the so-called sex wars over the representation of sexuality in pornography and over the sexual practices appropriate to feminists.[2] But, as I show here, this conflict was deeply rooted in the contention over underlying assumptions about female sexuality first expressed within the debate between French and American feminisms. Both French and American feminisms emerged through the youth (countercultural) revolution of the 1960s and the sexual revolution that began in the same period and reached its apex in the 1970s with the development and proliferation of singles bars. Within these movements the loss of virginity was considered initiatory. Popularized Freudianism determined the common understanding of what one was being initiated into.

As Foucault famously argues in his *History of Sexuality*, and much earlier in *Madness and Civilization*, the acceptance of Freudian psychoanalytic theory as official truth established sexuality as the essence of identity.[3] Thus the sexual revolution was understood by the majority of its participants as active experimentation to discover the nature of one's sexual desires and so as a journey of self-discovery. This attitude aligned with the youth movement's emphasis on discovering and revealing one's "true" self, formerly hidden by a socially imposed mask. But in the minds of those who moved from belief in this sort of self-actualization to follow anti-Freudian poststructuralist philosophies, such as Foucault's and those of Deleuze and Guattari, that argued against the existence of human essence and core identity, virginity lost its preconceived crucial relation to truth and became simply a construct of the dominant discourse that might or might not be relevant to the "bodies and pleasures" mobilized to combat regimes of sexual norming.[4]

For the general public, however, who are not followers of antipsychoanalytic poststructuralist thinkers, virginity has remained an important issue. Clearly, in French cinema virginity's loss has retained its 1960s and 1970s meaning as initiation into adult self-discovery, in keeping with a culture that is increasingly, as we put it in the United States, sex-positive, moving forward in providing birth control and education in disease prevention to the young and in decriminalizing pornography. A girl's loss of virginity has, unfortunately, garnered other meanings in the United States.

From the modern period up until the sexual revolution, American mainstream attitudes about virginity could roughly be described as reflecting a gender binary, according to which men were seen as appropriately active and knowledgeable and women as appropriately passive and innocent. Young men were assumed to lose their virginity as soon as possible given their access to sexually available women, ideally prostitutes. Young men who deliberately preserved their virginity were generally depicted in popular culture as emotionally or even mentally ill, with problems such as extreme immaturity, excessive timidity, overattachment to their mothers, or homosexuality, which was deemed a psychological ailment. In contrast, virginity in young women signified moral purity. Fellatio and anal intercourse were generally described as sodomy under the law and often criminalized even for married couples. The earnest discussions in marriage manuals of whether or not such acts could ever be acceptable as expressions of affection rather than disgusting perversity further suggest what is blatantly obvious in popular media of the times: young women who sought to keep their hymens intact by offering dates oral and/or anal access were not considered true virgins and were, in fact, often considered morally inferior to honest whores, who at least acknowledged their debased status. Technical virgins, often referred to as demi-vierges, were despised as duplicitous violators of the code of feminine innocence, not only because of their experience of what were considered perverse acts, but also because of their deliberate arousal and knowing manipulation of men.

As popular Freudianism gained influence in the United States, reactions against female "frigidity," meaning lack of responsiveness to vaginal intercourse, increased, and the desire for such intercourse with a loved partner was accepted as normal in young women, even when strong self-control was expected, as when the woman was not yet married to her partner. Technical virginity was considered even worse at this time, a violation of feminine innocence, honesty, and normal female sexuality. Male preservation of technical virginity was explicable only as homosexuality, conscious or latent.

The sexual revolution of the 1960s and 1970s reversed some of this coding and strengthened other aspects of it. Adult male virginity was represented in popular culture not only as illness but as sinister and a threat to others. Norman Bates in Hitchcock's *Psycho* (1960) is a case in point. Female virginity was depicted as most appropriate in the very young, with fear and ignorance, if not trauma-induced frigidity or some other emotional illness, such as latent lesbianism, accounting for virginity's preservation into adulthood. While oral and anal sex became more acceptable, along with other types of sexual play and experimentation, voluntary female participation in these acts was still considered a sign of advanced experience, the very opposite of virginity.

In the last twenty-five years, three forces have converged to change concepts of virginity in the United States more radically than has ever happened before. First, we saw the development and ultimate mainstreaming of a feminist backlash against the orthodox Freudian view of healthy female sexuality and against the sexual availability of women to men demanded by many proponents of the sexual revolution. The popularization of radical feminist advocacy of women's sexual self-determinacy and freedom from objectification, through movements such as the one against pornography that divided American feminists, often entailed an insistence that vaginal intercourse was always unsatisfying to women and that all representation of sex acts—and sometimes even all heterosexual sex acts—violated women. Consequently, teaching young women to resist heterosexual penetration became, for some, a feminist project.

Second, the hysteria over the AIDS pandemic in the United States has released floods of misinformation while we have suppressed actual information about sexuality, especially for the young, as ignorance is equated with safety. Abstinence-only sex education in U.S. schools is illustrative. As well as celebrating ignorance about sexuality, Americans have increasingly demonized gay men as disease bearers. Ironically, as numerous studies of young peoples' beliefs and practices reflect, oral and anal intercourse are no longer considered sex acts and, despite reality, are understood by what may be the majority of teens not to transmit sexual diseases, unless the participants in the acts are both male.

And finally, America has seen the rise of the religious right as a formidable political power. Central to current doctrine in such religious organizations is a sort of cult of virginity, complete with books, music, youth groups, and symbolic accessories.[5] Although the leaders of provirginity religious movements, such as Joshua Harris, frequently explain to their followers that virginity means abstention from all sexual and erotic activities—Harris even bans hand-holding—numerous studies show that religious youth are even more likely than secular youth to insist that indulging in oral and/or anal sex does not destroy one's virginity.[6]

Virginity thus seems to have come to mean, in the United States today, that one has not experienced vaginally penetrative intercourse. Virginity seems to signify to young people a state of being disease free, which equates to being virtuous. Since the majority of U.S. teens begin having some sort of intercourse between the onset of puberty and age fifteen, we may assume that most of our "virgins" are not particularly innocent about sexuality. Yet they inhabit a space of potent symbolization within national discourses of sexuality, representing, among other things, purity that must be legislatively protected and preserved within "the family," as figured in conservative politics.

One crucial way the development of feminism, in terms of philosophy and praxis, in the United States has differed from its development in France is that here it has taken place not simply against the background of an increasingly powerful form of fundamentalism defined by its determination to suppress nonnormative heterosexuality and extramarital sexuality but often, surprisingly, also in collaboration with it. The most notorious example of this was Andrea Dworkin and Catherine McKinnon's development of a model antipornography ordinance for Minneapolis and their subsequent involvement in Attorney General Edwin Meese's Commission on Pornography, both activities bringing them into collaborative agreement with members of the religious right.[7] Some radical feminisms, such as that of Dworkin and McKinnon, and some mainstream feminisms can and have been articulated in ways that include assumptions underlying the antisexuality of the new American fundamentalism, for example, that pornography constitutes a degrading attack on women, that the sexual revolution took place at the expense of women, that women need emotional connection and trust to feel arousal, and most pertinent to this chapter, that early heterosexual activity exploits girls to the extent that it should be considered rape.

The aims of the sexual liberation movement in the United States have been seriously forestalled through proponents of freedom from legal regulation of sexuality being forced into dialogue with both the religious right and antiheterosexual feminisms. Within the discourses of these cultures, virginity's loss for girls has come to signify the subordination of female truth to male fantasy, the girl's loss of access to the universal(ized) realities of the female body to masculine discourses of pleasure.[8] Within these circles virginity has come to represent women's truth.

This is most evident in the film *Thirteen*'s apparently naïve replication of the ideology of American abstinence education through its depiction of a teen girl gone to the bad. A central tenet of the abstinence education programs, developed by a coalition between the religious right and right-wing think tanks such as the Heritage Foundation, is that interest in sexual activity is not a natural, spontaneously occurring feature of puberty but rather a result of poor parenting—even including sexual molestation—and the influence of a decadent society saturated in sexual messages inappropriate for the young.[9] The decadence of contemporary society is implicitly associated with racial mixing in many abstinence education materials.[10] All of these ideas seem to structure *Thirteen*'s narrative.

Although Tracy, the film's protagonist, is clearly going through puberty and her personal and familial crises center on her drug abuse, some traditional features of narratives of female coming-of-age and of addiction are put aside here. There is no reference to menstruation or hormones or to any physical change linked to maturation to account for Tracy's sudden transformation from a childlike person who plays with Barbies and begs her mother, Mel (Melanie), to buy her a board game into a defiant teen obsessed with recreational drugs. All the changes in her behavior and personality are attributed to her early interactions and subsequent relationship with a slightly older girl, Evie, who first makes fun of her clothes as "Cabbage Patch" and then corrupts her. The film also departs from drug-abuse narratives in that Tracy's introduction to marijuana (dusted with stronger drugs as well as plain), cocaine (or some powdered drug), alcohol, psychedelics, and huffing aerosols does not seem to result in addiction, illness, overdose, or any problems at all beyond her naughty behavior while under the influence.

Instead of drug addiction, loss of virginity seems to be posited by the film as the only significant crisis threatening teen girls. Tracy desperately wants Evie's friendship because she assumes that Evie, perceived as "the hottest girl" in their school, has sexual power. Because all of Evie's sexual exploits are merely hinted at and take place off screen, the impression is conveyed that these dangers are too terrible to be seen. Once we see Evie sneak out of Tracy's bedroom during a sleepover in order to meet a boy, but we learn nothing of what ensues, nor, it seems, does Tracy. At another time, Evie emerges from the dressing room of a shop, smugly wiping what appears to be semen off her mouth, followed by the boy Tracy likes, looking sheepishly pleased. This would seem to be a perfect opportunity for the film to raise feminist questions about what constitutes heterosexual pleasure for teen girls. Does teenage female sexuality consist primarily of the desire to be desired, or of the desire to successfully compete for male attention? Is it about the girl's physical sensations or direct experience, or is it mainly psychological? Does it retain any connection to orgasm? A conversation between the two girls could have been used to bring out the implications of the replacement of intercourse by fellatio as the initiatory experience for girls. But it never takes place. The film's shying away from such topics gives the impression that, as for the heroine of *Deep Throat* (1972), fellatio is simply and naturally the means through which desires are best satisfied. Silence naturalizes here because there seems no need to explain why the characters behave as they do. Their sexual behaviors are presented as the only expressions of sexuality possible and thus are beyond being questioned. But even though naturalized, oral sex is presented as something to be avoided, not because it brings risk of sexually transmitted diseases, but because it is dangerous in some mysterious, unarticulated, and thus naturalized way.

Scenes in which the girls drink and take drugs in the company of boys are ominously lit and accompanied by portentous songs on the soundtrack that suggest, as do the abstinence brochures, that such practices are problematic primarily due to their weakening of teens' resolve to resist sexuality. Although Tracy does some very dangerous drugs with Evie, ones generally depicted in film as being instantly addictive, the implication is that because she comes through her association with Evie with her virginity intact, she comes through all right. Nothing else seems to matter.

Tracy's falling victim to Evie's pernicious influence is explained by Tracy herself and by the film, through flashbacks and reaction shots, as a result of parental failures, depicted in conservative terms. Tracy's home has been broken by divorce, and the film devotes a lengthy sequence to establishing the lack of a proper patriarchal presence in Tracy's life, as her father visits only to whine about his need to concentrate on his business and new family before abdicating parental responsibility and leaving his first son and daughter depressed and cynical about him. On top of this, Tracy's mother, a recovering substance abuser, leaves her daughter alone as she devotes her free time to her relationship with her boyfriend, also in recovery. Flashbacks emphasize the impossibility of Tracy's being able to respect this man whom she has seen brought low by an overdose.

Despite its ostensible feminist stance, the film never engages with the sexism of the world Tracy grows up in, which seems to offer women no pleasures except those of domesticity, shopping, and beauty rituals and no ego gratification beyond being desired by men and raising physically attractive children. Instead, Tracy's mother's work as a home beautician is represented as heroic, part of her virtue as a single mother doing the best she can for her children. One of most glaring areas of lack of analysis concerns the messages Mel's work and interests send to her growing daughter and that daughter's anxieties about her own appearance and ability to attract boys. The film makes no connection between Mel's obvious preoccupation with retaining the extreme slenderness of early adolescence and her substance abuse. There is also no connection suggested either visually by the montage or verbally through the narrative between Mel's patronizing attitude toward an ordinary-sized woman whose hair she dresses in her home beauty shop—and whom she obviously perceives as fat—and Mel's constant smoking, her ravaged face and withered skin often shown in close-up, and her nagging at Tracy to eat, as Tracy develops an eating disorder. How is Tracy supposed to remain below a size 2, the film industry standard for female beauty, if she eats normally, as Mel urges her to do?[11] Instead of addressing this problem, which currently spoils the health and happiness of so many adolescents, the film gives in to the usual Hollywood magical thinking, in which a body fat level so low as to stop menstruation signifies not only beauty but good health.[12]

In fact, rather than examine Mel as the primary force in Tracy's life for promulgation of American myths of health and beauty, the film uses Evie's mother, Brooke, as a foil to deflect our criticisms. Brooke's grotesquely exaggerated pursuit of youth is marked as unnatural by the scene in which, groggy and weepy from sedation, she reveals the hideous scars left by her recent face-lift. Her failure as a parental figure is reflected not only in Evie's wild behavior but in Evie's anxiety that Brooke not be referred to as her mother, but instead as her guardian or cousin. We may assume that Brooke conceals her true relation to Evie in order to seem younger both to keep alive her dream of a career as a "model-slash-actress" and to keep her very young lover. Brooke seems to be always on drugs, always unavailable to Evie, and lacking in any maternal feeling toward the girl. In contrast, Mel is shown to be maternal and caring both toward her lover, who is appropriately her same age and similar to her in background, and toward her two children. Because Brooke's preoccupation with beauty standards is so heavily coded as unnatural and immature, Mel's devotion to glamour is naturalized as normal female desire to look good and so to be loved. Thus we are urged to conclude that female narcissism is fine as long as it does not interfere with a women's performance of a traditional maternal/domestic role.

Because almost all the scenes are set either in shopping malls or house interiors, consumerism and domesticity are portrayed as the world of girls and women. An opposition is also set up between the two by Mel's insistence that the girls should entertain themselves wholesomely at home rather than getting into trouble in the shops they love. The emotional intensity of this opposition is ratcheted up when Tracy cruelly rejects as homemade the jeans with fake leopard fur side panels that Mel sews for her and prefers shoplifted panties imprinted with a suggestive message. Just as in the dichotomy between the nice home beauty salon and the nasty cosmetic surgery, one side of the binary is always naturalized. So domestic pursuit of glamour and fashion are depicted as natural, and apparently inevitable, despite the obvious fact that they are achieved merely at less cost to the consumer than the forms of buying beauty the film demonizes.

Other ways that the film naturalizes as inevitable the body issues that plague young women are even more alarmingly conservative. Racial concerns are always presented the way they are in abstinence brochures, where a wildly disproportionate number of the badly behaved young people we see are nonwhite.[13] Not only does Evie's surname (Zamora) suggest that she is Latina, but notably, the young men who pursue the girls are almost all not only African American but gotten up in threatening gang-style attire. Once the girls attempt to seduce a white boy, who almost gives in to their seductive posturing but then catches himself and rejects them because of his fear of being charged with statutory rape, or perhaps even out of a moral desire to obey the law. Dark-skinned boys in the film lack such impulses, freely taking advantage of whatever the girls offer them.

Despite Tracy and her brother's residence in Los Angeles and his involvement in surfing, both are strikingly pale, her pallor so profound that it seems it would be impossible for a normally active child to achieve. She is easily as white as if she assiduously avoided sun exposure. Through lighting that enhances the radiance of her light skin and blonde hair, the film suggests that an exemplary Anglo-Saxon appearance signifies virtue just as conformity to other cinematic beauty standards does.

Ultimately Tracy is saved by her mother's preservation of her white purity. Forcefully enfolding her daughter in her arms and lying in bed with her all night, as if to make sure Tracy is safe from sleeping with anyone else, Mel returns her daughter to the innocence of childhood, as the film's color palette and lighting let us know. The darkness that had gradually taken over the screen, making the scenes increasingly grey and dim, lifts, and as the long night of danger ends, the bright primary colors of childhood again blaze on the screen. Sexuality, figured as descent into darkness, as fearful miscegenation, has been banished, and Tracy is once again a happy child who we last see playing on a playground. This conclusion literalizes the "hugs not drugs" slogan that became so popular in the Reagan years, while displacing anxiety about drugs onto anxiety about maintaining sexual purity and emphasizing that redemptive physical intimacy can only come from a return to the maternal body.

This might be merely silly if the film were not heralded by influential feminist thinkers, such as Angela McRobbie, as a "hopeful" and accurate portrayal of female development that can "help us understand what it means to become a woman for the new generation."[14] If the latter is true, the film is certainly not hopeful. Because the possibility of heterosexual pleasure is decisively foreclosed for Tracy, we are left with a strange sense of what is natural for girls and what their futures as sexual beings should be. Lesbianism can hardly be considered a future solution because Tracy's attraction to Evie has been so aggressively pathologized, and Tracy's redemption begins with Mel's expulsion of Evie from their home. Asexuality or autoeroticism seem to be all that remain. But the surface of the film never acknowledges its own suggestion that girlhood is most properly a sexual dead end.

Instead, *Thirteen* ends by seemingly celebrating the protection of the image of innocent girlhood that has become a national obsession in the United States, what Lauren Berlant calls "the little-girl form that represents totemically and fetishistically the unhumiliated citizen" upon whose behalf Americans manage everyone's sexuality.[15] The film produces "paramnesias, images that organize consciousness, not by way of explicit propaganda, but by replacing and simplifying memories people actually have . . . [in order to veil] the means by which the nation's hegemonic contradictions and contingencies are constructed, consented to, displaced, replaced by images of normal culture" that in turn determine attitudes about the legal regulation of sexuality.[16] The film entreats its target audience to look back, as women and feminists, on our own puberty as a time in which we faced the threat of sexuality with only our mothers, and the domesticity they represented, to save us from being dirtied, rendered impure, and despoiled, and to (mis)remember our resistance to that maternal protection as a form of madness with no source other than the corruptive darkness of the world outside the familial home.

In contrast to *Thirteen*, the depiction of the family's interactions in *À ma soeur!* stresses the effects of the parents' narcissistic obsession with surfaces on the daughters. The excruciating scene around the breakfast table in which both parents humiliatingly berate Anaïs for eating despite being fat, and praise their thin daughter, Elena, for her lack of interest in food, suggests an explanation of Elena's belief that beauty and female worth must entail suffering and the suppression of desire. This belief obviously underlies her vision of her virginity as a commodity that she will finally exchange for an expensive piece of beauty. The film raises the question, how can she avoid thinking that for women beauty is worth and that male love is shown through the exchange of financial advantages for sexual favors when this is modeled to her by her parents? Through frequent returns to the conflict between the mother's need for reassurance of her beauty's power and the father's need to earn more to pay for the tributes she demands, the film provides an implicit analysis of traditional gender roles among the bourgeoisie. Far from being negligent, the parents are training their daughters to take on the cold vanity and the gender relations of barely suppressed hostility that characterize their own lives.

As is the case throughout French feminist theory, domesticity is ignored as unworthy of analytical attention. While the structuring opposition in Hardwicke's film is between domesticity and what is outside the home, in Breillat's film the central opposition is between what can be observed by anyone with even nascent feminist consciousness and dominant discourses, especially those of beauty and romance. In the latter, a woman's desirability determines how much she is loved, and she is desirable to the extent that she conforms to beauty standards and can tease and please men. Both teasing and pleasing are accomplished through disciplining the self in ways that require the suppression of one's own primal desires (i.e., all desires except the desire to be admired/desired). As current mainstream culture equates female beauty with thinness to the point of starvation, beautiful women must learn to stop responding to hunger. Likewise the truly lovable woman refuses to act on her own sexual desires and instead responds to the man's, sometimes frustrating him while still giving him hope of future fulfillment and at other times gratifying him with a "proof of love," as Elena's boyfriend describes the anal intercourse she permits in order to put off vaginal penetration.

In contrast, Anaïs provides a point of view roughly consonant with that of Breillat herself, that is, the viewpoint of someone developing into a contemporary French feminist observer. As such, she sees that being loved has nothing whatsoever to do with conforming to mainstream cultural beauty standards, and in fact she sees that some of the most lovely women are treated as objects or prizes to be seduced and abandoned, or at best acquired and then treated as convenient objects, as their mother is. Moreover, watching Elena gradually submitting more and more sexually, despite her physical pain and the fear it arouses, Anaïs sees that, in order to fulfill her role as a beautiful prize, her sister must not act on her own feelings at all but only attend to the man's. Anaïs becomes "scathingly knowledgeable."[17] And she "articulates with increasing clarity her rejection of the romantic delusions she sees at work in her sister's life."[18]

Just as Tracy functions in *Thirteen* to reinscribe current master narratives of female adolescence, both as a character within a narrative and as a symbol of what the dominant culture values, Anaïs functions in *À ma soeur!* to undermine such narratives, both through her role in the story as a critical observer and as a symbol of what is obscured by dominant narratives of female adolescence, especially those that dominate American popular feminism. But Breillat avoids treating Anaïs as representative of the desires—diffuse, fleshy, and impersonal—that were universally attributed to women by second wave French feminism. As a symbol Anaïs might best be described with Deleuze's term *demark*. Deleuzian demarks are images that denaturalize. In contrast to a mark that always "refers back to other terms in a customary series such that each can be 'interpreted' by the others," demarks "leap outside the web and suddenly appear in conditions which take it out of its series or set it in contradiction with it."[19] A demark pushes the viewer to reassess the context in which it is presented.

Anaïs's fatness provides an image disruptive of the narrative of thinness as youth/beauty, taking us into affect that resists conventional organization and so prepares us to receive the event of (her) virginity's loss otherwise than the way it occurs in her sister's story, structured as it is to Elena by a predetermined perspective, one that Deleuze and Guattari would call majoritarian.[20] In their theory of majoritarian languages and literatures, which derives from Foucault's genealogies of dominant discourses, these forms express the identities that result from the coding of experience by cultural and societal power structures. Through taking on the perspective of the despised sister, the one who is excluded from exemplary femininity, the film functions as minoritarian. Instead of reinscribing universalized identities in service of existent power structures, minoritarian arts resist them through focusing on the particularity of experience.[21] Claire Colebrook explains, "A minoritarian politics does not have a pre-given (or transcendent) measure or norm for inclusion or identity." Instead, "each addition to the group change[s] what the group is," without ever generating a naturalized norm.[22]

As Susan Bordo points out, "Pre-occupation with fat, diet, and slenderness . . . may function as one of the most popular normalizing mechanisms of our century, insuring the production of self-monitoring and self-disciplining 'docile bodies' sensitive to any departure from social norms and habituated to self-improvement and self-transformation in service of those norms."[23]

Breillat's comments on Anaïs elucidate her relation to this system of norming. She sees Anaïs as "beautiful" and her perspective as "magical."[24] In fact, if Elena's world view is determined by a false, majoritist romanticism based on lies about female sexuality, Anaïs's world view is romantic in a minor sense. Her obvious enjoyment of her own voluptuous body, especially as she swims, and her eager anticipation of her own virginity's loss, which she insists will be impersonal and allow her to focus on her own sensations rather than those of the initiatory stranger, evoke the attention to one's own specificity that gives childhood much of its romance for adults who have already capitulated to dominant ways of seeing. Here, too, Deleuze is instructive. As Ronald Bogue explains, for Deleuze, "the modern visual image . . . is the site of multilayered forces that materialize sensation and offer the possibility of various re-enchainments with other images, each conjunction of images forcing the viewer to read the image in terms of the re-enchainment actualized in that particular series of images."[25] As such an image, fat and beautiful Anaïs takes us back into the feeling of childhood openness to experience and wonder at the new. She provides us with a vision of "this world seen and thought 'otherwise.'"[26]

Nowhere is this more evident than in the film's shocking conclusion in which Anaïs, Elena, and their mother are assailed at a highway rest stop by a psychotic killer who immediately murders Elena and the mother and drags Anaïs into the woods and rapes her. The shock of the conclusion comes not from these events, horrifyingly depicted as they are, but from Anaïs's response to them as a satisfactory initiation into womanhood. Anne Gillian remarks, "Birth is ugly. She is born amidst the ugliness of rape."[27] Recognizing that her attacker is fulfilling her intention of having her first sexual experience with a stranger in a situation without romance or sentimentality, Anaïs not only embraces him companionably during the act but later denies to the police that she was taken without her consent. And perhaps even more disturbingly, her complaisant facial expression suggests that she feels freed by the removal of the two females whose presence always worked to assign her meaning—in Deleuze and Guattari's terms, to territorialize her—in the name of the majoritist vision.

Two feminisms, then. One upholds the value of the mother-daughter bond, but at the expense of the exclusion not simply of the "bad girl" (the aptly named Evie) but also of the possibility that a teenage girl could act to gratify heterosexual desires of her own without destroying herself and her natural(ized) environment, the maternal/domestic home. The other feminism is radically other. It rejects the norm violently, even to the point of valorizing the destruction of the women who embody it. But it allows for the possibility that teen girls can choose how they will experience their virginity's loss and can embrace and take pleasure even in acts that our current culture and society consign to the very fringes of criminality and unnatural evil. One feminism asks women to protect girls from sex in the name of a remembered—or misremembered—lost purity we are all assumed to mourn as the loss of the true, natural self. The other feminism ask us to dare to remember what each of us once was, complete with our often frighteningly different early sexualities. The choice presented by these feminisms goes far beyond how we want to remember our own pasts or what sorts of pleasures we want cinema to provide. It goes to the heart of what sort of futures we, as the women who articulate feminism for those who follow, and who advocate and often effect social, cultural, and legislative changes, want to create for girls now on the verge of womanhood.

Notes

1. Luce Irigaray, *This Sex which Is Not One,* trans. Catherine Porter with Carolyn Burke (Ithaca, NY: Cornell University Press, 1985), 24–26.

2. Lisa Duggan and Nan D. Hunter, *Sex Wars: Sexual Dissent and Political Culture* (London: Routledge, 2003); Alice Echols, *Daring to Be Bad* (Minnesota: University of Minneapolis Press, 1989); Pat Califia, *Public Sex: The Culture of Radical Sex* (San Francisco: Cleis Press, 1994); Elayne Rapping, *Media-tions: Forays into the Culture and Gender Wars* (Cambridge, MA: South End Press, 1994); Jill Nagle, ed., *Whores and Other Feminists* (London: Routledge, 1997); Marianne Hirsch and Evelyn Fox Keller, eds., *Conflicts in Feminism* (London: Routledge, 1991); Jane Gerhard, *Desiring Revolution* (New York: Columbia University Press, 2001); Adele M. Stan, *Debating Sexual Correctness: Pornography, Sexual Harassment, Date Rape and the Politics of Sexual Equality* (Surrey, UK: Delta, 1995).

3. Michel Foucault, *History of Sexuality,* vol. 1, *An Introduction* (New York: Pantheon Books, 1978); and Foucault, *Madness and Civilization* (London: Routledge, 2006).

4. Ladelle McWhorter, *Bodies and Pleasures: Pornography, Sexual Harassment, Date Rape and the Politics of Sexual Equality* (Indianapolis: Indiana University Press, 1999).

5. True Love Waits is probably America's best-known abstinence youth group, but many more, such as the Pro-Virginity Society, appear regularly on high school and college campuses. Many self-proclaimed virgins wear white wristbands to signify their purity and chastity, and "promise" and purity rings are popular with youth who want to announce their intention to remain virginal. True Love Waits even of-

fers a complete line of virginity jewelry. Recordings also capitalize on the trend, for instance Marcellus T's "Don't Give It Away" and Michael Sweet's "No Safe Way."

6. Sharon Lerner, "An Orgy of Abstinence: Federal Funding Pushes No-Sex Education into the Mainstream," *Village Voice*, August 7, 2001, 34–36; Cindy Patton, *Fatal Advice: How Safe-Sex Education Went Wrong* (Durham, NC: Duke University Press, 1996); Peter S. Bearman and Hannah Brückner, "Promising the Future: Virginity Pledges and First Intercourse," *American Journal of Sociology* 106 (January 2001): 859–912. See also press coverage of the study conducted by Buzz Pruitt, professor of health and kinesiology at Texas A & M University, who plans to publish the results in the near future.

7. Lisa Duggan, *The Twilight of Equality? Neoliberalism, Cultural Politics, and the Attack on Democracy* (Boston: Beacon Press, 2003).

8. Eve Ensler's feminist play, *The Vagina Monologues* (New York: Villard, 1998), exemplifies the popularization of this idea.

9. Judith Levine, *Harmful to Minors: The Perils of Protecting Children from Sex* (Minneapolis: University of Minnesota Press, 2002); Janice Irvine, *Talk about Sex: The Battle over Sex Education in the United States* (Berkeley and Los Angeles: University of California Press, 2002).

10. N. Dickson Reppuci and Jeffrey J. Haugaard, "Prevention of Child Sexual Abuse: Myth or Reality," *American Psychologist* 44 (October 1989): 1266–75.

11. An American size 2 is generally made to fit a woman with a bust measurement of 32 inches, a waist measurement of 24 inches, and a hip measurement of 34 inches.

12. Here, as in many other instances, Hollywood supports some of the most pernicious myths of our times. See Susan Bordo's classic study, *Unbearable Weight: Feminism, Western Culture, and the Body* (Berkeley and Los Angeles: University of California Press, 1993), for discussion of this problem.

13. Annette Fuentes, "No Sex Ed: Congress Pushes Abstinence in the Schools," *In These Times*, December 18, 1997, 16–18.

14. Angela McRobbie and Ryan Gilbey, "Sugar and Spice," *Sight and Sound* 13, no. 12 (2003): 9.

15. Lauren Berlant, *The Queen of America Goes to Washington City: Essays on Sex and Citizenship* (Durham, NC: Duke University Press, 1997), 62.

16. Ibid., 59.

17. Anne Gillian, "Profile of a Filmmaker: Catherine Breillat," in *Beyond French Feminisms: Debates on Women, Politics, and Culture in France, 1981–2001*, ed. Roger Celestin, Eliane DalMolin, and Isabelle de Courtivron (New York: Palgrave Macmillan, 2003), 207.

18. Colin Nettlebeck, "Self-Constructing Women beyond the Shock of *Baise-moi* and *À ma soeur!*" *FULGOR: Flinders University Languages Group Online Review* 1 (December 2003): 63.

19. Gilles Deleuze, *Cinema 1: The Movement-Image*, trans. Hugh Tomlinson and Barbara Habberjam Galeta (Minneapolis: University of Minnesota Press, 1986), 203.

20. Gilles Deleuze and Félix Guattari, *Kafka: Toward a Minor Literature*, trans. Dana Polan (Minneapolis: University of Minnesota Press, 1986), 16–27.

21. Gilles Deleuze, *A Thousand Plateaus: Capitalism and Schizophrenia*, trans. Brian Massumi (London: Athlone, 1988), 105–6.
22. Claire Colebrook, *Gilles Deleuze* (London: Routledge, 2002), 117–18.
23. Bordo, *Unbearable Weight*, 186.
24. Nick James, "Looks That Paralyse," *Sight and Sound* 11, no. 12 (2001): 32.
25. Ronald Bogue, *Deleuze on Cinema* (New York: Routledge, 2003), 190.
26. Ibid., 180.
27. Gillian, "Profile of a Filmmaker," 210.

Celestino Deleyto

The New Road to Sexual Ecstacy
Virginity and Genre in *The 40-Year-Old Virgin*

"Lovers, to bed," advises Theseus at the end of *A Midsummer Night's Dream*, one of romantic comedy's founding texts, flaunting the genre's traditional investment in the pleasures of the nuptial bed. While such pleasures can only be explicitly enjoyed in this and other Shakespearean green world comedies once the wedding ceremony of the final act has taken place, sexual heat is, as Stephen Greenblatt has convincingly argued, more pervasive in the genre, and it is transformed in these plays into the linguistic friction between the protagonists that occupies much of the stories and that is at the heart of the lovers' experience.[1] Cut to more than three hundred years later, and screwball comedy has similar pleasures on offer even if the invitation to bed after the final credits is generally much less explicit than in Shakespeare. The Production Code notwithstanding, the filmmakers continue to turn sexual desire into intricate verbal and visual metaphor of the kind that abounds, to mention two of the most obvious examples, in *The Awful Truth* (1937) and *Bringing Up Baby* (1938). There is no sex in these films (the reconstituted couple of *The Awful Truth* is about to have sex just before the end, but the narrative prefers to suggest sexual activity through the famous gag of the cuckoo clock), but, at the same time, sex is everywhere, conveniently translated into the verbal hostility of the lovers and a sophisticated pattern of symbols that pervades the body of the texts and turns them, to paraphrase Elizabeth Cowie, into celebratory mise-en-scènes of desire.[2]

Stanley Cavell has written about the ambivalence of the sexual references of *Bringing Up Baby*. He considers discussion of these references indispensable to understand what the film is about but, at the same time, is reluctant to press them too far for fear of betraying the film's subtlety of representation.[3] I find Cavell's comment appropriate not only for this particular film but, more generally, for much of romantic comedy. The genre's attitude to sex and its visibility in the films has been far from homogeneous in the course of its long cinematic history, but, with all the possible caveats, it could be said that sex has more often than not been a structuring absence in it. Romantic comedy is indeed about the vicissitudes of desire and, generally, about the inevitability of sexual fulfillment, and yet a certain coyness about it seems to be central to several traditions of the genre. Brian Henderson went so far as to suggest, in his analysis of *Semi-Tough* (1972), that romantic comedy is about fucking and its absence, and when for cultural reasons that absence stopped making sense, the genre threatened to disappear.[4]

On the one hand, while the aptly called sex comedies of the 1950s and early 1960s took advantage of a certain relaxation of the Production Code and, in accordance with cultural discourses of the time, brought sex to the fore (as, e.g., many of Lubitsch's films had done earlier), they still found important difficulties in making it explicit and even in naming it. Woody Allen's films of the 1970s and other comedies of the decade, on the other hand, managed to incorporate sex openly into their discourse. However, according to Tamar Jeffers McDonald, that surfacing of sex was more a flash in the pan than the consolidation of a new trend. For this critic, the commercially successful comedies of the last three decades, which she labels neotraditional romantic comedies, are characterized precisely by a de-emphasizing of sexuality and a substitution of a more vague intensity in the central relationship.[5] Sex thus continues to enjoy a bizarre status in the genre: both fundamental to understand what it is about and hardly ever there.

Virginity, as the absence of sex in a person's individual history and therefore a cultural concept that links sex and identity, has had a similar relationship to romantic comedy: because the characters of screwball comedy never have sex or even talk about having sex on the screen, we often assume that they are virgins or take their virginity more or less for granted, and even though it is impossible to associate, for example, the Barbara Stanwyck gold-digger protagonists of *The Lady Eve* (1941) and *Ball of Fire* (1941) with virginity, their male counterparts in these two films are certainly defined by their total lack of sexual experience, absorbed as they are, respectively, in snakes and books. Because this state of affairs is unacceptable for a genre so concerned with the joys of sexuality, the maturation of the heroes consists precisely in shedding their virginal condition, although this does not generally happen before the narrative is finished. Therefore virginity both is and is not what the films are about. Leaving aside the sex comedies and the nervous romances, its representational elusiveness makes it difficult for the critic to pinpoint the exact space it occupies in the films' signifying structures.

Conversely, romantic comedy, like any other genre, is less a group of films than a discursive construct.[6] Therefore the individual films, rather than belonging to a genre, are combinations of discourses associated with several genres. While both sex and virginity have had an unstable status in romantic comedy, they are most visible in the gross-out and the teen-pic comedy, two genres that have recently appeared in combination with romantic comedy in numerous films. Early 1980s landmarks of the teen-pic comedy, such as *Porky's* (1982), *The Last American Virgin* (1982), *Fast Times at Ridgemont High* (1982), or *Losin' It* (1983), may have had little to do with romantic comedy, but a particular blend of the two genres became the name of the game in such end-of-the-century hits as *Clueless* (1995) and *American Pie* (1999). Around the same time, *There's Something about Mary* (1998) inaugurated a tendency in romantic comedy in which its hybridization with the gross-out movie became more and more frequent. These recent alliances of the genre with concomitant categories had as a consequence the repositioning of an explicit concern and even an obsession with sex, and occasionally virginity, within romantic comedy, consolidating, according to William Paul and Leger Grindon, an important line of evolution in its contemporary history.[7] Thus in these cases both sex and virginity come into romantic comedy through the side door, so to speak, but their presence necessarily changes its approach to intimate matters.

Jeffers McDonald complains that the neotraditional romantic comedy has developed with its back to the culture to which it belongs, its virtual erasure of sex contrasting with the modern dating habits it purports to represent, and finds a small measure of hope for the future in the reemergence of sex in films such as *Along Came Polly* (2004), *Wedding Crashers* (2005), and *You, Me and Dupree* (2006), in which men rather than women are placed at the center of the narrative.[8] She labels these films "homme-coms" and, while decrying their ideologically traditional endings, links the opening and middle sections of their narratives to the "radical comedies" of the 1970s.[9] Among these, she briefly focuses on *The 40-Year-Old Virgin*, an unexpected sleeper hit of the summer of 2005, whose success may have been due to the mixing of elements from the gross-out and teen comedies with the conventions of romantic comedy. Through this specific combination, the film explores the cultural meanings of male virginity in a postmodern, post–sexual revolution, and postfeminist society, by pitting the unlikely presexual condition of its protagonist against the exaggerated sexual experience of his workmates. Yet the movie is extremely ambivalent about the relative worth of innocence and experience for the contemporary man. In this chapter, then, I discuss the ways in which *The 40-Year-Old Virgin* constructs its sexual and affective discourses around the issue of virginity from the generic perspective of romantic comedy and its by now formulaic association with the other two comic genres.

Although, in our patriarchal society, virginity has generally been linked with femininity and with the value of women as objects of property and exchange between men, male virginity has not been exactly rare in the history of romantic comedy, from the screwball examples mentioned earlier, through such 1950s male virgins as many of Jerry Lewis's characters or Bo Decker (Don Murray) in *Bus Stop* (1956), to the young heroes of many contemporary teen comedies or Howard Brackett (Kevin Kline), the closeted gay teacher of *In & Out* (1997). In this sense, not only does the protagonist of *The 40-Year-Old Virgin*, Andy Stitzer (Steve Carell), belong in a relatively long line of sexually inexperienced romantic comedy heroes, but his initial predicament, while more openly stated and more explicitly a matter of worry than in most cases, is relatively familiar to the spectator of the genre.

Because of the title, when we first see Andy we already know that he is a virgin, and we therefore associate all the information that goes toward the construction of his character in the first few scenes with his "condition." In case there is any doubt, his virginity is immediately conveyed, among other details, by means of gross-out comedy. Gross-out is part of the tradition of Aristophanic and Rabelaisian comedy, and, as such, it revels in the bodily explicit text and strives to challenge the limits of socially acceptable representation. The film starts with what is presented as the reasonable—that is, culturally understandable—profile of a forty-year-old male virgin: a grown man of extremely neat and healthy habits, surrounded in his bachelor apartment by a huge number of toys, posters, and other types of openly phallic representations of comic-book supermen, gets out of bed in the morning, after apparently having spent a sleepless night, with an obvious erection.

This unremarkable physiological circumstance becomes the centerpiece of the opening scene for several reasons. First, it identifies the film generically and sets the tenor of its take on sexual matters. Second, in combination with Carell's remarkable performance at this point, it signals the character's unwanted sexual abstinence as a problem that has become deeply entrenched as part of his identity. Finally, it defines Andy as a healthy, virile man with all the potential to become a good performer as soon as the opportunity arises. At the same time, while the mise-en-scène emphasizes Andy's teenage mentality as an integral part of his personality and therefore conventionally introduces him as a comic hero in urgent need of maturation, other traits of his character are more affirmative and prevent him from being seen as a ridiculous man or as an Aristotelian *alazon*. These assets will become gradually more apparent when set against the much more caricatured personalities of the other men in the film. What is more significant, the mildness of his attitude to other people, his relaxed politeness, his sense of humor, and especially his respect for women are all related to his virginity and openly celebrated by the film. Unlike, for example, in the cases of the virginal male heroes at the beginning of *Bringing Up Baby* or *The Lady Eve*, his is not a way of living and being that the romantic comedy would like to dispense with altogether.

This disturbing ambivalence toward virginity as maybe a curse and maybe a blessing finds a visual correlative, still in the credit sequence, when Andy, who does not drive a car out of principle, rides his impeccable and perfectly equipped bicycle to work in the morning. Riding along a lonely suburban street, he zigzags on the road with an expression of quiet contentment on his face. This action may have been included at this point to suggest the carefree happiness of the man who does not have to deal with the worries and anxieties of heterosexual relationships, an unobtrusive early celebration of the freedom he enjoys, which awakens in the spectator memories of the famous bicycle ride musical number from *The Sound of Music* (1965), more or less evoking the fullness of childhood and early adolescence. However, a lesser known filmic reference simultaneously comes to mind: the final scene of Luis Buñuel's *Él* (1953), in which the protagonist, ostensibly recovered from a very pronounced psychological imbalance produced by sexual repression, is visited in the convent to which he has retired by his ex-wife and her new husband. After projecting signs of the internal peace that he has reached, he says good-bye and walks away from them, zigzagging along the path, revealing that he is still seriously disturbed and that he will never get cured. Andy's riding flourish also has that implication: his sexual repression has affected him psychologically in a serious way, a fact that is verbalized later by his friend Cal (Seth Rogen) when he expresses his fears that Andy may be a serial killer.

This apparently irrelevant detail summarizes the film's approach to its protagonist's virginity, veering between gross-out macho mockery of his failure to measure up to received standards of masculinity and celebration of what are taken to be its positive aspects. That forty-year-old virginity may be seen as having positive aspects at all by an early twenty-first-century cultural text is in itself revealing, but equally revealing is the textual anxiety to have it both ways, to shamelessly use Andy's problem as an exploitation tactic—to talk about sex as much and as obscenely as possible—and, at the same time, to offer this problem as a solution to the nervousness provoked in the textual discourse by heterosexual relationships. This ambivalence is narratively feasible, at least partly, because of the generic transformations that had occurred in the previous years in the interface between romantic comedy, teenpic, and gross-out.

There is little doubt that one of the narrative and commercial goals of the centrality of Andy's sexual innocence is its exploitative potential: it becomes the perfect excuse for the deployment of a gross-out discourse on sexuality that is developed mostly through the attitudes toward sexual matters of Andy's workmates, including that of his boss Paula (Jane Lynch), and their constant talk of sex. This pattern is inaugurated in the first scene after the credits, when Andy and Cal, back at work on Monday morning, exchange their experiences of the weekend: while the protagonist spent most of the weekend obsessing about making himself an egg salad sandwich, his friend went down to Tijuana to see a show of a woman fucking a horse. After patiently and painfully listening to Andy's detailed account of his recipe, Cal comically expresses the extreme dullness of his friend's existence by pretending to shoot himself in the head, but, having heard Cal's account of his weekend, there is no reason to think this gesture cannot also be applied to the tediousness of his own weekend. Although the film appears to place the spectator closer to Cal at this point, that is, closer to the sexually "sophisticated" than to the sexually naïve, there is surely not so much difference in terms of excitement or adventure between their two experiences, and neither of the two entails a more mature or, from the point of view of romantic comedy, more fulfilling attitude toward sex and heterosexuality. This is a point that is gradually but forcefully driven home by the narrative. Andy's activities may characterize his life as immature, empty, and solitary, but, beyond being the cause of much gross-out fun, his sexually hyperactive friends are not much better off. In this early scene, the comic perspective gently pokes fun at both characters while making sure that the spectator does not overlook the potential pleasures of both behaviors. At the same time, as with the opening visual gag, Cal's narration of his weekend ensures that the spectator knows what to expect from the text in terms of graphic sexuality and profanity.

The explicit sexualized talk at the electronics store where most of the characters work never relents, and it is characterized by a blend of constant semi-infantile profanity and post-p.c. sexism and homophobia. When Andy's friends find out that he is a virgin, during a late-evening poker game in which they exchange anecdotes of "extreme" sexual experiences, Jay (Romany Malco) immediately expresses his solidarity: "Your dick is my dick. I'm getting you some pussy." The line suggests that Andy's condition is not a serious psychological problem—after all, this is a comedy—but rather an occasion to, on the one hand, construct one more narrative of male bonding and, on the other, use the kind of rude words that gross-out revels in and that much of its humor consists of. At the same time, Cal's almost permanent weed-induced stupor, Jay's recurrent infidelities, and David's (Paul Rudd) inability to get over his ex-girlfriend's leaving him two years ago define the male world of the film as seriously impaired and underline the glaring limitations of both the male bonding and the teenage giggling.

The textual distance from its male characters' behavior often appears as a self-granted carte blanche for its misogynist and antigay jokes. We will return to the film's attitude toward women later, but homosexuality is represented exclusively as part of the banter between the heterosexual males. There are no gay people in the film, but references to homosexuality abound in many of its jokes, climaxing in the scene in which David and Cal accuse each other of being gay while playing a violent video game against each other. The verbal sparring starts when David explains to his friend his decision to remain celibate, after his not so recent disappointment. Celibacy and gayness sound approximately the same to Cal (before realizing he was a virgin, Andy's friends also thought he may have been gay when he did not know what women's breasts felt like), and so the two friends engage in their "you know why I know you are gay?" routine, a dialogue that is mostly funny because of the stubborn repetition of the pattern by both characters and the text's blatant obliviousness toward the unfairness of stereotyping. The exchange of accusations of gayness alternates with a telephone conversation between Andy and Trish (Catherine Keener) during which they arrange to have their first date, the narrative thus establishing a contrast between David and Cal's regressive attitude toward sexuality and Andy's initiation of the "correct" route to adult heterosex. Homosexuality, therefore, is never seen as anything but an amusingly inappropriate sexual option. The immature behavior of the characters who indulge in homophobia does not cast a positive light on the sexual practices that they deride but rather absorbs them into their own limited attitude to sex. Set against this, Andy and Trish's relationship appears as the only viable option.

Romantic comedy on the one hand, and gross-out and teenpic on the other, do not complement each other but rather vie for dominance, emphasizing the cultural contradictions between them. Whereas the latter two stress the dominance of male homosocial desire that Eve Sedgwick correctly singled out as the central feature of patriarchal culture, romantic comedy has always been an exception to this rule in that it has generally considered male bonding as an immature state to be shed on the road to adult sexuality.[10] *The 40-Year-Old Virgin,* combining the two traditions, encourages the spectator to indulge in the pleasures of teenage male bonding while simultaneously poking fun at this adolescent behavior. In the film's discourse, these are men whose attitude to sex has arrested their psychological growth in more serious ways than virginity has affected Andy. Andy's virginity has allowed him to become a more mature man than the rest of them. That these are the only two available options for the spectator is part of the ideological work of the text, apparently averse, at least in its first half, to imagining other forms of sexuality that might be more in keeping with the age of the characters.

It could be argued, then, that *The 40-Year-Old Virgin* flaunts the amusing immaturity of gross-out, while exploiting its irreverence for commercial reasons, in order to convince the spectator of the advantages of radical, even if unwanted, abstinence. For this text, adolescent sexuality may be fun, especially when it is so convincingly articulated as it is here, but grown-up virginity is much better. This ideology situates the film within a general postfeminist discourse of entrenched anxiety about heterosexuality (and therefore also about homosexuality), which, according to such theorists as Neale and Krutnik and, more recently, Jeffers McDonald, has resulted in the neoconservative impulse of much contemporary romantic comedy.[11] Andy's last-reel success at finally shedding his virginity with the woman he loves may be seen not only as a backlash attempt on the part of the text to celebrate sex exclusively in the context of old-fashioned romantic love but, perhaps more interestingly, as a reaffirmation of the advantages of virginity, even for a forty-year-old. The protagonist says it all in a climactic summation of his past life when he finally confesses to Trish, "For so long I thought there was something wrong with me because it didn't happen. But I realize now that it was because I was waiting for you." This gender reversal of traditional patriarchal justifications of female virginity not only underlines the importance of love for successful sex but also suggests that a male virginity prolonged into middle age may well be the road to wonderful sexual performance and the answer to the crisis of masculinity.

Before this happens, Andy's humiliation when his virginity becomes a matter of public knowledge forces him to reassess his life and to see the childish, solitary pleasures that have made up his existence up to this moment as patently inadequate. It also reveals for the spectator the terms in which women are perceived not only by the characters of this male comedy but also by the text itself. On the one hand, the reappearance of the possibility of sex in his life reawakens Andy's anxieties about women's bodies when, on his way back home, he can see nothing but women's breasts and other eroticized body parts and is literally followed by a bus featuring an advertisement with a huge image of a woman in a provocative pose. On the other hand, his desperate explanation to David of the reasons why he is a virgin, minutes earlier, is, "I respect women, I love women. I respect them so much that I completely stay away from them." Since the wording of Andy's line practically forces the spectator to translate respect into fear, the gross-out comedy attitude of the other men toward women—seeing them exclusively as erotic objects and body parts—and Andy's "respect" are comically constructed as part of the same continuum, classically articulated by Freudian theory of (male) sexuality: the fetishization of women's bodies and their fragmentation in isolated parts as a psychological mechanism to allay male anxieties about female sexuality. It can be argued, therefore, that Andy's decision to stay away from women, like his sudden obsession with eroticized parts of their bodies, is not so different from the other men's objectification of femininity and post-p.c. lack of interest in anything but women's bodies and the pleasure they, and above all the pleasure that talking about them, can give them.

This larger-than-life sexism is a mechanism characteristic of gross-out comedy, probably even of those films, such as *The Sweetest Thing* (2002), with women as protagonists. The genre typically tries to get away with its barefaced celebration of male fantasies and its consequent lack of concern with women's interests and desires by framing its representations as hyperbolic and parodic—not to be taken seriously. In this film, this pattern is extended beyond the men's conversations to the construction of some of the female characters—including Paula, who repeatedly identifies herself to Andy as a "fuck buddy"; the drunken girl he picks up the first night he goes out with his friends; all the women at the dating game to which his friends take him; and, most obviously, the character of Beth (Elizabeth Banks), the sex-obsessed bookshop assistant, who, after masturbating in front of Andy, is about to have sex with him but, when he backs down, does not seem to mind settling for Cal instead. The one-dimensionality of Beth's character summarizes the construction of femininity by the gross-out comedy as little more than a teenage male fantasy. However, because, as we have seen, *The 40-Year-Old Virgin* is capable of exploiting its gross-out conventions while simultaneously presenting their pleasures as infantile, the text offers an alternative to these representations through the character of Trish.

Compared to all the other figures in the film, especially the women, Trish is a psychologically complex character and, from the moment she becomes narratively important, Andy's only rival for spectatorial identification. Even more clearly than Mary in *There's Something about Mary*, she does not belong in the gross-out comedy and has in fact practically no scenes with any of the other characters, tempering Steve Carell's comic excesses when they are together. The generally positive reviews received by the film when it came out constantly emphasized the balance between the gross-out irreverence and the depth of feeling unexpectedly introduced by this character and, more specifically, by Keener's performance.[12] A mother of three and even a grandmother in her midforties—a "hot grandma," according to Andy—her sexuality has been marked by her previous bad experiences with men, which have rendered her frail and insecure (although, conveniently for the narrative, sexually experienced). Andy's kindness and gentleness immediately establish his way to her heart, but his reluctance to have sex makes her eventually lose her patience and brings about the film's mild romantic crisis. Trish is a sexually active woman, but one that, unlike the rest of the men and women in the film, is not solely defined by her sexuality. For example, while Cal and David immediately realize that an adult woman will not appreciate the sight of Andy's apartment being full of toys and video games, but enjoy them as much as he does and sympathize with his hobby, Trish tries to make Andy grow up by turning his childish hobby into a business opportunity that will allow him to fulfill his dream of setting up his own electronics shop. She is also the believable mother of a sex-obsessed teenager and a businesswoman who has to make ends meet every month.

Still, for a film whose narrative drive consists of articulating the "proper" road to the end of its protagonist's virginity, Trish's main role is to provide that possibility. The specific way in which she facilitates the denouement becomes a central ingredient of the film's sexual ideology. Catherine Keener offers a pointed contrast to the hyperreal construction of the other female characters, even before her performance is, as it were, filled with ideological content.[13] Through this strategy, the text ensures the spectator understands that in its fictional world there are two types of women, even before we get a clear idea of what the differences between them consists of. More specifically, Keener's pedigree as an independent cinema icon of contemporary femininity and her naturalistic, laid-back approach to performance make the ordinariness of her sexual desire immediately credible and convincing, while going some way toward convincing the spectator that a forty-year-old virgin is a good option for a modern woman: if Catherine Keener falls in love with him, then the sexual discourse that Andy represents must be perfectly acceptable.

The urgency of Trish's initial desire to have sex with Andy is explained, on the one hand, as a counterpoint to his reticence, and on the other, as the healthy desire of a sexually mature woman, but it is soon tempered when she realizes that she loves him. Conveniently for Andy, the romantic comedy that becomes dominant in the second half of the film argues that when there is love in a relationship it is a good idea to postpone sex as much as possible. Without sex to confuse matters, love will become much stronger, and conversely, with love firmly in place, the sex when it eventually happens will be much better. This is made explicit, for example, when after twenty sexless dates, and in spite of Andy's procrastinating, Trish finally decides to take the initiative again. As when, in classical Westerns or gangster films the villain always has to shoot first and never have his back turned to the hero when the latter returns fire, just before sex Trish reminds Andy that she is in love with him, a perhaps unnecessary observation given the ample evidence that we have had of their love for each other. This remark narratively validates the impending sex as an acceptable activity and contrasts it with the more superficial and comically mechanical attitude of the gross-out characters. The clinch is thwarted on this occasion by Andy's nagging insecurities, but after the crisis, when he explains that he did not want to have sex because he was afraid of it not working properly, she again reassures him that, as long as there is love between two people, as is the case here, the sex will necessarily be great. And of course it is, the film unexpectedly changing its mode again for the final reel, translating sexual ecstasy into a fantasy musical extravaganza that, through a parodic performance of the song "Aquarius" from the countercultural musical *Hair*, suggests the sublimity of the combination of love and sex, even while gently undercutting its seriousness, perhaps in order to remind us that this is still, partly, a gross-out comedy and therefore that sex, love or no love, should not be taken too seriously.

Trish is extremely understanding of Andy's virginity, as had been, a little earlier, her daughter Marla (Kat Dennings) when she found out. In fact, beyond the female protagonist's rather forced revulsion when she finds in his apartment David's pornographic tapes and the plastic vagina he has apparently stolen from the family health control clinic, all the women in the film willingly accept and even embrace the only two options of male sexuality offered them by the narrative, even though they are both expressions of male infantile fears of their own sexuality. Just as Beth's cartoonish willingness and lack of inhibition sanctions the approach to sex of Andy's friends, Trish's patience and immediate discarding of his virginity as a problem for their relationship ensures that all male behavior in the film is seen as normal, reasonable, and even healthy. Beth probably gets what she was looking for when she got into the bathtub, even though the man has changed in the middle, and Trish's reward is not only the lasting happiness suggested by the wedding and the musical fantasy but also the most wonderful, fulfilling, and exhausting sexual experience she has ever had. That, of course, would not have been possible if Andy had been an experienced sexual partner.

The 40-Year-Old Virgin inscribes itself within a group of male-centered comedies that, following the template provided by *There's Something about Mary* and, to a certain extent, *American Pie*, attempt to temper the excesses of gross-out and teenpics by combining them with romantic comedy and to use this combination to suggest that men, for all their flaunted promiscuity and crass objectification of women, are also capable of love and romance. Judd Apatow's film, however, incorporates virginity into its narrative in order to separate these two impulses: the sex talk and the promiscuity are attached to some characters and the romantic attitude to others. It is perhaps the difficulty of finding romance in a postfeminist, homophobic, all-male world that has forced Andy to remain a virgin into early middle age, but the film, while never failing to provide its "natural" constituency the usual pleasures of gross-out in generous doses, manages to elevate virginity to a status so far uncommon either in romantic comedy or in gross-out.

While the sexual innocents of earlier romantic comedies had generally been placed in narratives whose objective was to present their sexual inexperience as a limitation to get rid of rapidly in order to achieve a mature identity and, as a consequence, to become a fit romantic partner, *The 40-Year-Old Virgin* posits male virginity as a definite asset and as good training for sexual happiness. Although theorists of romantic comedy have traditionally sought to allot it a specific ideology, the genre has proved time and again its flexibility and readiness to articulate very diverse sexual and affective discourses, adapting to a cultural climate that in matters sexual has been extremely changing and volatile for some time in Western societies. While no direct or simple association can be established between the ideology of a film, or any cultural text, and the historical moment in which it appears, a text's viability depends on the extent to which it can make itself understood and, in the case of a commercial film, entertaining. The success of Apatow's film confirms the contemporary resilience and good health of the gross-out/teenpic/romantic comedy combination and is instructive of the ways in which, through such combinations, genres can affect each other: the regular visibility of virginity in gross-out and teenpic comedy as an occasion of ridicule and obscene humor transforms its traditional elusiveness in romantic comedy and the genre's usual aversion to it into a celebration of its decisive contribution to the attainment of true love and even sexual excellence. *The 40-Year-Old Virgin* appears to affirm that, in today's intimate climate, virginity is not just better than casual sex: it is the best form of sex.

Notes

1. Stephen Greenblatt, *Shakespearean Negotiations* (Oxford: Clarendon Press, 1988), 89.

2. Elizabeth Cowie, "Fantasia," *M/f* 9 (1984): 70–105.

3. Stanley Cavell, *Pursuits of Happiness: The Hollywood Comedy of Remarriage* (Cambridge, MA: Harvard University Press, 1981), 116–17.

4. Brian Henderson, "Romantic Comedy Today: Semi-Tough or Impossible?" *Film Quarterly* 31 (Summer 1978): 22.

5. Tamar Jeffers McDonald, *Romantic Comedy: Boy Meets Girl Meets Genre* (London: Wallflower Press, 2007), 97.

6. James Naremore, *More Than Night: Film Noir and Its Contexts* (Berkeley and

Los Angeles: University of California Press, 1998), 6.

7. William Paul, "The Impossibility of Romance: Hollywood Comedy, 1978–1999," in *Genre and Contemporary Hollywood,* ed. Steve Neale (London: British Film Institute, 2002), 117–29; Leger Grindon, "From the Grotesque to the Ambivalent: Recent Developments in the Hollywood Romantic Comedy, 1997–2007" (paper read at the Chicago SCMS Conference, March 8–11, 2007).

8. Jeffers McDonald, *Romantic Comedy,* 97.

9. Ibid., 112.

10. Eve Kosofsky Sedgwick, *Between Men: English Literature and Male Homosocial Desire* (New York: Columbia University Press, 1985); Celestino Deleyto, "Between Friends: Love and Friendship in Contemporary Hollywood Romantic Comedy," *Screen* 44, no. 2 (2003): 172–73.

11. Steve Neale, "The Big Romance or Something Wild? Romantic Comedy Today," *Screen* 33 (Autumn 1992): 284–99; Frank Krutnik, "Conforming Passions? Contemporary Romantic Comedy," in *Genre and Contemporary Hollywood,* ed. Steve Neale (London: British Film Institute, 2002), 130–47; Jeffers McDonald, *Romantic Comedy,* 85–105.

12. Roger Ebert, "*The 40 Year Old Virgin,*" *Chicago Sun Times,* August 18, 2005, http://rogerebert.suntimes.com/apps/pbcs.dll/article?AID=/20050818/REVIEWS/50803002/1023 (accessed June 12, 2007); James Berardinelli, "*The Forty Year Old Virgin,*" *James Berardinelli's ReelViews,* 2005, www.reelviews.net/movies/f/40_year.html (accessed June 12, 2007); Carina Chocano, "*The Forty Year Old Virgin,*" *Los Angeles Times,* August 19, 2005, www.calendarlive.com/movies/chocano/cl-et-40virgin19aug19,0,4286369.story (accessed June 12, 2007).

13. Keener rose to prominence in the indie pictures *Walking and Talking* (dir. Nicole Holofcener, 1996), *Your Friends & Neighbors* (dir. Neil LaBute, 1998), and especially *Being John Malkovich* (dir. Spike Jonze, 1999).

Bibliography

Abbott, Elizabeth. *A History of Celibacy: From Athena to Elizabeth I, Leonardo Da Vinci, Florence Nightingale, Gandhi and Cher.* New York: Scribner, 2000.
Abraham, Karl. "Manifestations of the Female Castration Complex." *International Journal of Psychoanalysis* 3 (1922): 1–28.
Agee, James. Review of *Kiss and Tell. Nation,* October 27, 1945, 44.
Ansen, David. Review of *Little Darlings. Newsweek,* March 24, 1980, 78–79.
Archer, Jules. "Will She or Won't She?" *Playboy,* January 1956, 13 and 64.
Atkins, Thomas R. "Troubled Sexuality in the Popular Hollywood Feature." In *Sexuality in the Movies,* edited by Thomas R. Atkins, 109–31. Bloomington: Indiana University Press, 1975.
Auerbach, Nina. *Romantic Imprisonment: Women and Other Glorified Outcasts.* New York: Columbia University Press, 1986.
Austin, Joe, and Michael Nevin Willard. "Angels of History, Demons of Culture." In *Generations of Youth: Youth Cultures and History in Twentieth-Century America,* edited by Austin and Willard, 1–20. New York: New York University Press, 1998.
Babington, Bruce, and Peter William Evans. *Affairs to Remember: The Hollywood Comedy of the Sexes.* Manchester: Manchester University Press, 1989.
Basinger, Jeanine. *American Cinema: One Hundred Years of Filmmaking.* New York: Rizzoli, 1994.
———. *A Woman's View: How Hollywood Spoke to Women, 1930–1960.* London: Chatto and Windus, 1994.
Bearman, Peter S., and Hannah Brückner. "Promising the Future: Virginity Pledges and First Intercourse." *American Journal of Sociology* 106 (January 2001): 859–912.
Bell, Robert R., and Jack V. Buerkle. "Mother and Daughter Attitudes to Premarital Sexual Behavior." *Marriage and Family Living* 23, no. 4 (1961): 390–92.
Berardinelli, James. "*The Forty Year Old Virgin.*" *James Berardinelli's ReelViews,* 2005. www.reelviews.net/movies/f/40_year.html (accessed June 12, 2007).
Berlant, Lauren. *The Queen of America Goes to Washington City: Essays on Sex and Citizenship.* Durham, NC: Duke University Press, 1997.

Bernau, Anke. "Eternally Virginal." *Guardian,* July 18, 2007, 28.

———. *Virgins: A Cultural History.* London: Granta, 2007.

Betteridge, Thomas. "A Queen for All Seasons: Elizabeth I on Film." In *The Myth of Elizabeth,* edited by Susan Doran and Thomas S. Freeman, 242–60. Basingstoke: Palgrave Macmillan, 2003.

"B.G." Review of *Little Darlings. New Yorker,* March 31, 1980, 108, 111.

Blank, Hanne. *Virgin: The Untouched History.* New York: Bloomsbury, 2007.

Bogue, Ronald. *Deleuze on Cinema.* New York: Routledge, 2003.

Bordo, Susan. *Unbearable Weight: Feminism, Western Culture, and the Body.* Berkeley and Los Angeles: University of California Press, 1993.

Boston Women's Health Book Collective. *Our Bodies, Ourselves: A Book by and for Women.* 2nd ed. New York: Simon and Schuster, 1979.

Bradley, Laurel. "From Eden to Empire: John Everett Millais's 'Cherry Ripe.'" *Victorian Studies* 34 (1991): 179–203.

Brady, Lois Smith. "Vows: Ellen Fein and Lance Houpt." *New York Times,* Weddings/Celebrations, Sunday Styles, August 10, 2008, 13.

Branin, Larissa. *Liz.* New York: Courage Books, 2000.

Breines, Wini. *Young, White and Miserable: Growing Up Female in the Fifties.* Chicago: University of Chicago Press, 2001.

Bridgman, Joan. "Diana's Country." *Contemporary Review,* January 1999, 19–23.

Briefel, Aviva. "Monster Pains: Masochism, Menstruation and Identification in the Horror Film." *Film Quarterly* 58, no. 3 (2005): 16–28.

Brontë, Charlotte. *Jane Eyre.* New York: Modern Library, 1847.

Brown, Helen Gurley. *Having It All: Love—Success—Sex—Money, Even If You're Starting with Nothing.* New York: Simon and Schuster, 1982.

———. *Sex and the Single Girl.* New York: Bernard Geis and Associates, 1962.

Brown, Tina. *The Diana Chronicles.* New York: Random House, 2007.

Bruzzi, Stella. "Elizabeth." *Sight and Sound* 8, no. 11 (1998): 47–48.

Butler, Ivan. "The Horror Film: Polanski and *Repulsion.*" In *The Horror Film Reader,* edited by Alain Silver and James Ursini, 76–85. New York: Limelight Editions, 2001.

Califia, Pat. *Public Sex: The Culture of Radical Sex.* San Francisco: Cleis Press, 1994.

Campbell, Beatrix. *Diana, Princess of Wales: How Sexual Politics Shook the Monarchy.* London: Women's Press, 1998.

Campion, Thomas. *Cherry-Ripe.* 1600. www.poetry-archive.com/c/cherry-ripe (accessed August 24, 2006).

"Campus Love Left out in Cold." *Life,* March 11, 1957, 49–52.

Capp, Al. "The Day Dream." *Show,* December 1962, 72–73, 136–37.

Carroll, Noël. *The Philosophy of Horror or Paradoxes of the Heart.* London: Routledge, 1990.

Cavell, Stanley. *Pursuits of Happiness: The Hollywood Comedy of Remarriage.* Cambridge, MA: Harvard University Press, 1981.

"A Certain Smile." Review in *Saturday Review,* August 13, 1956, 13.

Chang, Donald. "Pillow Talk." Script and scrapbook accompanying soundtrack of *Pillow Talk.* Bear Family Records, Germany, 1996.

Chapman, James. *National Identity and the British Historical Film.* London: I. B. Tauris, 2005.

Chase, Alisia. "'Like Their First Pair of High Heels...': Continental Accessories and Audrey Hepburn's Cinematic Coming of Age." In *Abito E Identita: Richerche di Storia Letteraria E Culturale,* edited by C. Giorcelli. Palermo: Ila Palma 5 (Spring 2004): 215–43.

Chase, Chris. "At the Movies: Jennifer Leigh [sic] and Her Trip from X to R." *New York Times,* September 3, 1982, C6.

"Child Labor." Public Affairs News Service, *Bulletin* 4 (January 27, 1942): 11.

Chocano, Carina. "*The Forty Year Old Virgin.*" *Los Angeles Times,* August 19, 2005. www.calendarlive.com/movies/chocano/cl-et-40virgin19aug19,0,4286369. story (accessed June 12, 2007).

Church Gibson, Pamela. "From Dancing Queen to Plaster Virgin: Elizabeth and the End of English Heritage?" *Journal of British Popular Culture* 4 (2002): 133–41.

Clarke, Jane, and Diana Simmons. *Move Over Misconceptions: Doris Day Reappraised.* London: British Film Institute, 1980.

Clover, Carol. *Men, Women and Chain Saws: Gender in the Modern Horror Film.* London: British Film Institute, 1992.

Colebrook, Claire. *Gilles Deleuze.* London: Routledge, 2002.

Considine, David M. *The Cinema of Adolescence.* Jefferson, NC: McFarland, 1985.

Costantini, Maria Vittoria. "La rabbia impossibile." Unpublished paper, 1996.

Cowie, Elizabeth. "Fantasia." *M/f* 9 (1984): 70–105.

Coyne Kelly, Kathleen. *Performing Virginity and Testing Chastity in the Middle Ages.* London: Routledge, 2000.

Craddock, Jim, ed. Review of *Little Darlings. VideoHound's Golden Movie Retriever: The Complete Guide to Movies on Videocassette and DVD,* 431. Detroit, MI: Gale Group/Thomson Learning, 2002.

Cronin, Paul, ed. *Roman Polanski: Interviews.* Jackson: University Press of Mississippi, 2005.

Crowe, Cameron. *Conversations with Wilder.* New York: Alfred A. Knopf, 2001.

Damon, Virgil. "My Daughter Is in Trouble." *Look,* August 14, 1962, 26–28ff.

Davis, Lloyd. *Virginal Sexuality and Textuality in Victorian Literature.* Albany, NY: SUNY Press, 1993.

de Beauvoir, Simone. *The Second Sex.* Translated and edited by H. M. Parshley. New York: Vintage Books, 1952.

D'Emilio, John, and Estelle B. Friedman. *Intimate Matters: A History of Sexuality in America.* New York: Harper and Row, 1988.

Deleuze, Gilles. *Cinema 1: The Movement-Image.* Translated by Hugh Tomlinson and Barbara Habberjam Galeta. Minneapolis: University of Minnesota Press, 1986.

———. *A Thousand Plateaus: Capitalism and Schizophrenia.* Translated by Brian Massumi. London: Athlone, 1988.

Deleuze, Gilles, and Félix Guattari. *Kafka: Toward a Minor Literature.* Translated by Dana Polan. Minneapolis: University of Minnesota Press, 1986.

Deleyto, Celestino. "Between Friends: Love and Friendship in Contemporary Hollywood Romantic Comedy." *Screen* 44, no. 2 (2003): 167–82.

de Lisle, Rosanna. "The Original Elizabethan: What Was It Like Being Elizabeth I?" *Independent* (London), September 27, 1998, 2.

Denby, David. "Growing Up Absurd." Review of *Fast Times at Ridgemont High*. *New York*, September 27, 1982, 50–51.

———. Review of *Little Darlings*. *New York*, April 7, 1980, 86–87.

———. Review of *Risky Business*. *New Yorker*, August 22, 1983, 62.

"De St E., F." Review of *Bonjour Tristesse*. *Films in Review* 9, no. 2 (1958): 87–88.

Deutsch, Helen. *The Psychology of Women: A Psychoanalytic Interpretation*, vols. 1 and 2. New York: Grune and Stratton, 1944–45.

Doherty, Thomas. "Clueless Kids." *Cineaste* 21, no. 4 (1995): 14–16.

———. *Teenagers and Teenpics: The Juvenilization of American Movies in the 1950s*. 2nd ed., revised and expanded. Philadelphia: Temple University Press, 2002.

Dougherty, Philip H. "Drug Drive Outlined to First Lady." *New York Times*, October 12, 1983, D22.

Douglas, Susan J. *Where the Girls Are: Growing Up Female with the Mass Media*. New York: Times Books, 1994.

Downey, Fairfax. "The Care and Feeding of Fathers." *American Girl*, January 1940, 18–19, 50.

Driscoll, Catherine. *Girls: Female Adolescence in Popular Culture and Cultural Theory*. New York: Columbia University Press, 2002.

Duggan, Lisa. *The Twilight of Equality? Neoliberalism, Cultural Politics, and the Attack on Democracy*. Boston: Beacon Press, 2003.

Duggan, Lisa, and Nan D. Hunter. *Sex Wars: Sexual Dissent and Political Culture*. London: Routledge, 1995.

Dunning, John. *On the Air: The Encyclopedia of Old-Time Radio*. New York: Oxford University Press, 1998.

Dyer, Richard. *Heavenly Bodies: Film Stars and Society*. Basingstoke: Macmillan Press, 1986.

———. "Heritage Cinema in Europe." In *Encyclopedia of European Cinema*, edited by Ginette Vincendeau, 204–5. London: Facts on File, 1995.

Ebert, Roger. "*The 40 Year Old Virgin*." *Chicago Sun Times*, August 18, 2005. http://rogerebert.suntimes.com/apps/pbcs.dll/article?AID=/20050818/REVIEWS/50803002/1023 (accessed June 12, 2007).

Echols, Alice. *Daring to Be Bad*. Minnesota: University of Minneapolis Press, 1989.

Ehrenreich, Barbara, Elizabeth Hess, and Gloria Jacobs. *Re-making Love: The Feminization of Sex*. New York: Anchor Press, 1986.

Ensler, Eve. *The Vagina Monologues*. New York: Villard, 1998.

Farber, Manny. "Crazy over Horses." *Nation*, February 3, 1945, 175.

Farquhar, Michael. "As a Matter of Fact, Elizabeth Is a Pretender to the Throne." *Washington Post*, December 20, 1998, 4.

Fein, Ellen, and Sherrie Schneider. *All the Rules: Time-Tested Secrets for Capturing the Heart of Mr. Right* [*The Rules* and *The Rules II*, combined ed.]. New York: Grand Central, 1995, 1997.

Feinstein, Harvey. "The Queen and I." *Guardian* (London), November 28, 1998, 12.
Foreman, Jonathan. Review of *American Pie*. *New York Post*, July 16, 1999, 48.
Foucault, Michel. *History of Sexuality*. Vol. 1, *An Introduction*. New York: Pantheon Books, 1978.
———. *Madness and Civilization*. London: Routledge, 2006.
French, Philip. "Film of the Week: Another Fine Bess." *Observer* (London), October 4, 1998, 6.
Freud, Sigmund. *The Taboo of Virginity*. Vol. 11 in *Standard Edition*. London: Hogarth Press, 1918.
———. Totem and Taboo. Vol. 13 in *Standard Edition*. London: Hogarth Press, 1913.
———. "The Uncanny." In *Studies in Parapsychology*, edited by Philip Rieff, 19–60. New York: Collier Books, 1963.
Friday, Nancy. *Sex for One: The Joy of Self Loving*. 25th ed. New York: Crown, 1996.
Fuchs, Cynthia. "Framing and Passing in *Pillow Talk*." In *The Other Fifties: Interrogating Midcentury American Icons*, edited by Joel Foreman, 224–51. Urbana: University of Illinois Press, 1997.
———. Review of *The Virgin Suicides*. *City Paper* (Philadelphia), May 4, 2000. www.citypaper.net (accessed August 22, 2006).
Fuentes, Annette. "No Sex Ed: Congress Pushes Abstinence in the Schools." *In These Times*, December 18, 1997, 16–18.
Gardner, Harold C. Review of *Bonjour Tristesse*. *America: The National Catholic Review*, March 12, 1955, 623.
Gateward, Frances, and Murray Pomerance, eds. *Sugar, Spice and Everything Nice: Cinemas of Girlhood*. Detroit: Wayne State University Press, 2002.
"Gee, Is She Sophisticated!" *Seventeen*, January 1946, 82.
Gerhard, Jane. 2001. *Desiring Revolution*. New York: Columbia University Press.
Gibbs, John, and Douglas Pye. "Revisiting Preminger: *Bonjour Tristesse*." In *Style and Meaning: Studies in the Detailed Analysis of Film*, edited by Gibbs and Pye, 108–26. Manchester: Manchester University Press, 2005.
Giddens, Anthony. *The Transformation of Intimacy: Sexuality, Love and Eroticism in Modern Societies*. Cambridge: Polity Press, 1992.
Gillian, Anne. "Profile of a Filmmaker: Catherine Breillat." In *Beyond French Feminisms: Debates on Women, Politics, and Culture in France, 1981–2001*, edited by Roger Celestin, Eliane DalMolin and Isabelle de Courtivron, 201–12. New York: Palgrave Macmillan, 2003.
Gillis, Stacy, Gillian Howie, and Rebecca Munford, eds. *Third Wave Feminism: A Critical Exploration*. Houndmills, UK: Palgrave Macmillan, 2007.
Gitter, Elisabeth G. "The Power of Women's Hair in the Victorian Imagination." *PMLA* 99, no. 5 (1985): 936–54.
Gliberman, Owen. Review of *American Pie*. *Entertainment Weekly*, July 16, 1999, 44.
Goldstein, Laurence, ed. *The Male Body: Features, Destinies, Exposures*. Ann Arbor: University of Michigan Press, 1994.
Green, Janet. *Matilda Shouted Fire!* London: Evans Brothers, 1961.

Greenblatt, Stephen. *Shakespearean Negotiations.* Oxford: Clarendon Press, 1988.

Greene, Gael. *Sex and the College Girl.* New York: Dial Press, 1964.

Grindon, Leger. "From the Grotesque to the Ambivalent: Recent Developments in the Hollywood Romantic Comedy, 1997–2007." Paper read at the Chicago SCMS Conference, March 8–11, 2007.

Griswold, Robert. *Fatherhood in America: A History.* New York: Basic Books, 1993.

Hart, Nicky. "Of Procreation and Power." *New Left Review* 35 (September–October 2005): 79–91.

Haskell, Molly. *From Reverence to Rape: The Treatment of Women in the Movies.* Chicago: University of Chicago Press, 1987.

Hatch, Kristen. "Little Butches: The Tomboy Film in the 1970s." Paper presented at the Society for Cinema and Media Studies Annual Conference, Atlanta, GA, March 4, 2004.

Hechinger, Grace, and Fred M. Hechinger. *Teenage Tyranny.* New York: William Morrow and Co., 1963.

Hegarty, Marilyn E. "Patriots or Prostitutes: Sexual Discourses, Print Media, and American Women during World War II." *Journal of Women's History* 29 (Summer 1998): 112–36.

Henderson, Brian. "Romantic Comedy Today: Semi-Tough or Impossible?" *Film Quarterly* 31 (Summer 1978): 11–22.

Hengtes, Sarah. *Pictures of Girlhood: Modern Female Adolescence on Film.* Jefferson, NC: McFarland, 2006.

Higson, Andrew. *English Heritage, English Cinema: Costume Drama since 1980.* Oxford: Oxford University Press, 2003.

Hirsch, Marianne, and Evelyn Fox Keller, eds. *Conflicts in Feminism.* London: Routledge, 1991.

Hogan, David J. *Dark Romance: Sex and Death in the Horror Film.* Wellingborough: Equation, 1986.

Holtzman, Deanna, and Nancy Kulish. "Nevermore: The Hymen and the Loss of Virginity." *Journal of the American Psychoanalytic Association* 44 (1996): 303–32.

———. *Nevermore: The Hymen and the Loss of Virginity.* Northlake: NJ: Jason Aronson, 1997.

hooks, bell. "White Light." *Sight and Sound* 6, no. 6 (1996): 10.

Horney, Karen. "The Denial of the Vagina." *International Journal of Psychoanalysis* 14 (1933): 57–70.

Hotchner, Al, and Doris Day. *Doris Day: Her Own Story.* London: W. H. Allen, 1976.

Hudson, Rock, and Sara Davidson. *Rock Hudson: His Story.* New York: Morrow, 1986.

Inness, Sherrie A. *Tough Girls: Women Warriors and Wonder Women in Popular Culture.* Philadelphia: University of Pennsylvania State Press, 1998.

Irigaray, Luce. *This Sex which Is Not One.* Translated by Catherine Porter with Carolyn Burke. Ithaca, NY: Cornell University Press, 1985.

Irvine, Janice M. *Talk about Sex: The Battle over Sex Education in the United States.* Berkeley and Los Angeles: University of California Press, 2002.

Jackovich, Karen G. "Kristy McNichol Leaves the 'Family' Hour Behind for a Pad of Her Own and an 'R' Rating." *People*, March 31, 1980, 90–92, 94.

James, Nick. "Looks That Paralyse." *Sight and Sound* 11, no. 12 (2001): 20.

Jankowski, Theodora A. "Pure Resistance: Queer(y)ing Virginity in William Shakespeare's *Measure for Measure* and Margaret Cavendish's *The Convent of Pleasure*." *Shakespeare Studies* 26 (1998): 218–56.

Jeffers, Tamar. "Pillow Talk's Repackaging of Doris Day: 'Under all those dirndls ...'" In *Fashioning Film Stars: Dress, Culture, Identity*, edited by Rachel Moseley, 50–61. London: British Film Institute, 2005.

———. "'Should I Surrender?': Performing and Interrogating Female Virginity in Hollywood Films, 1957–64." PhD thesis, University of Warwick, 2005.

Jeffers McDonald, Tamar. *Romantic Comedy: Boy Meets Girl Meets Genre*. London: Wallflower Press, 2007.

Johnson, Albert. "Repulsion." Review in *Film Quarterly* (Spring 1966): 44–45.

Johnson, Nora. "Sex and the College Girl." *Atlantic Monthly*, November 1959, 56–60.

Joseph, Joe. "Sex Aplenty, But Little Sensibility." *Times*, October 21, 1998, 47.

Kael, Pauline. Review of *Fast Times at Ridgemont High*. *New Yorker*, November 1, 1982, 146, 149.

Kehily, Mary Jane. "More Sugar? Teenage Magazines, Gender Displays and Sexual Learning." *European Journal of Cultural Studies* 2, no. 1 (1999) 65–89.

Keller, Wendy. *The Cult of the Born-Again Virgin: How Single Women Can Reclaim Their Sexual Power*. Deerfield Beach, FL: Health Communications, 1999.

Kinsey, Alfred C., Wardell B. Pomeroy, Clyde E. Martin, and Paul H. Gebhard. *Sexual Behavior in the Human Female*. Philadelphia: W. B. Saunders Company, 1953.

Kleinhans, Chuck. "Girls on the Edge of the Reagan Era." In *Sugar, Spice and Everything Nice: Cinemas of Girlhood*, edited by Gateward and Pomerance, 73–90. Detroit: Wayne State University Press, 2002.

Knudsen, Dean D., and Hallowell Pope. "Premarital Sexual Norms, the Family, and Social Change." *Journal of Marriage and the Family* 27, no. 3 (1965): 314–23.

Krämer, Peter. "Women First: *Titanic*, Action-Adventure Films, and Hollywood's Female Audience." In *Titanic: Anatomy of a Blockbuster*, edited by Kevin Sandler and Gaylyn Studlar, 108–31. New Brunswick, NJ: Rutgers University Press, 1999.

Kroll, Jack. Review of *Fast Times at Ridgemont High*. *Newsweek*, September 20, 1982, 92, 96.

Krutnik, Frank. "Conforming Passions? Contemporary Romantic Comedy." In *Genre and Contemporary Hollywood*, edited by Steve Neale, 130–47. London: British Film Institute, 2002.

Lake, Eleanor. "Trouble on the Street Corners." *Reader's Digest*, May 1943, 43–46.

Lambert, Gavin. *Natalie Wood: A Life*. New York: Alfred A. Knopf, 2004.

Laqueur, Thomas. "The Social Evil, the Solitary Vice and Pouring Tea." In *Solitary Sex: A Cultural History of Masturbation*, edited by Paula Bennett and Thomas Laqueur, 155–62. New York: Zone Books, 2003.

Leaming, Barbara. *Polanski: A Biography; The Filmmaker as Voyeur.* New York: Simon and Schuster, 1981.

Lee, Robert G. *Orientals: Asian Americans in Popular Culture.* Philadelphia: Temple University Press, 1999.

Leibman, Nina C. "The Way We Weren't: Abortion 1950s Style in *Blue Denim* and *Our Time.*" *Velvet Light Trap* 29 (Spring 1992): 31–42.

Lerner, Sharon. "An Orgy of Abstinence: Federal Funding Pushes No-Sex Education into the Mainstream." *Village Voice,* August 7, 2001, 34–36.

Letter to Betty Marsh. January 14, 1915. Vertical file, folder 32. Margaret Herrick Library, Los Angeles.

Lev, Peter. *History of the American Cinema.* Vol. 7, *Transforming the Screen, 1950–1959.* New York: Charles Scribner's Sons, 2003.

Levine, Judith. *Harmful to Minors: The Perils of Protecting Children from Sex.* Minneapolis: University of Minnesota Press, 2002.

Lewis, Jon. *The Road to Romance and Ruin: Teen Films and Youth Culture.* New York: Routledge, 1992.

Loughlin, Marie H. *Hymeneutics: Interpreting Virginity on the Early Modern Stage.* Lewisburg, PA: Bucknell University Press, 1997.

Markel, Lester. "Why Parents Leave Home." *Good Housekeeping,* February 1943, 22.

Maslin, Janet. Review of *Fast Times at Ridgemont High. New York Times,* September 3, 1982, C6.

———. Review of *Little Darlings. New York Times,* March 28, 1980, C15.

Mast, Gerald. *A Short History of the Movies.* New York: Macmillan, 1986.

May, Elaine Tyler. *Homeward Bound: American Families in the Cold War Era.* New York: Basic Books, 1988.

May, Lary. "Making the American Consensus: The Narrative of Conversion and Subversion in World War II Films." In *The War in American Culture: Society and Consciousness during World War II,* edited by Lewis A. Erenberg and Susan E. Hirsch, 71–104. Chicago: University of Chicago Press, 1996.

McAdam, Ian. "Fiction and Projection: The Construction of Early Modern Sexuality in *Elizabeth* and *Shakespeare in Love.*" *Pacific Coast Philology* 35, no. 1 (2000): 49–60.

McCarthy, Todd. "Trick and Treat" (Interview with John Carpenter). *Film Comment* 16 (1980): 17–24.

McRobbie, Angela, and Ryan Gilbey. "Sugar and Spice." *Sight and Sound* 13, no. 12 (2003): 8–9.

McWhorter, Ladelle. *Bodies and Pleasures: Pornography, Sexual Harassment, Date Rape and the Politics of Sexual Equality.* Indianapolis: Indiana University Press, 1999.

Meyers, Laura. Letter. *New York Times Magazine,* June 10, 2007, 8.

Miller, Judith Graves. *Francoise Sagan.* New York: Twayne, 1988.

Monk, Claire. "Sexuality and Heritage." In *Film/Literature/Heritage: A Sight and Sound Reader,* edited by Ginette Vincendeau, 6–11. London: BFI, 2001.

Moseley, Rachel. "Dress, Class and Audrey Hepburn: The Significance of the Cinderella Story." In *Fashioning Film Stars: Dress, Culture and Identity,* edited by Rachel Moseley, 109–20. London: British Film Institute, 2005.

Moss, David Grant. "A Queen for Whose Time? Elizabeth I as Icon for the Twentieth Century." *Journal of Popular Culture* 39, no. 5 (2006): 796–816.
Mouton, Janice. "From Feminine Masquerade to Flaneuse: Agnes Varda's Cleo in the City." *Cinema Journal* 40 (Winter 2001): 3–16.
Mulvey, Laura. "Pandora: Topographies of the Mask and Curiosity." In *Sexuality and Space*, edited by Beatriz Colomina, 53–71. Princeton, NJ: Princeton Architectural Press, 1992.
Munford, Rebecca. "'Wake Up and Smell the Lipgloss': Gender, Generation and the (A)politics of Girl Power." In *Third Wave Feminism: A Critical Exploration*, edited by Gillis, Howie, and Munford, 266–79. Houndmills, UK: Palgrave Macmillan, 2007.
Nagle, Jill, ed. *Whores and Other Feminists*. London: Routledge, 1997.
Nairn, Tom. *After Britain: New Labour and the Return of Scotland*. London: Granta, 2000.
Naremore, James. *More Than Night: Film Noir and Its Contexts*. Berkeley and Los Angeles: University of California Press, 1998.
Nash, Ilana. *American Sweethearts: Teenage Girls in Twentieth-Century Popular Culture*. Bloomington: Indiana University Press, 2006.
National Velvet pressbook, microfiche, Margaret Herrick Library, Los Angeles.
Navarro, Mireya. "On Abortion, Hollywood Is No-Choice." *New York Times*, sec. 9, June 10, 2007, 1, 8.
Neale, Steve. "The Big Romance or Something Wild? Romantic Comedy Today." *Screen* 33 (Autumn 1992): 284–99.
Nettelbeck, Colin. "Self-Constructing Women beyond the Shock of *Baise-moi* and *À ma soeur!*" *FULGOR: Flinders University Languages Group Online Review* 1 (December 2003): 59–68. http://ehlt.flinders.edu.au/deptlang/fulgor/search.htm (accessed June 11, 2009).
"The New Doris Goes Sexy." *Hollywood Reporter*, September 16, 1959. Unpaginated advert after 3.
Newman, Kim. *Nightmare Movies: A Critical Guide to Contemporary Horror Films*. New York: Harmony Books, 1988.
"The New Pictures: *National Velvet*." *Time*, December 25, 1944, 44.
Nyqvist, Eva. Letter. *New York Times*, sec. 9, June 17, 2007, 11.
O'Sullivan, Michael. "Elizabeth: The Godmother." *Washington Post*, November 27, 1998, 59.
O'Toole, Lawrence. Review of *Little Darlings*. *Maclean's*, March 31, 1980, 50.
Parris, Robert. "Grin, Grimmer, Grimace." *New Republic*, August 20, 1956, 19–20.
Patton, Cindy. *Fatal Advice: How Safe-Sex Education Went Wrong*. Durham, NC: Duke University Press, 1996.
Paul, William. "The Impossibility of Romance: Hollywood Comedy, 1978–1999." In *Genre and Contemporary Hollywood*, edited Steve Neale, 117–29. London: British Film Institute, 2002.
Perkins, Adrath. "A Look at New Movies." *Seventeen*, January 1954, 14.
Pfiefer, Arnetta. "Movies Make Me Sentimental." *Seventeen*, January 1958, 12.
Pidduck, Julianne. "*Elizabeth* and *Shakespeare in Love*: Screening the Elizabethans."

In *Film/Literature/Heritage: A Sight and Sound Reader*, edited by Ginette Vincendeau, 130–35. London: BFI, 2001.

Pigeon, Renée. "'No Man's Elizabeth': The Virgin Queen in Recent Films." In *Retrovisions: Reinventing the Past in Film and Fiction*, edited by Deborah Cartmell, I. Q. Hunter, and Imelda Whelehan, 9–24. London: Pluto Press, 2001.

Pilcer, Sonia. *Little Darlings*. Based on the screenplay by Kimi Peck and Dalene [*sic*] Young. Story by Kimi Peck. New York: Ballantine, 1980.

Pinedo, Isabel Cristina. *Recreational Terror: Women and the Pleasures of Horror Film Viewing*. Albany, NY: SUNY Press, 1997.

Polanski, Roman. *Roman*. New York: William Morrow and Co., 1984.

Potter, Alicia. "Her Royal Slyness—Colorful Virgin Queen Ascends to the Screen Again in *Elizabeth*." *Boston Herald*, November 22, 1998, 60.

Preminger, Otto. *Preminger*. New York: Doubleday and Co., 1977.

Rapping, Elayne. *Media-tions: Forays into the Culture and Gender Wars*. Cambridge, MA: South End Press, 1994.

Reis, Pamela Tamarkin. "Exchange: Victorian Centerfold; Another Look at Millais's *Cherry Ripe*." *Victorian Studies* 35, no. 2 (1992): 201–5.

Reppuci, N. Dickson, and Jeffrey J. Haugaard. "Prevention of Child Sexual Abuse: Myth or Reality." *American Psychologist* 44 (October 1989): 1266–75.

Review of *Bonjour Tristesse*. *Time*, Books section, August 20, 1956, 94.

Review of *Pillow Talk*. *Hollywood Reporter*, August 12, 1959, 3.

Rich, Frank. Review of *Little Darlings*. *Time*, March 31, 1980, 84.

Richards, David. *Played Out: The Jean Seberg Story*. New York: Random House, 1981.

Riesman, David, with Nathan Glazer and Reuel Denney. *The Lonely Crowd*. Abridged ed. with a 1969 preface. New Haven, CT: Yale University Press, 1980.

Rowbothom, Sheila. *A Century of Women: The History of Women in Britain and the United States*. London: Penguin Group, 1997.

Sagan, Françoise. *Bonjour Tristesse*. New York: E. P. Dutton and Co., 1955.

———. "By a Charming Monster." *Newsweek*, March 7, 1955, 92.

———. *A Certain Smile*. New York: E. P. Dutton and Co., 1956.

———. *With Fondest Regards*. New York: E. P. Dutton and Co., 1984.

Schallert, Edwin. "Jane Withers Picture Given Budget Boost." *Los Angeles Times*, June 3, 1940, 9.

Scheiner, Georganne. "Look at Me, I'm Sandra Dee: Beyond a White Teen Icon." *Frontiers: A Journal of Women Studies* 22, no. 2 (2001): 87–106.

———. *Signifying Female Adolescence: Film Representations and Fans, 1920–1950*. Westport, CT: Praeger, 2000.

Schickel, Richard. *The Stars: The Personalities Who Made the Movies*. New York: Bonanza Books, 1962.

Schwartz, Kathryn. "The Wrong Question: Thinking through Virginity." *differences: A Journal of Feminist Cultural Studies* 13, no. 2 (2002): 1–34.

Scott, John. "Juveniles Bidding." *Los Angeles Times*, March 13, 1938, C1.

"The Second Jazz Age." *Newsweek*, October 29, 1945, 34–35.

Sedgwick, Eve Kosofsky. *Between Men: English Literature and Male Homosocial De-*

sire. New York: Columbia University Press, 1985.

Shary, Timothy. *Generation Multiplex: The Image of Youth in Contemporary American Cinema*. Austin: University of Texas Press, 2002.

Shone, Tom. "Romp without Pomp." *Sunday Times* (London), October 4, 1998, 6.

Shonfield, Katherine. *Walls Have Feelings: Architecture, Film, and the City*. London: Routledge, 2000.

Smith, Joan. *Misogynies*. London: Vintage, 1989.

Stan, Adele M. *Debating Sexual Correctness: Pornography, Sexual Harassment, Date Rape and the Politics of Sexual Equality*. Surrey, UK: Delta, 1995.

Starkey, David. "The Drama Queen." *Sunday Times* (London), September 20, 1998, 5.

"Star of Stars Award." *Motion Picture Herald*, January 28, 1961, 8.

Steinem, Gloria. "The Moral Disarmament of Betty Coed." *Esquire*, September 1962, 97, 153–57.

Stroud, Joanne, and Gail Thomas. *Images of the Untouched: Virginity in Psyche, Myth and Community*. Dallas, TX: Dallas Institute for the Humanities and Culture, Spring Publications, 1982.

Tasker, Yvonne, and Diane Negra, eds. *Interrogating Postfeminism: Gender and the Politics of Popular Culture*. Durham, NC: Duke University Press, 2007.

"Teen-Age Bill of Rights." *New York Times Magazine*, January 7, 1945, 16–17.

Therbon, Göran. *Between Sex and Power: Family in the World, 1900–2000*. London: Routledge, 2004.

Timson, Judith. "Teen Sex." *Maclean's*, March 31, 1980, 39–46.

Tuck, Greg. "Mainstreaming the Money Shot: Representations of Ejaculation in Mainstream American Cinema." *Paragraph* 26 (August–September 2003): 263–80.

———. "Of Monsters, Masturbators and Markets: Autoerotic Desire, Sexual Exchange and the Cinematic Serial Killer." In *Monsters and the Monstrous: Myths and Metaphors of Enduring Evil* 3, ed. Niall Scot. Amsterdam: At the Interface Publications/Rodopi, 2006.

Turim, Maureen. "Designing Women: The Emergence of the Sweetheart Line." Reprinted in *Fabrications: Costume and the Female Body*, edited by Jane Gaines and Charlotte Herzog, 212–28. London: Routledge, 1990.

Vidler, Anthony. *The Architectural Uncanny: Essays in the Modern Unhomely*. Cambridge, MA: MIT Press, 1992.

Vincendeau, Ginette, ed. *Encyclopedia of European Cinema*. London: Facts on File, 1995.

Wacker, Ronnie. "Suffolk Teen-Agers Find Responsibility Begins with an Egg." *New York Times*, February 14, 1988, A1.

Wald, Gayle. "Clueless in the Neocolonial World Order." In *Sugar, Spice and Everything Nice: Cinemas of Girlhood*, edited by Gateward and Pomerance, 103–24. Detroit: Wayne State University Press, 2002.

Walter, Natasha. *The New Feminism*. London: Little Brown and Co., 1998.

Warner, Malcolm. "John Everett Millais's *Autumn Leaves*: 'A picture full of beauty and without subject.'" In *Pre-Raphaelite Papers*, edited by Leslie Parris, 126–42.

London: Tate Gallery, 1984.

Warner, Marina. *Monuments and Maidens: The Allegory of the Female Form.* New York: Atheneum, 1985.

Weiner, Susan. *Enfants Terribles: Youth and Femininity in the Mass Media in France, 1945–1968.* Baltimore: Johns Hopkins University Press, 2001.

Weinraub, Bernard. "At the Movies: A Goofball Guy's Guy." *New York Times,* November 13, 1998. http://query.nytimes.com/gst/fullpage.html?res=9E04E1D D1431F930A25752C1A96E958260&sec=&spon=&pagewanted=1 (accessed July 5, 2007).

Weissman, Philip. "Psychosexual Development in a Case of Neurotic Virginity and Old Maidenhood." *International Journal of Psychoanalysis* 45 (1964): 110–20.

Wexman, Virginia Wright. *Roman Polanski.* Boston: Twayne, 1985.

Whyte, William H. *The Organization Man: The Book That Defined a Generation.* Philadelphia: University of Pennsylvania Press, 2002.

Willemen, Paul. "The National." In *Looks and Frictions: Essays in Cultural Studies and Film Theory,* 206–19. London: BFI, 1994.

Williams, Leslie. "The Look of Little Girls: John Everett Millais and the Victorian Art Market." In *The Girl's Own: Cultural Histories of the Anglo-American Girl, 1830–1915,* edited by Claudia Nelson and Lynne Vallone, 124–55. Darby, PA: Diane, 1994.

Williams, Raymond. *The Long Revolution.* London: Chatto and Windus, 1961.

Wilson, Susan N. "Teen-Agers and AIDS: Protection, Yes, But How?" *New York Times,* January 8, 1989, NJ24.

Wouk, Herman. *Marjorie Morningstar: A Novel.* New York: Doubleday, 1955.

Yates, Sybille L. "An Investigation of the Psychological Factors in Virginity and Ritual Defloration." *International Journal of Psychoanalysis* 11 (1930): 167–84.

Filmography

10 Things I Hate about You. Directed by Gil Junger. US, 1999.
The 40-Year-Old Virgin. Directed by Judd Apatow. US, 2005.
À bout de souffle. Directed by Jean-Luc Godard. France, 1959.
All the Real Girls. Directed by David Gordon Green. US, 2003.
Along Came Polly. Directed by John Hamburg. US, 2004.
À ma soeur! Directed by Catherine Breillat. France, 2001.
American Beauty. Directed by Sam Mendes. US, 1999.
American Pie. Directed by Paul and Chris Weitz. US, 1999.
An American Werewolf in London. Directed by John Landis. UK/US, 1981.
Animal House. Directed by John Landis. US, 1978.
The Apprenticeship of Duddy Kravitz. Directed by Ted Kotcheff. Canada, 1974.
Ascenseur pour l'échafaud/Frantic. Directed by Louis Malle. France, 1957.
As Good as It Gets. Directed by James L. Brooks. US, 1997.
As Virgins Fall. Directed by Natalie Barades. US, 2003.
Austin Powers: International Man of Mystery. Directed by Jay Roach. US/Germany, 1997.
The Awful Truth. Directed by Leo McCarey. US, 1937.
Bad Lieutenant. Directed by Abel Ferrara. US, 1992.
Ball of Fire. Directed by Howard Hawks. US, 1941.
The Ballad of Jack and Rose. Directed by Rebecca Miller. US, 2005.
Beach Party. Directed by William Asher. US, 1963.
Being John Malkovich. Directed by Spike Jonze. US, 1999.
The Big Bet. Directed by Bert I. Gordon. US, 1986.
Blackboard Jungle. Directed by Richard Brooks. US, 1955.
Black Christmas. Directed by Bob Clark. Canada, 1974.
Blade. Directed by Stephen Norrington. US, 1998.
Blue Denim. Directed by Philip Dunne. US, 1959.
Bonjour Tristesse. Directed by Otto Preminger. US, 1958.
Boyz N the Hood. Directed by John Singleton. US, 1991.

The Breakfast Club. Directed by John Hughes. US, 1985.
Bright Eyes. Directed by David Butler. US, 1934.
Bringing Up Baby. Directed by Howard Hawks. US, 1938.
Brother Sun, Sister Moon. Directed by Franco Zeffirelli. Italy, 1972.
Bus Stop. Directed by Joshua Logan. US, 1956.
Campus Flirt. Directed by Clarence D. Badger. US, 1926.
Can't Hardly Wait. Directed by Harry Elfont and Deborah Kaplan. US, 1998.
Carrie. Directed by Brian De Palma. US, 1976.
Cat People. Directed by Jacques Tourneur, 1942.
The Cell. Directed by Tarsem Singh. US/Germany, 2000.
The Champ. Directed by King Vidor. US, 1931.
Cherry Falls. Directed by Geoffrey Wright. US, 2000.
Un Chien Andalou. Directed by Luis Buñuel. France, 1928.
Citizen Kane. Directed by Orson Welles. US, 1941.
Class. Directed by Lewis John Carlino. US, 1983.
Clueless. Directed by Amy Heckerling. US, 1995.
Coming Soon. Directed by Colette Burson. US, 1999.
Cruel Intentions. Directed by Roger Kumble. US, 1999.
Curly Top. Directed by Irving Cummings. US, 1935.
Deep Throat. Directed by Gerard Damiano. US, 1972.
Diary of a High School Bride. Directed by Burt Topper. US, 1959.
Dirty Dancing. Directed by Emile Ardolino. US, 1987.
The Door in the Floor. Directed by Tod Williams. US, 2004.
Eighteen and Anxious. Directed by Joe Parker. US, 1957.
Él. Directed by Luis Buñuel. Mexico, 1953.
Elizabeth. Directed by Shekhar Kapur. UK, 1998.
Et Dieu créa la femme. Directed by Roger Vadim. France, 1956.
Eye of the Beholder. Directed by Stephan Elliott. Canada/UK/Australia, 1999.
Fast Times at Ridgemont High. Directed by Amy Heckerling. US, 1982.
Fear. Directed by James Foley. US, 1996.
Forgetting Sarah Marshall. Directed by Nicholas Stoller. US, 2008.
For Keeps. Directed by John G. Avildson. US, 1988.
Friday the 13th. Directed by Sean S. Cunningham. US, 1980.
The Full Monty. Directed by Peter Cattaneo. UK, 1997.
Gas, Food, Lodging. Directed by Allison Anders. US, 1992.
Gidget. Directed by Paul Wendkos. US, 1959.
Gidget Goes Hawaiian. Directed by Paul Wendkos. US, 1961.
Gidget Goes to Rome. Directed by Paul Wendkos. US, 1963.
Gigi. Directed by Vincente Minnelli. US, 1958.
Ginger Snaps. Directed by John Fawcett. Canada/US, 2000.

Girls Town. Directed by Jim McKay. US, 1996.
Goin' All the Way. Directed by Robert Freedman. US, 1982.
The Gold Rush. Directed by Charles Chaplin. US, 1925.
Good Luck Chuck. Directed by Mark Helfrich. US, 2007.
Grease. Directed by Randal Kleiser. US, 1978.
Hackers. Directed by Iain Softley. US, 1995.
Hair. Directed by Milos Forman. US/West Germany, 1979.
Halloween. Directed by John Carpenter. US, 1978.
Happiness. Directed by Todd Solondz. US, 1999.
Heathers. Directed by John Lehmann. US, 1989.
Hell Night. Directed by Tom DeSimone. US, 1981.
High School Confidential! Directed by Jack Arnold. US, 1958.
Hot Moves. Directed by Jim Sotos. US, 1984.
The House of Youth. Directed by Ralph Ince. US, 1924.
I Know What You Did Last Summer. Directed by Jim Gillespie. US, 1997.
Immediate Family. Directed by Jonathan Kaplan. US, 1989.
In & Out. Directed by Frank Oz. US, 1997.
The Incredibly True Adventure of Two Girls in Love. Directed by Maria Maggenti. US, 1994.
Invasion of the Body Snatchers. Directed by Don Siegel. US, 1956.
Invasion of the Body Snatchers. Directed by Philip Kaufman. US, 1978.
It Happened to Jane. Directed by Richard Quine. US, 1959.
I Was a Teenage Werewolf. Directed by Gene Fowler Jr. US, 1957.
Jane Eyre. Directed by Robert Stevenson. US, 1944.
Janie. Directed by Michael Curtiz. US, 1944.
Jeremy. Directed by Arthur Barron. US, 1973.
Joy of Sex. Directed by Martha Coolidge. US, 1984.
Julie. Directed by Andrew L. Stone. US, 1956.
Juno. Directed by Jason Reitman. US/Canada, 2007.
Just Another Girl on the I.R.T. Directed by Leslie Harris. US, 1993.
The Kid. Directed by Charles Chaplin. US, 1921.
kids. Directed by Larry Clark. US, 1995.
Kiss and Tell. Directed by Richard Wallace. US, 1945.
Knocked Up. Directed by Judd Apatow. US, 2007.
The Lady Eve. Directed by Preston Sturges. US, 1941.
Lassie Come Home. Directed by Fred M. Wilcox. US, 1943.
The Last American Virgin. Directed by Boaz Davidson. US, 1982.
The Last Emperor. Directed by Bernardo Bertolucci. China/Italy/UK/France, 1987.
The Last Picture Show. Directed by Peter Bogdanovich. US, 1971.
Last Summer. Directed by Frank Perry. US, 1969.

Last Tango in Paris. Directed by Bernardo Bertolucci. Italy/France, 1972.
Les Amants/The Lovers. Directed by Louis Malle. France, 1958.
Little Buddha. Directed by Bernardo Bertolucci. France/Liechtenstein/UK, 1993.
Little Darlings. Directed by Ronald F. Maxwell. US, 1980.
The Little Girl Who Lives down the Lane. Directed by Nicholas Gessner. Canada/USA/France, 1976.
Lolita. Directed by Stanley Kubrick. UK, 1962.
Losin' It. Directed by Curtis Hanson. Canada/US, 1983.
Love in the Afternoon. Directed by Billy Wilder. US, 1957.
Love Me or Leave Me. Directed by Charles Vidor. US, 1955.
Lover Come Back. Directed by Delbert Mann. US, 1961.
The Madness of King George. Directed by Nicholas Hytner. UK, 1994.
The Man Who Knew Too Much. Directed by Alfred Hitchcock. US, 1956.
Marjorie Morningstar. Directed by Irving Rapper. US, 1958.
Marnie. Directed by Alfred Hitchcock. US, 1962.
Married Too Young. Directed by George Moskov. US, 1962.
Mary, Queen of Scots. Directed by Charles Jarrott. UK, 1972.
The Mask of Satan/La Maschera del demonio. Directed by Mario Bava. Italy, 1960.
Midnight Lace. Directed by David Miller. US, 1960.
The Moon Is Blue. Directed by Otto Preminger. US, 1953.
Mrs. Brown. Directed by John Madden. UK/Ireland/US, 1997.
Mulholland Drive. Directed by David Lynch. France/US, 2001.
My Tutor. Directed by George Bowers. US, 1983.
National Velvet. Directed by Clarence Brown. US, 1944.
Never Been Kissed. Directed by Raja Gosnell. US, 1999.
A Nightmare on Elm Street. Directed by Wes Craven. US, 1984.
Notting Hill. Directed by Roger Michell. UK/US, 1999.
The Nun's Story. Directed by Fred Zinneman. US, 1959.
Ode to Billy Joe. Directed by Max Baer Jr. US, 1976.
The Omen. Directed by Richard Donner. UK, 1976.
Once Bitten. Directed by Howard Storm. US, 1985.
One, Two, Three. Directed by Billy Wilder. US, 1961.
The Opposite of Sex. Directed by Don Roos. US, 1998.
Our Dancing Daughters. Directed by Harry Beaumont. US, 1928.
Our Gang. Directed by Robert F. McGowan. US, 1922.
Paradise Motel. Directed by Cary Medoway. US, 1985.
Peeping Tom. Directed by Michael Powell. UK, 1960.
Peyton Place. Directed by Mark Robson. US, 1957.
Pillow Talk. Directed by Michael Gordon. US, 1959.
Pleasantville. Directed by Gary Ross. US, 1998.

FILMOGRAPHY

Please Don't Eat the Daisies. Directed by Charles Walters. US, 1960.
Porky's. Directed by Bob Clark. Canada, 1982.
The Port of Missing Girls. Directed by Irving Cummings. US, 1928.
Private Lessons. Directed by Alan Meyerson. US, 1981.
Private School. Directed by Noel Black. US, 1983.
Psycho. Directed by Alfred Hitchcock. US, 1960.
Psycho. Directed by Gus Van Sant. US, 1998.
The Queen. Directed by Stephen Frears. UK/France/Italy, 2006.
The Rage: Carrie 2. Directed by Katt Shea. US, 1999.
Rambling Rose. Directed by Martha Coolidge. US, 1991.
Ratcatcher. Directed by Lynne Ramsay. UK/France, 1999.
Rear Window. Directed by Alfred Hitchcock. US, 1954.
Rebel without a Cause. Directed by Nicholas Ray. US, 1955.
Repulsion. Directed by Roman Polanski. UK, 1965.
Risky Business. Directed by Paul Brickman. US, 1983.
River's Edge. Directed by Tim Hunter. US, 1987.
Rock around the Clock. Directed by Fred F. Sears. US, 1956.
Romance on the High Seas. Directed by Michael Curtiz. US, 1948.
Saint Joan. Directed by Otto Preminger. US/UK, 1957.
Saturday Night Fever. Directed by John Badham. US, 1977.
Saved! Directed by Brian Dannelly. US, 2004.
Say Anything . . . Directed by Cameron Crowe. US, 1989.
Scary Movie. Directed by Keenen Ivory Wayans. US, 2000.
Scream. Directed by Wes Craven. US, 1996.
Semi-Tough. Directed by Michael Ritchic. US, 1972.
Sheltering Sky. Directed by Bernardo Bertolucci. UK/Italy, 1990.
A Short Film about Love/Krotki Film O Milosci. Directed by Krzysztof Kieślowski. Poland, 1988.
The Silence of the Lambs. Directed by Jonathan Demme. US, 1991.
Single White Female. Directed by Barbet Schroeder. US, 1992.
The Sisterhood of the Traveling Pants. Directed by Ken Kwapis. US, 2005.
Skipped Parts. Directed by Tamra Davis. US, 2000.
Slums of Beverly Hills. Directed by Tamara Jenkins. US, 1998.
The Sound of Music. Directed by Robert Wise. US, 1965.
Splendor in the Grass. Directed by Elia Kazan. US, 1961.
Stealing Beauty. Directed by Bernardo Bertolucci. Italy/France/UK, 1996.
The Stepford Wives. Directed by Bryan Forbes. US, 1975.
Storm Warning. Directed by Stuart Heisler. US, 1951.
Summer of '42. Directed by Robert Mulligan. US, 1971.
A Summer Place. Directed by Delmer Daves. US, 1959.

Superbad. Directed by Greg Motola. US, 2007.
The Sure Thing. Directed by Rob Reiner. US, 1985.
The Sweetest Thing. Directed by Roger Kumble. US, 2002.
Take Her, She's Mine. Directed by Henry Koster. US, 1963.
Tammy and the Bachelor. Directed by Joseph Pevney. US, 1957.
Tea and Sympathy. Directed by Vincente Minnelli. US, 1956.
Teachers. Directed by Arthur Hiller. US, 1984.
The Texas Chainsaw Massacre. Directed by Tobe Hooper. US, 1974.
The Texas Chainsaw Massacre 2. Directed by Tobe Hooper. US, 1996.
There's One Born Every Minute. Directed by Harold Young. US, 1942.
There's Something about Mary. Directed by Peter and Bobby Farrelly. US, 1998.
Thérèse. Directed by Alain Cavalier. France, 1986.
Thirteen. Directed by Catherine Hardwicke. US, 2003.
Three Smart Girls. Directed by Henry Koster. US, 1936.
Titanic. Directed by James Cameron. US, 1997.
Trainspotting. Directed by Danny Boyle. UK, 1996.
Trojan War. Directed by George Huang. US, 1997.
Trust. Directed by Hal Hartley. UK/US, 1990.
Unwed Mother. Directed by Walter Doniger. US, 1958.
Valentine. Directed by Jamie Blanks. US, 2001.
Village of the Damned. Directed by Wolf Rilla. UK, 1960.
Virgin. Directed by Deborah Kampmeier. US, 2003.
Virgin High. Directed by Richard Gabai. US, 1990.
The Virgin Suicides. Directed by Sofia Coppola. US, 2000.
Virgin Territory. Directed by David Leland. Italy/US/UK/France/Luxembourg, 2007.
Waitress. Directed by Adrienne Shelly. US, 2007.
A Walk to Remember. Directed by Adam Shankman. US, 2002.
Walking and Talking. Directed by Nicole Holofcener, UK/US/Germany, 1996.
The Wanderers. Directed by Philip Kaufman. US, 1979.
Wedding Crashers. Directed by David Dobkin. US, 2005.
Welcome to the Dollhouse. Directed by Todd Solondz. US, 1996.
Where the Boys Are. Directed by Henry Levin. US, 1960.
The White Cliffs of Dover. Directed by Clarence Brown. US, 1944.
The Wicker Man. Directed by Robin Hardy. UK, 1973.
Wild Things. Directed by John McNaughton. US, 1997.
You, Me and Dupree. Directed by Anthony Russo and Joe Russo. US, 2006.
Your Friends & Neighbors. Directed by Neil LaBute. US, 1998.

Contributors

ALISIA G. CHASE is assistant professor of art history and visual culture at SUNY College, Brockport. Her recent publications include "'Draws Like a Girl': The Necessity of Old School Feminist Interventions in the World of Comics and Graphic Novels," in *Feminism Reframed: Reflections on Art and Difference*, ed. Alexandra M. Kokoli (Newcastle: Cambridge Scholars Publishing, 2008).

SHELLEY COBB is a teaching fellow at the University of Southampton, UK. She has recently published "Mother of the Year: Kathy Hilton, Lynne Spears, Dina Lohan and Bad Celebrity Motherhood," *Genders*, ed. Diane Negra and Su Holmes, special edition, no. 48 (2008), www.genders.org/, and "Adaptable Bridget: Generic Intertextuality and Postfeminism in *Bridget Jones's Diary*," in *Authorship in Film Adaptation*, ed. Jack Boozer (Austin: University of Texas Press, 2008).

CELESTINO DELEYTO is associate professor in film and literature at the University of Zaragoza, Spain. He has written and published widely on romantic comedy, his latest book being *The Secret Life of the Romantic Comedy* (Manchester: Manchester University Press, 2009). He is presently researching Mexican director Alejandro González Iñárritu.

LISA M. DRESNER is assistant professor of writing studies and composition at Hofstra University, New York. Her recent published work is her monograph *The Female Investigator in Literature, Film, and Popular Culture* (Jefferson, NC: McFarland and Co., 2007).

PETE FALCONER is a doctoral student at Warwick University, UK. His chapter titled "*3:10* Again: A Remade Western and the Problem of Authenticity" is forthcoming in *Adaptation in Contemporary Culture*, edited by Rachel Carroll, by Continuum.

TAMAR JEFFERS MCDONALD is lecturer in film at Kent University, UK. Her most recent published works include the monographs *Romantic Comedy: Boy Meets Girl Meets Genre* (London: Wallflower Press, 2007) and the forthcoming *Hollywood Cat-*

walk: Costume and Transformation in American Film, by I. B. Tauris. She is presently working on a full-length critical appraisal of Doris Day.

NINA MARTIN is assistant professor of theater and director of the film studies program at Connecticut College. She is the author of *Sexy Thrills: Undressing the Erotic Thriller* (Urbana: University of Illinois Press, 2007).

ILANA NASH holds a joint appointment with the English department and the gender and women's studies program at the University of Western Michigan. Her recent monograph is *American Sweethearts: Teenage Girls in Twentieth-Century Popular Culture* (Bloomington: Indiana University Press, 2006).

ANDREA SABBADINI is a psychoanalyst and chairman of the European Psychoanalytical Film Festival. He has edited *The Couch and the Silver Screen: Psychoanalytic Reflections on European Cinema* (2003) and *Projected Shadows: Psychoanalytic Reflections on the Representations of Loss in European Cinema* (2007), both for Routledge in association with the Institute of Psychoanalysis, London.

TIMOTHY SHARY is director of film and video studies at the University of Oklahoma. He is the author of *Generation Multiplex: The Image of Youth in Contemporary American Cinema* (Austin: University of Texas Press, 2002), *Teen Movies: American Youth on Screen* (London: Wallflower Press, 2005), and *Youth Culture in Global Cinema* (Austin: University of Texas Press, 2007).

CAROL SIEGEL is professor of English at Washington State University. Her publications include *New Millennial Sexstyles* (Bloomington: Indiana University Press, 2000), and *Goth's Dark Empire* (Bloomington: Indiana University Press, 2005). She also coedits the online journals *Genders* (www.genders.org) and *Rhizomes* (www.rhizomes.net).

GAYLYN STUDLAR is David May Distinguished Professor of the Humanities and director of the Program in Film and Media Studies at Washington University in St. Louis. She has published widely on issues of gender, sexuality, and Hollywood cinema.

REBECCA SULLIVAN is associate communications professor at the University of Calgary, Canada. She is the author of *Visual Habits: Nuns, Feminism, and American Postwar Popular Culture* (Toronto: University of Toronto Press, 2005) and, with Bart Beaty, of *Canadian Television Today* (Calgary: University of Calgary Press, 2006).

GREG TUCK is senior lecturer in film at the University of the West of England. He is the author of "Sex *with* the City: Urban Spaces, Sexual Encounters and Erotic Spectacle in Tsukamoto Shinya's *Rokugatsu no Hebi/A Snake of June* (2003)," *Film Studies* (Winter 2007) and is currently coediting a volume of essays on neo-noir for Wallflower Press.

Index

Abortion, 55, 59, 176, 186–88, 190, 193, 194, 195–96
Abstinence, sexual, 174, 194, 259, 262
Abstinence-only sex education, 242, 243–44, 245, 247
Adaptation, 68–71, 74, 84, 85, 86, 87, 91, 100, 204
Adolescence, 34, 39, 55, 167, 178, 196, 236, 246, 250, 259
Advertising, slogans, 13, 42; campaigns for films, 31; firms 77. *See also* Madison Avenue
Advice, 153, 178, 180, 191, 192
Agency, 45, 106, 112, 119, 130, 155; sexual agency, 3, 16, 106
AIDS, 57, 61, 187, 188, 193, 242
Alienation, 79–81, 130, 141. *See also* Anomie
Ambiguity, 81, 142
Ambivalence, to virginity, 124, 229, 255, 259, 260
America: cinema, 50, 65, 67, 160, 163–64; conflict with Soviet Union, 44; cultural stereotypes, 34, 47, 85; family, 39–40, 43; fantasies about itself, 34, 36, 38, 39, 41, 73; feminism, 239, 240, 242, 250; ideology, 49, 72; patriarchy 35, 48, 50; popular culture 35, 36, 45, 54; values, 35, 36, 38, 43, 49, 50, 53, 68, 73; woman or girl, 35, 72, 78, 96
American Beauty, 164–66, 236

American Pie, 64–65, 157–58, 266
Anal sex, 241–42
Anomie, 62, 79–81, 130, 141. *See also* Alienation
Anxiety, cultural, 35, 71, 80–81, 85, 93, 99, 126, 149, 164, 166, 168, 171, 176, 224, 247, 260, 262
Architecture, 138, 139, 142, 146, 207
Art cinema, 63, 223–24, 230–36
Autonomy, 41, 42, 80, 82, 90

Beauty: of child-woman, 16, 25, 27–28, 32; of child in Victorian paintings, 18–19, 22–23; of film heroine 69, 140, 145, 152, 232; of film villain, 126, 135, 140, 145, 152; myths, 246, 247, 248–49, 250; of stars (*see names of individual stars*)
Berlant, Lauren, 38–39, 44, 248
Bernau, Anke, 4, 5, 223–25
Binary (binary oppositions), 24, 35, 37, 117–18, 119, 123, 124, 135, 247. *See also* Duality
Birth control pill, 45, 59, 75, 104, 176–77, 186–90, 194, 195, 240
Black-and-white film stock, 85, 91, 92, 98, 170
Blank, Hanne, 4, 5, 6, 218
Blood, 60, 66, 124, 127, 128–29, 154–55, 225, 228, 231, 235
Bodily integrity, 132, 147
Body: alienated from one's own, 141, 225, 246; autonomy over, 98, 128,

INDEX

225, 243; child-woman, 27, 31, 47, 141, 148, 155; closed (possessing integrity), 127, 136; connoting innocence, 47; developing, 161, 243, 246; destruction of, 124, 125, 136; devirginized, 95; enjoyment of one's own, 251; evil legible on, 135; female interest in male, 181, 182; fetishizing of, 263; horror genre preoccupied with, 135; invisible parts of, 89; issues over, 246–47; language, enacting desire through, 114, 117, 119; passivity of, 138, 145, 151; sexual possession of, 153; star, 6; virginity legible on, 5, 6, 94, 95, 147, 213–14

"Body knowledge," 161, 163, 165, 171

Bonjour Tristesse, 83–102

Borders, 47, 138, 146, 225, 236

"Born-again virgin," 185, 186, 191, 192, 205

Boundary, 19–20, 29, 48, 158, 159, 234

Bourgeoisie, 72, 73, 75, 78–79, 80–81, 249

Box Office success, 15, 105, 106, 111; revenue 21, 68, 198

British, the, 16, 20, 21, 29, 50, 217, 221

British cinema, 206, 208

Brown, Helen Gurley, 13, 183, 198

Butler, Judith, 213, 215

Camera-work, 25, 31, 44, 71, 73, 91, 114, 127, 134, 140, 141, 142, 146, 150, 151, 153, 154, 155, 180, 182

Career woman, 46, 69, 106, 109, 111, 120, 187, 193, 216, 246

Carrie, 126–28, 130

Casting, 20, 27, 28, 31, 76, 168, 209, 265

Castration anxiety, 227, 228

Celibacy, 129, 130, 185–86, 261

Chastity, 5, 36, 43, 46, 66, 77, 203, 213, 225, 227, 233

Child: abuse of, 167; body, 31; denial of being, 88, 95; doomed, 23, 27, 210; as emblem of purity, 26, 29, 31, 43, 44, 47, 140, 210; English, 21; eroticized, 15–23, 25, 28; as ideal citizen, 38, 44; as inevitable outcome of marriage (or of sex) 80, 166, 190, 193; insistence on being, 147, 148, 149, 150, 151, 155; liminal position of 94, 95, 140, 147, 155, 225, 229, 244; monstrous, 126; pre-sexual nature of, 158–59, 263–64; problematic 41; similarity with, of killer, 131, 139; trauma experienced as, 230, 234; treating young woman as, 90, 95, 247

Child star, 15, 16, 17, 20, 21, 27, 31

Childhood, 18, 19, 21–23, 30, 32, 140, 146–48, 151, 152, 225, 247, 251, 259

City, 78, 91, 93, 106, 139, 141–42, 153

Claustrophobia, 140, 149

Clover, Carol, 123, 129, 131, 133–34

Color, as sign of sexual experience, 170–71; color film stock, 85, 91, 92, 93; color palette, 247; color usage, 109, 117, 118

Coming-of-age narratives, 60, 84, 94, 161, 244

Commodification, 18, 60, 193, 215

Condom, 164, 180, 187, 188, 189, 190, 194, 195. *See also* Safe sex

Conflict: American Cold War, 34, 44, 51; between different emotions, 111, 116, 128; between different views on sex, 175, 214, 224, 225; between different views on virginity, 229; between forms of femininity 68, 72, 89, 214; between French and American feminism, 240; between sexes, 249; father-daughter, 36; mother-daughter, 87, 89; Oedipal, 228, 229

Consumerism, 41, 51, 80, 117, 171, 225, 246, 247

Consummation, 24, 66. *See also* Defloration; Initiation (sexual)

Conventions (cinematic), 20, 22, 23, 29, 31, 90, 123, 129, 135, 168, 207, 258, 259, 264. *See also* Tropes

INDEX

Costume: bourgeois, 74, 80–81; French couture, 85, 93, 94; "period," 28–29, 201–2, 208; provocative 176, 180, 247; symbolic of desire, 77, 105, 107, 116, 141, 143, 247; symbolic of innocence, 49, 74, 95, 118, 134, 141, 166, 180–82, 191, 201–2, 211; symbolic of intellectualism, 92, 96; symbolic of loner status, 197; symbolic of the nation, 221; symbolic of repression, 128–29, 148, 201–2, 213; symbolic of sophistication, 93, 95, 98, 195, 107, 143, 150; T-shirt, 83, 145–46; typical teen 47, 96, Victorian, 18, 21, 23

Credits, credit sequence, 126, 140, 143, 201, 255, 259, 260

Crying, 27, 177, 230, 231

Day, Doris, 103–21
De Beauoir, Simone 84, 93, 138, 146
Death: as ending virginity, 224, 227; in horror genre, 123, 124, 128, 132, 135; of child, 23, 27; of mother-figure, 91, 92, 98; of Princess Diana, 209, 210, 220; of sibling, 204; of soldiers, 36, 41; symbolic, 77; virginity as matter of life or, 60, 61, 65, 147, 148

Decadence: of American society, 244; of contemporary youth, 62; of Europe, 50, 86, 92, 97, 23

Definitions of virginity, 5, 125, 129, 130, 139, 158–59, 160, 171, 206, 214, 225, 224, 227, 234, 242, 256

Defloration, 46, 57, 62, 63, 65, 95, 138, 140, 177, 180, 227–28, 235. *See also* Consummation; Sexual Initiation

Delinquency, 39, 41, 45, 51, 54, 55, 62, 189, 230, 234

Demi-vierges, 226, 241. *See also* Technical virgins

Deneuve, Catherine, beauty of, 155

Desire: for acceptance, 25–26, 244; audience's, 92; for control, 181; female sexual, 22, 29, 74, 79, 84, 85, 88, 89, 90, 91, 93, 97, 98, 99, 105, 106, 109, 111, 113–20, 121, 126–27, 145, 163, 171, 179, 182, 214, 241, 245, 251, 263, 265; for historical authenticity, 208; Hollywood's, 22, 95, 96; to look good, 246; male sexual, 79, 109, 129, 130, 138, 143, 145–46, 151, 153, 165, 166, 230, 245; for possessions, 66, 79, 80, 190; to remain pure, 76, 144, 147–48, 154, 155; repression of, 129, 130, 248, 249; teen boys', 64, 157, 158, 169; taboo 27, 29, 32, 167, 229, 230

Diana, Princess of Wales, 204–12, 216; beauty of, 212

Divorce, 161, 172, 187, 192, 210, 211, 245

Domesticity, 39, 44, 68, 75, 80, 245, 246, 248, 249

Door (symbolic), 75, 89, 98, 117, 118, 138, 139, 140, 146–47, 150, 151, 153, 154, 155, 228, 232, 233, 235. *See also* Limenality; Threshold

"Double standard," 3, 75, 78, 144, 241

Dracula, 125, 225

Dream, 23, 30, 36, 49, 127, 128, 133, 142, 233

Drug use, 62, 65, 175, 244–46

Duality, 131

Dyer, Richard, 98, 219

Editing, 89, 154, 165, 201
Ejaculation, 65, 167, 168, 169, 231
Experience, sexual: already achieved, 63, 76, 81, 86, 91, 106–8, 111, 113, 129, 213; commodification of, 60, 179; emptiness of, 75, 90, 168, 178, 184; enjoyment of, 59, 113–14, 170; female 56, 163, 165, 171, 178, 191, 244, 252, 264; first time of, 65, 66, 112, 115, 120, 158, 167, 171, 214, 224, 229, 230, 234, 238, 242, 251, 266; male, 60, 64, 65, 66, 163, 167–68, 230, 258, 261; teenage 57, 178

Family: abnormal, 128, 133, 235; appropriate focus for women, 45, 235; association with suburbs of, 78; as audience within film, 30, 50, 168–69, 248; disapprobation of, 72; disintegration of, 65, 66, 248; importance of individual over, 72, 81; nuclear, 35, 38, 39, 42, 140; portrait, 146–48, 149, 152, 155; sanctity of, 42, 44, 69, 81, 188; symbolic of nation, 40, 41, 42, 46
Fantasy, 29, 30, 32, 117, 117, 140, 147, 150, 165, 170, 185, 214, 229, 243, 264, 266
Father: absent or uninvolved, 190, 245; angry, 66; companionate, 40, 41; "facts of life" talk by, 163; financing, 80, 249; head of family, 35, 40, 44, 46, 55; link with heroine, 133; Oedipal feelings towards, 227, 228, 229, 232, 233–35; role in career promotion, 16; sexuality of, 86, 94, 166, 167, 169, 186; undead, 128; witness to child's sexual misadventures, 157; worrying about daughter's chastity, 36–38, 42, 45, 48, 49, 50, 55, 66
Femininity: adult, 147, 150, 155; childhood, 21; extreme, 27; male objectification of, 263, 264; millennial, 265; 1960s, 152–53; performance of, 217, 218; "proper," normative, 46, 139, 149, 151, 213, 214, 250; symbols of, 189; traditional association with virginity of, 258; work as detrimental to, 73; youthful, 47, 150, 215
Feminism, 171, 187, 215, 217, 220–21, 238–43, 250, 251–52
Feminist; agenda, 185, 200, 214, 242, 244, 248; audience, 206, 210; backlash, 242; belief in gender performativity, 204, 213; chastity as empowering to, 192; French vs. American, 238, 239, 240, 249; icon, 210, 217–18; medical literature, 188; Second Wave, 162, 183; sitcom, 199; Third Wave, 215
Fetish, 23, 27, 37, 44, 208, 248, 263
Film score, 26, 90, 114, 128. *See also* Music; Soundtrack
Final Girl, 128, 131–34, 162
France, 49, 84, 243
French, The, 50, 84, 85, 86, 94, 96, 107
French feminism, 239, 240, 249, 250
Freud, 142, 227, 240, 263; Freudian symbols, 133, 138
Frigidity, 205, 241

Gender, 18, 19, 32, 66, 73, 94, 160, 169, 188, 204, 212, 213, 214, 215, 217, 224, 239, 249, 263
Gender performativity, 204, 213, 215
Gender politics, 66, 212, 239
Genre, 16, 34, 44, 157, 219, 223, 255, 256, 257, 258, 263, 267
Girl: as emblem of nation, 38, 42, 44, 49, 51, 248; as emblem of purity, 21, 28, 44, 46, 47, 51, 74, 96, 119; English, 20–22; friendship of, 24, 26, 193, 224; and horses, 30; immature body of, 27, 141, 148; sexual maturation of, 22, 36, 38, 41, 44, 45, 50, 55, 58, 64, 66, 71, 84, 98, 161, 174–222, 225, 228–29, 238–52; stars, 15–17, 25; taboo desire for, 29; Victorian "cult of the girl," 18–20. *See also* Final Girl; Girl Power
Girl Power, 215–18
Gross-out, 157, 257, 258, 260, 261, 262, 263, 264, 265, 266, 267

Heterosexuality, 24, 26, 152, 158, 159, 166, 168, 178, 179, 193, 228, 242, 243, 248, 251, 259, 260, 261, 262
Home: children's changing place within, 40; of couple, 107; place of father's dominance, 35, 37, 38, 39, 41, 42, 44, 98; place of women's containment, 76, 78, 80, 81, 86, 143, 144, 147, 149, 187, 196, 246; sanctified, 43; as site of sexuality, 157, 167, 170; suburban, 78, 80;

threats to virginity as threats to, 50, 59, 144, 231, 245, 248–49, 252
Homophobia, 179, 261, 262, 266
Homosexuality, 55, 57, 241, 261, 262
Horror, 60, 123, 124, 125, 126, 128, 129, 130, 134, 135, 136, 139, 151, 162, 172, 223
Hymen, 22, 35, 36, 47, 125, 138, 146, 200, 202, 214, 228, 229, 235, 241
"Hymen rejuvenation," 202, 226

Identity: American, 34, 36, 38, 39, 45; English, 207; as father, 50; of father, 233, 235; female, 27, 201–22; in flux, 127; sexuality as essence of, 240; teenage sexual, 157, 226, 256; true, 107–9, 112, 120; as virginal heroine, 126; virginity as integral to, 256, 259, 267; women's sexual, 72, 213
Ignorance, sexual, 123, 157, 158, 166, 241, 242
Immaturity, 39, 166, 167, 241, 262
Independence, 76, 97, 104, 105, 120, 210
Individuality, selfhood, 69, 72, 73, 78, 81, 124, 126, 166, 167, 171, 172, 202, 214, 215, 217, 223, 224, 225, 227, 239, 256
Inexperience (sexual), 64, 106, 120, 131, 214, 258, 267
Ingénue, 29, 68, 96, 104
Initiation (sexual), 59, 60, 65, 180, 190, 213, 238, 240, 251, 262. *See also* Consummation; Defloration
Innocence: and eroticism, 18–20, 24, 32; girlhood, 20–21, 28, 29, 37, 39, 43, 47, 50, 51, 95, 127, 140, 216, 225, 229, 247; loss of, 49, 66, 85, 89, 92, 93, 110, 146, 147, 229, 241; male, 258, 260; performed, 114–15, 119, 126; and purity, 29–30, 43, 47, 51, 115, 140, 145, 157, 224, 247
Insanity, 139, 152, 169
Intimacy, 24, 26, 27, 120, 140, 144, 152, 191, 231, 248

"Kinsey Report" (*Sexual Behavior in the Human Female*), 78, 83, 87

Lacan, Lacanian theory, 239
Lesbianism, 78, 93, 159, 179, 241, 248
Liminality, 130, 158, 165. *See also* Door; Threshold
Looking, 18, 72, 83, 101, 114, 131, 132, 134, 177, 180, 182, 184, 213, 244, 266
Loss of virginity as sacrifice, 54, 57, 58, 59, 62, 66, 67, 85, 90, 93, 99, 148, 158, 159, 167, 225, 229, 239, 240, 244

Madison Avenue (advertising), 77
Madness, 139, 140, 149, 150, 151, 152, 155, 161, 206, 228, 248
Makeover, 105, 213
Make-up, 211
Male virginity, 241, 258, 263, 267
Marriage, 45, 46, 48, 49, 56, 70, 73, 75, 78, 109, 111, 165, 167, 172, 183, 192, 210, 217, 224, 241
Masquerade, 108, 111, 112, 156, 214
Masturbation, 127, 157–73, 183, 185, 228, 229, 231, 264
Maturity: girlish, 26, 43, 127; hymen as threshold between innocence and, 146; sex and, 76, 81, 107, 202; teen progress toward, 54, 60, 127
Menstruation, 124, 126, 227, 228, 244, 246
Metaphor, 3, 35, 42, 60, 91, 134, 139, 171, 255
Mise-en-scène, 2, 3, 8, 85, 86, 92, 95, 112, 117–18, 134, 255, 259
Misogyny, 6, 169, 239, 261
Moon Is Blue, The (1953), 83, 84, 99. *See also* Production Code
Mother: advice from, 73, 87, 91, 191, 193, 247; bad role model, 190, 244–45, 246, 249; bourgeois, 77, 93, 170; concerned, 84–85, 87, 88–89, 99, 189, 247, 248; film role as, 104, 121; permissive, 30, 164, 189; in horror genre, 126–29, 130, 133,

Mother (*continued*)
162; in psychoanalytic theory, 228–29, 230, 231–33, 235; punished, 169, 251; repressive, 66, 86, 87, 88, 99, 126–27, 193; saintly, 210, 211, 217; sexualised, 164, 170–71, 264; as ultimate goal of woman, 46; upper-class, 28–19

Murder, 123, 125, 126, 130, 132, 133, 135, 151, 154, 162, 251

Music, 25, 26, 42, 55, 89, 93, 109, 117, 128, 168, 201, 208, 221, 242, 259, 266. See also Film score; Soundtrack

National identity, 34, 36, 39, 207

Neurotic behaviour, 120, 160, 161, 212, 225, 227, 228

1950s: attitudes towards sex, 73, 84, 104, 156, 170, 256, 258; audiences, 92; baby boom, 45, 172; Cold War America, 34, 44; delinquent films of, 55–56, 62; filmmakers, 94, 126; literary canon of, 78, 84; New York telephone line shortage, 106; perceived as conformist, 71, 72, 104, 170, 256; periodicals, 86; virginity dilemma films of, 68, 85

1980s: political moment of, 57, 174–96, 204, 206, 297, 240, 257; teen-sex quest films of, 54–61

Nostalgia, 20, 21, 172

Nudity, 126, 181–82

Oedipal scenarios, 226, 228, 229, 233, 235

Orgasm, 64, 158, 160, 161, 162, 163, 164, 167, 168, 169, 170, 171, 172, 182, 183, 184, 185, 190, 244

Parody, 65, 136, 151, 264, 266

Passivity, 25, 114, 153, 241

Patriarchy, 35, 36, 42, 48, 50, 51, 166, 167, 168, 171, 172, 214

Penetration, 35, 47, 48, 129, 133, 138, 139, 140, 144, 145, 146, 147, 157, 158, 159, 162, 164, 165, 168, 224, 230, 233, 235, 242, 249

Performance: of desire, 116–19, 121; of domestic roles, 246; of experience, 113–15; of girlish femininity, 215, 217; of repression, 129; screen, 20, 26–29, 31, 68, 92, 101, 105–6, 211, 259, 264–65, 266; sexual, 263; of virginity, 111, 116–19, 166, 208, 210, 212, 213, 214

Pleasure: from career, 109, 217; of comedy, 261, 264, 267; of domesticity, 245; female sexual, 65, 85, 89, 96, 98, 99, 146, 150, 163, 169, 170–71, 183, 185, 228, 231, 239, 244, 248, 252; of friendship, 59, 144, 262; from looking, 182; from power, 217; self, 162, 163, 165–66, 168, 169, 170–71, 183, 231, 263 (*see also* Masturbation); sensual, 54, 58, 62, 78, 92; sexual, 159, 160, 164, 166, 172, 183–84, 240, 243, 255

Pornography, 61, 85, 163, 167, 168, 179, 240, 242, 243, 266

Pregnancy, 38, 43, 48, 56, 57, 58, 59, 61, 66, 72, 73, 76, 83, 88, 98, 149, 156, 176, 180, 182, 186–90, 193–96, 199, 200, 226

"Pregnancy melodramas," 72–73

Premarital sex, 57, 87, 90, 105, 176

Primal scene, 146, 235

Production Code, 2, 6, 54–56, 83, 85, 90, 95, 99, 255, 256. See also Moon Is Blue, The

Promiscuity, 36, 58, 76, 100, 135, 162, 230, 266

Promise rings, 12, 225, 252

Psycho killer, 125, 129, 130, 131, 132, 133, 160, 241, 251, 260

Psychoanalysis, 125, 224, 236

Psychoanalytic concepts, 223, 226, 227, 228, 231, 235, 236, 239–40

Psychosexual development, 30, 79, 130, 131, 227, 228

Puberty, 45, 129, 238, 242, 243, 244, 248

Purity, 3, 5, 11, 21, 26, 29, 30, 36, 51, 66, 103, 127, 136, 210, 224, 241, 243, 247, 252

INDEX

"Rabbit test," 149, 156
Rape, 62, 129, 136, 162, 167, 224, 243, 247, 251
Reagan era, 57, 59, 174, 196, 247
Representing virginity, difficulty of, 3, 91, 95, 115–20, 124, 126, 134, 223, 224, 234, 241, 256, 257
Representations (visual), codes of, 16, 18, 22, 168, 169; of masturbation, 160, 161, 162, 165, 167, 169–71; of mental state, 142; nineteenth-century art, 18, 19, 21; of past, 207, 208; of virginity, 86, 126, 134, 158, 166, 229; screen, 22, 34, 152, 231, 264; sexual, 64, 152, 160, 166, 167, 168, 180, 228, 240, 242, 256, 257, 258, 263
Repression, 27, 129, 130, 167, 207, 225, 228, 235, 259
Reputation, 49, 91, 99, 103, 204, 209
Rite of passage, 12, 66, 81, 178, 229
Ritual, 45, 65, 132, 227, 229, 245
Romantic comedy, 70, 255–58, 259, 260, 262, 265, 266, 267

Sacrifice, 21, 55, 116, 135, 216, 229
Safe sex, 65. *See also* Condom use
Seberg, Jean, beauty of, 96
Self-control, 118, 119, 241
Semen, 168–69, 231, 235, 244
Sexism, 245, 261, 263
Sexlessness, 170, 171, 216, 265
Sexual fulfilment, 107, 256
Sexual identity, 12, 157, 213
Sexual intercourse, 57, 87, 100, 157, 161, 162, 164, 166, 176, 213, 214, 224, 227, 228
Sexual Revolution, 68, 71, 72, 81, 172, 176, 224, 240–43, 258
Silver Ring Thing Movement, 66, 225
Slasher movies, 123, 129, 130, 131–36, 162
Soundtrack, 25, 117, 118, 245. *See also* Film score; Music
Spice Girls, 208, 215, 221
Spirituality, 24, 26, 27, 71, 100, 225
Split-screen, 109, 111

Star, 2, 4, 5, 6, 8, 13, 15, 50, 68, 95–97, 104, 106, 107, 111, 120, 176, 211
"Star persona," 5, 8, 103, 104, 121
Stardom, 3, 16, 60, 105
Stereotype, 31, 47, 159, 165, 215, 261
Subjectivity, 69, 130, 158, 172, 239
Suburbs, 43, 73, 76, 78, 79, 80, 81, 131, 172, 259
Symbolism: around costume, 95, 101, 145; around girlhood, 18, 46, 47, 50; of existentialism, 92; of mise-en-scène and setting, 117, 134, 135, 140, 255; of nation by family, 40, 42; of nation by female, 35, 51, 250; props, 133, 149, 155, 189, 217, 225, 235, 242; around virginity, 125, 126, 129, 146, 210

Taboo, 6, 16, 29, 31, 32, 54, 55, 91, 227, 235
Taylor, Elizabeth, beauty of, 16, 24, 25
Technical virgins, 3, 158, 226, 241. *See also* Demi-vierges
Teenage: boy, 54, 60, 64, 65, 157–63, 259, 261, 262, 264; girl, 34–37, 39, 40–44, 45–51, 54, 56, 57, 58, 84, 88, 99, 100, 101, 127, 131, 164–65, 174–96, 244, 251; sexuality, 54–55, 57, 61, 62, 65, 66, 85, 88, 99, 104, 127, 157–59, 160, 170, 174–96; slasher movie, 135–36, 162–63
Teen sex, 45, 55, 57, 58, 61, 62, 63, 65, 67, 175, 176, 195, 196. *See also* Masturbation
Teen sex quest film, 54–67, 164, 174–200
Thatcher, Margaret, 10, 204, 209, 216–18, 221
Threshold, 4, 128, 138, 146–48, 151, 154, 155, 225, 231, 234, 235. *See also* Door; Liminality
Tropes, 23, 125, 134, 152, 167, 168. *See also* Conventions
True Love Waits (abstinence youth group), 252

Uncanny, the, 142, 156, 227
Uncertainty, 115, 124, 125, 175

INDEX

Vampire, 60, 126, 128, 129, 130, 134, 225

Violence, 41, 57, 61, 121, 124, 129, 133, 140, 147, 154, 155, 251, 252, 261

Virgin/whore dichotomy, 119, 139, 182, 229, 241

Virginity, definition of, 5, 125, 138, 158–59, 206, 224, 234; faking 6, 166, 202, 214; female, 35, 43, 46, 47–48, 50, 64, 65, 66, 68, 69, 71, 73–75, 78, 84, 87–88, 89–90, 95, 103–4, 111–12, 116–19, 126–28, 130–34, 138–55, 161, 166, 170, 174–200, 223, 231–33, 234–35, 238, 244–49, 251; male, 54, 57, 64, 69, 81, 111–12, 128–30, 131, 135, 157–58, 160, 163–64, 167, 223, 230–31, 234–35, 241, 256, 258–66

Virginity-loss plots, 54–55, 57–62, 64–65, 66, 67

Voice-over, 24, 27, 37, 39, 98, 108, 113–14, 118, 165

Voyeurism, 37, 146, 152, 167, 182, 230, 233, 234, 235

White (color associated with purity), 74, 77, 95, 126, 148, 182, 191, 197, 201–2, 221, 252

White (skin), 13, 55, 82, 160, 172, 201–2, 221, 247

Window (symbolic), 131, 132, 139, 142, 190, 230–31, 232, 235

Woman: achievement of individual, 30, 209, 212, 217; as audience member, 27, 93, 94, 99; birth control for, 75, 76, 188–89; career woman, 109, 187, 193, 216, 265; physical appearance of, 15, 16, 22, 26, 27, 94, 144, 148, 168, 246; sexuality of, 32, 38, 51, 55, 74, 76, 78, 80, 83–86 88, 89–90, 94, 99, 105, 107, 108, 111, 113, 118–20, 144, 148, 152, 171, 185, 233, 241, 249, 264